THE BEST OF
HAWAII

THE BEST OF
HAWAII

Jocelyn K. Fujii

Crown Publishers, Inc.
New York

Published by Crown Publishers, Inc., 201 East 50th Street, New York, New York 10022. A member of the Crown Publishing Group.

CROWN is a trademark of Crown Publishers, Inc.

Cartography by Jacques Chazaud.

Manufactured in the United States of America

Library of Congress Cataloging-in-Publication Data

Fujii, Jocelyn.
   The best of Hawaii.

   Includes index.
   1. Hawaii—Description and travel—1981—   —Guidebooks.   I. Title.
DU622.F82   1988   919.69'044   87-20182
ISBN 0-517-56729-6

10 9 8 7 6 5 4

For my father and Nana

Contents

Introduction

My friends reacted in one of two ways when they heard I was writing this book: envy or sympathy. Envy because they envisioned me luxuriating in the lap of haute cuisine, sunset sails, and glorious, mountainous hinterlands, all in the name of research. And sympathy because they anticipated, too, the unspeakable hazards accompanying such an endeavor. After all, they argued, does the discovery of a great new Ethiopian restaurant run by a Latvian chef in the eastern quarter of Chinatown compensate for the squabbles, hostilities, and suspicion I would endure from those who disagree with my choices?

Besides, they persisted, what *is* the best anyway, and how could you presume to define it? I can't answer those questions. I will, however, say this: Arguments and disagreements are part of the turf and contribute enormously to the fun. We are not in the business of milk-toast, and in the end we're just sharing opinions. The purpose of this book is to lessen the travail of discovering these islands by doing some of the searching for you. Rather than adding to the swelling volume of books on "Hawaii from A to Z," I hope to steer you to only those products, services, sights, and experiences I feel have a special quality.

The selections were made on the basis of quality, uniqueness, service, consistency, reliability, and other inexplicable elements. A finely woven *lauhala* basket or a fresh, flawless lei of indigenous Hawaiian plants, made with joy and skill, expresses the best of Hawaii as surely as does a candlelight, oceanside dinner of champagne-poached *opakapaka* drenched on a bed of mango purée. There is no system of bells, toques, points, or any of the usual rating methods employed by professional critics. I did not inspect remote corners of restaurant kitchens or dissect a meal according to its Bocusian leanings or the origin of its quenelles. Rather, I approached this as a reporter, seeking out experts, knowledgeable sources, and people whose opinion I respect and complementing their suggestions with my own explorations. Rounding out the equation were the insights I have gained in a lifetime of living in Hawaii and writing about it.

Many of these finds have a high price tag, but many don't. From dining to finding gifts, a special effort was made to uncover noteworthy and distinctive offerings to satisfy good taste in all budgets, on and off the beaten track. There are enticements aplenty, from nature walks in historic valleys to hula festivals of the highest order. There are ethnic foods, ancient petroglyphs, and pockets of local color everywhere you look. Some of the selections are celebrated favorites, many are the favorites of the future. And some of them—such as old mom and pop restaurants or backwoods craftsmen of great talent—are nostalgic and anachronistic, throwbacks to a bygone Hawaii and precious in their innocence and tenacity. They exist side by side with a twentieth-century, glamorous Hawaii, a Hawaii of luxury South Kohala hotels, opulent cruises, and posh continental restaurants catering to worldwide celebrities, many of whom wind up buying land and residing in a newfound paradise such as Hana or Hanalei.

This book contains many of the reasons we live here, move here, visit, and return. Whether you're a first-time visitor or a lifelong resident, you will find new things to discover and old favorites with a new twist. Whatever your inclination, budget, hometown, or expectations, I hope you will savor this journey.

As you wend your way through our suggestions, you will notice the use of the glottal stop in some Hawaiian words. Sacrificing consistency for simplicity, I have used the symbol primarily in cases where its absence would result in severe mispronunciations. If this license offends, my apologies. And, because businesses and services are changeable and may even disappear without notice, I strongly recommend that you call ahead whenever possible. If you disagree with the choices, or if conditions are not as reported, please let us know. Information such as this is transitory, and books such as this are never complete. As one wise writer once noted, books are never finished . . . only abandoned.

Jocelyn K. Fujii
Honolulu, Hawaii

BEFORE YOU GO: TIPS ON PLANNING YOUR STAY

HOW TO USE THIS BOOK

Because this is a selective guide, it does not direct you to everything you can see and do in Hawaii. It directs you only to the best in various categories. There are, however, exceptions. For your convenience, some general, nonselective information has been provided in areas of practical interest to the traveler. This information, on such things as car rentals and airlines serving various islands, is generally included in the section of each chapter called Getting Around.

Several features have been included to give you a general orientation to island ways and cuisine. Most notably, they are included in a chapter called Hawaii: Hawaiian Style, which describes the nuances and culinary idiosyncrasies of Hawaii—plate lunches, luaus, leis, tropical fruit, island seafood—and includes a glossary of commonly used Hawaiian words. This is the chapter that will give you a little more information to help you feel a little less of a *malihini* (newcomer) when you arrive.

Each island is treated as a separate part in this book, with highlights and subjects that differ according to the island's specialties and particular strengths. Given this liberty, we have attempted nevertheless to maintain a fluidity and consistency among the parts. Each part begins with a brief history of the island before Hawaii became a territory. Practical information and a geographical orientation of the island follow in the section called Getting Around, which will make it easier to assimilate the information that follows. Hotels and certain other categories are reviewed geographically when appropriate and in the simplest format possible.

The Dining Out section for each island covers not only restaurants, but informal takeout stands, diners, and isolated taste treats, such as shave ice, as well. The restaurants are listed alphabetically. Many of the restaurants, shops, and businesses, particularly on the neighbor islands, do not have street addresses but are on the main highway and easy to find. Therefore, when you see a business listed with only the address "Kaunakakai" or "Lanai City," rest assured it'll be easy to find because the towns without street addresses are small.

The Special Outings sections (on land and water) are varied, covering a wide variety of known and little-known activities, indoors and outdoors, bound only by the threads of quality and adventure. Special outings are listed alphabetically by topic. Unless specified, the Special Outings sections are not broken up by region but rather cover the entire island.

Because this is a selective guidebook, some of the anticipated standard attractions are not included. Instead, you will find many new items never before approached or mentioned in a guidebook. Also of note is the emphasis on Hawaiian crafts and artists. Through the recommendations in the sections The Best in Hawaiiana and Gifts to Go, we hope to steer you to the fine talent and works in these islands.

Finally, a word on place names. Sources for the names of places in this book were *Place Names of Hawaii,* by Mary Kawena Pukui, Samuel Elbert, and Esther Mookini, the *Atlas of Hawaii* by the University of Hawaii Department of Geography, *The State of Hawaii Data Book* by the State Department of Planning and Economic Development, and the series of topographic maps by the University of Hawaii Press. These are reliable sources whose spellings and names, accepted and used in Hawaii, may differ from more prominent national sources. Where names differed I have given precedence to the locally used names since they are what the visitor is likely to encounter.

PRACTICALITIES

Weather and Clothing

You can travel light when you come to Hawaii. A sweater or jacket is recommended for evenings, but this is the tropics, where your most important items will be a swimsuit for day and something more elegant for evenings out. Except for a few fancy restaurants that require jackets for men, most of your Hawaii outings can be as casual or dressy as you want them to be. That's one of the pleasures of Hawaii—a sartorial freedom that may find aloha wear (muumuus and aloha shirts, for but heaven's sake, not the matching ones), cocktail dresses, Italian linens, and denims at the same event in the same room.

There are two seasons in Hawaii: April to November, when the temperature is a balmy 73°F. to 88°F., and the rest of the year, when sweaters and extra blankets are unfurled for damper, cooler weather in the 65°F. to 83°F. range. During some rare winter evenings the mercury may drop into the high fifties, and in high-altitude areas such as Kokee State Park on Kauai and the Haleakala summit on Maui, it can get *very* cold, in the forties and fifties. If you plan to visit these mountainous attractions, especially Maui's Haleakala or the Big Island's Mauna Kea, it's recommended you come equipped with warm clothing.

Hawaii is blessed with a natural cooling system in the form of tradewinds that blow in from the northeast to rustle the palm fronds and cool off city streets. On those rare occasions when the tradewinds cease it is noticeably less pleasant, particularly when the humidity is high. Occasionally a condition called "Kona weather" prevails, when strange winds blow in from the south or west and the days are markedly sticky and humid.

One of Hawaii's abiding delights is the temperature of its surrounding waters. Much of the year the water is a constant and pleasant 75°F. to 80°F. In Waikiki, for example, average water temperatures in the month of March are 75°F. in the morning and 77°F. in the afternoon. In the month of August, one of the warmest months in Hawaii, the water temperature in Waikiki averages 77°F. in the morning and 82°F. in the afternoon.

You can imagine, then, the heat of the sun on those bodies lolling on the beach. If you don't bring a sunscreen lotion, be sure to purchase one here.

5

Because the tropical sun can wreak havoc on sensitive skin, an effective screen or block is essential to a good vacation in Hawaii.

It is also suggested that you bring, or purchase when you get here, appropriate footwear for the beach. Those top-of-the-line Reeboks may be suitable for almost anything, even most restaurants, but sneakers at the beach are about as comfortable or appropriate as ice skates in the Serengeti. Highly recommended for beach goers is a pair of rubber flip-flops, called zoris, available everywhere, from drugstores to supermarkets and trendy surf shops.

Money and Medicines

Although you'll be able to find just about everything you'll need in Hawaii, you should bring your prescription medicines and anything for unusual medical needs if you plan to travel to the islands outside of Oahu, called the neighbor islands. Although there are banks and drugstores on all the islands except Lanai, which doesn't have a drugstore, to save yourself some trouble it's recommended you do your money exchanging, camera repairs, and filling of prescriptions at home or on Oahu. It can be difficult to procure these services on some of the neighbor islands.

Time and Telephoning

Hawaii time is three hours behind California and six hours behind New York when the mainland states are on Daylight Savings Time. The rest of the year, Hawaii is two hours behind the West Coast and five hours behind the East Coast. When calling Hawaii from out of state, remember that the area code for all the Hawaiian Islands is 808.

Agricultural Requirements

On the airplane coming into Hawaii, you'll be asked to declare incoming plant materials so they can be inspected for pests and diseases. Some plant items coming into Hawaii may need permits, certificates, or quarantine. These plants include sugarcane and grasses, pineapples and bromeliads, pine plants, coconut plants and parts, corn, fruits or berries from Florida, and banana plants. State plant quarantine officials are required to examine the incoming plant materials at the airport.

Upon leaving Hawaii, you're prohibited from taking cactus, citrus plants or parts, selected fresh fruits and vegetables, mango seeds, rose plants, gardenias, maunaloa and jade vine flowers, sugarcane cuttings, onions, and other plants unless inspected. Most cut flowers are acceptable but should have the U.S. Department of Agriculture stamp of approval from the place of purchase. If you wish to have your plants preinspected before leaving Hawaii, contact the State Department of Agriculture, Plant Quarantine Branch, 701 Ilalo Street, Honolulu, HI 96813-5524; telephone (808) 548-7175.

A NOTE ON HOTELS

Hotels make up a category with many variables and considerations. Consider the numbers: Hawaii has more than 65,000 hotel rooms, with 34,000 of them in Waikiki alone. The sheer volume of hostelries, their variety and competitiveness, and the differing needs and budgets of travelers make this a difficult and subjective area to cover.

Even with a sky's-the-limit pocketbook, you'll have to consider the locations, rates, and services of individual hotels. Once you've selected one, you'll have to make the same decisions about the rooms because a single hotel is likely to have several room categories.

Prices fluctuate anywhere from $2 to $30 a night, depending on the season and the proprietor's conscience. "Peak season," when prices are highest, is from December, to mid-April. The rest of the year is a grace period of sorts, when slower tourist trade means lower room rates. Regardless of the season, make reservations as early as possible.

In Hawaii, a hotel's prices are directly related to its proximity to the beach. The closer you are to the ocean and the better the view, the higher the room rate. But even in a luxury oceanfront hotel—and you can't get better than that—you'll have rooms with mountain or parking lot views as well as rooms by the elevator or generator that are noisier and less desirable than the others.

A good measure of vigilance will be your greatest ally in selecting a hotel. Some tricks to watch for: "Garden view" may mean just that, but it is often used as a catch phrase to denote the less desirable views in the hotel. Occasionally a "garden view" room will show a patch of green and high-rise neighbors. Also, "ocean view" is quite different from "oceanfront," and you should be aware of the difference. An oceanfront room has the best placement—right on the ocean—but the less expensive (but often prohibitive nonetheless) ocean-view room may have a distant view of the ocean, even a meager sliver of blue between neighboring high-rise towers. In rare cases, an ocean-view room may be close to the ocean, more expensive, and with a better view than oceanfront. The room categories and sliding rate scale are tricky enough to warrant attention so you can assess value as accurately as possible.

Even with the hotels that aren't right on the beach, a view of the ocean is a luxury factor that costs more. This causes considerable overlap in listing the hotels. For example, just about every hotel has several room categories, often determined by the floor and view rather than the actual physical layout of the room. This means that with many hotels, the rooms on the higher floors command higher prices. This also makes it difficult to place some hotels in a single category in our book, because their sliding room rates could easily place them in several categories.

The recommendations in this book are based on the strongest offering of the individual hotel—in one it could be service and atmosphere, in another, an extraordinary view or sumptuous amenities. For example, we found that in budget and less expensive hotels, the distressing decor could often be overlooked in favor of cleanliness and the cordial family feeling that prevailed in many of them. In deluxe hotels, fewer things were forgivable because of the price attached and the presumption of excellence put forward by the establishment.

For your convenience, the selected hotels have been divided into four categories: budget, moderate, superior, and deluxe. The budget category encompasses rooms up to $40 a night; moderate, $40 to $90; superior, $90 to $150; and deluxe, $150 and up. Except where specified, the prices quoted are for 1988 and do not include the 9.4 percent hotel room and excise tax.

Unless otherwise noted, most hotels operate on the European Plan, which means meals are not included in the room rates. Some of the deluxe hotels offer the American Plan, which means that meals are or can be included for a fixed price, or the Modified American Plan, including breakfast and dinner daily. Family Plan means there is no extra charge for children if they stay in their parents' room.

At the end of each hotel listing is a category called "Alternatives." This list includes condominiums, vacation rentals, and other isolated accommodations outside of the hotel category. Remember, though, that condominiums these days often include maid service and most of the amenities of hotels except for restaurants. In fact, except for residential kitchen facilities, in many condominiums you will not be aware of the difference. In addition, Hawaii has a growing roster of bed and breakfast accommodations that may present good alternatives at prices ranging from $25 to $60 a night.

A good directory to Hawaii's B & B scene is *Bed and Breakfast Goes Hawaiian* by Evie Warner and Al Davis of Bed and Breakfast Hawaii, a well-known and reliable organization founded in 1979. They can be reached at B & B Hawaii, Box 449, Kapaa, HI 96746; telephone (808) 822-7771. Another B & B accommodation network is Pacific Bed and Breakfast, 19 Kai Nani Place, Kailua, HI 96734; telphone (808) 262-6026.

HAWAII: HAWAIIAN STYLE

Hawaii has more than the usual quota of idiosyncrasies. Remember, this is a polyglot culture, so there are ethnic nuances and cross-cultural traditions that may be neither Hawaiian, Japanese, Chinese, Portuguese, Caucasian, Filipino, or Samoan, but all of them combined. "Local style" is what it's called, an ethnic hybrid in style and manner that began with the Hawaiian race and the blending of its ways with the waves of immigrants who came to these shores to create the Hawaii we know today. From pidgin English to plate lunches, from aloha wear to pirie mangoes, local style is uniquely Hawaiian and is everywhere in evidence today.

This is a primer for enjoying some of the finer aspects of local style, from food, fruit, and leis to the classic—and endangered—Hawaiian luau. Enjoy.

EATING AS THE LOCALS DO

In Hawaii you can dine at the world's most romantic restaurant—Michel's—or have a *manapua* lunch in your swimsuit, at a hand-painted lunch wagon by the sea. In between is a wide variety of choices, from weird-looking diners with good food to family-style ethnic eateries and that prevailing new genre of Yuppie-style restaurants that proclaims itself "casually chic."

There is also a category called "local food." That's a catch-all phrase for such things as plate lunch, *saimin, bento,* and the above-mentioned man-apua. Although they are identified in Hawaii as the diet of the hoi polloi, they are also the favorites of business-suited professionals and CEOs. Herewith, then, is a guide to eating "local," something you will want to explore if you're in any way adventurous.

If you're a malihini, or newcomer, you will no doubt encounter mahima-hi, a popular game fish that apears on fancy menus and the humblest plate lunches. At the busy lunch wagons that dispense them apace, a typical encounter may go like this:

"May I help you?"

"One mahi (short for you-know-what) special with two scoop [sic] rice, three manapua and one saimin. Plus one *teri* (short for teriyaki) chicken bento to go."

Translated, that means a piece of mahimahi, usually breaded and fried, with two scoops of rice (one scoop of macaroni salad is de rigueur as well) to accompany the few leaves of the obligatory green salad and finely julienned cabbage. The plate lunch, as you can see, is a euphemism for carbohydrates. It's a paper plate overflowing with potato or macaroni salad, rice, and the entrée of beef, fish, or chicken, which is sometimes slathered with greasy gravy. It's favored among famished surfers and gangly adolescents. In the world of cuisine, it's camp.

The rest of the order consists of three round pieces of steamed Chinese pastry filled with sweetened pork (manapua), a steaming bowl of broth in which have been plopped noodles, green onions, and fishcake (saimin), and the bento, the Japanese version of the plate lunch.

The bento is also ubiquitous, dispensed everywhere from corner delis to department stores. Contrary to what you may think, it does not refer to a crooked part of the foot but rather to a compact assortment of picnic fare, such things as chicken or fish with sushi or rice balls, pickled vegetables, and various neatly arranged condiments. Bento are great for picnics at the beach.

Now we get to the nuances. Dim sum, for example, is a petite, more refined version of manapua. Both are Chinese, and both are dumplings. But in the words of one connoisseur, "Manapua is what you'd serve your teenagers when they're dying of hunger, and dim sum . . . well . . . dim sum is tiny, minute, dainty, made of the freshest ingredients, very refined." Manapua, on the other hand, is hefty and bready, a munchie on the run. Dim sum comes in various forms, with delicately seasoned fillings of seafood or pork enveloped in noodle dough wrappings and then cooked in bamboo steamers. Dim sum, say the connoisseurs, was made for tea. When prepared authentically, it could be approached with jade chopsticks.

What you would not approach with chopsticks is *shave ice*, another island favorite. (Grammarians call it *shaved ice*.) It's a local version of the snow cone, an icy treat topped with tropical fruit syrups and dispensed with great abandon from antiquated North Shore grocery stores and the slick, tiled stores that now appear in Waikiki. The shave ice aficionados go for the kind with sweetened black azuki beans and ice cream ensconced in the bottom of the mound of ice.

Malasadas are also worth watching for, especially on the Big Island where everyone from the Mauna Lani Bay Hotel to a Honokaa roadside stand sells them to an eager public. Malasadas are a Portuguese delicacy, a donutlike dumpling popularly sold at school carnivals and outdoor fairs and featuring a yeasty batter fried and rolled in sugar. As you can see, this genre is not for the health conscious.

There's a lot more. No doubt you'll encounter *kal bi* (Korean barbecued short ribs), *limu* (seaweed), and *poke*, a sashimilike dish of raw fish seasoned with soy sauce or seaweed and occasionally with kukui nut.

Whatever you do, don't fall prey to the mistaken notion that Hawaii's barefoot-in-the-sand approach precludes fine dining. Hawaii has many excellent, world-class restaurants where you can dress up and dine over breathtaking views, good professional service, and imaginative cuisine that utilizes the best fresh ingredients from Hawaii in classic and innovative culinary traditions.

A GUIDE TO ISLAND SEAFOOD

Hawaii has an enviable selection of fresh seafood to enhance the menus and chalkboards of its fine restaurants. At daily predawn fish auctions, chefs and wholesalers bid among dozens of species of snapper, trevally, tuna, and gleaming, multicolored reef and bottom fish that come pouring in on the fishing boats. However, because local menus often list the fish by their Hawaiian nomenclature, ordering seafood in a restaurant can be confusing.

There are certain things it's helpful to know if you're a seafood lover in Hawaii. Often you'll see a sign that says "*kiawe* grilled." That means the fish is grilled on kiawe—or mesquite—charcoal, the ne plus ultra of barbecuing that imparts an exceptionally pleasing flavor. It also helps to know which fish are running when, and, especially if you're from the mainland, what the English equivalents of *ono, ulua,* and other Hawaiian-named species would be. Also, the fish that are running, or in season, are usually the best buys in restaurants and markets.

Here are some definitions.

Ono, or wahoo, is usually available in fall and winter. It's most often available in fillet form and is prized in restaurants, which serve it poached, broiled, and in any number of gourmet preparations. Ono means delicious in Hawaiian and this fish is aptly named. Ono is versatile, appearing with equal appeal in everything from kiawe-grilled ono sandwiches to entrées poached in champagne sauce.

Mahimahi, the universal favorite, is a dolphin—the popular game fish, not our friendly mammals by the same name. Mahimahi has a firm, light texture and is versatile, giving it top billing in restaurants. A caveat: Many restaurants feature mahimahi on their menus year-round, but it may be frozen and from other than local waters. If it matters to you, ask specifically if the mahimahi is fresh and from Hawaiian waters. Mahimahi runs in Hawaiian waters from February through the end of May.

Opakapaka, or pink snapper, is the darling of the seafood set, the one that has become synonymous with continental preparations in fine restaurants. It is what those in the business call a "high-dollar" fish. Poached op-akapaka, opakapaka Provençale, blackened opakapaka, and other such dishes appear commonly on island menus. Opakapaka is more plentiful from January through February and September through December but is generally in good supply in island restaurants year-round.

Uku is the Hawaiian name for gray snapper, a close relative of the pink snapper. All the snappers from island waters are prized bottom fish. Uku is not as pretty as the pink snapper and not as glamorous or well known, but it's a great-tasting fish, often less expensive than opakapaka but prepared in similar ways. Like the other snappers, uku may be caught year-round, but its availability depends partly on weather conditions. Uku's flesh tends to be firmer than the other snapper species.

Ehu, or the red snapper, is also delicious but not as well known or well promoted as its snapper cousins. Like all the other snappers, ehu is a delicacy with a flaky white meat that lends itself to many preparations. It's a pretty, bright, carp-red fish. Although it may be available year-round, it is more abundant during winter months if weather conditions are conducive to fishing.

Aku, or skipjack tuna, is important to Hawaii not only for its restaurant appeal, but also because it's commonly used by local families for sashimi, poke, and in home cooking. It can be caught in abundance, and if there's a big haul of large aku, the price will be very good for the consumer. Aku has a dark red flesh and runs April through September in Hawaiian waters.

Ahi, which could be yellowfin tuna or bigeye tuna, is another important local fish and a favorite for sashimi and sushi. It's a lighter red than aku, more refined, and very versatile. The bigeye tuna run most abundantly from January through April and the yellowfin tuna from the last half of April through the first half of October. When ahi is in abundance, it affects everything from upscale sushi bars to the local bar that serves happy-hour sashimi appetizers (called *pupus*).

Papio, of the jack trevally family, is a popular local fish that can reach hundreds of pounds. When it's small it's called papio; the larger papio are called *ulua.* Hawaii has seven or eight different types of papio, each with its own culinary qualities. The flesh is white, firm, and flavorful and is often prepared sautéed, broiled, and with various lightly seasoned sauces. Types of ulua include white ulua, *butaguchi, papa, omilu,* and freckled trevally. The differences between them are very subtle and the menu is likely to say just ulua.

Kumu is a highly prized fish. Pink on the outside and very expensive, it's a goatfish the Chinese like to steam with garlic, ginger, green onions, peanut oil, and soy sauce. Kumu is one of the top-of-the-line eating fishes and is served whole when prepared oriental style. It is not a species that is always available, and certainly not in large quantities, hence the high prices.

These basic, reliably good fish are those you will encounter in better restaurants, most often in the "catch-of-the-day" or "fresh catch" category. But there are some new names you'll be seeing as well, not necessarily in upscale restaurants but more likely in family-style eateries. Emergent trends in seafood center around marketing, hybridizing, and supply. *Tilapia* and *taape,* two déclassé trash fish no one would have touched ten years ago, are appearing on some island menus. The hybridized tilapia is appearing in some Chinese restaurants as the Hawaiian sunfish, and the taape—a striped yellow perch introduced into Hawaiian waters—is undergoing a promotional blitz as well.

If you seek more detailed information on seafood, look for the *Hawaii Seafood Buyers' Guide*, put out by B.T. and Associates. Funded by the federal government and state legislature, it's an informative book on island fish, their seasons, suggested preparations, and other useful tidbits.

TROPICAL FRUIT: WHAT'S BEST WHEN AND WHERE

Your vacation pleasure can be enhanced by knowing the ins and outs of Hawaii's fruit. Wouldn't you just love to roam the marketplace asking such questions as, "Where can I find Lanai pineapple?" or "Is it too early now for lichee?" Such questions would immediately elevate the conversation to a much more savvy level, for here in Hawaii it is the multifarious world of fruit that really marks the seasons. Here are some basics.

First, the seasons. Papayas and pineapples grow year-round. Pineapples are sweetest in the summer, and the sweetest papayas are from whichever areas are sunniest at the time of fruiting. This means that the rainier, denser areas (such as Kauai) may not produce the same caliber of the queenly papaya as the drier areas of Hawaii, such as Puna on the Big Island or Oahu's Kahuku and Laie.

Mango season starts around May and continues through the summer months.

Lichees, rare as they are these days, come during summer and are most abundant in Hilo. You will, however, find them on just about every island. Your best chance of finding this quintessential fruit is at fruit stands along the roadside, or at the city's People's Open Markets around Oahu, or at ethnic marketplaces such as the Oahu Market on Kekaulike Street.

Bananas grow year-round.

Avocados grow in the winter months but can be picked year-round from wild trees in the mountains—such as on Oahu's Tantalus, where you can practically pick them from your car—and even along the roadside on the Big Island's Hamakua coast. Anything too close to the roadside should be avoided, however, because of pesticides.

The Best Papayas

Fierce competition continues among Puna papayas, Kauai sunrise, solo papayas, and so forth. If the truth be known, it is the Kahuku papaya, specifically the Kamiya papaya, that reigns supreme. These exalted fruit are grown in Kahuku on Oahu's north shore, which has good year-round conditions for high sugar content—dry weather, lots of sun, and good soil

16

conditions. Taste a Kamiya papaya and it will set new standards for you. Breakfast menus that specify Kamiya papaya are to be taken seriously. Kamiyas are fleshy, often with a smaller seed cavity than other types, juicy, assertive, deeply colored, and sweet. If you happen to be on the Big Island, Puna papayas will do.

The Best Pineapples

No one will say it, but winter pineapples do not pass muster. Winter weather conditions usually produce sour, regrettable, pale yellow clones that fall sorrowfully short of the real thing. Of the summer pineapples, Lanai pineapples are the best, particularly the small, bright yellow ones. The yellower the fruit, the sweeter it is. On any single pineapple, the bottom section is always sweeter. Also, keep your eyes peeled for the stellar newcomer, the deliciously sweet, organically grown, and allegedly acid-free white pineapple, grown on the Big Island by Hawaiian Sugerloaf.

The Best Mangoes

Again, the best mangoes are produced in the sunniest, driest areas. Haydens are abundant, juicy, and elegant, but they're not the best. When you can find them, white piries surpass them all. They're sweet, extremely juicy, with a refined, string-free texture that melts in your mouth. And the flavor—the white pirie has a sweetness that is sharp, not cloying, a delicate ambrosial caress with a fragrance all its own.

The areas that usually produce the best mangoes are Kaimuki (renowned for its mango trees), Waianae on Oahu, Kauai's west side, and the drier leeward side of most of the islands.

The Best Bananas

Unlike other fruit, bananas generally don't vary in quality according to season. What's important for bananas is high rainfall and humidity and the quality of care and handling after harvest. Locally grown apple bananas, available from many locations, are the most popular, and so are the blue fields. Every island has its own good sources of bananas—the closer they're sold to where they're grown, the fresher and better they are.

The Best Watermelon

Oahu's Kahuku has the best watermelons, sold from roadside stands during summer months. Also a hot item is the Kahuku canteloupe, a newcomer to the produce world. Those in the know say Kahuku canteloupe will ascend rapidly in the local fruit hierarchy.

The Best Oranges

Undoubtedly, the best oranges come from the Big Island. Generically called Kona navel oranges or Ka'u oranges, they're grown in the sunbelt of

Kona and in Ka'u near Ka Lae, commonly called South Point. They're ugly creatures, often brown and lumpy, with thin skins, but the fruit is fleshy and juicy. The oranges are tree-ripened and will put any mainland counterpart to shame.

THE LUAU

The most difficult thing to find in Hawaii is its own indigenous food. *Poi*, the pasty staple of the Hawaiians, is available in ample supply, but Hawaiian restaurants are not and a genuine luau is even rarer.

A luau is a Hawaiian feast, called *pa'ina* in the old days and characterized by a pig roasted in an *imu*, or underground oven of lava rock, and a plethora of dishes gathered from the seashore, ocean, and mountains by friends and relatives of the hosts. In the old days, the luau was a family affair in which the preparation and camaraderie were as important as the eating. A birthday, especially a baby's, was a good occasion for a luau. While Aunty Honey from Kauai might have sent *taro* and *opihi* (limpet) for the feast, Uncle Sonny from the Big Island would donate the pig or *limu* (seaweed) and Cousin Maile would make the *haupia* (coconut pudding). "Aunty Tillie made the *lau lau* and Sonny picked the opihi," the emcee would announce enthusiastically. Each would be acknowledged with appreciative applause.

Fathers, sons, and nephews would dig the imu days beforehand, to be lined with kiawe wood, lava rocks, and banana stumps for moisture. On the day of the luau the pig, stuffed with sizzling rocks, would be placed into the steaming pit, then covered with more rocks, leaves, burlap, and soil, and left to steam, bake, and cook for hours in the primordial heat and smoke. Sweet potatoes, yams, breadfruit, lau lau (pork wrapped in taro leaves), and other delicacies would be placed in the imu as well, to be unveiled en masse in a great, smoky, momentous unearthing representing days of sweat and labor. The table would be set with ferns and banana leaves, the family trio would pull out their ukeleles, and the party would begin.

Poi was always, and still is, a necessary ingredient in any Hawaiian gathering. Made from the bulbous taro described by Mark Twain as a "corpulent sweet potato," this sticky purple paste comes in varying consistencies and shades of purple. The thicker poi was called "two-finger poi" because two digits, extended, were enough to transport a mouthful to the lips without dripping. The thinner version was called "three-finger poi." As the immigrant groups arrived in the islands, ethnic specialties such as chicken long rice and the lomi salmon introduced by whalers were added to the spreading roster of dishes.

19

Such was the Hawaiian luau—festive, collaborative, full of humor and generosity.

Today luaus in the old style are few and far between, reserved for baby birthdays and backyard family gatherings. Except for a few benefit luaus by Hawaiian churches such as Kawaiahao and Kaumakapili, anything resembling the real thing is difficult for the visitor to experience.

To be sure, there are many operations that offer commercial luaus that are successful at it. Some of them cart tourists off to remote beaches in large buses, led by tour guides who tell bad jokes in insulting and condescending ways. People who attend these luaus often pay $35 to $40 for watered-down Mai Tais, a smattering of Hawaiian food with mahimahi or chicken, and the opportunity to go up on stage and wiggle their hips in the hula. Others refine the event into a polished gourmet repast barely recognizable as a luau.

There are several reasons for this sad decline. One is that the backyard family luau was never meant to be a money-maker. It was, after all, a traditional gathering of the clan in a culture that had no currency. In today's scheme of things, it's time-consuming, labor-intensive, and impossible to produce for large numbers on an ongoing basis. With a few exceptions, this gives rise to a cheapening and exploitation of the event among many of the current purveyors.

The second reason is that Hawaiian food is not immediately palatable to newcomers, causing most operators to want to alter the food, or offer western alternatives for the mostly *haole* (Caucasian) guests.

These somber facts aside, the rare, authentic luau remains one of Hawaii's abiding delights, an affair with leis, entertainment, and the fond remembrance of the way it was. (And the truth of the matter is that most people who attend even the tackiest of luaus appear to be having a ball.) I assessed Hawaii's luaus with a critical awareness and identified the best in the Oahu, Maui, Kauai, and Big Island chapters.

LEIS

Everyone who comes to Hawaii wants to wear a lei. Why not? The tradition of wearing and giving leis has been with Hawaii since the beginning, and still the art evolves. Never before have there been so many types of leis made of so many kinds of materials for so many different occasions.

In Hawaii's earliest days, leis of *maile*, a fragrant leaf from the mountains, were given as offerings to *Laka*, the goddess of the dance who is still acknowledged among hula dancers today. Leis were worn as ornaments, as they are today, and given as gifts and ritual offerings to the gods, to friends, at temples and in the home. When a lei is placed around your neck, many centuries of tradition surround you.

The style most immediately apparent to the visitor is the *kui* lei, the strung version that covers the arms of the prearranged, commercial airport "lei greeters" and the relatives and friends who await their guests at airport arrival areas. Fragrant plumeria, pikake, tuberose, carnations, orchids, and a host of colorful blossoms are strung end to end into simple garlands that greet, say good-bye, or express any sentiment desired. Kui leis also dangle from the walls and refrigerators of the streetside lei stands and can appear in more elaborate versions, such as the blue jade lei, the thick, double-strung *akulikuli* (ice plant), and the intricate, thousand-blossomed cigar plant lei with its tiny, tubular red and orange blossoms strung in a spiral pattern.

The *haku* lei is made of flowers, leaves, berries, vines, ferns, and other materials braided into a full, textured garland. Haku leis often dry well, and some include dried materials to begin with. Like the other techniques, haku is time-consuming and sophisticated, resulting in hat bands, neck leis, and head leis that are richly textured with *liko lehua* (the shiny young red leaves of the *ohia* tree), pansies, and an infinite variety of colorful materials. Leis made in the haku or wili method are available in better flower and lei shops but are often best ordered ahead.

The *wili* lei is another in the designer lei category. *Wili* means wound; a wili lei is made by winding the materials onto a base with thread or fiber, a technique that is quite different from the haku but which may appear indistinguishable to the inexperienced eye. Wili leis may be simpler as well, as in some types of maile leis in which strands of the vine are simply wound around each other.

Other techniques include the *hili*, in which a single material is plaited in a triple strand, and the *humupapa*, in which the lei maker uses needle and thread to sew the materials to a base.

Shell leis are another genre of this art, a style that reaches its pinnacle in the Niihau shell leis, strung in various patterns and lengths and worn in everything from dainty chokers to long ropes worn by the dozen. Niihau shell leis are lasting, expensive, and usually found in high-caliber gift shops and museums.

Some of the most pleasing leis are the simplest, such as the strung *pikake* with its heady fragrance of sweet jasmine, or the *puakenikeni*, a Tahitian bloom with a creamy blossom that deepens in color by the day. Some would walk the earth for a puakenikeni lei. Its sharp, enrapturing fragrance is impossible to forget and it blooms year-round, although not in abundant supply. Pikake, on the other hand, is unavailable in the winter months, when its prices escalate sharply before its annual disappearance.

Pakalana, a small, light green blossom with a firm texture, is an old favorite among lei lovers. "Give me a full moon and a pakalana lei and I'll say yes to anything" is one favorite saying. Pakalana is only available in the spring and summer months, when it appears in selected lei shops in simple strands that can be tied in pairs, triples, ropes, and in combination with other flowers. Gardenia, also a spring flower, is sewn in the kui technique when especially abundant.

It's customary for a lei to be presented with a kiss, a custom introduced when a World War II entertainer was dared to kiss an officer publicly. Embarrassed, she kissed him and presented her lei and then claimed it was a Hawaiian custom. It was immediately accepted and has endured, and to this day no one has been known to complain.

For more information on leis, Marie McDonald's *Ka Lei* is the definitive resource.

GLOSSARY OF
HAWAIIAN TERMS

Ahi: yellowfin tuna
Akamai: smart, clever, wise
Aku: skipjack tuna
Aloha: hello, good-bye, love, welcome
Auwana: modern hula
Diamond Head: east
Ehu: red snapper
Ewa: west
Halau: a Hawaiian long house where hula and other Hawaiian arts are taught; a school
Haole: Caucasian
Heiau: Pre-Christian place of worship
Hukilau: fishing with a large fishing net that is pulled in to shore
Hula: Hawaiian dance
Imu: underground oven
Kahiko: ancient hula
Kalua pork: pork cooked in an underground oven, or imu
Kamaaina: old-timer, native, local or longtime resident
Kane: man
Keiki: child
Kokua: help, cooperation, assistance
Kumu: teacher, model, guide
Kumu: a type of goatfish
Kupuna: grandparent, real or adopted; ancestor; a respected elder

Lanai: veranda, porch, balcony
Laulau: pork, beef, or fish steamed in taro leaves
Lomi salmon: a dish of salt salmon worked with the hands and mixed with onions and seasonings
Lua: bathroom
Luau: Hawaiian feast
Mahalo: thank you
Mahimahi: dolphin, a popular game fish
Makai: toward the sea
Malihini: newcomer, tourist, visitor
Mauka: toward the mountains
Ohana: family
Ono: wahoo, a popular game fish
Opakapaka: pink snapper
Paniolo: Hawaiian cowboy
Papio: small trevally
Pau: finished
Pa'u: type of long, voluminous skirt worn by women horseback riders
Poi: Hawaiian staple, a paste made of cooked taro
Poke: seasoned raw fish
Punee: movable couch
Pupu: appetizer
Uku: gray snapper
Ulua: a fish of the trevally family
Wahine: woman
Wikiwiki: quick, hurry, soon

OAHU

OAHU

Ka'ena Pt.

Mokule'ia

Haleiwa

Sunset Beach Co. Park
Ehukai Beach Co. Pk.
Shark's Cove
Waimea Bay
Sunset Beach
Pupukea

Kahuku

Malaekahana Bay
Pounders Beach

Hau'ula

Punalu'u

Kahana Bay
Ka'a'awa

Kualoa Co. Regional Park

Waikane
Waiahole
Kahalu'u

Kaneohe

Makua

Makaha

Waianae

Nanakuli

WAIANAE MTN. RANGE

KO'OLAU MTN. RANGE

Wahiawa

Pearl City

Pearl Harbor

Barber's Point

Ewa
Beach

Ala Moana
Beach Co. Park
Aina Moana
St. Rec. Area

HONOLULU INT'L AIRPORT

HONOLULU

Waikiki

Diamond
Head

Kahala

Maunalua
Bay

Koko Head

Hanauma Bay

Sandy Beach
Co. Pk.

Makapu'u Pt.

Waimanalo Beach

Waimanalo Bay

Lanikai

Kailua

LIKELIKE HWY.
PALI HWY.

0 2 4 6 Miles

A BRIEF HISTORY

Welcome to Oahu, the Rodney Dangerfield of the Hawaiian Islands. Often underrated, maligned for its traffic-choked corridors and dense urban skyline, this bustling metropolis is considered by the other islands as the mistake they don't want to make. Jokes abound about Waikiki, about the sinking of the earth beneath its tons of concrete, about how the Hawaii state bird is the construction crane.

Honolulu elicits such reactions, for it is a city of extremes. On one extreme you have a cosmopolitan paradise of golden-skinned children, sophisticated restaurants, world-class boutiques, and romantic, palm-fringed skylines against the backdrop of Diamond Head. Another extreme is the image of a commercial, developed, and often crowded outpost of the nouveau riche and foreign investment.

But those who know Oahu would have you remember another factor. They point to the island's inherent natural beauty, its sharply carved Koolau Range, its waterfalls, wilderness, and networks of hiking trails just minutes from downtown Honolulu. A drive to windward Oahu, a ride up to Tantalus mountain, or a peek over the Nuuanu Pali Overlook would drive the point home immediately. There is also the spectacle of Oahu's beaches. Predominantly white sand, many of them are accessible around every corner.

According to the *State of Hawaii Data Book*, there are more than 50 miles of sandy shoreline around Oahu, 12.5 of them safe, clean, accessible, and generally suitable for swimming. Oahu also has 103 sandy beach sites and nearly 600 of the state's 1,600 surfing spots. Some of these beaches are crowded, others less so. A 1-hour drive, at the most, is all it takes to reach the splendid seclusion of a north shore beach.

True, much of Oahu's beauty has been lost, but much of it is merely hidden. Those who would venture beyond Waikiki have more than they think awaiting them. Unlike the island of Kauai, which has most of its beauty hidden from view in the shrouded interiors of Waialeale mountain, Oahu is fairly straightforward. The Koolau Range can be hiked, seen, and driven through. Cultural activities are centered in downtown Honolulu, and the beaches are generally accessible. There is a windward side, a leeward side, a Honolulu, a north shore, and a freeway system connecting all of it.

And there are many people crisscrossing the thoroughfares and districts daily.

If the freeways seem crowded, it's because they are. There is a rush hour taxing a society wholly dependent on two freeways and badly in need of mass transit. On this island, only the third largest of the Hawaiian islands, live 80 percent of Hawaii's population. At 617.6 square miles—44 miles long and 30 miles wide—Oahu is actually smaller than Maui and only slightly larger than Kauai. Yet 814,640 of Hawaii's 1,054,000 residents live and work on this angular mass of shoreline and mountain.

Located on the southeastern coast of Oahu, Honolulu is the state capital; the largest and most densely populated city in Hawaii; the business, commercial, and industrial headquarters of the state; and the county seat as well. Honolulu is the developed, urban sector of Oahu and also the name of the county, which encompasses the whole island.

In the downtown government district sits the State Capitol. The $25-million building is only yards away from Iolani Palace, this country's only palace and a living reminder of Hawaii's royalty. It was there that King David Kalakaua and his sister, Queen Lili'uokalani, reigned in the final days of the Hawaiian kingdom, until it was dismantled by armed American forces in a coup d'etat in 1893. Only steps away from the palace is City Hall, where the machinations of urban planning and municipal government continue apace.

Several blocks away, in the heart of downtown Honolulu, neatly squared blocks sprout mirrored buildings and skyscrapers while business-suited professionals march off to banks, offices, and board rooms. Compare this to the Honolulu of 1866, described by Mark Twain:

> The town of Honolulu (said to contain between twelve thousand and fifteen thousand inhabitants) is spread over a dead level; has streets from twenty to thirty feet wide, solid and level as a floor, most of them straight as a line and a few as crooked as a corkscrew; houses one and two stories high, built of wood, straw, 'dobes, and dull cream-colored pebble-and-shell conglomerated coral cut into oblong square blocks and laid in cement, but no brick houses; there are great yards, more like plazas, about a large number of the dwelling houses, and these are carpeted with bright green grass, into which your foot sinks out of sight; and they are ornamented by a hundred species of beautiful flowers and blossoming shrubs, and shaded by noble tamarind trees and the "Pride of India," with its fragrant flower, and by the "Umbrella Tree," and I do not know how many more.*

Inland from this civic center is the Koolau Range, dramatic but relatively low-lying mountains that cut through the center of the island, dividing it into Honolulu on one side and windward Oahu on the other. The highest point of the Koolaus is the 3,150-foot Konahuanui near the famous Nuuanu Pali Overlook, where Kamehameha the Great ran his rivals off the cliffs to take control of Oahu in 1795. The Koolaus are a dominant presence on

*From Mark Twain's Letters from Hawaii, edited by A. Grove Day, University of Hawaii Press

Oahu, the younger and wetter of the two shield volcanoes that formed the island. The other, the west side's Waianae Range, contains the highest point on the island, the 4,020-foot Kaala, a mere dimple when compared to Maui's 10,023-foot Red Hill in Haleakala National Park or the Big Island's 13,796-foot Mauna Kea.

Further embellishing the city's topography are three geological latecomers: Diamond Head, Punchbowl, and Koko Head. These volcanic tuff cones, among the city's most scenic features, are the result of eruptions that came long after the island was formed by the connecting lava flows of the Waianaes and Koolaus.

Today the Punchbowl crater houses the National Memorial Cemetery of the Pacific, where astronaut Ellison Onizuka and other heroes are buried. Koko Head commands the eastern tip of Oahu, its picturesque crater spilling to the shore in a series of striated hills and undulating rhythms. In between is Diamond Head, the silent, queenly sentinel of Honolulu.

More than any other feature on Oahu, Diamond Head evokes passion and nostalgia. It was the backdrop in those old, sepia-toned photographs showing Duke Kahanamoku and the Waikiki beachboys as they surfed the waves on their gargantuan koa surfboards. In the halcyon days of the Matson liners, the sight of Diamond Head as they turned the corner prompted a loud whistle from the ship. Passengers on board and those on shore, at the Royal Hawaiian or Moana hotels, would hoist high their glasses in a mutual toast. Today Diamond Head is still visible as a landmark from as far away as leeward Oahu, from incoming planes, from sunset cruises off Waikiki beach. Surrounded as it is on one side by the high rises of Waikiki, it is still Fantasy Island.

A resident of Lanai, who moved to Hawaii from New York nearly thirty years ago, recently described the effect of this landmark. "Hell, I thought I knew Hawaii, and like every other local person, I never gave much thought to Waikiki, never even went near it," he explained. "I thought I was beyond all that corny stuff. But I had a meeting in an oceanfront Waikiki high rise not too long ago, and I stood out on the balcony with my glass of wine, looked out at Diamond Head with the palm trees and the moonlight, felt the salt air on my face, and it just hit me. I thought, My God! This is what they mean! This is everyone's fantasy!"

Between this angular, nostalgic image and Honolulu Harbor toward the airport is a stretch of beaches, hotels, shopping centers, streets, two boat harbors, the Ala Moana Beach Park, theaters, restaurants, and the usual unglamorous, teeming niches of a city in action. Looking at this, the most densely developed stretch in all of Hawaii, it is hard to imagine that Oahu emerged as a center of island life as late as the mid-1800s, long after Captain Cook discovered the islands in 1778. In fact, Maui (and the Big Island) overshadowed Oahu as a cultural and social center until 1845, leaving Oahu to become the late bloomer of the Hawaiian islands.

Honolulu Harbor, small and innocuous looking, was easily overlooked by early explorers. Not until a fur-trading captain named William Brown stumbled upon it in the early 1790s did Honolulu Harbor, named Kou, reveal itself to the rest of the world. Brown met his demise at this harbor he called Fair Haven, when he was killed by Oahu's covetous king, Kalanikupule. Kalanikupule sought to defeat Kamehameha with Brown's military weapons, but instead, months later, had his own forces decisively beaten. In the historic Battle of Nuuanu Valley, Kamehameha's warriors drove their opponents off the cliffs of the Nuuanu Pali, effectively claiming Oahu as the fifth island in his spreading kingdom. Kalanikupule, the son of Maui's former chief Kahekili, lost a skirmish to Kamehameha a year later in Moanalua Valley. On an altar in Moanalua Valley, he was sacrificed to Kamehameha's war god, Kukailimoku.

With Oahu under his belt, Kamehameha the Great moved to this island, and Waikiki became the center of the kingdom. He prepared his men to invade Kauai—an attempt that failed—on the shores of Waikiki, then a flatland of bogs overrun with bullfrogs, waterfowl, fish ponds, and taro fields. After Kamehameha died on the Big Island in 1819, nine years after Kauai joined the kingdom by agreement, the advent of whaling, trade, and the missionaries wrought dramatic changes in the island's social fabric.

On Oahu, downtown Honolulu grew swiftly. The famous Kawaiahao Church was dedicated in 1842 after an arduous seven years of construction. It is by far Hawaii's most impressive church and still conducts services in Hawaiian. The Mission Houses Museum, with the oldest frame house in Hawaii, is a short walk away from Kawaiahao. The frame house, built in 1821, is now a museum of missionary history, with an annex in which the Hawaiian language was first printed in 1822.

One block away is Iolani Palace, built by King Kalakaua in 1882 and today a gleaming, inspiring tribute to Hawaii's monarchy. It was there, at Iolani Palace, that Queen Lili'uokalani, Hawaii's last ruling monarch, composed the poignant song "Aloha Oe." The palace was the seat of government during the period of territorial government, through the first years of statehood beginning in 1959, and until the new State Capitol was completed in 1968.

Across town in Chinatown, the ethnic flavor of Honolulu emerges in full flower. Nestled between ancient noodle shops, acupuncture and herbal stores, and tiny, fragrant lei shops are some new galleries and boutiques lending momentum to ongoing revitalization efforts. Toward the mountains is the Chinese Cultural Plaza, a newer Chinatown with an array of bookstores, restaurants, and Chinese businesses.

Directly over the Pali from Chinatown is windward Oahu's Kailua, a bedroom community of homes clinging to the shoreline or to the lakeside plains of Enchanted Lakes. The drive north from Kailua is one of Oahu's most scenic, coursing through valleys and villages where Hawaiians still grow taro and bananas, where fruit stands vending lichees, papayas, bananas, and mangoes appear around occasional corners. The Kahana River valley, near a fish pond and wide-mouthed bay, is still home to a community of Hawaiians who continue to fish, plant, weave, and live by the ways of the ancients, as they have for generations.

The north shore is reached by following the highway north from windward Oahu or by cutting through central Oahu on the H-2 freeway. However you approach it, it will unfold like a bouquet of beaches before you.

North shore towns are reminiscent of old surfer days, of Beach Boys music mingling with the strains of Ravi Shankar sitar and the pungent fragrance of incense. Haleiwa, the major north shore town, was the hippie haven of the 1960s after insatiable surfers discovered the powerful north

shore waves in the 1950s. For years the north shore towns fairly reverber-
ated with surfer-hippie energy as paradise seekers from all over arrived to
participate in the social ritual of "dropping out."

Haleiwa has retained some of that flavor, but for the most part it has
entered the 1980s with some new wooden buildings, a less seedy look, and,
happily, the rustic charm it has always possessed. It remains the ultimate
getaway on Oahu for those who would escape the urban crush of downtown Honolulu.

The north shore and its stellar beaches are one of four things without
which no trip to Oahu is complete. Another is a drive to Waimanalo Beach
around the southern shoreline, with a long, lingering look at the coast from
Makapu'u Beach overlook. The third is a drive up the old Nuuanu Pali road
to the Nuuanu Pali Lookout, stopping to smell the gingers on the way. The
fourth necessary thing is a drive up Tantalus mountain, high above the city
where the sweet mountain mists descend from the Koolaus. These four
simple outings will give you new perspectives on this island, an island that
has made its share of mistakes, but that is still pretty wonderful.

In fact, Oahu has so many things going for it that water sports, although
present in great abundance, are neither as crucial nor as central to knowing
this island as they are on the neighbor islands. There are boat cruises,
windsurfing operations, and diving expeditions galore here, but like the
streets, the waters are more crowded. Also, a plethora of cultural and
recreational activities on land compete for the visitor's time. If you visit
Oahu, you must be prepared to work harder to find the Hawaii you're
looking for; but remember, too, that Oahu offers diversity, convenience,
and cultural activities unmatched in Hawaii.

WAIKIKI

Honolulu Zoo

Monsarrat

To Kahala

Kapiolani Park

To Diamond Head

Kuhio Ave.

Kapahulu

Kalakaua Ave.

Paoakalani

Ohua

Kealohilani

Liliuokalani

Kapuni

Kapili

Tusitala

Cleghorn

Prince Edward

Uluniu

Kaiulani

Koa

Kanekapolei

Kaiulani

Walina

International Market Place

Kuhio Ave.

Nahua

Nohonani

DIAMOND HEAD

MAUKA

MAKAI

EWA

Seaside

Royal

Hawaiian

Kalakaua Ave.

Kalia

Lewers

Kaiolu

Kuhio Ave.

Launiu

Beach Walk

Saratoga

Kalaimoku

Olohana

Namahana

Kuamoo

Fort DeRussy

Keoniana

Pau

Niu

Kalia

Kalakaua Ave.

Ena

Hobron

Hobron

Ala Moana Blvd.

McCully

Ala Wai Blvd.

Ala Wai Canal

Ala Wai Canal

Kapiolani Blvd.

Ala Moana Shopping Center

Atkinson

Ala Moana Beach Park

Ala Wai Yacht Harbor

BEACH

WAIKIKI

GETTING AROUND

Oahu has one airport, the Honolulu International Airport, wedged between Pearl Harbor on one side and Keehi Lagoon on the other. The five-hour flight from the West Coast ends here at the shoreline runway. During certain approaches you can see Diamond Head from the air; it's a sight to behold in the light of sunset, even for those who have returned many times. When you land, the mountains you see before you are the Koolau Range. On the other side of the Koolaus is windward Oahu, dominated by sprawling stretches of suburban residences and military communities wrapped around a string of white-sand beaches. The other mountains on Oahu, the Waianae range, loom high and purple to the west of the island.

If you're heading for Waikiki, you will be traversing the southwestern flank of the Koolaus as you wend your way through the industrial corridor heading south. Unfortunately, the route from the airport to Waikiki is the least attractive on the island—some have called it industrial purgatory—and hardly a suitable welcome. It is dingy, crowded, and usually hot, but don't take it as a sign of things to come.

The island of Oahu is generally divided according to its shoreline areas: the north shore, which yields the mammoth waves for winter surfing; the south shore, which includes Ala Moana, Waikiki, Hanauma Bay, Sandy Beach, and up to Makapu'u; the windward side, which is the stretch north from Makapu'u on the other side of the Koolaus; and the west side, the dry leeward coast separated from the rest of Oahu by the Waianae mountains.

Honolulu is the name of the county, but it is also the name of the town. Honolulu, the town, refers to the area from the Honolulu International Airport through downtown Honolulu, Ala Moana, Waikiki, Diamond Head, Kahala, and Hawaii Kai. On the other side of the highway from these shoreline towns is a string of residential areas that creep up the valley walls and line the valley floors like blankets of lights at night.

There are four terms you should learn as quickly as possible, because they'll appear relentlessly in local parlance: *makai*, which means toward the sea, *mauka*, which means toward the mountains, *ewa*, which means west, and Diamond Head, which refers to the east. These directional terms are centered in Honolulu, where Diamond Head is at the east, the town of Ewa is to the west, and the ocean and mountains are on either side. Having learned all this, you might then instruct the cab driver to take you to the Diamond Head–makai corner of King and Kalakaua streets, or to the mauka side of such-and-such street heading ewa.

The H-1 freeway cuts through Honolulu proper and heads out west. The H-2 meets it and leads you out toward the north shore (follow the Wahiawa sign), through the plains of central Oahu. In Wahiawa, near Schofield Barracks, the H-2 terminates, and you'll find yourself on Kamehameha Highway. Past the Wahiawa Reservoir is a sign to Haleiwa; that route will lead you through the pineapple fields to the north shore, where you can go east to Waialua and Mokulei'a or north to Waimea Bay, Sunset Beach, and the fabled north shore beaches. Kamehameha Highway curls around the shoreline north and then down the windward coastline, where beautiful bays, rural villages, and the breathtaking Koolau range offer one stunning sight after another. Kamehameha Highway meets the Kahekili Highway near Kaneohe; at the Likelike Highway you can go left and follow the signs to Kailua. Where the Pali Highway ends in Kailua, follow the Waimanalo signs on Kalanianaole Highway, and you will find yourself on a long, scenic drive around the eastern tip of the island. Try not to resist that name, Kalanianaole Highway—it, too, will appear to haunt you, for it covers a large part of east and south Oahu. Kalanianaole Highway is the coastal route sweeping around Makapu'u Beach Park, Sandy Beach, and Koko Head until it meets the H-1 freeway in Kaimuki. If you don't want to take the coastal route, you can drive through the Koolaus.

There are two tunnels, the Wilson and the Pali Highway, which cut through the Koolau mountain range and connect windward Oahu with Honolulu. Both are exceptionally scenic, but the Pali Highway goes through rain forest and the gorgeous Nuuanu Valley, where you can stop at the Nuuanu Pali Lookout. Besides being a historic spot—the spot where Kamehameha ran his Oahu rivals off the cliffs to win Oahu in 1795—the Pali Lookout will give you a wide, panoramic view of windward Oahu at its most splendid.

ARRIVAL

Honolulu International Airport is a bustling gateway to Asian and Pacific destinations and, for eastbound passengers from Asia, to western cities and Europe. The following airlines are among those landing in Honolulu: American, Continental, Delta, Japan, United, Western, Air Canada, Air Micronesia, Air New Zealand, Canadian Pacific Air, Wardair, Trans World, China, Qantas, Singapore, UTA, and Northwest.

Interisland airlines are Aloha Airlines, telephone (808) 836-1111; Princeville Airways, telephone (808) 833-3219; Hawaiian Air, telephone (808) 537-5100; and Mid Pacific Airlines, telephone (808) 836-3313. For several years in a row, U.S. Department of Transportation surveys have found Aloha Airlines to be the airline with the fewest passenger complaints among all the major carriers in the country. Aloha flies 737s exclusively, so the planes are the most comfortable, the flights are brief, and the service is noticeably superior. Hawaiian Air flies to the mainland and the South

Pacific as well as interisland, has the largest number of scheduled interisland flights, and has a fleet of DC-9s and Dash-7 Turboprops. Mid Pacific flies F-28 jets or turboprops, and Princeville's planes are 18-passenger De Havilland Twin Otters.

CURRENCY

If you need to exchange currency, better do it in Honolulu and not wait until you get to the neighbor islands, where you'll be lucky to find anything resembling a foreign currency exchange. Citicorp has four offices scattered throughout the Honolulu airport, with the main one in the line of shops facing the main lobby. The hours at the four locations vary, but the main office is open from 8:00 A.M. to 4:00 P.M. and from 5:00 P.M. to 1:00 A.M.

If you miss Citicorp, A-1 Foreign Exchange has an office in the Hyatt Regency, corner of Kalakaua and Kaiulani in Waikiki, second floor, ewa (west) tower, telephone (808) 922-3327. A-1 also has an office in the Royal Hawaiian Center, Building C, 2301 Kalakaua Avenue, telephone (808) 922-4761.

Deak Hawaii has four locations outside of Waikiki that will handle currency exchange: 841 Bishop Street downtown, Suite 140, telephone (808) 523-1321; 1450 Ala Moana Boulevard, in Sears at the Ala Moana Center, telephone (808) 947-0405 and 946-7888; 1585 Kapiolani Boulevard, telephone (808) 949-4613; and Pearlridge Center, telephone (808) 487-9696.

For traveler's checks, American Express customers have four locations to serve them: Hyatt Regency, corner of Kaiulani and Kalakaua avenues in Waikiki, telephone (808) 922-4718 and 926-5441; Hawaiian Regent Hotel, telephone (808) 924-6555; Hilton Hawaiian Village, telephone (808) 947-2607; and Discovery Bay, 1778 Ala Moana Boulevard, telephone (808) 946-7741.

TRANSPORTATION

Airport Service

Arriving passengers heading from the airport to Waikiki have a choice of taxi, a ride on Waikiki Express, a Gray Line bus ride, or limousine service. Waikiki Express charges $5 per person to and from the airport. Although they like at least one day's advance notice, in which case they'll be waiting for you at the baggage claim area, they do have direct lines at the baggage claim areas for those without reservations. Just pick up the Waikiki Express line and it'll take about ten minutes for one of their air-conditioned, eleven-passenger vans to pick you up. The smaller size of their vehicles gives them access to the ramps and more remote corners of Waikiki for drop-offs. Call (808) 942-2177 for more information.

Gray Line has large buses at the baggage claim areas to transport arrivals to Waikiki hotels. The buses run every half hour in the morning, beginning at 6:45 A.M., and every twenty minutes in the afternoon. The last run from the airport to Waikiki is at 12:15 A.M. The charge is $5 per person. Call (808) 836-2669 for more information.

Those wishing to ride a taxi can find Sida Taxi dispatchers near the baggage claims. Sida is the only one with a state contract allowing them to keep a fleet at the airport. Their fleet is large, well-maintained, and consists largely of station wagons and spacious, late-model sedans. Sida's limousines will carry up to seven passengers in one car. If you have lots of luggage, there will be a charge of $.30 a bag. It costs about $15 to take a cab from the airport to Waikiki. Call (808) 836-0011 for information.

TheBus

You can traverse the island for $.60, but you must have exact change. Children pay $.25, but if they're under five they can sit on their parents' laps and ride free. Seniors can register with the MTL Inc., 650 South King Street, and obtain passes that will enable them to ride free. For current bus information, call TheBus, (808) 531-1611.

The Beach Bus

People in Waikiki should know about the Beach Bus. Run by MTL, which also runs the city bus system, the Beach Bus is loved by surfers and beach goers. Except for the summer months, it runs Saturday, Sunday, and holidays. During summer months, it runs weekdays too.

It starts at the corner of Monsarrat and Kalakaua in Waikiki and goes to Sea Life Park near Makapu'u Point, stopping at all the beaches on the way, from Hanauma to Sandy Beach and Makapu'u. The buses run thirty to fifty minutes apart and cost $.60 for adults and $.25 for children.

Limousine Service

The Rolls-Royce Silver Cloud Limousine Service will deliver you to the gangplank of selected airlines or meet you there. You hire chauffeur and car by the hour for anywhere from $28 to $60 per hour, depending on the car and duration. There is a two-hour minimum on all rentals, and the longer the rental, the cheaper the hourly rate.

Silver Cloud has also expanded its services to include car rentals of the most opulent vehicles on the road: Ferrari, Porche, and Mercedes, among others. For getting around on the water, there's a 40-foot sailing yacht for charter. Luxury homes are part of the Silver Cloud service, too. Oceanside vacation homes in the exclusive Diamond Head area are among Silver Cloud's offerings for rent. For information: Silver Cloud Limousine Service, P.O. Box 15773, Honolulu, HI 96830-5773; telephone (808) 524-7999.

Taxis

There are many smaller cab companies that are reliable, but Sida and Charley's stand out—Sida for its large, comfortable, well-maintained vehicles, and Charley's because it takes credit cards and, in most of its cabs, personal and traveler's checks too. Cab rates are regulated by ordinance so the maximum allowable charge, which is what most taxis charge, is $1.40 for the first ½ mile and $.20 for each ½ mile thereafter. Sida Taxi, telephone (808) 836-0011; Charley's Taxi, telephone (808) 531-1333.

Waikiki Trolley

It looks like a San Francisco cable car, but it's battery run and it cruises the shoreline instead of the hills. The Waikiki Trolley's route takes you from Ward Warehouse to Diamond Head, making many stops on the way. The trolley appears every forty-five minutes at each of the stops and makes a loop around the Ala Moana and Waikiki areas. A $5 pass is good all day; you can hop off, shop, and have lunch, hop aboard, and continue. For more information, call E Noa Tours, (808) 941-6608.

Pedicabs

Many people consider them nuisances and traffic hazards, but they're still on the road and popular in Waikiki, the only area in which they operate. The pedicab is more modest than other forms of transportation, but not necessarily less entertaining. Athletic pedalers with surfer tans drive their rickshawlike vehicles with radios blaring and a streetside chutzpah—people either adore them or deplore them. Prices vary, so be sure you ask the fare beforehand.

Moped Rentals

Aloha Funway Rentals is the oldest moped operation in Waikiki, with a large fleet of Suzuki mopeds for rent. The day rate is $10.95 from 8:00 A.M. to 4:30 P.M., and $13.95 for twenty-four hours. Hopefully you won't need this, but they will service mopeds without charge anywhere between Pearl City and Sea Life Park. The mopeds are prohibited on the freeways, but they are economical. You can get 40 to 50 miles on a tank of gas, which costs about a dollar. Open 8:00 A.M. to 4:30 P.M. Aloha Funway Rentals, 2025 Kalakaua Avenue, Waikiki; telephone (808) 942-9696.

Car Rentals

Car rentals vary considerably in terms of service, rates, and availability. The large national operations (Hertz, Avis, Dollar, Budget) have counters at the airport, and many have offices and car lots in Waikiki. Among those with offices in Waikiki are Avis, (808) 924-1688 or (800) 331-1212; Budget, (808) 922-3600 or (800) 527-0700; Dollar, (808) 926-4200; Hertz, (808) 836-2511 or (800) 654-3131; Honolulu, (808) 941-9099 or 942-7187; Maxi Car Rentals (used and low cost), (808) 923-7381; Odyssey (exotic cars such as Ferraris and Maseratis), (808) 947-8036; National, (808) 922-3331 or (800) 227-7368; Robert's Hawaii, (808) 947-3939; Sears, (808) 922-3805; Thrifty, (808) 923-7383; Tropical, (808) 922-2385. There are other car rental agencies in other parts of town, including Ugly

Duckling, (808) 538-3825; Kapiolani Mules Rent-a-Car, (808) 538-0209; and Alamo, (808) 833-4585 or (800) 327-9633. Be sure you inquire about airport or hotel pickup; most of these companies offer such services.

TOURS

There are several noncommercial tours that are unique, informative, and entertaining. The Hawaii Geographical Society offers a sociological tour of Honolulu as well as three archaeological tours that go into Nuuanu, the north shore, and Makaha on the west side. Some of the tours require fairly strenuous hiking. Prices vary according to the tour, and a minimum of three is required. For information: Hawaii Geographical Society, P.O. Box 1698, Honolulu, HI 96806; telephone (808) 538-3952.

The Chinese Chamber of Commerce offers guided tours of Chinatown every Tuesday. Guests assemble at about 9:20 A.M. and the group soon leaves on a two-and-a-half-hour tour of the stores, temples, pharmacies, fishmarkets, noodle shops, and other colorful stops in Chinatown. There is a lunch stop at Wo Fat's restaurant. Larry Ing is one of the guides—he's colorful, knowledgeable, and enthusiastic. Cost is $3 for the walking tour alone, plus $4 if you plan to have lunch. For information: Chinese Chamber of Commerce, 42 North King Street, Honolulu, HI 96813; telephone (808) 533-3181.

You might also want to check into the Lyon Arboretum's Chinatown tours. They're offered sporadically and when Bea Krauss is the guide, it's not to be missed. Bea Krauss is an ethnobotanist and one of Hawaii's treasures. For information: Lyon Arboretum, 3860 Manoa Road, Honolulu, HI 96822; telephone (808) 988-3177.

In the realm of standard sightseeing tours, there are more tour companies on Oahu than you could imagine. These are the leaders: Trans Hawaiian Oahu, (808) 735-6467, offers personalized small-van tours daily to all major attractions on the island. They also have fifty-seven-passenger air-conditioned motorcoaches as well as vans and Cadillac/Chrysler Fifth Avenue sedans for charter tours and transfers. Trans Hawaiian specializes in tours to the Polynesian Cultural Center and offers five different tours there, including motorcoach, small van, U-drive, or chauffeur-driven tours. Robert's Hawaii, (808) 947-3939, and Gray Line, (808) 836-1883, are also leaders in bus and van tours.

Small van tours carrying twelve to seventeen passengers are very popular, and some find them more personalized than the larger group tours. The leaders in small van tours are Akamai Tours, (808) 922-6485, and E Noa Tours, (808) 941-6608. Also popular is Polynesian Adventure Tours, (808) 922-0888, which offers a large variety of tours in air-conditioned minicoaches.

If you'd like to expand your horizons and take a quick sightseeing tour of the outer islands, there are various tours that will take you from hotel to airport to several other islands in one day. It may suit your time schedule, but it can be exhausting and is not the ideal way to see the islands. If time restrictions make this the tour of your choice, however, you can inquire at your hotel or travel agency.

MAPS AND GUIDEBOOKS

There's some helpful information—particularly the maps—in the complimentary tourist magazines that appear in racks on the sidewalks of Waikiki. Surveys have found *This Week* magazines the leader among the free tourist publications. Also, the Hawaii Visitors Bureau, (808) 923-1811, offers free brochures of all the individual islands, which include several maps of each island with its basic points of interest.

The two best maps of Oahu are the University Press of Hawaii's and Bryan's Sectional Maps. The first of these features street names on one side and a large scale map of such points of interest as hiking trails, parks, beaches, waterfalls, peaks, and even a listing of rain-forest drives on the other. A new feature is the inserts with details of Kahala-Makapu'u, Honolulu, and Kaneohe-Kailua. The map is as attractive as it is functional. Bryan's Sectional Maps are a must for every resident and are best utilized by those who have some general knowledge of Oahu's layout. Published by EMIC Graphics, they come in a spiral-bound book with highly detailed, well-indexed, and up-to-date information on every conceivable nook on Oahu. It even tells you about the exceptional trees on the island.

Both these maps are available at most bookstores, but try Maps and Miscellaneous, a tiny, offbeat, eccentric nook containing everything you'd need to get around, except the car, of course. Located at 404 Piikoi Street, Suite 213, it contains topographical maps of every island by the U.S. Geological Survey, as well as many common and uncommon maps for everything from hiking to flying. Owner Claire Shultis loves her work, fawns over her maps, and is extremely helpful and knowledgeable as well. There is also an array of flashlights, Silva Explorer hiking compasses, quartz timers, and digi-walkers for hiking, sailing, or just meandering. For more information call (808) 538-7429.

Hidden in the recesses of the Hamilton Library on the Manoa campus of the University of Hawaii, the Map Collection Room holds treasures that will give you new perspectives on the world. The 120,000 maps housed here include reference, topographic, thematic, road, and street maps of cities around the world. You can find World War II maps, reproductions of Captain Cook's maps, and other historical Hawaiian maps, census documents, and ocean and wind charts. Although you won't be able to buy or borrow the maps, they do have special copying machines. The map collection is located in the Hamilton Library, room 6, 2550 The Mall, University of Hawaii, Manoa, and is open 8:30 A.M. to 4:30 P.M. Monday through Friday. For more information, the telephone number is (808) 948-6199.

The Hawaii Geographical Society is especially useful in helping you get your bearings before you arrive in Hawaii. They encourage people to write ahead and will respond to every inquiry with a form letter and a list of maps and books, and with specific responses to any inquiries you may have about the wheres and whys of Hawaii. The HGS sponsors movies, lectures, trips, and has a small store that's bursting with books, maps, and current information on hiking trails, camping, and backpacking in Hawaii. There are also books on Hawaiiana and Hawaii's wildlife and flora. The maps specialize in

Hawaii and the Pacific and include the coveted recreation maps and hard-to-find trail guides. Their address is P.O. Box 1698, Honolulu, HI 96806. Since office hours are sporadic, please call before going. The telephone number is (808) 538-3952.

....

CAMPING

People who know Oahu often feel it's underrated, particularly by those who never venture beyond Waikiki and then bemoan the congestion they find here. In truth, Oahu has great beaches, consummate hiking only minutes above downtown Honolulu, and some camping spots worth looking into. When it comes to camping, however, some caveats are in order. There have been enough vandalism and serious crimes on Oahu to warrant extreme caution among campers. Never leave your valuables around, and avoid keeping them in the car trunk if possible. Gangs of youths often prey upon visitors by prying open and robbing the trunks of the easily identified rented cars. Also, you're advised to use common sense in camping—although it's desirable to camp in isolated areas, it's safer to camp among others and never get too isolated.

Oahu has some beautiful camping spots administered by the city and the state. The best state parks for camping are the Malaekahana Bay State Recreation Area in Kahuku on the north shore, Waimanalo Bay–Sherwood Forest in gorgeous Waimanalo on the windward side, and the Keaiwa Heiau State Park in the hills of Aiea.

Malaekahana is a wooded beach park with swimming and shore fishing. There are picnic areas, developed campgrounds, and housekeeping cabins for rent. Malaekahana is one of the island's most popular camping spots because of the shoreline beauty and the extent of its facilities. Waimanalo Bay–Sherwood Forest is newly opened, on windward Oahu's most gorgeous stretch of beach—Waimanalo Bay. The forest is thick with ironwoods and there are bathrooms and indoor showers. Keaiwa Heiau is for the mountain camper. A gorgeous, peaceful campground near the 4.8-mile Aiea Loop Trail allows you to combine camping and hiking with Hawaiiana. There are the remains of a medicinal *heiau* (ancient Hawaiian stone temple) in the area and specimens of medicinal plants on display.

All three state campgrounds have comfort stations, tables and stands for cooking, wash areas, developed campgrounds, and indoor showers. Camping permits are free but must be applied for in person at the Division of State Parks, 1151 Punchbowl Street, Suite 310, Honolulu, HI 96813; telephone (808) 548-7455. Go between the hours of 8:00 A.M. and 4:15 P.M. You can apply no more than five weeks in advance of your camping date.

The city also maintains some great beach parks for camping, but unlike the state system, city parks don't have resident caretakers except for Waimanalo, which has one. The best city parks for camping are Kualoa County Regional Park in windward Oahu, Bellows Field Beach County Park in Waimanalo (also on the windward side), Waimanalo Beach Park in Waimanalo, and Mokuleia Beach Park on the north shore.

Mokuleia is isolated, very beautiful, with a white-sand beach and some ironwoods. It's not heavily wooded and is not ideal for swimming, but it is one of the most popular camping sites. Bellows is a white-sand, protected area of Waimanalo Bay that is thickly wooded with ironwoods. It's very pretty, popular for bodysurfing, and, like Kualoa, has the added advantage of extra security. The gate locks at 8:00 P.M. at both Bellows and Kualoa, making them a bit safer for campers.

Waimanalo is not far from Bellows, on the same wide, long, white-sand bay overlooking Rabbit Island. It's not to be confused with Waimanalo Bay–Sherwood Forest, which is also in the same stretch of the bay but which is administered by the state. Waimanalo Beach Park is a large, grassy area with a generous sweep of beach popular among local residents and canoe clubs. Waimanalo is the only city park with a resident caretaker. In spite of the allure of this stunning beach park, campers are advised to be cautious because there have been some incidents of crime in this area.

Kualoa County Regional Park is also popular, with a large park overlooking Chinaman's Hat, which is a small offshore island. Kualoa is on the windward shoreline between the rural communities of Waikane and Kaaawa. The water here is shallow and swimming is not glorious, but the beach is great for families and group outings. Kualoa is one of the more popular rural parks.

All the city parks—and there are many more than these bests—have showers, bathrooms, and areas for camping. Most of them have picnic grills and tables as well. Permits are free and must be obtained in person from any Satellite City Hall or the Parks and Recreation Department, Permit Section, 650 South King Street, Honolulu, HI 96813; telephone (808) 523-4525. During holidays and long weekends, go to the main permit department on South King Street because satellite city halls are not allowed to issue permits on those days. The earliest you can obtain a permit is two Fridays before the weekend you wish to camp.

Both the city and state have recreational maps and lists of parks and facilities that may be helpful to you in your plans. The State Parks Division has a marvelous map with detailed descriptions of all the state facilities; it should be obtained by anyone who enjoys the outdoors.

HOTELS AND ALTERNATIVES

HONOLULU AND WINDWARD OAHU

Oahu's hotels are concentrated in Waikiki, a 1½-mile stretch of gleaming shoreline on or near which are planted some 34,000 hotel and condominium rooms. That's more than half of the total number of accommodations in the entire state.

Not all 34,000 units are covered here, but rather only the best in four categories: budget, moderate, superior, and deluxe. Except for a vacation rental in Kailua and three recommendations on the north shore, all are in Waikiki. Although the north shore is a major Oahu attraction, there is only one hotel in the area and accommodations on the shoreline are few. There are hostel-type accommodations on the north shore to handle the droves of winter surfers, but for the most part they can be rather primitive and appeal only to those seeking bare-bones shelter when they're not in the waves.

There are also several condominiums and a hotel on the west side of Oahu, in Makaha. West Oahu is beautiful and in fact is the home of professional surfing; however, because the area is known for not being particularly cordial to visitors—with a noticeably high incidence of crime—we have neither listed it as a section nor made many recommendations in the area. West Oahu is alive and well, but if you choose to explore it you must do so on your own. There are a few restaurants and stores and a Hawaiian cultural center that cater primarily to local residents.

Hotel room rates throughout Oahu and all the islands vary considerably between peak and off-peak months—up to $30 a month in some cases. For the sake of consistency they are listed at peak season rates (December through April), which are higher.

Budget Hotels

MALIHINI HOTEL
217 Saratoga Road
Honolulu, HI 96815
Telephone: (808) 923-9644

This is a no-frills, low-rise, strictly budget hotel, but it's clean and personable and very close to DeRussy beach. The location is a big plus, it's off Kalakaua Avenue, close to the bus route, not too far from Ala Moana Center and Ala Moana Beach Park, and also walking distance to Waikiki's major attractions.

The office consists of a desk near the courtyard, which has a small lava rock wall and monstera plants—a nice change from Futura Stone and concrete. The two-story buildings house studios and one-bedrooms, all with kitchenettes. The large studio has a little patio, three twin beds, and a ceiling fan. The regular studio has two twin beds put together, with a small patio enclosed by a lava rock wall and laua'e ferns. The one-bedroom units are larger, with extra beds, a small table, and chairs.

The rooms are spare and basic, and you'll have no view and no amenities. You can't, however, beat the prices. The studios rent for $30 without lanai, $42 with lanai for two people, and the one-bedrooms go for $52 for two people, with $2 for an extra person.

THE ROYAL GROVE
151 Uluniu Avenue
Honolulu, HI 96815
Telephone: (808) 923-7691

The Royal Grove is the darling of the budget traveler. People from as far away as England return year after year and stay for months. They book their next year's reservations when they leave. It's two blocks from Waikiki Beach and it is clean, comfortable, and inexpensive.

The lobby is cordial, with sofas, a dining table, a piano, and ceiling fans—much like a modest living room. Owner Leonard Fong and his family take pride in the operation and go to great ends to make things comfortable for guests.

The hotel consists of an older mauka wing, forty-five years old with about thirty rooms, and the main makai wing, six floors with fifty rooms. The Fongs also book in the Pacific Monarch condos across the street, where there are seven high-rise units for rent.

Any room in the hotel is a bargain, because all are clean and equipped with the essentials. From some corner units with the wraparound lanais, you can even see a patch of ocean. The cheapest room offers bath, black-and-white TV, a small refrigerator, two twin beds, a fan, and a spotless new bathroom—for $30 and $32 a night. The standard rooms in the newer building range from $34 to $52, depending on size and whether they have a lanai. The $48 room, a large studio with a king-size bed, carpet, dresser, sofa, table, and a lanai that runs the length of the room, is an astonishing value. You also get a price break on weekly rates.

The rooms in the Pacific Monarch across the street run from $60 to $80, but most guests want to stay in the main complex. They like the family feeling there and enjoy the gregariousness of the Fong family, one of the reasons they keep returning.

Moderate Hotels

THE BREAKERS
250 Beach Walk
Honolulu, HI 96815
Telephone: (800) 426-0494; (808) 923-3181

For those who want a low-rise, offbeat hotel with a more Hawaiian than modern touch, the Breakers is a great find. It's located on a small street on the ewa end of Waikiki, within walking distance to the popular DeRussy beach. The brown wooden rooms surround a large, well-landscaped pool area.

The rooms, in two-story walk-ups, are impeccably clean. The studio on the second floor is a good buy at $65, or $70 for two people. The studios have small refrigerators, kitchenettes, ovens, two-burner stoves, one double bed or twins, carpets, dressers, desks, air-conditioning, color TVs, telephones, and electronic safes.

There are the usual hotel amenities, but no restaurant. The hotel is, however, planning to install a snack shop and a bar. Complimentary coffee is offered every morning. There are free parking, free beach towels, free mats, and laundry facilities for guests, as well as bell service.

Rates are $71 to $77 for a single, $74 to $80 for a double, and $108 to $132 for the larger garden suites.

THE HAWAIIANA HOTEL
260 Beach Walk
Honolulu, HI 96815
Telephone: (800) 367-5122; (808) 923-3811

It's much like the Breakers next door, with two-story walk-ups, a pleasant grassy lawn, palm trees, and philodendrons surrounding two pools. The landscaping is wonderful, accented by lava rock walls here and there for a tropical Hawaiian touch.

The rooms are air-conditioned, with a kitchen, two-burner stove, small refrigerator, small sink, carpet, and electronic safe. They're also a half-block from the beach on what is one of the quieter streets in Waikiki.

Complimentary coffee is served poolside in the mornings, and there's just about every service you could need except a restaurant. Some rooms, such as the superior rooms upstairs, do not have lanais. All rooms have crisp upholstery and decor and are spotless.

The rates are $72 for a single superior; $75 for a double superior; and $83 to $85 for a deluxe. The charge for an additional person is $11. Suites are $125 for up to four. Be sure you ask about their eight-day, seven-night package, and others; the packages offer incredible deals.

NEW OTANI KAIMANA BEACH HOTEL
2863 Kalakaua Avenue
Honolulu, HI 96815
Telephone: (800) 421-8795; (808) 923-1555

This is Honolulu's favorite hotel. Located on prime beachfront land near Diamond Head and Kapiolani Park, it has the best location, the best beach, and the most comfortable, endearing feel of any of the Waikiki hotels.

It's informal and unpretentious, with a nondescript lobby and an atrium-style configuration that has the rooms arranged in a quadrangle around a center well. There are a staggering eighteen room categories for its 138 rooms and suites, all located on the third to ninth floors.

The hotel recently underwent extensive renovations that spruced up its rooms and suites with Pegge Hopper paintings, fancy tape decks, brass planters and lamps, as well as lavenders, taupes, blues, and powdery colors that are very attractive. This is the best the Kaimana has ever looked.

All the rooms have balconies and small refrigerators. Some have studio kitchenettes, and the corner suites have wraparound lanais with spectacular views of Kapiolani Park, the mountains, Waikiki, and all the way up the leeward coastline of Ewa. In these suites, even the mountain views are fabulous because Kapiolani Park and Diamond Head have kept the view free from construction and therefore free from neighboring high rises. The noisiest rooms are by the elevator.

The restaurant is notoriously forgettable, but efforts are being made to introduce Hawaiian entertainment by leading Hawaiian musicians on a regular basis. Upstairs is The Miyako, a recommendable Japanese restaurant. The Hau Tree Lanai, as the coffee shop and main restaurant are called, is practically on the sand and overlooks all the beachgoing festivities of the Honolulu habitués who frequent this popular beach. The water is brilliant turquoise, with good swimming. Although the beach is small and crowded, it's a magnet for locals who sport the "Kaimana tan" from hanging out at "Dig me" beach, as Kaimana has come to be called.

Room rates are $81 for the standard rooms, $97 for ocean-Waikiki view, $145 for the ocean studio superior, and on up to $315 for the two-bedroom Pacific suite. Garden apartments can be had for $98 to $120. Most of the rooms are in the $80 to $100 price range. And from April to December, each room costs $10 less. Even the lowest priced, run-of-the-house rooms are a good deal here because this is the closest to the water you can be in Waikiki. You can wake up and walk right into the water. If you can afford the luxury suites, so much the better, you'll have unsurpassed views as well.

OUTRIGGER PRINCE KUHIO
2500 Kuhio Avenue
Honolulu, HI 96815
Telephone: (800) 367-5170; (808) 922-0811

The Prince Kuhio is one of Waikiki's newer hotels, located one long block away from the beach and slightly on the Diamond Head side of Waikiki. Like many of the Outrigger hotels, it has rooms that span several different categories, from its moderately priced standard rooms up to its deluxe-priced king suites. The hotel's strongest offerings are its attractive lobby and rooms, the good taste in design and landscaping, and the fact that you can have all the amenities and a pleasing room for under $100.

The lobby has high ceilings and overlooks a landscaped terrace and waterfall. The popular restaurant Compadres has opened up here, its first foray into the Waikiki market.

There are 626 units, from standard, at $95; to moderate, at $100; up to the ocean-view Kuhio Club for $145; and finally the two-bedroom King Suite for $375. Rooms cost considerably less during the low season.

Superior Hotels

THE HAWAIIAN REGENT HOTEL
2552 Kalakaua Avenue
Honolulu, HI 96815
Telephone: (800) 367-5370; (808) 922-6611

The 5.3-acre complex is attractively designed around a courtyard that opens onto Kalakaua Avenue directly across from the beach. This is also a huge hotel—1,346 rooms—with wide-open spaces, fountains and waterways, and a general feeling of luxury.

The Hawaiian Regent is known for its extensive convention facilities; its popular continental restaurant, The Third Floor; and its pleasant design and decor. There are two swimming pools, tennis courts and instruction, and rooms with varying views and in various sizes, ranging from the standard mountain-view room for $99 to $105 for high mountain view, $120 for partial ocean-view, and on up to $165 for ocean-view and oceanfront rooms. Deluxe rooms and suites go for $322 to $700.

Although the higher-priced rooms are attractive, it's the lower-priced rooms that are recommended. Anything in the higher, deluxe-priced categories in this (and the following) hotel would have to compete with the Colony Surf, Kahala Hilton, and Halekulani in the deluxe category, and would not hold a candle to them.

HYATT REGENCY WAIKIKI
2424 Kalakaua Avenue
Honolulu, HI 96815
Telephone: (800) 228-9000; (808) 922-9292

The Hyatt is large—1,234 rooms—and impersonal. It's flawed in taste and service, but some opt for its glamorous image and exciting restaurants over smaller hotels with nicer rooms and views, but fewer amenities. It's across the street from Waikiki beach, and some of the rooms have an unobstructed view of the ocean while others have no view. Although the overall feel of the hotel is that of glamour and luxury, there's a wide range of offerings here, determined by location, floor, and view rather than size and layout of the room. Because this is in a developed area of Waikiki, the higher you go the better it is. Except for the suites, most of the rooms are of similar size and layout.

The city view is the bottom of the line here, with no view to speak of and a $105 price tag. The rates go up for high mountain ($130), ocean view ($160), and oceanfront rooms ($175) until they hit the suites for hundreds of dollars. The Regency Club, at $185, offers special privileges and top-floor rooms with special elevator keys, concierge, complimentary cordials, coffee, and other amenities.

With its waterfall, labyrinthine construction, and plethora of shops and restaurants in its block-long complex, this hotel is not exactly low-key. One of its strongest features is its amenities, including the excellent Bagwells 2424 continental restaurant.

Deluxe Hotels

COLONY SURF HOTEL
2895 Kalakaua Avenue
Honolulu, HI 96815
Telephone: (800) 367-8047; (808) 923-5751

About 70 to 75 percent of the Colony Surf guests are repeat guests or recommendations, which tells you a lot about its quality. This is the kind of hotel guests return to year after year, to the same room on the same floor with the same housekeeper. It doesn't have a lot of amenities, but it's a beautiful, tasteful, intimate hotel in a prime Diamond Head location with service that's considered among the best in Hawaii. It is also in a category of its own because one building is run as a co-op and the other as a hotel. (Guests would not perceive the difference in the operation.) The main building on which its reputation is based, the Colony Surf Hotel, is on the beach; the other building, the Colony Surf East Hotel, is directly behind it, off the beach, with 50 units for rent.

The lobby is small and unpretentious, but the rooms are huge and lavish. The beachfront units may be 900 square feet in size, with balconies, breathtaking views, and a decor of white, beige, camel, and light blue, which adds to the visual expansion. There are white shutters, white carpets, a dining room, full kitchen, touches of rattan, wicker, and bamboo, twice-daily maid service, complimentary newspapers, grocery delivery if desired, and a variety of other personalized services, not the least of which is room service from the renowned Michel's. The main building is twenty stories high. When you are this close to the beach, the views just get wider and larger but the ocean is always present.

For luxury travelers with a penchant for quiet, personalized service in the most tasteful surroundings, this is a wonderful choice. The one-bedroom units in the preferred building rent for about $125 to $275, but there are two-bedroom suites in an adjoining building from $500 to $600.

HALEKULANI HOTEL
2199 Kalia Road
Honolulu, HI 96815
Telephone: (800) 367-2343; (808) 923-2311

Since it reopened in 1983 with its new luxury image, the Halekulani has been garnering awards as the most elegant hostelry on Waikiki Beach. Certainly it has been very creative in its amenities, and its elegance in motif, decor, cuisine, and image are hard to beat.

It's located on Gray's Beach; there is a seawall between the property and the ocean. There are 456 rooms on 5 acres, located in 5 buildings from 2 to 17 stories high, and the main building is built in the atrium style. The original coconut trees are still there, and so is what is touted as Waikiki's only kiawe tree, more than a century old.

The service is plush all the way, from the welcome chocolates, made at the hotel as your greeting, to the personalized check-in where you are escorted to your room and registered there in privacy. Plush white terry cloth robes await you in the room, where there are fresh flowers and three phones. (The hotel has its own full-time house florist.) Room service brings out such touches as your personal tableside toaster.

This is the second oldest hotel on the beach, built in 1917, but you'd never know it. Amenities range from the continental restaurant, La Mer, to Orchids, (the less expensive, but still elegant, restaurant below it), to the House Without a Key lounge, where Hawaiian entertainment is offered from sunset on.

As you can imagine, the rooms are flawless, with extra-deep bathtubs, teal- or oyster-colored wool carpets, honor bar (which stocks the full range of alcoholic beverages in your room, for a price) and all the rest. The bathrooms are white tile with marble basins and separate showers and tubs—very elegant.

Rates begin at $175 for a garden view to $210 for a courtyard view, $245 for an ocean view, $270 for oceanfront, and $300 for a Diamond Head oceanfront unit. Suites go up to $2,300.

KAHALA HILTON
5000 Kahala Avenue
Honolulu, HI 96816-5498
Telephone: (808) 734-2211

Five minutes outside of Waikiki, on a secluded beach at the end of Honolulu's most posh residential community, the Kahala Hilton still reigns as a very special luxury resort. It's small—370 rooms—and has a personalized, understated elegance that sets it apart from Oahu's other luxury hotels.

This is where presidents of the United States, premiers of China, rock stars, poets, European designers, and the world's celebrated personalities stay when they come to Hawaii. They like its privacy and its elegance; its excellent taste in decor, landscaping, and design; and the gentle, uncrowded beach. The amenities figure prominently too: the Maile Restaurant is one of the city's best, and serves the best Sunday brunch overlooking a lagoon of cavorting porpoises. The Plumeria Cafe, the Danny Kaleikini Show, and the oceanside Hala Terrace all have their own independent followings among residents and guests. The Kahala Hilton is also affiliated with the Maunalua Bay Club, a posh new health facility only five minutes away by shuttle bus.

Sweeping renovations have upgraded the rooms, corridors, halls, and the famous high-ceilinged lobby with its floral sculptures. What have not changed are the large, pleasant lagoon, the porpoises that put on daily shows, and the waterfall and garden area.

The rooms face mountain or ocean, and many have views of the sprawling Waialae golf course surrounding the hotel. There are also suites wrapped around the lagoon. Rates start at $165 for the mountain-view rooms, without balconies and on the lower floors. Mountain view on the higher floors, without balconies, is $185, and on up to the $280 rooms with ocean views. There are fifteen room categories and as many rates, going up to $1,500 for a two-bedroom, deluxe ocean-view suite.

Alternatives

JOHN GUILD INN
2001 Vancouver Drive
Honolulu, HI 96822
Telephone: (808) 947-6019

This three-story mansion was teetering at the edge of demolition when Honolulu businessman Rick Ralston, an avid restorer of old homes, bought it. He restored it, filled it with antiques from his considerable personal collection, obtained Hawaii's first and only commercial bed and breakfast license, and opened in 1984.

Built in 1915, the building is on the Hawaii and National Registers of Historic Places. It's two miles from Waikiki, in a residential area near the University of Hawaii in beautiful Manoa Valley. There are seven rooms for rent, each furnished in a distinctive style and named after someone who was prominent in Hawaii during the days of John Guild, the businessman who bought the home in 1919 and transformed it into the architectural marvel it is today.

The home is maintained and furnished impeccably, with priceless antiques and memorabilia: a wooden upright 1920s Philco radio, a nickelodeon, organ, and crank phonograph that work; a collection of antique hula dolls; an extensive collection of Maxfield Parrish prints; and such rich, nostalgic touches as four-poster beds, brocade chairs and old marble tables, antique porcelain shower heads, white cotton eyelet bedspreads, antique quilts, high ceilings, and a large stone fireplace.

There are three floors, with comfortable sitting rooms on each. The third-floor rooms have lower ceilings and share a bathroom; the second-floor units are airier and more spacious, with their own baths.

This is the kind of house you'll want to linger in and explore. It's like an old English country inn, with dark woods, polished wood floors, abundant windows, floral wallpaper, and soft velvet banquettes and sofas. Continental breakfast is offered in the mornings, refreshments are available all day, and at five o'clock every day complimentary wines, champagne, pâtés, and imported cheeses are offered on the patio.

Prices range from $80 to $110 and $145 for the largest suites, and $125 for the private cottage on the grounds. For someone desiring a quiet alternative to a Waikiki hotel and the most pleasant environment possible, this inn is highly recommended.

KAILUA BEACHSIDE COTTAGES
Patrick O'Malley
204 South Kalaheo Avenue
Kailua, HI 96734
Telephone: (808) 261-1653

There are few places like it in Hawaii—six cottages, island style, under a huge banyan tree with lava rock walls, picnic tables, full kitchens, and all the rest—and it's right next to Kailua Beach Park in windward Oahu.

This is one of Kailua's hidden delights, just yards away from the island's leading windsurfing beach. The cottages offer studios or one-bedrooms for

$55 a day, a spacious two-bedroom for $65, and two two-bedrooms for $70 a day. This is a small operation, and those who know about it book months in advance.

All cottages come with fully equipped kitchens, carpets, color TV and cable. There are laundry facilities nearby in the same complex.

The proprietors also rent units down the street, bordering the same beach park. They range from a $45 studio to a $65-a-day two-bedroom, one-bath house, or a $100-a-day two-bedroom, two-bath house. The largest house in this complex is $140 a day, with three bedrooms, but it's on a corner and is subject to traffic noises.

The O'Malleys, who own the property, also manage and rent others along Kailua Beach. Heartily recommended, however, are the beachside cottages described above for $55. They're utterly charming and perfect for reclusive beach goers who want to remain outside of Waikiki.

Kailua is about a thirty-minute drive from Waikiki, over the Pali Highway, on the windward side.

THE NORTH SHORE

The north shore is a forty-five-minute drive from downtown Honolulu via first the H-1, and then the H-2 freeway. You can also reach the north shore by winding up the windward coastline heading north on Kamehameha Highway. Although the windward route is much more scenic, the H-2 is much quicker. The north shore is a string of beaches—Sunset, Ehukai and its Banzai Pipeline waves, Waimea—and a shorter string of towns that curl around the fabled coastline where the north shore surfing contests are held. The north shore is where you go to escape the city, a place where all you unpack is your swimsuit (except in the winter, when swimming is not advised) and where you can feel far, far away from Waikiki. There is only one hotel on the north shore, but there are several vacation rentals. The only hotel and the two best vacation rentals are listed here.

TURTLE BAY HILTON
P.O. Box 187
Kahuku, HI 96731
Telephone: (808) 293-8811

This is the only hotel on the north shore, located on a windy point of 880 acres of land, where it accommodates an eighteen-hole golf course, ten tennis courts, and a three-wing hotel with 486 rooms, suites, and cottages. The best features of this hotel are its small, sheltered beach for swimming and snorkeling, Kuilima Point (a petite finger of lava that juts out to the sea), and the picturesque Turtle Bay where turtles are still sighted frequently. Other than that, the rooms are prosaic and, except for the view, you could be in any other Hilton.

The lowest-priced rooms are in the bay-view or ocean-view categories, which overlook either Turtle Bay or the small lagoon in front of the hotel. You'll pay prettily for these rooms, yet some of them don't even have a balcony, only a railing you can peer over. Like most hotels in Hawaii, the rooms in the different categories and price ranges differ only in location and view. The more expensive ocean-lanai rooms have a small balcony with chairs and a small table overlooking the north shore and Turtle Bay. It's supremely ironic that some of the oceanfront rooms, in a higher price category still, have a stunning view over Kuilima Point but can be directly over or very close to the loudly whirring air-conditioning unit. Be sure to request a room that is not close to this unit. The most attractive units—and most expensive—are the split-level cottages, with high cathedral ceilings and king-size beds.

The Bay View Lounge is one of the north shore's more popular spots, with a disco at night that attracts people from Haleiwa as well as students from the nearby Brigham Young University, a Mormon college.

Rates range from $120 for a bay-view room (it's less expensive but the view is prettier than the ocean-view rooms) to $145 for an ocean-view room, $165 for an ocean-lanai room, and $175 for an oceanfront room. Cottages, much larger, go for $245 a night.

Vacation Rentals

KE IKI HALE
59-579 Ke Iki Road
Haleiwa, HI 96712
Telephone: (808) 638-8229

Ke Iki Hale sits serenely on the most magnificent piece of shoreline on Oahu. There, at the edge of the sand, sunsets unfold in a daily spectacle that will leave you breathless at your cottage door. During the summer, waves roll in gently on a gorgeous white-sand beach dotted with shells, where you may sunbathe, run, play in tidepools, and forget the cares of the world. During the winter, waves as high as twenty and thirty feet crash upon a rocky shoreline as the sand has been pulled away for the season. At any time of the year, Ke Iki Beach is unforgettable.

The 1½ acres of beachfront land are ringed with coconut palms and ironwoods and dotted with twelve lovely cottages. The beachfront cottages have picnic tables overlooking the ocean with full barbecue facilities. At Ke Iki Hale you can even rinse off under a shower attached to a coconut tree.

There are one- and two-bedroom cottages on the beach and duplex one-bedrooms off the beach. There is no room service, bell service, or restaurant, just the immaculate, fully equipped beach homes and the considerable hospitality of owner Alice Tracy, who is as much of a draw as the property.

Although the units differ, all are fully stocked with four-burner stoves and full kitchens, clean linens, tables, sofas, and plants. The cottages are warm and inviting, and the beachfront cottages have picture windows framing stupendous ocean views beyond the palm trees. The decor is modest, but the view and feeling of openness give Ke Iki Hale a sense of luxury and well-being.

There are no telephones or televisions, but they'd be an intrusion anyway. If you need them, there are two pay phones on the grounds.

Ke Iki Hale is minutes away by car from the north shore's major eateries, not to mention the fabled Waimea Bay. Ke Iki Hale is highly, in fact unequivocally, recommended. The cost is $125 for the new one-bedroom beachfront cottage; $95 or $110 for the two-bedroom beachfront cottages; $80 for the one-bedroom beachfront duplex; and $65 for the one-bedroom streetside unit. There are lower weekly and monthly rates for all the units.

VACATION INNS
59-788 Kamehameha Highway
Haleiwa, HI 96712
Telephone: (800) 367-8047; (808) 628-7838

The best units of Vacation Inns are right over a dazzling north shore beach called Three Tables. Three Tables is right off the main highway, and so are these units, but the view is stunning and you can't get much closer to the water.

The beach is small and the building is a two-story concrete walk-up with eight studios. All the units have a view, but the best are the corner units.

In truth, this recommendation is made with several reservations. These are not the cleanest accommodations, nor are they impeccably furnished. They are recommended strictly because of their price and location, for those wishing to be on the beach on the north shore without paying luxury prices.

The corner studios have a double bed, dresser, a small desk, sofa, color TV, a small table with chairs, ceiling fan, bathroom, and kitchen facilities. There is ample closet space; a unit can sleep up to four. The interior studios are similar but have two twin beds and appear to be smaller. The small balconies look over the beach and add light and space to the otherwise marginal units. The corner units are $65 a night; the interior units, $55. Weekly and monthly rates are also available.

....

EXPEDITIONS

Expeditions are a noticeable new market in Hawaiian travel. They offer a way to see Hawaii past the clichés, beyond the high rises, and into the backwoods, rarely traveled paths that reveal the raw and untouched beauty of Hawaii. Health-conscious, nature-conscious travelers are among the burgeoning numbers seeking expeditions as an alternative way of traveling.

Herewith, then, are the four best expedition leaders in Hawaii. All are based in Honolulu but offer treks to all the islands.

ADVENTURE KAYAKING INTERNATIONAL
P.O. Box 61609
Honolulu, HI 96822
Telephone: (808) 988-3913

After years of hard work and experimentation, John Gray and Bob Crane developed an extensive program offering kayak trips to remote regions on all the islands. They offer an opportunity to approach by water some of the otherwise unapproachable—and most beautiful—areas of Hawaii, such as Halawa Valley, the Na Pali Coast, Oahu's Kahana Valley, the Huleia Stream on Kauai, and others. That's not to say that the ordinary, accessible areas aren't kayak material as well; the Waikiki sunset paddle is one of the easiest and most romantic of the kayak adventures.

The company recently decided to put a fleet of signature model inflatable boats on every island, which means expanded services on all the islands. There's also a South Pacific program offering kayak trips to Fiji, Rarotonga, Tonga, and other South Pacific islands.

The Hawaii expeditions range from a $30 river trip on Kauai or a Waikiki sunset kayak trip to $200-a-day charter service for one person. The standard expedition costs $125 a day per person, which includes air transportation between islands, food, ground transportation, guides, and camping gear. A five-day Hawaii expedition costs $625 round trip from Honolulu, and a new package offers round-trip air travel from the West Coast, a day in the hotel at the start and finish, and a five-day expedition (making it a seven-day package), for $999. The kayak trips have won the hearts of many adventure travelers because of the access they offer to hidden regions, and because the service takes the fuss out of planning. And the planners are quick to point out that the kayaks are easy to maneuver and have been used by children and seniors.

MARK COLLINS
Hawaiian Sunrise Expeditions
P.O. Box 62011
Honolulu, HI 96839
Telephone: (808) 988-4851

The trips offered here have enormous appeal to naturalists, nature lovers, and bird-watchers. In fact, Collins gets many referrals from the Audubon Society and has worked for years as a natural history guide for International Expeditions, one of the country's largest natural history tour companies.

His credentials are impeccable: He has a degree in wildlife biology and has worked for the U.S. Fish and Wildlife Service and the Institute of Pacific Island Forestry. You can imagine, then, the excitement and authority of his natural history tours when he personally guides you into the premier bird-watching spots in the state.

The emphasis on this expedition is Hawaiian forest birds. Collins leads trips into the forest interiors of all the islands, such as the Hakalau National Wildlife Refuge on the Big Island, the best place to see rare and endangered Hawaiian forest birds. He leads you toward the Mauna Kea summit and down to a ranch at the 6,000-feet elevation. The all-day bird-watching field trip costs $150 plus expenses, which may include transportation costs. The $150 is his fee regardless of the size of the group.

Collins's other major offering is a fourteen-day natural history expedition on Hawaii, Maui, Kauai, and with extensions on Oahu. On this trip, a small group travels inter-island, stays at an attractive hotel, and pursues educational adventures galore. On the Big Island, for example, you could study tidepools near the Pu'uhonua O Honaunau National Historic Park, observe invertebrates and small fish, and bird-watch near the petroglyphs at Pu'uhonua. Then on to meet the jovial members of the Ka'u Hawaiian Civic Club, who will put on the most authentic backyard luau you can hope to see in Hawaii. A few nights at the Volcano House, hiking in rain forests and old lava tubes, and down to the historic Waipio Valley before flying on to Maui for whale watching and a trip to Haleakala National Park.

The natural history expedition follows a similar course on the other islands selected, offering the best routes with the best opportunities for learning about Hawaii. The expedition is obviously not for the everyday traveler, but it is for the curious and the mature who like to stop and smell the flowers.

The expedition costs $2,000 for two weeks, which covers most meals, ground and air transportation between the islands, all admissions, and hotel accommodations. Collins can also offer excellent fares to Kona, on the Big Island, from any mainland city. For information on the natural history expeditions, write International Expeditions, Suite 104, 1776 Independence Court, Birmingham, AL 35216; telephone (800) 633-4734.

DESTINATION HAWAII
P.O. Box 90295
Honolulu, HI 96835

Anyone interested in scuba diving in Hawaii should contact this organization. Destination Hawaii represents thirty of the most professional and reputable dive and snorkeling operations throughout the state and is the best resource on water sports, particularly diving and snorkeling, in Hawaii.

Although Destination Hawaii is headquartered on Oahu, it has active members on all the islands. And although Destination Hawaii will not take you on an expedition, it will lead you to those operations that offer dive-travel packages and dives at the most exotic and exciting underwater attractions in Hawaii. Besides their up-to-the-minute information on the dive-travel packages in Hawaii, they offer the invaluable *Dive Hawaii* guide, a twenty-four-page, full-color booklet mapping out more than forty of the top diving and snorkeling sites throughout Hawaii. All the sites were selected by the dive operators themselves.

Hawaii's dive sites attract more than 50,000 scuba divers a year and countless more if you count snorkelers. The state's isolated position in the northern Pacific and the volcanic origins of the land forms here have created a marvelous underwater world of unusual reef and pelagic life, fertile ground for the avid diver.

THE NATURE CONSERVANCY OF HAWAII
1116 Smith Street
Suite 201
Honolulu, HI 96817
Telephone: (808) 537-4508

In an ongoing effort to protect Hawaii's rare and endangered wildlife, the Nature Conservancy has acquired nearly 17,500 acres in Hawaii's most important wilderness regions. The areas include the Big Island's Hakalau on the slopes of Mauna Kea, east Maui's Kipahulu Valley, Molokai's remote Pelekunu Valley, and other areas on Maui, Molokai, and Kauai. Recently the Conservancy developed a field trip program that offers a week in Hawaii with a naturalist guide and access to two of the Conservancy's preserves on Maui and Molokai.

The limit is eight to a group; besides the guide, other experts join the tour at intervals to discuss Hawaii's birds, plants, and endangered species. And there are many of them: More than 25 percent of the country's endangered species are in Hawaii.

The trips begin in Honolulu with a stay at the charming New Otani Kaimana Beach Hotel, one of Oahu's favorites, move to Maui for three nights, and then to Molokai for two nights. In the course of the five days the group explores the Waikamou preserve on Maui, Haleakala, and the Kamakou preserve on Molokai. The tour ends on Oahu, at Waikiki; guests are invariably invigorated by the natural beauty they've witnessed in hidden Hawaii.

The tour costs $1,850 double occupancy or $2,100 single occupancy for the seven days, including accommodations, some meals, and transportation.

PACIFIC QUEST
P.O. Box 205
Haleiwa, HI 96712
Telephone: (808) 638-8338

Pacific Quest plans two types of expeditions: an eight-day trip and a fourteen-day trip. Each offers a unique and complete vacation with a strong natural history bent. The two-week expedition covers Kauai, the Big Island, Maui, Lanai, and Oahu. The Kauai trip, for example, would entail a visit to the Na Pali Coast and the Kokee State Park, camping overnight at Kahili Mountain Park, with great meals using local fish, fresh local produce, and healthy foods. Snorkeling in Poipu and a trip to the Waimea Canyon are included, and in the summer months the group stays in Haena on the north shore. The trips to the other islands have a similar flavor, entailing hikes, swims, cabins, and excursions just slightly off the beaten track but manageable by anyone who's activity oriented. The eight-day trip is a softer adventure that includes stays in hotels and cabins on Kauai and Maui.

Zane Bilgrave has been doing this for eight years, with enormous success and satisfied guests. The youngest on the trips has been a nine-year-old and the oldest, in the mid-eighties, with the majority of adventurers in the thirty- to forty-five-year-old range.

The eight-day adventure costs $745, which includes accommodations, transportation, and about half the food. The fourteen-day excursion costs $1,175, or about $84 a day, which covers all transportation, equipment, food, gear, and camping or accommodations.

WILDERNESS HAWAII
Shena Sandler
P.O. Box 61692
Honolulu, HI 96839
Telephone: (808) 737-4697

The offerings here are extensive and quite daring. Not everyone would dare to backpack through the Ka'u Desert and up 14,000 feet to the summit of Mauna Loa. Shena Sandler's trips are often like that—vigorous, demanding, and challenging.

The premier summer offering is a twenty-one-day wilderness course in the Hawaii Volcanoes National Park that includes four nights at a 10,000-feet elevation or higher. Part of that trip is what they call a "solo," where you spend two to three days alone in the wilderness with no watch, flashlight, or book. One day is kept free to rappel, what else? This is called roughing it, and for this trip most takers are teens. The average age is thirteen to eighteen; they gain stamina and self-confidence.

Sandler also offers women's wilderness courses, executive and adult courses (challenge the urban dweller to go on a hike), simpler four-day courses with an introduction to wilderness skills, with some snorkeling thrown in.

Obviously, this isn't for everyone. But those who do go have great things to say about it, about how the beauty and challenge of the wilderness helped them to grow in other ways. The twenty-one-day course costs $1,175 for food and all gear. The shorter courses range $275 and up.

DINING OUT

Honolulu residents eat out a lot. Here, in alphabetical order, are where Honolulu residents may or may not be dining. Some of the following are recognized favorites, others less well known. All are good, not all are fancy, and some are downright humble. Each appeals in its own way, whether it offers a lot for your money or the most lavish feast in town, or whether it makes one thing better than anyone else. Herewith, then, the best of dining and eating on Oahu, starting with the restaurants of Honolulu and windward Oahu, of which there are many more than on the north shore—but the restaurant scene there is blossoming, so don't overlook it!

RESTAURANTS
Honolulu and Windward Oahu

L'AUBERGE SWISS RESTAURANT
117 Hekili Street
Kailua
Telephone: (808) 263-4663

L'Auberge serves a wide-ranging continental menu whose offerings include the traditional sausages (bratwurst), pasta, sautéed scallops, and other traditional European specialties. Chef and owner Alfred Mueller combines the best of German, French, and Italian cuisines and applies a seasoned hand to the veal, seafood, chicken, and beef dishes on the menu. There are smoked salmon, clams, oysters Rockefeller, and escargots as delicious as in any fine continental restaurant. There are two soups and two salads nightly, with light dinners. Although the menu is à la carte, two chef's specials are offered each night. One time it could be lamb chops, another time roast sirloin; whatever it is, it will be good. Mueller makes a wonderful osso bucco, and you'll rave about his scallops and opakapaka special. For the extent and quality of the meal it serves, L'Auberge is not at all expensive. Entrées range from $11 to $14.50, and specials such as the lamb chops go for $19. Open 6:00 P.M. to 10:00 P.M. Tuesday through Saturday, and from 5:30 P.M. on Sunday. Closed Monday. Major credit cards accepted.

AZTECA MEXICAN RESTAURANT
3569 Waialae Avenue
Kaimuki
Telephone: (808) 735-2492

Family-style Mexican food is the fare here, great bountiful platters of refried beans, rice, heavy steaks and meats, and the old standbys, tostadas, burritos, and enchiladas. The decor is regrettable, but no one comes here for that and the food is consistent. The enchilada platters are reliably good, and the salsa is generally, but not always, hot enough. The vegetarian burrito, guacamole, and flan are highly recommended.

Moderately priced and very informal. Open 11:00 A.M. to 10:00 P.M. daily, except Sunday, when it's open 5:00 P.M. to 10:00 P.M. Major credit cards accepted.

BACI
2255 Kuhio Avenue
Waikiki Trade Center
Waikiki
Telephone: (808) 924-2533

They will not kill you with kindness at the door, nor will they go out of their way to make you feel welcome, but the service is efficient enough and the food is marvelous.

Baci's extensive menu features northern Italian cuisine with many exceptional dishes. Fresh pasta is made daily and the sauces are made to order, which means maximum flavor and freshness. The Frutti di Mare is a favorite, with scallops, clams, squid, shrimp, and a wide, flat pasta in a zesty red tomato sauce. It's exceedingly popular, as are the fresh fish dishes—ono, mahi, or ahi—sautéed in a cream sauce with mushrooms and shrimp. And the Baci garlic bread is memorable—warm and buttered bread with a whole head of soft baked garlic served separately. The idea is to gently coax the tender, sweet garlic out of its skin and then spread the savory paste over the bread. Marvelous.

There are pastas with white sauces too, a host of attractive salads, and veal and chicken dishes galore. One acceptable way to tackle the menu is for two to share a salad, pasta, and entrée. The servings are enormous and shared orders are perfect for moderate eaters.

The desserts are equally enticing, with Chocolate Decadence Cake leading the pack and a White Chocolate Brioche with Strawberries and Cream a close second. From start to finish, you can have a convincing Italian meal here.

Two can dine handsomely for about $40, not including wine. Open nightly for dinner and weekdays for lunch and dinner. Major credit cards accepted.

BAGWELLS 2424
Hyatt Regency Hotel
2424 Kalakaua Avenue
Corner Kaiulani
Waikiki
Telephone: (808) 922-9292

This posh continental restaurant, one of Honolulu's best, has been completely renovated and has a new menu. The room is lighter and prettier than ever before, with a white baby grand piano in the center and a luxurious ambience of soft whites and beiges highlighted with etched glass and exotic palms inside and outside the floor-to-ceiling glass windows.

The emphasis is on fresh local produce and fish, and there is an extensive à la carte menu. The chilled cucumber soup with sorbet is excellent, and so are the lobster raviolis. For entrées, the ulua served with a passion fruit beurre blanc wins rave reviews; so do the lamb chops. Another new feature is the chef's surprise, a six-course meal designed according to the availability of ingredients and the chef's mood.

Desserts include passion fruit soufflé, double chocolate pâté with warm orange zabaglione, burgundy poached pear with wild honey ice cream, and mango puree in season.

Adding to the room's appeal are the displays of raku pottery by local and California artists. Also, the sumptuous Bagwells wine bar has been remodeled and now offers more than four hundred different labels.

Bagwells is expensive; dinner for two could easily run about $120. Open nightly for dinner. Major credit cards accepted.

THE BALI
Hilton Hawaiian Village Hotel
2005 Kalia Road
Waikiki (ewa end)
Telephone: (808) 941-2254

Chef Yves Menoret, formerly of Bagwells, continues to serve continental cuisine with his characteristic light touch. Trained in Brittany, he's well schooled in the preparation of light sauces to complement the fresh seafood, such as the opakapaka in a fresh basil sauce or the opakapaka in a ginger sauce reduced in beurre blanc. Diners rave about his game sauces as well and the sauce of fresh papaya with macadamia nut liqueur he so skillfully concocts to accompany the venison or lamb. The dessert headliners are the fresh sorbets in guava, lilikoi, papaya, and fresh lime—again, light and refreshing, nothing cloying.

The restaurant is at water's edge, in a beautifully appointed room of antiques and glorious etched glass. It sets an elegant mood for oceanside dining in what is the loveliest and most tranquil spot at the alarmingly large Hilton Hawaiian Village Hotel.

Expensive. Entrées cost from $19 to $26. Open nightly for dinner. Major credit cards accepted.

BAN ZAI RAHMEN
1103 South King Street
Corner Pensacola
Telephone: (808) 533-2033

A mere counter with stools on a street corner, this is still a worthy stop. It's ideal for an after-movie snack or a light meal of fried noodles or ramen when you're too hungry for a smoothie and not famished enough for a three-course meal. The specialty is noodles: fried, in soups, with vegetables, with seafood, chilled, hot, with seaweed, with butter, you name it. The takeout is great on those chilly evenings when you're too tired to cook, and if you request no monosodium glutamate, they'll accommodate as best they can.

Inexpensive—about $4 per person. Open 11:00 A.M. to 3:00 P.M. and 5:00 P.M. to midnight weekdays; 11:00 A.M. to midnight weekends. No credit cards accepted.

BERNARD'S OF NEW YORK
2633 South King Street
Across from Puck's Alley
University area
Telephone: (808) 946-3633

Finally, a place that serves matzoh ball soup. And blintzes, latkes, smoked sturgeon, and all the rest. Bernard's also has great sandwiches, from chopped liver to turkey and pastrami—and the bagels and desserts are not to be missed. The flavored cheesecakes are quite the rage.

The small, neatly tiled deli has a few tables, a large counter, and a brisk takeout business. The smoked sturgeon, Nova Scotia lox, and sable are flown in from Brooklyn. The kippered herring, kippered salmon, and roll-mop herring add even more authority to the menu.

For a deli, though, it's expensive, and worse, that sacred cow of kosher food—matzoh ball soup—is inconsistent. Hopefully this will improve, because there's nothing better than sitting down to a bowl of soup, a sky-high sandwich, and a bottle of Dr. Brown's Cel-Ray tonic. For some people, though, the zenith of the meal is the dish of rice pudding, which Bernard's does well enough.

Informal but expensive—a sizable meal for two can cost about $20. Open 11:00 A.M. to 9:00 P.M., Monday through Friday; 9:00 A.M. to 9:00 P.M. Saturdays. Major credit cards accepted.

BON APPETIT
Discovery Bay
1778 Ala Moana Boulevard
Waikiki (ewa end)
Telephone: (808) 942-3837

Guy Banal, the chef and owner, has remarkable staying power. His creativity is unflagging and his classic French bistro is still one of the quiet corners for good dining in Honolulu.

There are pink linens, a beveled glass screen, fresh flowers, and cane-backed chairs—nothing elaborate, but very quietly tasteful. There are fixed-price "gourmet dinners of the week" that are invariably a good value: roast rack of lamb or the fresh catch of the day, with fresh asparagus flan, tomato bisque, cucumber salad with smoked salmon, vegetables, and dessert. There's also an ample à la carte menu that includes escargots in puff pastry (excellent), bouillabaisse with rouille, soft-shelled crabs, fresh fish, and various offerings in beef, duck, and chicken. There are pasta and vegetarian dishes and cold and warm appetizers—the Tahitian salad is great. No palate is neglected.

An added feature is the wine list, not extensive but very well selected.

There's an excellent selection of French wines and you also have a choice of about three dozen fine wines by the glass. Desserts—profiteroles, clafoutis of pear and black cherries, with hot raspberry sauce, tarte tatin, and others—are a fitting finale to an exceptional meal.

Moderately expensive—$19.95 to $27.95 per person for the "gourmet dinner of the week." Dinner nightly except Sunday. There's validated parking in the Discovery Bay parking lot. Major credit cards accepted.

BUENO NALO
41-865 Kalanianaole Highway
Waimanalo
Telephone: (808) 259-7186

The newly expanded Bueno Nalo still serves superior chimichangas, enchiladas, and burritos along with many other Mexican specialties. The appetizers here are fantastic, from the nachos to the quesadillas served with a delicious, hearty salsa. For the entrée, you can't go wrong with the chimichangas or chile rellenos. It's safe to order anything here, for the quality is consistent and they take their cuisine seriously.

Informal and inexpensive. No liquor, but you can bring your own. No reservations either, so be prepared to wait during peak hours. Open daily except Monday for dinner. No credit cards accepted.

CASTAGNOLA'S ITALIAN RESTAURANT
Manoa Marketplace
2752 Woodlawn Drive
Manoa
Telephone: (808) 988-2969; 988-2971

It could be said that this is the best restaurant in town. In terms of quality, it's unrelenting and uncompromising. To wit, they make their own sausage (people love to buy it to take home); *everything* is made with extra-virgin olive oil; the hand-picked, vine-ripened, thin-skinned canned tomatoes are shipped in from Italy; and the pasta is made with natural mineral water in the Abruzzi region of Italy. The cheeses, too, are from Italy, where the milk for the Parmesan comes from cows that are not allowed to graze outdoors but are fed strictly in their stalls to avoid impurities. The chicken is freshly grown on the island, the herbs and produce are fresh from Oahu, and the Italian bread is baked twice a day, using unbleached flour, kosher salt, honey instead of sugar, and no shortening.

Needless to say, the food is flawless. The Caesar salad is the best in town, the scampi is impeccable, the fresh catch is always sublime. For lunch and for dinner, from fresh ono sandwiches to linguini al pesto, you can count on top quality here.

The restaurant is informal, always busy, and scrupulous in its ethics. Unlike the exclusive New York restaurants where a big name is entrée enough, Castagnola's has been known to decline Ronald Reagan and the mayor simply because the tables were full. This is New York–style Italian food, the best in town, from a New Jersey Italian family who brought the best of Italy to Hawaii.

Moderately expensive, about $60 for dinner for two. The restaurant serves without a break and is ideal for any kind of snack throughout the day. Open 11:30 A.M. to 10:00 P.M. Tuesday through Saturday, closed Sunday, open for lunch only on Monday. Major credit cards accepted.

CHE PASTA
3571 Waialae Avenue
Kaimuki
Telephone: (808) 735-1777

Che Pasta makes its own noodles and prepares Italian food with a light touch, with only the freshest ingredients. Everything is made from scratch, including the tomato sauce from tomatoes that are roasted daily. The cuisine is only lightly salted, a pleasant departure from most, and most of the dishes are flavorful and satisfying.

You can tell a lot by the way Che Pasta makes its Spaghetti Pomodoro, a basic tomato sauce with the perfect touch of garlic and herbs. Many restaurants oversalt or underseason this great Italian staple, but here it's done beautifully. The Linguini with Clams is also notable, and the Primavera is excellent, although a little on the rich side. Che Pasta's pastas, including the green spinach pasta, are consistently well done even though the sauces may not always be consistent.

Specials may include fresh lobster ravioli with leeks, mushrooms, and ricotta cheese in a cream and walnut sauce. The fresh catch is usually excellent, prepared in a number of ways, using wine, capers, and herbs.

Che Pasta is one of the more pleasant luncheon rendezvous. (They have just begun serving pizza, but I have not yet tried it.) The changing art exhibits adorning the walls, the tasteful, clean lines of the room, and the expansive gray motif make this a soothing place to have lunch or dinner. Che Pasta also has a downtown restaurant, but it is singularly noisy, with tables so close together you have to hide your notes.

Moderately expensive, about $60 for dinner for two. Open Monday through Friday for lunch, and for dinner nightly. Major credit cards accepted.

CHIANG MAI
2239 South King Street
McCully
Telephone: (808) 941-1151

The nice thing about most Thai and Chinese restaurants is that you can feast like a sultan and not dress up. Cleanliness, good cuisine, and a skilled hand at the seasonings are crucial, and who cares about the decor? Chiang Mai is one of those places—spare, functional, with great northern Thai food.

There are many seafood dishes—hot spicy clams, golden calamari with fresh lemon grass, seafood casserole—and the traditional green papaya salad, which Chiang Mai does quite well. The fresh catch of the day is always popular, and you can count on the Evil Jungle Prince, a concoction of sautéed vegetables in basil, coconut milk, and spices. They are unstinting with their coconut milk and fresh lemon grass, and the chef has a seasoned hand with the creamy, herb-filled sauces that grace the curries. Their

Cornish game hens are also popular; forty were served in a single night recently. One thing everyone orders here is the sticky rice, a rather tasteless regional favorite that accompanies anything.

You can expect slow service when it's busy, but at least the food will be hot. Two can dine abundantly for $22. Lunch Monday through Saturday; dinner nightly. Major credit cards accepted.

CHOI'S YAKINIKU
1736 Kapiolani Boulevard
Waikiki/Ala Moana
Telephone: (808) 947-6861

Choi's is the true Korean restaurant, with spicy food and lots of little appetizers. You sit at Formica tables and Naugahyde booths in a smoky, crowded room with lit-up beer signs and watch the habitués pour in for their favorite dishes. Although you may have a long wait during busy hours, they fill the table with many dainty dishes of appetizers to keep you busy: tiny saucers of marinated bean sprouts, eggplant, turnip, watercress, seaweed, kim chee, and marinated dried fish. The eight different kinds of appetizers are hot, pickled, or poached in sesame oil and very delicious.

The entrées range from the familiar Man Doo Soup to buckwheat noodles with sashimi, homemade noodles with julienned vegetables, fish and clam stews, and the familiar barbecued meats and ribs. The soups come in iron kettles and the servings are generous.

The appetizers are the stars of the show here. If you're not in a rush and don't mind a wait during rush hour, you should have an enjoyable evening.

Inexpensive. Open 10:30 A.M. to 10:00 P.M. daily. Major credit cards accepted.

COMPADRES MEXICAN BAR AND GRILL
Ward Centre
1200 Ala Moana Boulevard
Across Ala Moana Park
Telephone: (808) 523-3914

The light, upbeat ambience is accented with bright wooden parrots hanging from odd corners, large Mexican vases and urns, and hardwoods with brass trim. It's informal, very Yuppie, with young, hip waiters and waitresses who provide efficient service.

Their margaritas are famous, and the menu provides many options in seafood, traditional Mexican dishes such as the burritos and chimichangas, and some heavier meat and pork dishes. The choices are vast, and the dinner servings are enormous.

The recently introduced breakfasts are also terrific. The huevos rancheros are noteworthy, the cinnamon-fried tortillas are great, and the chilaquiles (tortillas sautéed with garlic, chilis, onions, and tomatoes) are certainly worth a try.

The food is moderately priced and highly recommended. The only problem is getting in. Compadres does not take reservations and is always packed, with a small waiting area not capable of handling the numbers usually waiting.

Moderately priced. Open daily for breakfast, lunch, and dinner. Major credit cards accepted.

CREPE FEVER
Ward Centre
1200 Ala Moana Boulevard
Across Ala Moana Park
Telephone: (808) 521-9023

Certainly one of the more pleasant lunchtime stops, Crepe Fever offers sandwiches, salads, and a "grain and green express bar," which is an oasis for the health-conscious. There are only a few tables and a counter at this popular sandwich and crêpe bar, so it can get busy.

The choices: crêpes (tuna, spinach, vegetarian, chicken, etc.), stuffed croissants, wonderful homemade soups, sandwiches on cracked wheat bread with the best locally grown produce and the fresh pea spreads and other imaginative offerings of the grain and green bar.

The food is inexpensive and the choices are healthy, delicious, and wide-ranging. You can't go wrong with Crepe Fever for an informal, light, and satisfying lunch or dinner.

Inexpensive. Open for breakfast, lunch, and dinner Monday through Saturday, with shorter hours and no dinner service on Sunday. Major credit cards accepted.

DOONG KONG LAU—HAKKA RESTAURANT
100 North Beretania Street
Chinese Cultural Plaza
Chinatown
Telephone: (808) 531-8833

"Hakka" refers to a style of cooking used by the poor people in China who live on boats. The cuisine is less spicy than Szechuan and uses many different kinds of seafood, served sizzling on heated platters. Doong Kong Lau has excellent sizzling platters, from the scallops to mixed seafood, and its black bean sauces are honorable as well. There are nearly a hundred items on the menu, from fresh steamed kumu to noodle dishes and spicy eggplant, the best. Moreover, the prices are exceedingly low.

Very inexpensive. Open daily from 9:00 A.M. to 9:30 P.M. Major credit cards accepted.

EGGS 'N THINGS
436 Ena Road
Waikiki (ewa end)
Telephone: (808) 949-0820

This Honolulu old-timer is still kicking, with the same great pancakes and excessive omelets that gave it its reputation years ago. A handful of tables fills the small room and eccentric night owls file in at all hours. It can be rowdy here late at night. In the morning, quiet early birds restore themselves with the specials: the early-riser and late-riser specials of three pancakes and two eggs for $1.75, offered between 5:00 A.M. and 9:00 A.M., 1:00 and 2:00 A.M. and 1:00 and 2:00 P.M.

The omelets are sinfully rich, just wallowing in butter. The pancakes are reliably good, and the lemon crêpes, although very rich, are worth the calories.

The usual menu items, pancakes and omelets, are not inexpensive, but the specials and the generous servings make Eggs 'n' Things a deal any time of the day.

Omelets cost $4.75 to $6.50. Open from 11:00 P.M. at night to 2:00 P.M. the following day. No credit cards or checks accepted.

FIVE SPICE
432 Ena road
Waikiki (ewa end)
Telephone: (808) 955-8706

This Chinese restaurant is a sleeper. Little known and unobtrusive, it sits quietly on noisy Ena Road and serves wonderful Mandarin, Shanghai, Szechuan, and Cantonese food, and the best vegetarian Chinese food around. The menu is extensive, covering the full range of spicy shrimp, chicken, pork, noodle, and even lamb dishes in various preparations. But when you get to the vegetarian menu, what a surprise! Vegetarian gyoza (fried dumplings), vegetarian spring rolls, vegetarian roast duck, vegetarian char siu, vegetarian chicken with broccoli, monk's food, vegetarian mu shu pork—everything a non–meat eater has ever desired but couldn't have is on this marvelous menu. The chef has mastered the art of making tofu and gluten taste like anything, so the ersatz meat dishes have their own lively integrity. The gyoza is superb, with a nutty flavor. The mu shu pork without the pork (they'll substitute shrimp for the pork if you wish) is divine on its bed of plum sauce and wrapped in the tender crêpe.

The restaurant has a knotty pine interior and odd painted murals. It's endearingly eccentric and homely. The owner, a pleasant, serene woman who radiates warmth, makes you feel entirely at home. You will eat well, feel welcome, and surely you'll want to return.

Parking is a problem, but you can park in the nearby Wailana Coffee Shop parking lot for a nominal charge. Street parking is scarce here. Inexpensive—dinner for two would be about $20. Open 11:00 A.M. to 10:30 P.M. daily. Major credit cards accepted.

GOLDEN DRAGON
Hilton Hawaiian Village
2005 Kalia Road
Waikiki
Telephone: (808) 946-5336

After you walk through what may be the most gorgeous black lacquer door in the world, you see the 6-foot-tall antique vases, the teak floor, and the silk and lacquer screens. Every visual detail is elegant and the room literally oozes with opulence. And then, suddenly, you see the waitress/ fortune teller with an elaborate upswept coif in which are ensconced blinking lights and what look like miniature pagodas. She's reading tea leaves.

It is an abrupt incongruity, but when she sweeps you to the other side of the room you can settle down to the menu and reflect upon Chef Dai Hoy Chang's latest ingenuities. Complimentary appetizers appear: smoked duck with sauce and condiments. Behind you is a glassed-in room where they smoke their own fowl. The smoked duck salad with tangerine dressing is popular, but the surrounding greens aren't as fresh as they could be. (Endive should never be bruised, especially at these prices.)

Nevertheless, the menu is impressive, with a wide range of dishes that bring to mind "California Chinois" or "nouvelle Chinese" or something equally cross-cultural. The Imperial Beggar's Chicken, wrapped in lotus leaves and baked in clay, is the best known of the chef's creations, but it must be ordered twenty-four hours in advance and for at least two people. There's also a group of smoked oven specialties, from pork and fish to lamb and duck. The lobster in Chinese black bean sauce is delicious, and the Hawaiian touches of taro, lotus, and haupia in the cooking provide an added plus.

The dinner is expensive—about $70 for two—which puts it in a different category from what we normally think of as Chinese food, where decor is inconsequential and the sole concern is hearty, unpretentious, and inexpensive fare. The Golden Dragon is for those to whom price is no object and who don't mind paying exorbitant prices for a visual and esthetic experience in dining. Open for dinner nightly. Casual to dressy. Major credit cards accepted.

GREEK ISLAND TAVERNA
2570 Beretania Street
Moiliili
Telephone: (808) 943-0052

It's a small rectangular room above a parking lot and copy service where you can find the best Greek food in town. To start with, the Greek bread is marvelous and the mezethes kries, cold appetizers, are entertaining and satisfying. One could dine all evening on the appetizers here: escargots, deep-fried squid, fresh eggplant salad, stuffed grape leaves, and the Kasseri cheese flamed in brandy. Dinners range from the Greek bouillabaisse, kakavia, to the catch of the day and various types of chicken and fish kebabs. The lamb and gyros are favorites among meat eaters. The Greek music builds through the night as the retsina flows, and by the time you leave there will be Greek dancing on the tiny floor. They know how to eat well and have fun here.

Two can dine heartily for $25 to $30. Open for dinner nightly and for lunch weekdays. Major credit cards accepted.

HAMBURGER MARY'S ORGANIC GRILL
2109 Kuhio Avenue
Waikiki
Telephone: (808) 922-6722

Count on having the best sandwiches of your life here, and homemade soups to match. The atmosphere does its part too—an eclectic amalgam of tropical funk, Deco Hawaiian, and a pervasive humor that expresses itself in such details as baby-bottle milk dispensers. The sandwiches are wholesome: good breads with fresh vegetables and generous tuna, shrimp, avocado, or beef fillings. The raw-milk cheddar offered here is impressive. Of course, Hamburger Mary's has the best hamburgers, and its salads are great too. Sautéed mushrooms with raw-milk cheddar are an old favorite offered nowhere else.

Real crowd pleasers are the desserts, from the cheesecake to the walnut pie. They also make the best vegetarian Eggs Benedict on whole-wheat English muffins here. It's usually noisy and is quite the hangout for trendies and gays, but others should not be intimidated. This is wholesome, good food you'll come back for.

Sandwiches run $4.25 to $7.25. Open daily from 10:00 A.M. to 2:00 A.M. Major credit cards accepted.

HARD ROCK CAFÉ
1837 Kapiolani Boulevard
Corner Kalakaua
Waikiki (ewa end)
Telephone: (808) 955-7383

The people who brought hamburgers to London and cultism to café dining have opened in Honolulu. The Hard Rock Café, known for combining rock and roll memorabilia with hamburgers and smokehouse ribs, have opened at the site of the old Coco's at the gateway to Waikiki.

The café features loud music, seats 250, and is highlighted with surf memorabilia from the most coveted collections in Hawaii. It is a raucous and popular hang-out. The rock and roll collectibles that are the Hard Rock insignia are there too, and so are the Hard Rock chili, ⅓-pound hand-patted hamburgers, and some fresh island fish as entrées and sandwiches. The black bean soup is excellent. The prices are moderate, and already this new Honolulu eatery has the same cult appeal exhibited at the other eight Hard Rock Cafés.

The Hard Rock will be moving into Hawaii's surf scene in a big way, too. It's the new sponsor of the World Cup of Surfing, one of the lead events in Hawaii's Triple Crown of Surfing each winter on the north shore.

Hamburgers cost $5.75 to $6.75, so lunch would run about $10 per person. Open 11:00 A.M. to 1:30 A.M. Fridays and Saturdays; to 1:00 A.M. on Mondays through Thursdays, and until midnight on Sundays. Major credit cards accepted.

HATA RESTAURANT
1740 South King Street
Pawaa/McCully
Telephone: (808) 941-2686

Hata Restaurant is one of those secrets you want to keep. Like an old soda fountain that's been upgraded to a diner, it's small, inexpensive, and very informal, with a loyal cadre of fans whose word-of-mouth business keeps it going. Expect Formica tables and a kitschy interior; this is not Japanese haute cuisine, but simpler folk dishes with no pretensions. The traditional New Year's mochi soup, called *ozoni*, is served here, and so are crab in a broth served in an earthenware pot (kani nabe), salmon in a few preparations, butterfish, saimin, cold saimin, kalua pig tofu, and fresh ahi or aku sautéed in soy sauce. Hata's serves no dessert and no liquor.

Open Monday through Saturday from 10:30 A.M. to 9 P.M. No credit cards accepted.

HEALTHY'S NATURAL FOODS
2425 South King Street
Moiliili
Telephone: (808) 955-2479

Healthy's is a godsend for those concerned with eating healthy food but having little time. It is that ingenious new discovery, a health-food fast-food restaurant. And it is fast. You can have breakfast, lunch, or dinner here, beginning with scrambed tofu for breakfast with a whole-grain honey-cinnamon roll. You can also have whole-grain waffles; and as the day moves into lunchtime, vegetarian chili, vegetarian pizza, spaghetti, sanwiches, and a host of tangy specials. No meat or animal products are used in the food here, so you're eating pure vegetarian food.

You can order to go or eat at any of the tables set up in the cafeterialike setting. It's strictly efficient eating, with not much of an atmosphere, and a bustling health food store next door. But who cares? This is fast food, remember, and Healthy's delivers.

Inexpensive. Open 7:30 A.M. to 11:00 P.M. Monday through Saturday and until 9:00 P.M. on Sunday. No credit cards accepted.

HELENA'S HAWAIIAN FOOD
1364 North King Street
Kalihi
Telephone: (808) 845-8044

Helena Chock's Hawaiian restaurant is *the* place to go if you're looking for the real thing. She's served three generations from her Kalihi restaurant—grandchildren are returning now for the homemade lau lau, pipikaula, kalua pork done in an imu, the lomi salmon, and all the Hawaiian specialties homemade here. Since it opened in 1945, Helena's has been known as the most authentic Hawaiian restaurant, not widely known, but known among Hawaiian food fans. The specialty here is the pipikaula, sort of a Hawaiian jerky that's seasoned, dried, and fried.

Inexpensive. Open Tuesday through Friday from 10:30 A.M. to 7:30 P.M. No credit cards accepted.

HY'S STEAK HOUSE
Waikiki Park Heights Hotel
2440 Kuhio Avenue
Waikiki
Telephone: (808) 922-5555

Dark woods, leather banquettes, tapestried booths, shirred velvet curtains, classical paintings, and a dark, Yale Club–like atmosphere set the mood here. And the cuisine, with its ample selection of steaks and seafood, is excellent. The Only, a 13-ounce New York steak enhanced with a mysterious sauce, is very popular, as are the kiawe-broiled rack of lamb and the sirloin and lobster plate. For the more slender appetites, the Fettucine Primavera (with tricolored pasta, snow peas, and other vegetables) competes with the best of them, and the Scampi Sicilian is fiery and good. There are some nice touches in the appetizers, too. The French bread slathered with melted cheese is a cordial welcome, but the French onion soup is a trifle too salty.

Other than that, Hy's delivers on the food and the service, which is exceptional. They're also very accommodating with children, a rare trait in fancy restaurants and something grateful parents never forget. Moderately expensive, with entrées in the $11 to $26 range. Open for dinner nightly. Major credit cards accepted.

IDETA RESTAURANT
620 Kohou Street
Kalihi
Telephone: (808) 847-4844

Ideta isn't as well known as its counterparts, but those who know sushi swear by it. It's authentically Japanese, down to the Japanese-speaking customers who line the sushi bar and drink the exotic snail shell soup popular in Japan but little known in Hawaii. The sushi is exceptional, very fresh and served by competent, conscientious chefs. There's no razzle-dazzle here, just honest sushi made of the best ingredients. Ask for the mountain yam with ume (plum paste) and chiso leaf—it's not to be missed. The restaurant also serves popular Japanese items, from the usual tempura dishes to various combinations of chicken, tonkatsu, and bento-style clusters of appetizers.

Moderately priced. Ideta opens Monday through Saturday for lunch, and for dinner Tuesday through Sunday. Major credit cards accepted.

IL FRESCO
Ward Centre
1200 Ala Moana Boulevard
Across from Ala Moana Park
Telephone: (808)523-5191

Il Fresco is one of those chic restaurants with a long list of celebrity customers they like everyone to know about. But the menu stands on its own and the lunches and dinners are creatively prepared, making it a nice stop anyway. If you don't mind paying the price.

There are so many other temptations on the menu that it's curious the pizza has so much appeal. The ahi pasta is always superb, a tasty melding of fresh ahi and herbs in an olive oil base with Greek olives, herbs, and capers. The goat cheese salads and appetizers also have some appeal, but the grilled eggplant, topped with crisp fried garlic and with a goat cheese spread, is the most successful of all. The meats and fish, cooked on Il Fresco's famous kiawe grill, are reliable.

For dinner, the blackened opakapaka is the mainstay of the menu, cooked with Cajun spices and served tender and moist inside. Although Il Fresco was one of the first in Honolulu to start serving this Paul Prudhomme specialty, this is not the best blackened fish around. The blackened ahi, however, is superb. A fillet of ahi—essentially sashimi—is seared quickly and served, still raw inside, with a marvelous sauce. This is one of Il Fresco's most notable dishes.

This is a fine place for lunch, with a pleasant, airy ambience and a selection that will satisfy. Informal and moderately expensive—dinner can run $40 a person. Open Monday through Saturday for lunch and dinner. Major credit cards accepted.

INDIA HOUSE
2632 South King Street
University area
Telephone: (808) 955-7552

Ram Arora, who brought naan to Hawaii, is still serving the best Indian food from his modest little restaurant near the university. Ever since he left The Third Floor restaurant, where his naan was legendary, Arora has established himself as a consummate Indian chef.

Very popular is the chicken shahicorma, fresh chicken cut into pieces and cooked in a special spicy sauce with fresh grapes and cashew nuts. People also love the maharaja dinner, a colorful composite of soup, lamb, tandoori chicken, fish, curry, and condiments. For vegetarians, there is an ample selection of vegetarian curries. Leave room for dessert—the halvah and rose-flavored sweets are delightful.

Moderately priced; entrées are $10.75 to $14.95. Open weekdays for lunch and nightly for dinner. Major credit cards accepted.

IRIFUNE RESTAURANT
563 Kapahulu Avenue
Kapahulu
Telephone: (808) 737-1141

With its Japanese folk decor and its simple but exquisite fare, Irifune remains one of the city's favorite low-profile winners. The menu here is unique, with dishes that have been adapted to suit Irifune's distinctive cuisine. The shish kebabs are popular, and the shrimp tempura is exceedingly light and delicious. The garlic dishes are something you'll find nowhere else: garlic vegetables, garlic chicken, garlic ahi. Just wonderful, and there are tasty vegetarian dishes as well. The sashimi is always fresh, and what they have accomplished with tofu in their appetizers and entrées is staggering. Best of all, the food is incredibly reasonable, and you can be sure it'll be prepared just right. A second big plus is that Irifune uses no MSG. Although Irifune does not serve liquor, you're welcome to bring your own.

No reservations and very inexpensive—a hearty meal may cost $5 to $6 per person. Open for lunch Tuesday, Wednesday, Friday, and Saturday, as well as for dinner every day except Monday. Major credit cards accepted.

JACK'S COFFEE HOUSE
Aina Haina Shopping Center
Aina Haina
Telephone: (808) 373-4034

Everyone who knows about Jack's adores it. It's often crowded in the mornings with bleary-eyed diners discussing last night's game or meeting, and fortifying themselves for the day ahead. Jack's is famous for its home-baked biscuits, fresh fish dishes, and inexpensive, home-cooked meals. The omelets are not fancy as in most breakfast restaurants, but they are appealing, tasty, and wholesome.

There are only a few tables in the restaurant so you may have to wait during peak hours. It will be worth it. It's inexpensive, straightforward, and a delight any time. Open daily for breakfast, lunch, and dinner. Major credit cards accepted.

KAMAAINA SUITE
The Willows
901 Hausten Street
McCully
Telephone: (808) 946-4808

The continental dinner is very elegant, served on the second floor overlooking lovely bromeliads, hanging ferns, and a thatched hut beside a carp pond. It's very understated; they impart a feeling of *kamaaina* ("native born" in Hawaiian) grace with the hospitality and the few pieces of artwork.

Chef Kusuma Coray unleashes her creative vigor in the courses that unfold before you. First, the hot, fragrant brioche with brie appears, and then the appetizer, spinach timbale with lemon butter glaze, perhaps, or roast quail with foie gras pâté in a nest of mountain yams. The entrée could be fresh onaga with lobster mousse, coulis de tomate, with either watercress saffron sauce or with chutney butter sauce, or medaillons of roast veal with lemon-kumquat glaze and saffron spinach. A mint sorbet as intermezzo, perhaps, and then a salad of cumin-flavored, slivered breast of duckling. It's all quite splendid, delivered with the sterling touches of one of Honolulu's master chefs in an environment that is like a comfortable living room. It's surprising, then, to hear Helen Reddy and other thoroughly un-Hawaiian sounds coming across the sound system. Although you are treated to a brief interval with a lovely strolling Hawaiian trio, the taped music before and after them do not do the cuisine justice.

If you prefer a vegetarian meal or one with seafood and no meat, let them know ahead of time and they'll accommodate your preferences.

The moderately expensive dinner is $42.50 per person, plus tax and gratuity, which for a six-course dinner of this quality is not excessive. Open for dinner nightly except for Sunday. Major credit cards accepted.

KENGO'S ROYAL BUFFET
1529 Kapiolani Boulevard
Near Ala Moana Center
Telephone: (808) 941-2241

There are two parts to Kengo's: the coffee shop–diner and the buffet restaurant next door to it. Both offer incredible value, but it's the buffet that is notable.

From breakfast on, Kengo's coffee shop provides great meals at budget prices. This is no gourmet restaurant, rather it's simple, very local, with booths and a nondescript ambience, the kind of place you can come to in your T-shirt and Zoris.

The dinner buffet offers a sampling of local dishes; try the lobster in black bean sauce, kal bi, shrimp tempura, deep-fried ahi, french fries, and many other delectables for a modest $12.95, which also includes beverage and dessert. It has a diverse and wonderful salad bar with all the trimmings. The luncheon buffet has a selection nearly as vast as the dinner buffet, delicious and a bargain at $7.95.

There are no pretensions here, just good, honest food at unbelievably low prices. The restaurant is open from 6:00 A.M. to 9:00 P.M. daily. The buffet is open from 11:00 A.M. to 2:00 P.M. and 5:00 P.M. to 9:30 P.M. daily.

KEO'S THAI CUISINE
625 Kapahulu Avenue
Kapahulu
Telephone: (808) 737-8240

Keo's is the glamour restaurant of Honolulu, where everyone from Tina Turner to Jimmy Carter tries the Evil Jungle Prince or a mango daiquiri. Everyone loves Keo's. It has a style all its own, a sort of oriental-deco-baroque-tropical ambience that features bronze statues and gold Thai figurines lolling about amid oceans of lovely orchids.

There are hundreds of items on the menu, from the famous Evil Jungle Prince to green, yellow, and red curries in various styles and soups with the familiar lemon grass–basil fragrance. The herbs are fresh and are used with ingenuity here. There are many recommendable dishes: the green papaya salad, Bangkok stuffed chicken wings, Thai crispy noodles, Evil Jungle Prince with ulua, and of course the spring rolls. Vegetarians have ample choices here as well.

Moderately priced—about $20 per person, without wine. Open for dinner nightly and for lunch weekdays. Major credit cards accepted.

KYO YA
2057 Kalakaua Avenue
Waikiki
Telephone: (808) 947-3911

The neon sign of the pagoda is still here, and the good food is still being served. Kyo Ya is a classic Japanese restaurant that hasn't changed much in the thirty years it's been on Kalakaua.

There are tables and tatami dining areas, with kimono-clad waitresses bustling around wielding platters of sashimi, pots of yosenabe, and the delicate curls of tempura that are esthetically arranged. They do very well with the shabu-shabu, the beef and vegetables cooked in a zesty broth, and with the yosenabe served in earthenware pots, and the ever-popular sukiyaki. The forte here is the specially arranged dinners in the tatami rooms upstairs, where groups can dine teahouse-style.

Moderately priced—dinner for two costs about $35 to $40. Open for lunch daily except Sunday; open for dinner nightly. Major credit cards accepted.

MAILE RESTAURANT
Kahala Hilton
5000 Kahala Avenue
Telephone: (808) 734-2211

The orchid-covered walls of the lava rock stairway set the mood for this dining adventure. You're greeted by a kimono-clad hostess and led through an attractive room highlighted with huge bromeliads and elaborate floral arrangements. The service is impeccable, and the wine list has been voted one of the country's top 100 by *Wine Spectator* magazine.

For starters, the opakapaka soup is exceptional—a clear broth with morsels of fish, perfectly cooked, with julienned vegetables adding color and texture. Sautéed fiddleheads follow, and then a salad and a sorbet of cumin, or champagne, or some exotic fruit or spice. There are roast rack of lamb, chateaubriand, and the classic duckling Waialae. The Scallops Orientale are served with ginger and oyster sauce, tofu, mushrooms, and snow peas. The Opakapaka Kahala is consistently a winner, perfectly done in a butter cream sauce and surrounded by a medley of vegetables. Since the restaurant introduced its new menu recently, however, some of its seafood dishes have had mixed reviews.

The table d'hôte menu, at $38, changes according to what's available. Selections may include freshly smoked salmon medaillons, curry-oyster soup, collar of sole fillets, salmon parfait with salmon caviar, and the finale—baked coconut pudding, called *haupia* by the Hawaiians, with lime sauce and strawberry ice cream.

For dessert, large, clear vases of fresh fruit in season accompany the pastry cart, and you face having to choose between stawberry flan, chocolate-almond squares, profiteroles, and a host of other temptations. If you're lucky, a Grand Marnier or chocolate mint soufflé is on the menu and should absolutely not be missed.

The Maile Restaurant is in the luxurious Kahala Hilton hotel, one of Oahu's long-standing favorites, which lists among its clients rock stars, U.S. presidents, Chinese premiers, and other international celebrities. But it also has a large following among local residents who have come to expect consistently good service and cuisine. Jackets are required for men. Expensive—dinner for two could cost about $100. Dinner nightly. Major credit cards accepted.

MAKAI MARKET FOOD COURT
Ala Moana Center
Makai side

It used to be that shoppers would wander around Ala Moana Center looking for a decent place to eat. It was a problem and a serious deficiency.

Since they built the Makai Market, however, residents make special trips to the shopping center to dine in this crowded arcade.

The Food Court is the largest in Hawaii and one of the largest in the United States. It has 850 seats, is always crowded, and has a surprisingly good assortment of acceptable, and even wonderful, eateries. There are 21 restaurants with takeout service. You order, pay at the counter, and find a place among the throngs of people, like you, dining at the plastic tables.

If you can handle the noise level, you'll find some great meals here. The Korean takeout is fabulous, as is La Rotisserie with its vegetable kebabs, potato salads, and other good deals. Although the seafood kebab is a deal for under $5, it would be great if they told you the crab was imitation crab—that's the biggest transgression here. And Sbarrro offers the best pizza on the island, real thin-crust, New York–style pizza. Healthy's is here too, with its fast-food vegetarian fare, and there are yogurt bars and the famous Patti's Chinese Kitchen. Wander around and you're sure to find something to suit your palate.

MAPLE GARDEN
909 Isenberg Street
Moiliili
Telephone: (808) 941-6641

Maple Garden still serves great smoked tea duck and an excellent eggplant garlic, two of the things that made it famous. The Szechuan favorites here are the hot and sour soup and the Chinaman's hat, but the seafood in black bean sauce is good too. It may be crowded, so be prepared—it's a small restaurant with a big name among Szechuan food lovers.

Moderately priced—dinner for two costs about $25. Major credit cards accepted. Open for lunch Monday through Saturday and for dinner daily.

MATTEO'S
364 Seaside Avenue
Marine Surf Hotel
Waikiki
Telephone: (808) 922-5551

The wine cellar is a stellar feature and was recently expanded to include hundreds of labels that have garnered it the highest distinction in Hawaii from *Wine Spectator* magazine. Although the interior has been redone completely to give it a warm, intimate ambience, the menu, which established Matteo's in the first place, hasn't changed much. The filet mignon is a classic winner here, and so is the cannelloni manicotta. The Caesar salad and pasta dishes are ever popular too. A new pastry chef is putting out such marvels as marbled cheesecake, the headliner in the dessert category.

Moderately expensive; dinner for two would cost about $65. Open for dinner nightly. Valet parking. Major credit cards accepted.

MEKONG I RESTAURANT
1295 South Beretania Street
Pawaa
Telephone: (808) 531-2025

Thai food lovers know this as the restaurant that established Thai food in Hawaii. It opened years ago with little to-do and quickly established itself as the best Thai eatery on the island. While the glamorous Keo's in Kapahulu gets all the attention these days, Mekong, run by the same family, sits quietly in its modest, crowded quarters and still makes the best Thai food on the island.

Mekong makes consistently good Thai food using the best fresh ingredients. You can taste the generous basil, coconut milk, lemon grass, and herbs in its curries and sauces, unwavering in their excellence. From the old classic, the Evil Jungle Prince, to the green papaya salad that many have butchered, to the Thai noodle curries and Bangkok chicken wings, Mekong will do the job right.

No alcohol is served; you can bring your own. Moderately priced—dinner for two is about $30 to $40. Open weekdays for lunch and nightly for dinner. Major credit cards accepted.

LA MER
The Halekulani
2199 Kalia Road
Waikiki
Telephone: (808) 923-2311

The setting is unbeatable and they go to great pains to present flawless continental cuisine. Yet there's something so serious and somber, perhaps self-important, about La Mer that many who enjoy its cuisine are nevertheless not encouraged to return.

The offerings include appetizers of creamy bisque of sea urchin, asparagus custard with lobster sauce and fresh mint, seaweed salad with shrimp, Maui onion and lemon grass—honorable, creative introductions. The opakapaka is broiled and filled with black olives and nestled in a seafood sauce; the medaillions of lamb are accompanied by artichokes, duck liver, truffle juice, and basil. There are many nice touches, including two prix fixe selections that include sautéed moana, breast of duck with fresh pears, poached oysters, roasted venison, and other offerings for either $44 or $56, depending on the selection. The à la carte offerings include several types of fresh fish, medaillions of lobster, stewed breast of wild duck, and bouillabaisse, at prices ranging from $26 to $36.

This is one of Honolulu's most expensive restaurants, set in the premier oceanside setting of a well-known luxury hotel, the Halekulani. It strives for excellence and pays great attention to detail in both service and cuisine. For the price you pay, it should be flawless. Yet it may not be a particularly enjoyable dining experience; it suffers from too much restraint and affectation. A more relaxed attitude, a little more levity, would serve La Mer well.

Expensive. Jackets are required. Open nightly for dinner. Major credit cards accepted.

MICHEL'S AT THE COLONY SURF
2895 Kalakaua Avenue
Waikiki
Telephone: (808) 923-6552

At Michel's, excellence is the order of the day. In terms of service, cuisine, ambience, and consistency, this oceanside Diamond Head eatery continues to lead all others as the best of Hawaii's restaurants.

That's a lot to live up to, and it does. Whether you come for breakfast, lunch, or dinner, you will be pampered with excellent food, service, and a pristine setting on the ocean where the sun shines blindingly on the water or, at night, the moon glows beyond the coconut trees just outside the window. Formally attired waiters are sensitive to your every need as you dine under crystal chandeliers, with wall-to-wall windows open to the sea breeze.

The rack of lamb here is legendary, labeled by connoisseurs as the best in town. The opakapaka simmered in champagne sauce is also a long-time favorite, and so is the Long Island duckling. Although a classic French restaurant, Michel's does deviate with some pleasing variations to suit island tastes, such as fresh onaga in an Oriental sauce.

Breakfast choices range from chanterelles omelet to continental breakfast, eggs Florentine, or fresh opakapaka. The nice thing is that you can order light or order extensively without feeling intimidated. The croissants and fresh-squeezed orange juice are wonderful. For lunch, the soufflé, seafood crêpes, salads, and changing specialties continue the tradition of excellence.

The restaurant is located in one of Hawaii's top luxury hotels, the Colony Surf, which offers its guests the supreme luxury of room service from Michel's. When you drive up, there's valet parking; a short walk through the lobby and down the stairs will bring you to this thoroughly enchanting restaurant.

Jackets are required for men in the evenings. Dinner is expensive, but two can have lunch or breakfast for $20 to $30. Open daily for breakfast and dinner, weekdays open for lunch. Major credit cards accepted.

NICK'S FISHMARKET
Waikiki Gateway Hotel
2070 Kalakaua Avenue
Waikiki
Telephone: (808) 955-6333

Nick's continues to offer fine seafood and an enjoyable dining experience. Its atmosphere is not the most memorable, but it's in good taste and the emphasis is on fresh, imaginatively prepared seafood. Fresh ono, mahimahi, opakapaka, ulua, abalone, and lobster are offered in various preparations, with lobster being the prime specialty. The legendary seafood chowder is as good as it's always been, and the scampi appetizer is excellent.

You can hardly go wrong with the seafood dishes at Nick's; only the freshest fish obtainable is used, so you can take your choice. There have been raves about the filet mignon and about the desserts, as well, particularly the carrot cake and cheesecake.

After dinner, the dance floor is a mecca for the beautiful people who gather for the entertainment and live music. Nick's is one of those celebrity haunts that attracts the high-flyers, but it's also one of the few late-night places where sophisticated partyers can go.

Expensive. Open nightly for dinner. Major credit cards accepted.

ONO HAWAIIAN FOODS
726 Kapahulu Avenue
Kapahulu
Telephone: (808) 737-2275

Ono's is always crowded, with a line that curls around the entrance auspiciously. It's a long-time favorite for Hawaiian food and is especially noted for its pipikaula and the Hawaiian classics of kalua pig, lau lau, and beef stew. Its squid luau, however, is not the best. This is the place to go if you want a taste of local color and native cuisine. You'll find yourself among the many waiting to get in for an inexpensive, hearty Hawaiian meal.

Inexpensive—two can dine here for about $14. Open 11:00 A.M. to 7:30 P.M. daily except Sunday. No credit cards accepted.

ORCHIDS
The Halekulani
2199 Kalia Road
Waikiki
Telephone: (808) 923-2311

The white linens are blinding, the view of the ocean is soothing, and the service matches the cuisine. Orchids delivers elegance.

Orchids is recommended for breakfast, lunch, or dinner. The Japanese breakfast of grilled fish, vegetables, and miso soup is impeccable, the best of its kind on the island. There are omelets, the famous Halekulani popovers, eggs benedict, and lox and bagels. For lunch, the broiled opakapaka with watercress sauce, shrimp pasta, and cold poached salmon with dill sauce are notable. The best item on the menu, however, is the Halekulani shrimp with garlic, Pernod, and saffron seasoning.

The menu is spare, but it combines Oriental and continental traditions gracefully. Even among the dinner items, the chef uses a noticeably light touch. Dinner features bouillabaisse, roast prime rib, shrimp pasta, scallop mousse with lobster sauce, and some satisfying salads and soups.

Not to be forgotten is the view. Diamond Head is in the distance, and the ocean is a stone's throw away. Although it's situated on what may be the least attractive stretch of beach in Waikiki, Orchids is still romantic.

Expensive. Open for breakfast, lunch, and dinner Monday through Saturday, with breakfast, brunch, and buffet on Sunday. Major credit cards accepted.

PEOPLE'S CAFE
1310 Pali Highway
Downtown/Nuuanu
Telephone: (808) 536-5789

The small, humble restaurant still bustles with the faithfuls who come for the "squid" luau (octopus in a coconut milk–taro leaf stew), the beef stew and teriyaki butterfish, and the usual kalua pig, lau lau, and lomi salmon. Some of the dishes are unexceptional, but some, like the squid luau, are famous.

Informal and inexpensive—dinner for two is about $12. Open 10:00 A.M. to 7:30 P.M. daily except Sunday. No credit cards accepted.

PHILLIPPE PAOLO'S
2312 South Beretania Street
Moiliili
Telephone: (808) 946-1163

You may have to wait because it's always so busy, but once you get seated it's smooth sailing. The menu is satisfying, the service is eminently professional, and the food—well, you'll know why it's always so busy.

The restaurant is in an old home that still has a pleasantly eclectic feel to it, something between grand funk and ultimate bordello, but in good taste. There are tables indoors; outdoors, under a tarp, candlelit tables are placed between palm trees, under umbrellas, and next to a large lichee tree.

The Frutti di Mare is excellent, and so is the opakapaka sautéed in butter with grapes. Phillippe Paolo's excels in seafood, from its seafood lasagne with smoked salmon and crab to its Alaskan king salmon and, if you're lucky, fresh Dungeness crab done to perfection. The calamari marinara is a must—exceptionally tender, with fine slivers of vegetables and the perfect medley of herbs. There are many others, from soft-shell crabs to lobster, from fettucini to cannelloni to the classic linguini with white clam sauce. After all that, the dessert choice is simple: cheesecake.

Phillippe Paolo's biggest fault lies in the excessively large servings. Casual attire. Dinner for two costs about $55, without wine. Open nightly for dinner only. Major credit cards accepted.

THE PLUMERIA CAFE
Kahala Hilton
5000 Kahala Avenue
Kahala
Telephone: (808) 734-2211

The Plumeria Cafe has one of the more imaginative menus around. The chef has included some bold local items, such as seaweed and opihi, and prepared them with sophisticated continental savvy so the dishes take on an international flavor. The Korean man doo, won ton, and spring rolls add a local twist, and the hot appetizer of deep-fried crab claws and beef and chicken saté make this a menu worth exploring.

The salads are great, especially the Hawaiian chicken salad with sesame oil and ginger dressing. It has a large following, and so does the lobster salad with asparagus and gazpacho. The pastas offer a nice alternative, and the entrées include pizza, sautéed scallops in coulis de tomate, pan-fried opakapaka meunière, and sandwiches. The desserts, including the Kahala Hilton's famous coconut layer cake, are hard to resist. The island-sized brownie with ice cream and hot fudge sauce is a meal in itself.

Whether for lunch or dinner, the Plumeria is a good bet. The surroundings are pleasant, the food reliable, and the service is cheerful. You can dine lightly or more substantially here, with good results. Moderate to moderately expensive, with entrées from $6.50 to $19.25. Open 11:30 A.M. to midnight daily. Major credit cards accepted.

RESTAURANT SUNTORY
Royal Hawaiian Center
2233 Kalakaua Avenue
Waikiki
Telephone: (808) 922-5511

Suntory excels in all aspects of Japanese cuisine, from the sushi bar to the teppanyaki grill. The ambience and cuisine are utterly refined, reflecting the best of Japanese esthetics. This is a world-class Japanese restaurant and certainly the finest Japanese eatery in Honolulu.

About half of the dining area is devoted to teppanyaki presentation and is very popular. Also popular is the Beef Sashimi, thinly sliced strips of steak arduously prepared. The meat is seared quickly on the outside on an open flame, then soaked in ice water to stop the cooking so it's raw inside. It's sliced thin and served with garlic, wasabi, and ginger in shoyu.

The house specialty is another sashimi dish, the fresh white fish (opakapaka, onaga, sea bass) sliced very thin, arranged prettily on a platter, and served with a grated turnip and chili pepper sauce. Add to this the very popular shabu shabu—seafood and vegetables in earthenware soup pots— and the excellent sushi bar, and you have a memorable dining experience. Not to be forgotten is the tempura ice cream, ice cream dipped in batter and deep-fried so it's cold on the inside—exotic, rich, and unforgettable.

Expensive—dinner for two could run about $60 to $70. Open daily for dinner and for lunch Monday through Saturday. Major credit cards accepted.

SADA'S RESTAURANT
1432 Makaloa Street
Ala Moana
Telephone: (808) 949-0646

Sada's is always the place for sushi, with sushi chefs obviously well-trained and professional. Lately, however, the sushi has been disappointing and inconsistent in a few cases, perhaps because of the chefs' changing shifts. Hopefully that will be or has been remedied, because Sada's is otherwise an excellent restaurant with a long-standing reputation to uphold.

The other favorites are the famous nabe dishes with their combinations of vegetables, seafood, and chicken cooked in individual pots; the chawanmushi, the marvelous custard with shiitake; the sukiyaku and shabu shabu. All the mainstays on the menu are reliably good, but watch for the specials too. Occasionally you'll find some rare dishes worth trying. When the right chefs are on, Sada's makes the best salmon-skin and the best scallop-with-crab-egg sushi. They can make the most esoteric sushi with panache. If it's not already your favorite hangout, it's definitely worth a try.

Moderately expensive—dinner for two could run about $50. Open 11 A.M. to 2 P.M. and from 5:00 P.M. to midnight Monday through Saturday. On Sunday it opens from 5:00 P.M. to 11:00 P.M.. Major credit cards accepted.

SERENDIPITY
1827 Palolo Avenue
Palolo
Telephone: (808) 735-1543

It took some cheek to open a gourmet restaurant in the heart of Palolo, not exactly known for its ambience extraordinaire. But "Bones" Yuen did it, and years later Serendipity is better than ever, dishing out sumptuous cuisine from its hole in the wall next to a rundown grocery store.

You dine in a room that feels like a comfortable living room, with only a few tables, pink tablecloths, and a courteous waitress. The menu offers green pepper steak with mango chutney, bouillabaisse, poached lobster and oysters in caviar sauce, rack of lamb, chateaubriand, and scampi. The menu is slight but wholly satisfying, and although you may wait awhile between courses, the food is extraordinary.

The scampi is recommended, and so is the opakapaka en papillote, moist and cooked to perfection. The stuffed lobster is another favorite, and many have raved about the green pepper steak. Dessert, cherries jubilee or bananas Foster, is skillfully flambéed as the grand finale.

If there's any fault with Serendipity, it is only in the wait. That's because they prepare everything to order, and occasionally an entrée may take twenty minutes to prepare. It's not a problem if you're prepared to wait, but for those in a rush it may detract from the meal. Otherwise, Serendipity is a satisfying and enjoyable dining experience. It's also a wonderful surprise to go from the rundown parking lot to the restaurant and sit down to a sumptuous repast.

No liquor is served, but guests may bring their own. Expensive—dinner for two costs about $80. Open for dinner nightly. Reservations a must. Major credit cards accepted.

SERGIO'S
Ilima Hotel
445 Nohonani Street
Waikiki
Telephone: (808) 926-3388

Sergio Battistetti is one of the deans of Italian cuisine in Hawaii, and his restaurant tells you why. From the service to the cuisine, the experience is memorable; only the dark, cavelike dining room is forgettable.

Beginning with the appetizers, the choices are difficult. The fresh shiitake is excellent, swimming in butter and garlic, something much like an escargot sauce. The calamari marinara is also noteworthy, very hot and assertive.

The bugili puttanesca's wide noodles in tomato sauce are spiced with anchovy, capers, bay leaf, chili, and what tastes like a touch of fennel. It's a unique combination that works; the saltimbocca and osso bucco are recommended too.

Sergio's also has an impressive, wide-ranging wine list and knowledgeable waiters to assist you. The dining experience here is delightful; you'll certainly want to return.

Moderately expensive—dinner for two is about $60. Open nightly for dinner. Major credit cards accepted.

SWISS INN
5730 Kalanianaole Highway
Niu Valley Shopping Center
Telephone: (808) 377-5447

This is one of the few places in town with elegant cuisine and an unstuffy, family atmosphere. That makes it enormously popular among families and the loyal returnees who like chef Martin Wyss's cooking. It is also not frightfully expensive, which adds to the appeal.

The seafood chowder and steamed clams are marvelous. The Scallops Madascar, sautéed with fresh mushrooms, tomatoes, and green peppercorns, are also memorable, and there have been raves over the veal chop with morels. The fresh catch of onaga, prepared in a lemon butter sauce, is tender, steaming, perfectly seasoned, and like the rest of the menu's selections, done well.

For such elegant fare, you may pay something ridiculously low, such as $55 for two, including drinks, three courses, and dessert. Open for dinner nightly except Monday. On Sunday there's a buffet brunch. Major credit cards accepted.

THE THIRD FLOOR
Hawaiian Regent Hotel
2552 Kalakaua Avenue
Waikiki, Diamond Head end
Telephone: (808) 922-6611

People love this restaurant for its service, for its nicely balanced environment, and for its cuisine. With its high-backed wicker chairs it affords more privacy than most dining rooms; and in spite of being an expensive continental restaurant, it makes everyone, even children, feel at home.

And the cuisine has improved with age. Where the appetizers and desserts were the show stealers before, now the entrées have come of age and you can expect a smooth, high-quality meal from start to finish. The age-old darling of the meal is the "promising start" appetizer buffet, but the frog legs and salmon are also tremendous. The scampi Provençale, a casserole of lobster, shrimp, and opakapaka; tenderloin of beef à la Niçoise; and a full gamut of toothsome possibilities round out the menu. Very popular are the medaillions of veal topped with mushrooms, chanterelles, and buttered egg spaetzle. The Third Floor's wine list is exceptional as well.

Like the appetizers, the desserts are exquisite. Black Forest cake, assorted French pastries, an ice soufflé with fresh hazelnuts and a caramel sauce, international cheeses, and fresh fruit make for a wonderful finish to a fine meal.

This is an expensive proposition: with wine, dinner can be $60 or $70 per person. Jackets are suggested for men. There's valet parking. Dinner is served nightly. Major credit cards accepted.

WOODLANDS
1289 South King Street
Near Keeaumoku
Telephone: (808) 526-2239

In its old location, which was about the size of a postage stamp, diligent women would be in a corner kneading the dough all evening for your pot stickers and gau gee. Most of the customers spoke Chinese and many would read Chinese language newspapers as they waited for their pan-fried dumplings. Woodlands had a good, loyal following among those who knew Chinese food.

And then, without warning, the building was razed and almost overnight, Woodlands was gone. A hushed whisper blew around town among worried Chinese food lovers.

Well, Woodlands did resurface. And when it did, you could almost hear the sigh of relief that went up among its fans. People are also relieved to see that it is still serving the best dim sum, gau gee, gyozas, and dumplings in town, and perhaps in the entire Pacific. Admittedly, it's new location, a few blocks from the original, is fancier and has lost some of its former intimacy. The dough, however, is still made fresh every day and the black bean fried noodles, the gau gee noodle soup, the saimin, and the black bean chicken are as good as they've always been. As for the gyoza (pot stickers) and the pan-fried dumplings, well, you'll have to see for yourself. Also flawless are the fish and chives gau gee, dainty morsels of seafood and seasonings wrapped in dough and then steamed.

The menu has all the old items and a few new ones. There are fewer kids around to help the business now. The gau gee and pot sticker business has been so good it's sent three of the kids off to college, two of them on the mainland. Owners Man Bing Yu and Kwei Fong Yu don't take that for granted, not at all.

Inexpensive—two can dine handsomely for $20. Open 11:00 A.M. to 2:00 P.M. and 5:00 to 9:00 P.M. every day except Wednesday. Major credit cards accepted.

YANAGI SUSHI
762 Kapiolani Boulevard
Punchbowl/Downtown
Telephone: (808) 537-1525

Yanagi's has changed little in recent years. It still has great sushi and tempura and it's still a crowded, comfortable place for lunch or dinner. The Tokyo-style cuisine is served in an unpretentious atmosphere, but the choices are bountiful and the chefs are reliable. With recent inconsistencies in the quality at Sada's more people are coming to appreciate the steady, seasoned touch of Yanagi's chefs.

Moderately priced—about $30 for two. Open daily for lunch and dinner, which is served until 3:00 A.M.. Dinner only on Sunday. Major credit cards accepted.

The North Shore

CAFE HALEIWA
66-460 Kam Highway
Haleiwa
Telephone: (808) 637-5516

This could be described as the north shore's homeliest and best restaurant. You'll dine on Formica tables, under fluorescent lights, with north shore art on the walls, and a concrete floor. But this is the best breakfast you'll find on this half of the island.

The Surf Rat breakfast is $1.89, the Dawn Patrol consisting of two eggs, three pancakes, or two pieces of French toast, is also $1.89. You can order the veggie omelet for $5.50 or the huevos rancheros, which may be the best you'll every have, for $4.50. Mahimahi, home fries, and all the old favorites, such as homemade refried beans, make this a memorable stop, and one you won't forget.

Inexpensive. Open for breakfast and lunch daily; closes at 2:00 P.M. No credit cards accepted.

COUNTRY DRIVE-INN
66-200 Kam Highway
Haleiwa
Telephone: (808) 637-9122

This is a takeout stand—one of the busiest spots in Haleiwa—with a few plastic tables for diners. It offers the best plate lunches on the north shore and a hefty array of island specialties at low prices. You can tell it's good by the habitués—a healthy mix of local surfers, tourists, local working folks, and Haleiwa residents.

There are twenty different kinds of plate lunches. The mahimahi plate is excellent, and so is the shaka-min, with won tun, shrimp tempura, and teriyaki beef. Also offered are plate lunches of shoyu chicken, veal cutlet, Korean plates with highly spiced vegetables and meats, and daily specials such as spaghetti and Chinese, Korean, Japanese, Filipino, and Hawaiian plates.

Prices range from $2.85 for a hamburger deluxe to $4 for a gargantuan plate lunch. Open 7:00 A.M. to 9:00 P.M. daily. No credit cards.

JAMESON'S BY THE SEA
62-540 Kam Highway
Haleiwa
Telephone: (808) 637-4336

Jameson's is the best restaurant on the north shore, certainly with the north shore's best view because it is the only one with tables facing the sea. You can sit on the lanai and watch the sunset over the water, which is across the road but still gorgeous, while enjoying margaritas and appetizers. Dinner is served upstairs, and it could be anything from fresh catch sautéed, broiled, or poached, with garlic hollandaise sauce, to something like lobster or filet mignon.

Dinners run from $16.95 to $22.95. Open 11:00 A.M. to 5:00 P.M. daily for lunch and 5:00 P.M. to 10:00 P.M. daily except Monday for dinner. Major credit cards accepted.

KUA AINA SANDWICH
66-214 Kam Highway
Haleiwa
Telephone: (808) 637-6067

Kua Aina has a tough reputation to uphold, and it does it so well. It's known to have the best sandwiches on the island, and this is true.

Kua Aina uses fresh buns into which are stacked the best homemade hamburger patties on the island. You can also order a gargantuan mahimahi or tuna sandwich or any number of other simple sandwiches, which will come with sprouts, fresh vegetables, and spreads you can live with forever.

Inexpensive, with sandwiches in the $3 to $4 range. Open daily from 11:00 A.M. to 8:45 P.M.. No credit cards accepted.

ROSIE'S CANTINA
Haleiwa Shopping Plaza
Hakiwa
Telephone: (808) 637-3538

You can start off with huevos rancheros, graduate to a burrito at lunch, and finish off the day with an enchilada. Rosie's serves all day, beginning with full Mexican breakfast specials as well as the standard breakfast fare of pancakes and waffles. Although the cuisine is not consistent, Rosie's is eminently popular. The margaritas have a following too.

Inexpensive—two can dine here for $15. Open daily. Major credit cards accepted.

....

LUNCH FAVORITES

All of the restaurants mentioned in the dining section are of course great places for lunch, especially Michel's and the Halekulani. The following are places of a different order, places that have a particular luncheon atmosphere, or provide the best luncheon music, or offer something special at midday that's not offered anywhere else. Also included are the universal favorite, pizza, and some uniquely local specialties, such as plate lunches and the Chinese delicacy called dim sum, a luncheon ritual in some corners. With the exception of Kemoo Farm in central Oahu, these establishments are found in Honolulu proper.

Restaurants

GARDEN CAFÉ
Honolulu Academy of Arts
900 South Beretania Street
Near Thomas Square
Telephone: (808) 531-8865

The Garden Café is set in a garden courtyard of the Honolulu Academy of Arts, so you know it's attractive. The small corner café faces glorious sculptures, a large plumeria tree, and a pleasantly shaded walkway. You don't really come here for the food, although the soups and desserts are marvelous; it's the dining ambience that's so pleasant.

Volunteers serve a fresh puréed soup every day (pumpkin is excellent), a salad, and usually, sandwiches of breads, cheeses, and meats. The sandwich ingredients are the least desirable part of the meal, but this is followed by home-baked brownies or cookies, and ice cream with candied ginger and fresh fruit toppings.

The café is staffed by volunteers because it's strictly a fund-raising effort. Proceeds from the café go toward the purchase of new art, and the volunteers are quite proud of that. Last year the soups and salads made over $20,000.

It's inexpensive—lunch is under $5. Reservations are required, and it closes from May until September. The café has two seatings a day, Tuesday through Friday, 11:30 A.M. and 1:00 P.M.. Open for supper on Thursday. No credit cards.

KEMOO FARM
1718 Wilikina Drive
Wahiawa, across the main gate from Schofield Barracks
Telephone: (808) 621-8481

The food is adequate, but that's not why it's recommended. The Kemoo Farm is one of the few places in Oahu with great Hawaiian music provided by Hawaii's top contemporary musicians. On Sundays, Kemoo Farm comes alive with a Sunday brunch, which includes some Hawaiian items, and entertainment by performers such as Charles K. L. Davis, who usually invites his friends for expanded Hawaiian entertainment. The show will vary by the week; one week it may be Dennis Pavao, another, Emma Veary or Haunani Apoliona. Just know that whoever is featured at Kemoo Farm will be an excellent Hawaiian artist and someone you won't always have a chance to hear. The brunch consists of a buffet with salads and entrées.

Moderately priced—about $10 for Sunday brunch and $12 for dinner. Open for Sunday brunch, for lunch daily except Saturday, and for dinner Friday and Saturday nights. Major credit cards accepted.

QUEEN KAPIOLANI HOTEL
150 Kapahulu Avenue
Kapahulu/Waikiki
Telephone: (808) 922-1941

Every Tuesday, the Queen Kapiolani Hotel offers a Hawaiian buffet lunch with entertainment. You won't find many shows better than the one here, with Charles Davis and friends. (When they're not at Kemoo Farm, they're at Queen Kapiolani.) The buffet will give you a good sampling of Hawaiian food while the music showcases some of the best talent in Hawaii. The shows change by the week, but if Genoa Keawe is performing, she's not to be missed. Nor are Nalani Olds, Jay Larrin, Emma Veary, Haunani Apoliona—musical luminaries who appear periodically at the Tuesday buffet to share traditional and contemporary Hawaiian music.

Moderately priced—the Tuesday buffet with entertainment is $12, but there is an à la carte menu as well. Open daily for lunch from 11:00 A.M. to 2:00 P.M., but Tuesday only is recommended. Major credit cards accepted.

SEPARATE TABLES
1028 Nuuanu Avenue
Downtown
Telephone: (808) 524-7787

In terms of cuisine, this is by far the best place to have lunch. It would no doubt be the best place for dinner too, if they would ever open after 2:00 P.M. This is downtown's sleeper, a small restaurant with tables indoors and outdoors. The outdoor tables are on a pleasant deck with a roof of banana thatch. There is a small yard in which jars of fresh mint tea steep cheerfully in the sun.

This is by far the most imaginative and satisfying luncheon menu in Honolulu. It is not extensive, but what is here is exceptional. There are arranged platters of chicken, shrimp, or tofu, for which nine or ten different sauces are available. Therefore, you can order shrimp Bombay or shrimp in black bean sauce or the tofu in the Oriental ginger-sesame sauce, or you can switch the sauces around. When the plate arrives, it's a celebration: couscous, linguini, or saffron rice surrounded by the salad of your choice made with only the best ingredients, perfectly steamed or sautéed vegetables, and the light entrée in your choice of sauce or preparation. The platters are colorful and artistic, a feast for the eyes. The desserts are fresh and homemade as well, from the ginger ice cream to the fresh berry sauce surrounding it. No matter how you may wish to resist, give in.

Highly recommended, but reservations are a must. Informal. Lunch costs from $7.95 to $9.95. You're welcome to bring your own wine. Open 11:30 A.M. to 2:00 P.M. Monday through Friday. Major credit cards accepted.

THE WILLOWS
901 Hausten Street
McCully
Telephone: (808) 946-4808

The Thursday Hawaiian lunch is a must for any visitor or resident. The Willows has an ambience that's noteworthy in itself, and when combined with a special Hawaiian feast and Hawaiian music by Genoa Keawe or Puamana, the combination is unbeatable.

Thursday's affair is called Poi Thursday, and it's hosted by Irmgaard Aluli, the noted island composer and the matriarch of a talented musical family. Her group, called Puamana, has a loyal island following, and when friends appear at the lunch they often entertain too. On alternate weeks, noted Hawaiian falsetto Genoa Keawe hosts the party. The menu includes lau lau, poi, lomi salmon, plus the Willows' popular curries and sandwich alternatives.

The pavilion in which the luncheon is held is part of the enjoyment, with ohia log pillars and Hawaiian quilt backdrops. Maile-scented ferns grow out of the ohia pillars and create the aura of old Hawaii. Outside, a lagoon full of carp lights up the walkways as diners lunch in thatched huts hanging over the water. It's so picturesque and lovely.

Cost: $12 for the Thursday lunch and program. Lunch in the regular dining area ranges from $8 to $12 per person and includes the Willows' famous curries and pies. Open Monday through Saturday for lunch and nightly for dinner. Major credit cards accepted.

Pizzerias

SBARRO
Makai Market
Ala Moana Center
Telephone: (808) 955-1665

Sbarro is setting new standards for pizza in Hawaii. It is the best pizza of all, made according to the recipe of a Brooklyn family that's been making pizza for thirty years. The sauces are made from imported Italian peeled tomatoes, onions, fresh garlic, olive oil, Romano cheese, and herbs, simmered for hours. The dough, of course, is made fresh too, hand-stretched as all good pizza crusts should be. When it's finally done, the crust is perfect: chewy, not too airy, with the perfect flavor and texture. When sauce, crust, and toppings meld together in the baking, the result is a flawless piece of pizza. All this, and a slice is $1.39. Heartily recommended.

Inexpensive—whole pizzas range from $7.95 to $10.95. Open 9:00 A.M. to 9:00 P.M. weekdays, 9:30 A.M. to 6:00 P.M. Saturday, and 10:00 A.M. to 5:00 P.M. Sunday. No credit cards accepted.

ZORRO'S NEW YORK PIZZA
2310 Kuhio Avenue
Waikiki
Telephone: (808) 926-5555

2128 Kalakaua Avenue
Waikiki
Telephone: (808) 924-8808

You can actually get a terrific slice of pizza for under a dollar. That's not why we mention Zorro's; we'd mention it even if it cost $2. It's a good, decent pizza with hand-stretched, New York–style crust, toppings that range from Maui onion to Italian sausage, and a zesty, authoritative sauce. A plain cheese-and-tomato pizza is terrific here, better than fancier combinations elsewhere and entirely satisfying.

Inexpensive—whole pizzas cost about $8 to $16. Open 8:00 A.M. to 4:00 P.M. daily. Major credit cards accepted.

Plate Lunches

GRACE'S INN
1192 Alakea Street
Downtown
Telephone: (808) 537-3302

2227 S. Beretania Street
McCully
Telephone: (808) 946-8020

The plate lunches here are varied, with choices ranging from beef curry and sweet-sour chicken to teriyaki beef and the ever-popular mahimahi. The entrée of your choice comes with two scoops of rice (the plate lunch signature), one scoop of macaroni salad, a small kim chee (pickled, peppered cabbage), and some noodles. You can also order bento (various pickled vegetable appetizers and rice) and kim chee on the side, and the more standard hamburgers and chili bowls.

Grace's plate lunches taste good and cost little: you can spend as little as $2.60 for a plate lunch, or you can splurge on a $4.55 mixed seafood plate. Open 6:00 A.M. to 8:00 P.M. daily at the Alakea Street location, 10:00 A.M. to 10:30 P.M. daily at South Beretania Street. No credit cards accepted.

MYONG'S TAKE OUT
1505 Young Street
Pawaa (in front of the police station)
Telephone: (808) 944-9075

Myong's soaks its chicken in a secret marinade, then barbecues, slices, and serves it with kim chee, macaroni salad, and rice. This plate lunch is outstanding. They also put together a man doo plate consisting of noodle soup, fried squid, and the Korean classic, kal bi, or barbecued short ribs. Myong's has a bold way with the Korean seasonings and spices up the plate lunches with kim chee and sesame vegetables.

The prices are unbelievable: $3.50 for the barbecued chicken plate, $4.25 for the kal bi, $2.75 for the bibim noodle. Vegetarians can choose assorted pickled vegetables for their plate lunch and come away perfectly happy. Open 8:00 A.M. to 7:00 P.M. Monday through Friday, 8:00 A.M. to 5:00 P.M. Saturday, closed Sunday. Cash only.

TED'S DRIVE-IN
2820 South King Street
Moiliili
Telephone: (808) 946-0364

Follow the scent of barbecued meats and garlic and you'll wind up at this corner takeout stand, where you have a wide selection of plate lunches prepared with a Korean touch. Ted's seasons its food assertively, as in bulgogi, thinly sliced marinated beef, and in kim chee, the Korean short ribs, and a host of other tasty, barbecued delicacies. The plate lunches are legendary assortments combining mahimahi, chicken, barbecued ribs, Korean-style vegetables, bulgogi, and the obligatory rice and macaroni salad.

Ted's is hard to find, however. It's located next to the freeway on King Street, slightly ewa of where King Street meets Kapiolani.

You can get a hefty plate lunch for $4 or less, and it will be tasty. Open 9:30 A.M. to 10:00 P.M. daily. No credit cards.

Dim Sum

Dim sum is a Hong Kong delicacy, a more refined version of manapua. Various fillings of fish, pork, and vegetables are wrapped in fresh dough and steamed in bamboo steamers. What emerges is a delicate dumpling that can then be fried (pot stickers) or enjoyed as is. Dim sum is a ritual in some corners of Honolulu, where people like to gather over several varieties for lunch, much as a San Franciscan would glory over a steaming bowl of cioppino and a slice of sourdough bread. The very best dim sum is available at Woodlands, listed under Restaurants.

CHINA HOUSE
1349 Kapiolani Boulevard
Ala Moana
Telephone: (808) 949-6622

China House is gargantuan and has a menu to match, but the dim sum is why people come here. It's served daily, only for lunch, and it comes in several varieties. The translucent skin of the wrapping holds the fillings tenderly so you can pick up the dumpling with chopsticks and daintily dip it in a sauce. Favorites are the shrimp filling and the custard tart.

Inexpensive—dinner for two costs about $15, dim sum about $1.50 per serving. Open 10:00 A.M. to 9:00 P.M. daily, but serving dim sum only for lunch. Major credit cards accepted.

YONG SING
1055 Alakea Street
Downtown
Telephone: (808) 531-1366

Yong Sing is always amusing because the waitresses are brusque, the room is noisy, and you sometimes wonder why you came here. The reason, of course is dim sum.

Here you order the dim sum individually, but if you order a steamerful you can watch it being unveiled. The usual varieties prevail here, as they have for years, but the shrimp and pork dumplings are the bestsellers.

Inexpensive—lunch for two costs about $15. Open 7:30 A.M. to 9:00 P.M. daily, but dim sum served only before 2:00 P.M. Major credit cards accepted.

....

COOL TREATS

It can get very hot in Hawaii. During the blistering days of summer, long lines form around Oahu's biggest attractions, the frozen yogurt, shave ice, and ice cream houses that are busy year-round but frenzied during the warmer months. Like pizza in Little Italy and frozen bananas on Catalina Island, icy delights are one of Oahu's trademarks. Be it frozen yogurt, ice cream, or a Matsumoto's shave ice, it's loved by residents and visitors, who think nothing of standing in interminable queues only to have to slurp their way through rapidly melting mounds. Here they are, Oahu's best and coolest.

Frozen Yogurt

PENGUIN'S PLACE FROZEN YOGURT
1035 University Avenue
University area
Telephone: (808) 941-1446

Every kid with a Duncan Yo-yo and every freckled adolescent is heading for Penguin's. It's quite the rage, a place where Yuppies can mingle with aspiring Yuppies and all can trundle off with the latest in yogurt couture. The selection of toppings is dizzying: fudge brownies, chip mix, chocolate chips, cinnamon streusel, gummy bears, jelly bellies, crushed Oreos. There are fruit toppings as well, from wild berries and peaches to banana melba and kiwi mix.

The yogurts come in many flavors and are combined in power shakes, custom shakes, sundaes, and fruit salads. It's so "in" and enthusiastic that one tends to shy away, but the yogurt is the best.

Prices range from $.88 for a "baby yogurt" to $2.55 a quart. Open 11:00 A.M. to 10:00 P.M. on weekdays, weekends from 11:00 A.M. to 11:00 P.M. No credit cards accepted.

TCBY
Nuuanu Shopping Center
Nuuanu
Telephone: (808) 521-2301

What's called the country's best yogurt came to town, and it's giving ice cream a run for its money. TCBY has smoothies, shakes, sundaes, crêpes, deluxe Belgian waffles, hot fudge sundaes, banana splits, and other lively expressions of this culinary fad. The yogurt tastes remarkably like ice cream, but it's lighter and less caloric. Flavors such as peach, strawberry, and French vanilla offer endless possibilities in sundaes, cones, pies, and even the yogwich, sandwiched between two cookies. Chocolate lovers also have a Dutch chocolate yogurt with hot fudge to soothe their aching sweet tooth. The yogurt is touted as being 96 percent fat free and with 98 percent less fat than most ice creams.

Prices range from $.75 for a "kiddie scoop" to about $5 for a quart. Open 11:00 A.M. to 10:00 P.M. Monday through Thursday, 10:00 A.M. to 11:00 P.M. Friday and Saturday, and 10:00 A.M. to 10:00 P.M. Sunday. No credit cards accepted.

The Best Ice Cream

BUBBIES HOME MADE ICE CREAM AND DESSERTS
1010 University Avenue
University area
Telephone: (808) 949-8984

Bubbies has the best lichee ice cream, bar none. It's creamy and delicious and they didn't cop out and make sherbert—they made creamy, rich ice cream instead. On the other hand, the papaya sherbert, Oreo, and mocha chip are also notable. The bananas royal and other homemade desserts on the counters are unfailingly popular, for instance: homemade apple pie in individual crocks, cinnamon twists, cookies, and hand-dipped cones. A single cone is $1.50, and it's huge.

Prices range from $.75 for a "kiddie cone" to $6.70 a quart. Open noon to midnight Monday through Thursday, to 1:00 A.M. Friday and Saturday, to 11:00 P.M. Sunday. No credit cards.

DAVE'S ICE CREAM PARLORS
Nuuanu Shopping Plaza, telephone: (808) 538-7918
Ward Warehouse, telephone: (808) 523-3692
Pearlridge Center, telephone: (808) 488-2552
702 Kapahulu Avenue, telephone: (808) 735-2194
1901 Kapiolani Boulevard, telephone: (808) 955-7609
and other locations

Dave's has grown like wildfire since its humble beginnings in Waianae. In those days ice cream fanatics would drive 50 miles from town to stock up on Dave's nutty buddies, ice cream dipped in chocolate and rolled in fresh roasted almonds. Today you can find a Dave's around every corner, and the ice cream is just as good. The tropical-fruit flavors include poha, guava, passion fruit, mango, banana, lichee, papaya, and others.

Favorite flavors include banana-strawberry, green tea, passion fruit frozen yogurt, Kona coffee, strawberry frozen yogurt, and lichee sherbet. They are all exceptional, and each cone costs about $1.25.

Prices range from $.96 for a "kiddie scoop" to $5.46 a quart. Open 10:30 A.M. to 10:00 P.M. Sunday through Thursday, 10:30 A.M. to 11:00 P.M Friday and Saturday. No credit cards.

HAAGEN-DAZS
1541 South Beretania Street, telephone: (808) 942-0981
801 Kaheka Street, telephone: (808) 955-1227
2330 Kalakaua Avenue, telephone: (808) 923-6877
2356 Kalakaua Avenue, Shop A2, telephone: (808) 924-9336
2586 Kalakaua Avenue, telephone: (808) 923-5177

Haagen-Dazs has more competition now, but it still hasn't lost its touch. The ice creams are creamier than ever and the toppings have evolved. There is still the fresh whipped cream for the sundaes, however, and no artificial flavors or colorings are used. Maple Walnut, Choco-Choco-Chip, Cookies 'n Cream, Orange/Vanilla sorbet, and Honey Vanilla remain classic favorites.

A scoop costs $1.15 to $1.40. Open seven days a week. No credit cards accepted.

Shave Ice

MATSUMOTO'S
66-087 Kam Highway
Haleiwa, North Shore
Telephone: (808) 637-4827

The long lines winding around the corner are for an island delicacy called shave ice. Matsumoto's has been dispensing these towering treats for generations, so there's a lot of loyalty involved.

The ice is shaved, piled into a mound, and topped with a fruit flavor. The real fans request sweetened black azuki beans and ice cream, to be mixed up with the icy mixture. Shave ice is perfect for the north shore; everyone from ravenous surfers to exhausted sightseers gets a chance to freshen up with it before the long drive back. Matsumoto's is the favorite in this field because of the consistency of its ice, the quality of their syrups, and the evenness of their pourings.

Prices are $.60 to $1.10. Open 8:00 A.M. to 5:00 P.M. every day. No credit cards accepted.

THE BEST LUAU

PARADISE COVE
Campbell Estate
Ewa
Telephone: (808) 945-3539

For a large luau—up to 1,300—Paradise Cove does a tremendous job. It's not ideal, because no commercial luaus are. But there are several factors that make this a luau worth mentioning.

First, the location. They bus you out to a gorgeous cove in leeward Oahu, where you can partake of a *hukilau* (net fishing), from the shore or watch demonstrations of Hawaiian crafts. You can also play *ulu maika*, a Hawaiian game much like lawn bowling, Tongan shuffleboard, and other Polynesian games, or you can simply enjoy the tranquil shoreline. The crafts demonstrations in thatched huts by the ocean add immeasurable pleasure to this luau as you watch cordial people demonstrate lei making, coconut husking and weaving, coconut tree climbing, and fiber weaving. When the pig is ready to be removed from the *imu* (underground oven), the smoky spectacle is something to be seen. There are no other buildings in sight and it's as if you're at a private estate designed exclusively for your enjoyment.

The food is adequate. It's not special, but it offers a sampling of Hawaiian foods: lomi salmon, poi, kalua pig, and the substitutes, short ribs and teriyaki chicken. As the sun sets you fill your plate and take your seat at long banquet tables to await the program. With the palms along the shore, it's quite pretty.

Sam Kapu, the emcee, is funnier than he thinks, and the program moves quickly enough. There are three stages for the dancers, who perform everything from Tahitian to ancient hula and modern hula. The fire dancer—fast, dangerous, and showy—is the best. What really makes the evening, however, is the guests' enjoyment. They parade up to the stage in unselfconscious lines quite eager to wiggle their hips and attempt the hula. It's impossible to be too critical when you see people having such fun.

If you can ignore the tour drivers' jokes on the bus and concentrate on the setting, the ocean, and the drumbeats of the hula, you can have a marvelous time. You will certainly have more fun at Paradise Cove than at any other location; this is the best location for a luau on Oahu. Cost is $37.50 for adults and $19.27 for children.

NIGHTLIFE AND ENTERTAINMENT

The favored bars in Waikiki are the Library (922-6611) at the Hawaiian Regent, Harry's Bar (922-9292) at the Hyatt Regency, and the Mai Tai Bar (923-7311) next to the ocean at the Royal Hawaiian Hotel. People also love the bar at the Chart House (941-6669), where there's a view of the harbor and a small, intimate crowd enjoying the music. The Mai Tai Bar is by far the favorite because you can sit in starlight and gaze at Diamond Head while sipping the town's best chi chis.

The best lounges are Trappers at the Hyatt Regency (922-9292) and Bagwells' wine bar (922-9292). Both are elegant and each has its own style. Trappers always has a good show (it was Herbie Mann for a while) and a lively crowd, albeit a smoky, crowded room. Bagwells has a more subdued, elegant ambience as people gather for expensive wine over the gentle riffs of a classical pianist or guitarist.

There's been a spate of new discos, ranging from the hi-tech, futuristic Zone Seven (941-5277) to the newly renovated Pink Cadillac (942-5282), the haven of the hip, the disenchanted, and the punkers-come-of-age. Across the street from Pink Cadillac is the most alluring of Honolulu's rock and roll nightclubs, The Wave Waikiki (941-0424), a small, entertaining club with a huge following and occasionally stupendous shows by visiting artists. Hula's Bar and Lei Stand (923-0669) is still popular after all these years, holding forth under the gaily lit banyan tree on Kuhio Avenue, an active mecca for gays. The Shore Bird (922-6906) has a lower profile, but it has the most attractive location, right on Waikiki beach, with open sides and an ocean breeze.

The more sophisticated after-dinner dance spots include Rumours (955-4811), Rascals (922-5566), Scruples (923-9530), and the most popular, Nicholas Nickolas (955-4466) and Nick's Fishmarket (955-6333). At the latter two you can dress up, have dinner, and hit the dance floor for some good times.

Way off in Moiliili is one of Honolulu's best casual spots, Anna Bannanas (946-5190), a small cavelike mecca for reggae lovers. Pagan Babies, Honolulu's best reggae band, plays third-world music to a full house there.

No doubt you will also hear about the Cazimeros, the dynamic duo, and their talented hula troupe performing at the Royal Hawaiian Hotel's Monarch Room. Theirs is a Hawaiian extravaganza with modern and ancient hula, very glitzy, slick, and nostalgic. Although the Cazimeros and their other-worldly harmony are the best-known entertainers in Hawaii, their show can get touristy at times.

Honolulu's best contemporary singers and musicians also include the Peter Moon Band, Brother Noland and the Pacific Bad Boys, Haunani Apoliona and Jerry Santos of Olomana, Melveen Leed, Steve and Theresa, and Emma Veary with her classically trained soprano voice singing Hawaiian songs.

Andrew's (523-8677) at Ward Centre shines with the talent of Mahi Beamer, one of Hawaii's foremost Hawaiian composers and musicians. Another name to remember is the Makaha Sons of Niihau, Hawaii's favorite group with a vast, soulful harmony. The Sons, as they're called, sing traditional Hawaiian songs but have their own inimitable contemporary style.

Not to be missed are Brad White and Lee Eisenstein, who call themselves White Eisenstein and who are arguably the most pleasing musicians around. On guitar and recorder, the duo plays everything from Bach and Renaissance classics to Simon and Garfunkel.

Jazz lovers have more than their share of entertainment here. Jeff Linsky is an excellent jazz guitarist. Keep an eye out for Gabe Baltazar, a jazz saxophonist of worldwide renown. The Ollie Mitchell band is also popular for its Big Band sound with contemporary arrangements. The leading ladies of jazz are the Jive Sisters: Shari Lynn, Azure McCall, and Annie MacLachlan. Some say McCall has the best jazz voice in town; with the three big talents here, the show is unstoppable.

The big name in island comedy is Frank De Lima. You must watch out for him. He usually plays at the Noodle House, where his raucous, outrageous humor reveals the best and worst of Hawaii.

If you ever see Genoa Keawe's name on a program, don't miss it. She's a classic Hawaiian falsetto who always brings the house down with her "cha-lang-a-lang" music, the best.

SPECIAL OUTINGS: ON LAND

Gardens and Valleys

FOSTER BOTANIC GARDENS
180 North Vineyard Boulevard
Nuuanu/Vineyard
Telephone: (808) 533-3214

You can come here for a moment of peace in a busy day. Shaded by large, rare trees and botanical specimens from all over the world, this 20-acre botanical garden is an idyllic spot for quiet lunches and picnics. You can wander among the rare hybrid orchids, palms, bromeliads, and historical Hawaiian plants, and you can learn about the Coco de Mer, a palm that yields 50-pound fruit requiring ten years to mature. The Foster Garden is one of Oahu's lasting treasures. Free guided tours are offered Monday through Wednesday at 1:30, and there are ongoing programs such as plant sales and annual moon walks by the Friends of Foster Gardens. There is a $1 admission charge; open 9:00 A.M. to 4:00 P.M. daily.

HART AND TAGAMI
Kahaluu
Windward Oahu
Telephone: (808) 239-8146

You could not imagine what awaits you here. Richard Hart and Hiroshi Tagami call their windward Oahu sanctuary a "zoological shelter and gallery." The two are foremost artists, Hart a ceramist and Tagami a renowned painter, who have opened their garden, aviary, and gallery to those fortunate enough to find them.

The mood is set before you enter. The entrance is marked by a bamboo ladle with water dripping into a stone basin, its gentle sounds mingling with the songs of birds. A large, vertical, moss-covered rock stands like a stone temple, and a flowering ohia tree yields sphagnum moss and bromeliads from its graceful trunk nearby. Hiroshi Tagami will greet you; he has a strong, radiant presence, the inescapable kindness of a man at peace.

The baby bird nursery is bustling with blue and gray cockatoos, two new blue and gold macaw babies, and various multicolored exotics that Tagami breeds and ships internationally. In the yard is an enormous cage containing a friendly, full-grown macaw that has been hand-fed by Tagami since it was 12 days old. In another corner of the property is a large aviary in a garden setting in which sixty brilliantly colored birds thrive. Twenty-five rare species are represented here, including peacock pheasants, a fairy bluebird, and a bleeding heart dove from the Philippines.

Buddhas and antiques are placed strategically throughout the garden, making a simple stroll an esthetic experience. Priceless artwork hangs unpretentiously in surprising corners. When you get to the gallery it will astound you with its simple majesty. Antiques, pottery, sculptures, Tagami originals, an antique Gambian wood sculpture, and Sepik mask from New Guinea are arranged in Japanese rooms with gleaming, dark woods and touches of tatami.

In the gardens you will see Tagami's own daylily hybrids, some 300 of them, soon to be registered and named after his friends. There are rare bamboo, 12 different kinds of apple trees, soft-shelled macadamia nut trees, breadfruit trees, rare palms, and brilliant crimson bromeliads. The gardens are another canvas for the artist, who personally planted every tree, flower, bush, vine, and bulb on the lush and verdant property.

Every Saturday, Sunday, and Monday, Hart and Tagami open their gallery and gardens to the public, but they ask that you make an appointment. There is no charge. This is an experience of uncommon beauty, a humbling experience indeed.

LYON ARBORETUM
3860 Manoa Road
Manoa
Telephone: (808) 988-3177

One of Oahu's most valuable resources, the Lyon Arboretum offers its generous grounds for public touring three times every month. The 124-acre arboretum is nestled deep within Manoa Valley, where clouds drift in and obscure the waterfalls like changing Chinese paintings. The gardens flourish with Hawaii's native and endemic plants and the state's largest taro collection—more than 200 species. Economic plants such as coffee, spices, vanilla, and cinnamon thrive among the luxuriant palms, heliconias, gingers, and countless other types of flora.

The Arboretum also offers educational programs in a wide variety of subjects, from native Hawaiian crafts to ethnic cookery. The grounds are lush and gorgeous, with quiet paths amid the generous foliage in the very womb of this valley. The Lyon Arboretum is a unit of the University of Hawaii and is highly recommended as a special outing. The free guided tours of the grounds, offered by staff and trained volunteers, occur the first Friday, the third Wednesday, and the third Saturday of every month. The Friday and Wednesday tours begin at 1:00 P.M.; the Saturday tour begins at 10:00 A.M. Call ahead to reserve a place, and take some mosquito repellent.

MILTON WARNE ORCHIDS
260 Jack Lane
Nuuanu
Telephone: (808) 595-2660

Milton Warne, the dean of orchid growers in Hawaii, has been cultivating this orchid nursery for more than fifty-five years. It's the oldest orchid nursery in the country, existing quietly in this valley where the cool mists of the Koolaus drift by daily to nourish the plants. There are rare hybrids here, original blooms, blooms that exist nowhere else in the world. When a desirable hybrid emerges, it can be mericloned, named, and added to the family tree.

Some have mysterious fragrances, others have surreal colors such as a chartreuse orchid, or a reddish-brown with magenta; still others have large, fluffy petals and unheard of color combinations. Warne works with cultures and petri dishes and often waits years to see the results. When an orchid blooms for the first time, it's a historic and momentous event. Then, when ready, it's displayed in Warne's large greenhouse among his other brilliant creations.

This is a collector's stop and a connoisseur's delight, but you don't have to be an expert to appreciate it. Because Warne is certified by the state Department of Agriculture to pack and ship flowers out of state, many an orchid lover's trip home begins with a stop here. Although visitors are always welcome, the nursery is not equipped to handle large busloads or groups. Please call before going.

WAIMEA FALLS PARK
59-864 Kam Highway
Waimea, North Shore
Telephone: (808) 638-8511

It's a developed park, but it is scenic, with peacocks wandering around and swarthy young men leaping off 60-foot waterfalls five times every day. There are botanic gardens to be explored, streamside hikes to be taken, picnic grounds everywhere you look.

You go at your own speed here, so you can linger to your heart's content. Not to be missed is the ancient hula, called kahiko, presented daily by the Halau 'O Waimea, the park's resident hula troupe. The dancers perform several times daily in the Upper Meadow, an area rimmed with rock walls and lush greenery. The area, the Waimea Valley on the north shore, is a historic valley in which major archaeological finds have been made. Stone bowls, bone fish hooks, poi pounders, and fiber mat remnants have been found in this 1,800-acre natural park.

At the Waimea Arboretum and Botanical Garden, some thirty-four botanical gardens featuring more than 5,000 species of plant life are maintained for public viewing, including the finest collection of ginger and heliconia in the world and an extensive hibiscus hybrid collection. The park is open from 10:00 A.M. to 5:30 P.M. daily. Admission is $7.50 per adult, $5.25 for 7- to 12-year-olds, $1.75 for 4- to 6-year-olds.

Hiking

Oahu doesn't have a Haleakala or Mauna Kea or other such geological giant, but it does have wilderness. Oahu's wilderness and forest reserves are in the Koolaus, in the Nuuanu, Tantalus, and Manoa areas, only minutes from downtown Honolulu. Trails in these areas lead to various vistas of Oahu's interior and deep into forests of bamboo, ginger, eucalyptus, and are full of native plants such as maile, kukui, ohia, and even taro. These trails are astoundingly beautiful and are a surprise to many a visitor, who might entertain the mistaken notion that Oahu has nothing but concrete to offer.

Both the Sierra Club and the Hawaiian Trail and Mountain Club lead regular hikes that are open to visitors. The Sierra Club, Hawaii Chapter, leads hikes every Sunday and on some Saturdays, for a $1 fee. For information, write the Sierra Club, 1212 University Avenue, Honolulu, HI 96822; telephone (808) 946-8494.

The Hawaiian Trail and Mountain Club leads hikes every Sunday except for an occasional "clubhouse day" (about every six weeks) when members congregate to clean their Waimanalo clubhouse. Except for those days, the hikes usually begin at 8:00 A.M. every Sunday. Hikers meet on the mauka side of Iolani Palace downtown. About twice a month, Saturday hikes are offered too. They usually begin at 9:00 A.M. There is a $1 charge for nonmembers. For information, write the Hawaiian Trail and Mountain Club, P.O. Box 2238, Honolulu, HI 96804; telephone (808) 734-5515, 488-1161, or 262-2845.

These two clubs are the principal hiking resources in the state. They know the latest on the state's hiking trails and even partipate in trail blazing and clearing when necessary. The Sierra Club and the Hawaiian Trail and Mountain Club offer opportunities for all residents and visitors to explore Oahu's wilderness safely and knowledgeably.

The first step for any hiker is to make a trip or write to the State Department of Land and Natural Resources, Division of Forestry, 1151 Punchbowl Street, Room 325, Honolulu, HI 96813; telephone (808) 548-2861. There you can pick up any of numerous publications on hiking, fishing, forestry, and camping. As of this writing, the most valuable publication, the Island of Oahu Recreation Map, is out of print, but it is available for viewing at this office. It has detailed maps and descriptions of Oahu's hiking trails. You can also write or call (or visit, but call first) the Hawaii Geographic Society (see Getting Around, Maps and Guidebooks), phone (808) 538-3952. They have an extensive selection of books and maps on hiking and other outdoor subjects. Finally, there are the trusty guidebooks, the most handy of which are *Hawaiian Hiking Trails* by Craig Chisolm and *Hawaii's Best Hiking Trails* by Robert Smith.

Because the trails in the Tantalus area all connect and even lead to the Manoa Falls Trail in the next valley, the following list (except for the Moanalua trail) only describes the major trails in the network. Be sure to take mosquito repellent, and never leave valuables in the car.

JUDD TRAIL
Nuuanu

This trail begins off Nuuanu Pali Drive (the old, wooded route, not the highway), near a bridge with a spillway beneath it at Alewa Heights Spring, just past Poli Hiwa Place.

There are large eucalyptus trees, bamboo, and a Norfolk pine forest in this densely wooded area. The lower part of the loop passes the popular Jackass Ginger, a freshwater swimming hole made famous by its ti leaf sliding of old. Kids sat on ti leaf bundles and slid down the slippery rocks in what was a favorite, and dangerous, local pastime. This is an easy trail, but it can be muddy and it does involve some stream crossings. Proper footwear would help, and the hiker should be sure-footed.

MOANALUA VALLEY
Moanalua

The Moanalua Gardens Foundation offers guided hikes into this historic valley twice a month, on the second Saturday and fourth Sunday. The hike is a leisurely, informative walk along a graded Jeep road that crosses seven eighty-year-old stone bridges, a petroglyph rock, and the remains of two ancient house sites. The 2½-mile walk usually begins at 9:00 A.M. and goes for four hours; it's so easy anyone in reasonable health can do it.

The value of this hike is the narration and information of the guide, who will explain the valley's historic sites, the plants and vines used by Hawaiians, and even how they made the rope, sandals, and other necessities from the plants that grew and still grow in the valley. The petroglyph rock is often cited by historians because it's the largest boulder on Oahu with petroglyphs on it.

The valley is not as lush as the upland forests of Tantalus, but it was an important agricultural and social center for the Hawaiians of old. The area was literally an oasis for travelers, who stopped to refresh themselves with water from its springs and streams. In the old days there were fishponds and taro fields, as well as bloody battles among rival chiefs. Not the least of those was the one in which Kamehameha defeated, and then sacrificed on an altar, the son of the Maui chief who aspired to rule Oahu.

To reserve a place on these guided hikes, call the Moanalua Gardens Foundation, telephone (808) 839-5334. A $1 donation is also asked, and you will be asked to bring your own lunch.

PU'U OHIA
Tantalus

This is a significant trail in the Tantalus system, and it is also magnificently and astoundingly beautiful. A walk on Pu'u Ohia will dispel forever the notion that Oahu is no longer naturally beautiful.

The trail winds through bamboo and eucalyptus groves and eventually connects the Aihualama Trail with the Manoa Falls Trail leading into the next valley. It is also the most direct route to what is called the meadows, a popular scenic stop through bamboo forests and wild guava and fruit trees. Pu'u Ohia is the highest peak of Tantalus. Several separate trails intersect with this one. If you take the Manoa Cliffs Trail off of Pu'u Ohia, you'll reach the Pauoa Flats Trail. Pauoa Flats connects with the Aihualama Trail as well, which takes you all the way into Manoa Falls. It's time-consuming, but it's not a difficult hike. And it is scenic beyond words. On this trail system you are surrounded by guava, hapu'u fern, bamboo, paper bark, banyan, a few stands of koa, and many fruit trees.

To get to Pu'u Ohia, first find Makiki Street, which crosses Wilder Avenue near Punahou School. Take Makiki to Round Top Drive and drive to its highest point, where it meets and becomes Tantalus Drive. Park opposite the avocado tree.

MANOA FALLS
Manoa

The Manoa Falls can be reached either through the trail described above or by driving past Paradise Park in Manoa, to an undeveloped parking area at the end of the road.

The hike crosses Aihualama Stream and winds its way through the forest, following and crossing another stream, until you find yourself at a small mountain pool, the first of three known as Manoa Falls. This is a stunning trail, but Manoa is a wet area and the trail can be muddy. However, on a clear day the dappled light through the kukui trees lends a magical charm to the trail, which traverses areas where ancient Hawaiian taro terraces can still be discerned.

WA'AHILA RIDGE
St. Louis Heights

Waahila Ridge is a different sort of experience. It's an easy 2½-mile hike along a ridgeline that overlooks Manoa Valley on one side and Palolo Valley on the other. It's cool, shaded over by immense Norfolk pines, with picnic tables and bathroom facilities. (See also Free for All.) The trail leads down into a valley and passes a campground before emerging on Alani Drive in Manoa Valley below, or you can do what many do—turn and hike back the same way. This is a lovely, loping, easy trail that wanders through koa, ohia, mountain naupaka, and even isolated clumps of 'ie'ie, a rare woody grass used in weaving by the ancient Hawaiians. The trail eventually leads to the very top of the Koolau Range, but hiking to that area is difficult and highly discouraged.

Museums

THE BISHOP MUSEUM AND PLANETARIUM
1525 Bernice Street
Kalihi
Telephone: (808) 847-3511

This garguantan stone structure is the most respected repository of Pacific artifacts in the world. Photographs, canoes, feather capes, implements, hundreds of thousands of shells, specimens, and artifacts are just a small part of the museum's offerings. Besides the exhibits, which could take days to peruse, there are planetarium shows and hula performances by the Atherton Halau. The halau performances are at 1:00 P.M. daily; there are periodic crafts demonstrations by the leading artisans in the traditional Hawaiian arts.

The museum is also an active scientific research facility with ongoing projects in archaeology, anthropology, and other disciplines. What you see in the gleaming, dark halls and display rooms is merely a glimpse of the Bishop Museum's work in Hawaii. But take a look—you can imagine the migration, origins, and development of this island culture by peering into the displays and exhibits.

Open Monday through Saturday, 9:00 A.M. to 5:00 P.M. Admission is $4.75 for adults and $2.50 for 6- to 17-year-olds.

IOLANI PALACE
Corner of King and Richards streets
Downtown
Telephone: (808) 538-1471; (808) 523-0141 for reservations

The palace, the official residence of Hawaii's last monarchs, King Kalakaua and Queen Lili'uokalani, has never looked better. A $6-million restoration of the building is complete, revealing the gleaming interior of precious polished woods, regal hand-carved stairways, and priceless artifacts. The Friends of Iolani Palace are still attempting to retrieve palace artifacts that have been lost in the community, and they are slowly trickling back. The palace is a powerful reminder of Hawaii's monarchy and the grandeur of its reign. A trip through the palace also brings home the extent of the European influence on Hawaii. Tours are given Wednesday through Saturday from 9:00 A.M. to 2:15 P.M., leaving every fifteen minutes and continuing for forty-five minutes. Admission is $4; children under five not allowed, but $1 is charged for children five to seven years of age.

BEACHES

Oahu's beaches are for everyone's enjoyment, but they must be approached with caution. Because surf and tide conditions can be unpredictable, all swimmers are advised to heed the warning flags posted by the lifeguards. You should also be aware of the possible presence of riptides and unseen currents.

The beaches of the islands undergo dramatic changes with the seasons. Every October, the onset of turbulent winter surf begins to pull away sand. The erosion continues throughout the winter months—reefs and tidepools are exposed, beaches narrow considerably, and the entire character of the coastline is transformed. This is particularly evident on the north shore, where wide, expansive, sandy shorelines can turn into rocky ledges of sharp reef and crashing surf. Sometime between February and April, the sand begins its annual return, and the shoreline begins reconstructing itself. During the summer months, there is once again a sandy shoreline and the waters are calm. The cycle begins anew.

These extreme changes in surf and beach conditions must be considered by anyone approaching Hawaiian waters. Also to be considered is the presence of unseen currents and riptides, the ever-present danger of the ocean. Obviously the best surf is not necessarily the safest—more often, the opposite is true.

Oahu has 112 miles of shoreline. Much of that shoreline is white-sand beach, and much of it is accessible. As developed as Oahu is, it is still full of beautiful coves and beaches where you can hunt for seashells, snorkel, swim, or watch the big-time bodysurfers ride the tubes. Beaches here are for swimming and recreation, but they're also great for the spectator sport of watching surfers ride waves. Beginning on the north shore and moving west, south, and east, here they are, in an island roundup. Most of these beaches have restroom and shower facilities and are easily accessible. If you want more information on Oahu's beaches, the best resource is John Clark's *The Beaches of Oahu*.

SUNSET BEACH
North Shore

Sunset Beach is famous for its high winter waves and in the summer, for its good swimming and snorkeling. Its famous shorebreak has been televised and filmed in many a professional meet, and its waves are considered among the most treacherous on the north shore. Sunset was the first north shore beach to be discovered by surfers, who were busy riding Makaha waves in the early days. You can park on the roadside and watch from the shore—or in the summer, if it's calm, you can actually swim where there were once 20-foot waves.

EHUKAI
North Shore

Ehukai is the most popular north shore bodysurfing beach and is the site of the annual bodysurfing championships. It offers a good front-row seat for watching the island's best surfers and bodysurfers. For most of the year it's wide and sandy, and during summer when the waters are calm, it's ideal for swimming. Just to the left of Ehukai, where the waves curl crisply, are the north shore's most formidable waves. This is the Banzai Pipeline—a surfing phenomenon with legendary tubes that have challenged the world's best wave riders. Stories abound about Pipeline, about strange disappearances and mysterious things floating ashore. One story describes a phantom surfboard that washed ashore covered with seaweed, with no sign of its long-vanished rider.

Indeed, the Pipeline swell is powerful, rising rapidly and steeply to form a wall and then turning into a tube as it thunders into the reef. Surfers claim the Pipeline tube offers the biggest thrill possible in the sport. When the waves get as high as 15 feet, the speed and shape are unbelievable. The waves are to be tackled only by the pros, but what a show it is for spectators!

SHARK'S COVE
North Shore

It may not sound like an auspicious name, but it isn't what you think. Shark's Cove is named after the shape of its rock formations and not from the presence of sharks. It's a very small cove, but it's the best snorkeling and dive spot on the north shore during the summer months. In winter it's too rough. Shark's Cove is a marine sanctuary with underwater shelves and ledges, teeming with colorful tropical fish. The only trouble is that it's so popular among scuba divers and snorkelers it can be downright congested at times.

WAIMEA BAY
North Shore

This is the granddaddy of the behemoth wave, where winter surf can yield 40-foot monsters that thunder into the bay, sometimes with surfers riding them. The biggest waves to be seen are at Waimea Bay, but it's gorgeous when it's not churning too. Waimea can be glassy and sweet during summer months, when its broad white curve is a perfect swimming spot. Just off the road above Waimea is a ledge that affords a good vantage point for watching Waimea's waves roll in and the kids jumping off a big black rock for kicks.

HALEIWA
Alii Beach Park
North Shore

The shallow reef visible from the shoreline can be dangerous for surfers, and so can the unseen currents known to be in the deeper waters. On a gentle day, however, this is a great spot for beginning surfers and families. They love to come here for picnics and for lazy days at the beach. When the surf picks up, the more accomplished surfers can tackle waves that can get as high as 15 feet. The shoreline of the park is known to be fertile ground for small, colorful "sunset shells" that bake in the sand and are avidly hunted by kids and shell lovers.

MAKAHA
West Oahu

Makaha, the birthplace of professional surfing, has a wide, sandy shore at the beach park where the surfers' cars and rubbernecking spectators invariably pile up on weekends. This is another world-famous, big-wave surfing spot and the site of the first professional surf meet in 1952. The shoreline undergoes extreme seasonal changes and the waves can get as high as 25 to 30 feet. Makaha is popular even when the waves aren't monstrous, and it's also a great spectator beach any time of the year. During summer, when the beach is wide and the ocean is calm, Makaha waters are great for swimming.

ALA MOANA
South Shore

Ala Moana is a long, wide curve with a well-used beach park and, on the Diamond Head side of the beach, a man-made peninsula with its own cove and seawall. Ala Moana's 76-acre park is a mecca for local residents, who dot the park and shoreline from predawn hours throughout the day to jog, picnic, swim, play volleyball, play tennis, exercise, and play. The beach is always crowded, especially on weekends. The water is shallow and protected by a reef, but there is a channel offshore that should be approached with caution.

The park contains food concessions, an outdoor pavilion for concerts and special programs, and full bathroom and shower facilities. The showers in the public restrooms in the center of the park are the nicest on the island. You can shower in privacy, in enclosed tile chambers hidden from the park, with the sun or stars shining overhead.

This is a city beach, so don't expect Bali Hai. There will be lots of well-oiled bodies baking on the sand. Right across the street is Ala Moana Center, a social and commercial center of the island.

HANAUMA BAY
East Oahu

You will no doubt hear about Hanauma Bay. Lying between two volcanic craters, this marine sanctuary is an underwater adventure for snorkelers. It is unbearably crowded, however, with throngs of beachgoers crowding its shores and waters. If you attempt this outing—and most people do—steel yourself for the masses. And, if you take some bread to feed the fish, they'll eat it out of your hand.

A walk around the bay to the right will take you across some tidal pool areas to the cauldronlike Witches Brew, the most turbulent area of the bay. The walk over the rocky shoreline is invigorating, and the view will be your reward.

SANDY BEACH
East Oahu

Sandy's, as it's called, is synonymous with bodysurfing. The waves are clean, fast, and hard-breaking, making a treacherous shorebreak that's anathema to novices but nirvana for the serious bodysurfer. Don't be fooled by the apparent ease with which the accomplished surfers tackle the waves. Unless you're accomplished at bodysurfing, this is better viewed from a distance than attempted.

The beach is on one of Hawaii's most stunning stretches of shoreline, an area cradled by Koko Head Crater, the Blow Hole, and a long scenic drive toward Makapu'u, where the whole windward coastline unfolds.

MAKAPU'U
East Oahu
South Shore

Makapu'u is the name bodysurfers love to drop. It is exclusively a bodysurfing beach; no boards are allowed. It's Hawaii's best-known and most popular bodysurfing spot, with "clean definition" and long, smooth breaks culminating in a vigorous shorebreak. The cove, visible from the lookout above, is ensconced between the steep Makapu'u cliffs and the ocean, with its famous waves and Rabbit Island offshore.

Makapu'u is also one of Oahu's prettiest beaches. During some months, the area is shaded over early in the day as the sun sinks behind the cliffs. The water changes color with the changing light, and a lighthouse at the point holds vigil. Overhead, you may see hang gliders soaring, enjoying the view below them.

WAIMANALO BEACH
Windward Oahu

When the skies are clear, Waimanalo is the picture-perfect beach, the beach of everyone's dreams. As you approach Waimanalo from Makapu'u you can see it stretch some 3½ miles into the distance, making it Oahu's longest continuous sand beach. Luxuriously white and wide, the bay occupies a large part of the southern windward shoreline, nestled in the shadow of the 2,200-foot Pu'u o Kona. The cliffs above are sharply carved by erosion and surround the bay on the mauka side with a protective wall of purple and green. A large, grassy park attracts families, softball teams, practicing bagpipers, and canoe clubs that practice and compete here.

The water is a gentle turquoise that takes on a purple tint against the white sand. On some days the waves are perfect for beginning bodysurfing; on others, for taking a long, luxurious swim in the open ocean.

LANIKAI
Windward Oahu

Lanikai is harder to get to because it's hidden in a residential area. If Waimanalo is a diamond in the rough, Lanikai is a polished gem—crystalline, refined, with a palette of blues and whites that will dazzle you for days. The two islands offshore, called the Mokuluas, are seabird sanctuaries occasionally reached by kayak, surfboard, or boat. Here, the powder-fine sand is firm when wet, making a good shoreline jogging path for the energetic.

Come here for swimming and lolling, but not for anything terribly active. There are public rights-of-way but neither facilities nor a developed park. The beach is lined with expensive homes, and the sand is peppered with people who live in them. But if you find a spot on this magical beach, especially for its dazzling sunrise, you won't want to leave. Like Waimanalo, Lanikai is a windward Oahu beach, best in the morning and early afternoon before the Koolaus' shadows hit the beach.

KAILUA BEACH
Windward Oahu

Kailua Beach is two miles long, consisting of the Kailua Beach Park at one end, Kalama Beach in the middle, and ending at Oneawa Beach on the other end. It is a gorgeous stretch of white sand with waves that are strongest toward the center. At the 30-acre Kailua Beach Park by the boat ramp on the south end of the beach, local families and windsurfers gather every weekend for volleyball, swimming, and windsurfing. Kailua Beach Park is often crowded, but a short walk along the bay will take you to less crowded shores.

At this and all other windward Oahu beaches, beware of the blue Portuguese man-of-war, a jellyfish that stings.

POUNDERS BEACH
Laie
North Shore/Northeast Oahu

Pounders is the north shore version of Makapu'u—extremely popular, with good waves, a nice cove, and a strong shorebreak. Pounders doesn't offer the strength and speed of Makapu'u, but surfers enjoy the high winter waves and, on the eastern end, the intimidating, forceful shorebreak just the same. It is small but offers perfect viewing for spectators. The beach is just off the main highway and is situated below a limestone bluff that was used in the old days for spotting fish.

MALAEKAHANA
North Shore

Malaekahana has a different quality from most other Oahu beaches. It's lined with ironwoods and false kamani trees, with more than a mile of sandy beach and safe swimming along the shoreline. Although popular as a camping facility (it has housekeeping cabins for rent from the state), the beach is never crowded and you feel you're at a remote country beach. The waves are small, the waters are calm, and the park has all the conveniences.

FREE FOR ALL

T he following list is only a beginning. Enjoyable things to do, see, and explore are scattered throughout other chapters, particularly in Special Outings: On Land.

The Best Night Drive

The best night drive has several criteria: roadside scenery and greenery, a vantage point over the city, and a special quality of air, namely fragrance. Nights still smile favorably upon Round Top Drive on Tantalus, where the enrapturing fragrance of night-blooming jasmine and ginger wafts through the clear, moist mountain air. The city unfolds before and below you while the fragrances change at every corner and, if you're lucky, the night-blooming cereus bloom at the bends of the road. If you look up, you'll see mile-high trees framed by night and the best of a starry, bright Hawaiian sky.

This drive takes you up Honolulu's most distinctive natural feature, a rapidly ascending mountain surrounded on either side by a steep valley, with the entire Honolulu skyline before it.

A caveat: Keep moving on this night drive. For safety reasons, stopping or lingering is not wise.

The Best Place to View the Sunrise

Lanikai on the windward side or Waimanalo Bay a short drive away make the best spots for viewing sunrise. The Lanikai sunrise is a spectacular daily light show only thirty-five minutes from downtown Honolulu, over the Pali and beyond Kailua. Lanikai is a turquoise stretch of gentle beach with white, powder-fine sand that reflects light as nowhere else. The morning begins with a glow beyond the two sphinxlike islands offshore, and as the sun rises the water and sand take on opalescent shades like mother-of-pearl.

Waimanalo's view is equally sublime, except that you view Rabbit Island instead of the Lanikai islands. The windward Oahu beach is a white sand curve flanked by the Makapu'u mountain ridge on one side and the ocean on the other. When the sun rises out of the ocean, it looks as if a golden glow is pouring out of the sky.

The Best Place to View the City

The drive up to Pu'u Ualakaa Park on Round Top Drive, about halfway up Tantalus mountain, is a worthy event in itself, but you couldn't possibly anticipate the view once you get up there. With the Koolaus behind you, you have an unobstructed view of the city, from Koko Head to Diamond Head, Manoa Valley, Waikiki, downtown Honolulu, Pearl Harbor, the Waianae Mountains, and Ewa Beach. That's half the island.

This is the consummate panorama, a majestic stretch of coastline framed by mountains moving to sea. If you're really lucky, the moon will rise to your left while the sun sets before you.

A note of caution: Do not leave valuables in the car, and be sure to lock it. The park gates are locked at 7:40 P.M. during the summer months and an hour earlier from November through April.

The Best Place to View Waikiki

The Diamond Head Crater is in its glory. A Diamond Head hiking club, complete with certificate, has been launched by the New Otani Kaimana Beach Hotel to encourage people to go up there. And indeed, the steep hike is worth it.

Although it's not recommended for young children, it's an otherwise superior outing. In less than an hour and a mile's distance you find yourself perched hundreds of feet above Waikiki, with a sweeping vista of the southern shoreline. Because the hike is steep and at one point goes up the steps of a bunker, caution is advised.

The entrance to the crater begins sightly east of the intersection of Diamond Head Road and Alohea Avenue. From Waikiki, follow Monsarrat past Alohea and turn where the entrance to the crater is marked. Drive through the tunnel to the parking lot, and then proceed to the marked trail.

The Best Place to Stay Cool

The Wa'ahila Ridge State Recreation Area, at the top of St. Louis Drive, is a trusty retreat at any time of the year. But on steamy summer days when the high temperatures become unreasonable, the park takes on an even more special quality. Here, high above Honolulu, temperatures are lower and the sky-high Norfolk pines and ironwoods offer quiet, shaded areas for hiking and picnicking. The best grove of strawberry guavas is here also, and those in the know come regularly during the season for their share of the bounty. Lining the road into the park are rose apple trees with flowers like white lehua blossoms. When fruiting, the trees are an oasis of pleasure—the yellow, ambrosial fruit actually taste like sweet roses!

Carp Feeding at the Pagoda Hotel

This hotel and floating restaurant, at 1525 Rycroft Street near Ala Moana Center, has the most impressive collection of carp—the colorful and price-less Japanese fish—for public viewing. The restaurant is built over a large pond filled with these multicolored creatures, with bridges and pathways that allow close viewing. Carp feeding times are 8:00 A.M., noon, and 6:00 P.M. daily, but it's advisable to call beforehand (941-6611) in case they are cleaning or treating the pond. The fish anticipate their meal and gather in a feeding frenzy at the designated spot. It may be the most dynamic and colorful fish scene you'll see here.

East-West Center

The grounds adjoining the University of Hawaii's Manoa campus, off Dole Street on East-West Road, are a gardenlike setting shaded by rare trees and picturesque ponds. The area around Jefferson Hall, the center of this institute's activity, has the tranquility of a Japanese garden, with rare plants, a pond and brook, and quiet paths for strolling and lingering.

Kodak Hula Show

This is a well-known and well-attended tourist event that is surprisingly enjoyable. Some of the best aspects of Hawaii are featured here, including fresh flower leis, real ti-leaf skirts, and gracious, large ladies in cotton muumuus who have been singing here for decades. There's ancient and modern hula, Tahitian dance, and demonstrations of poi pounding and the use of traditional implements. But be prepared for the busloads of people. It will be hot as well, so be prepared for the sun—bring sunscreen and sunglasses. If you'd like to participate in the free hula lessons that are a big part of the program, be sure to come with a sense of humor and a good dollop of chutzpah.

Hula Lessons at the Royal Hawaiian Center

One of Hawaii's foremost hula instructors, the late Auntie Ma'iki Aiu Lake, began giving free hula lessons in the heart of Waikiki. They were successful and she was well loved. Today her daughter and her halau carry on the tradition with hula lessons at the center, 2201 Kalakaua Avenue. Show up on Monday, Wednesday, and Friday, from 10:30 A.M. to 11:30 A.M., if you want to learn the basics of the hip-swaying hula to take back with you.

The Royal Hawaiian Band

Founded by King Kamehameha V, the band continues its historic tradition with free concerts under the trees at the Iolani Palace, this country's only palace. Every Friday at 12:15, the band gathers, as it has for decades, to fill the air with music of the monarchy and give the whole town an excuse for a picnic. The grassy lawn is shaded by large trees and the palace's majestic front is in view; surely this is one of downtown Honolulu's most scenic and historic spots.

Shirokiya

For years they have provided a phantasmagoria of treats for the adventurous palate. The upper floor of this large Japanese department store is largely devoted to food, with an atmosphere like a country fair. Exotic seafood and pastries steam, smoke, and smolder behind counters, while curious shoppers are encouraged to taste. Dainty food samples line the counters with many choices, from pickled vegetables to Japanese tea cakes to strange seaweeds and dumplings. It's all very exotic and enjoyable.

Besides being one of the premier taste-testing spots in town, Shirokiya is noted for its demonstrations of the arts and crafts of Japan. Visiting masters arrive periodically to demonstrate everything from calligraphy to pottery, carving, and the culinary arts. The demonstrations are announced in newspaper advertisements beforehand.

Shirokiya is in the Ala Moana Center.

Urasenke Foundation Tea Ceremony

The tranquil Japanese garden offers a peaceful respite from the crush of the city. The Urasenke Foundation's teahouse is open to the public every Wednesday and Friday from 10:00 A.M. to noon at 245 Saratoga Road on the ewa end of Waikiki. It's a haven and an education. The dignity, simplicity, and grace of Japanese esthetics are demonstrated through the ceremonial serving of tea in a spotless tatami room.

This is Waikiki's most tranquil spot, made available to the public as a service from dedicated practitioners of the ancient art. It's an informal version of a highly formal ritual, so there are explanations along the way. Guests participate in the drinking of the tea and are offered exquisite sweets made in Kyoto. The rooms accommodate only about twenty-five people at a time, so groups of ten or more should call (808) 923-3059 for reservations.

People Watching

Selective people watching can be a full-time preoccupation. You can pick your spot according to what you'd like to see, and usually the place will deliver.

Kalakaua Avenue, for example, is the consummate spot for people watchers seeking variety and volume. The teeming throngs of people from all corners of the world wear everything from pareus to bikinis to saris and kilts. Of course, you get more than your share of polyester aloha shirts and matching muumuus, which is the price one pays for being in Waikiki.

If you're looking for a lively street scene with offbeat characters and lots of surprises, the hot spot is the Kuhio District on Kuhio Avenue. It offers a colorful melange of red-light chic, continental panache, and a parade of people of all inclinations, sexual preferences, and walks of life. The area is flourishing with new eateries and shops, so you can walk around purposefully as well.

For a more comfortable spot over a cup of coffee close to an artificial waterfall, you might consider Harry's Bar at the Hyatt Regency. You can read foreign newspapers over espresso coffee while you behold the passing parade of visiting sheiks, honeymooners, celebrities, and ordinary folks watching people just like you.

For celebrity spotting, it's the Kahala Hilton, hands down. The Kahala Hilton also offers the added benefit of four porpoises in its lagoon, a spectacle that usually upstages the celebrities.

Finally, for local color nonpareil, it's Ala Moana Center. The mall level, by the fountain and escalator, is a hot spot for watchers, and so is the downstairs area by the stage. Everyone is watching everyone else here, and you will probably be watched as you watch. If that's not enough, go across the street to Ala Moana Beach Park and watch the joggers, picnickers, volleyball players, and kite flyers as they frolic among the well-oiled sunbathers and swimmers.

Watching Porpoises

Keeping in mind that porpoise viewing may be simply a matter of timing and good fortune, there are two noteworthy stops that make it easier for you to see them.

Portlock Point at the end of Hanapepe Place, a primordial stretch of ledge looking out to the southern sea, provides a spectacular panorama that includes a rarely seen side view of Diamond Head. This enchanting spot is often enhanced by the sight of frolicking porpoises or whales as they move across the horizon. During whale season, this is one of the throughways for the humpback mothers and calves as they move across island waters. For directions on how to get there, see Watching Surfers. And watch your footing.

If you're lucky enough to be dining at the Hanohano Room on the thirtieth floor of the Waikiki Sheraton, you will look through large, wall-to-wall picture windows at a breathtaking view of the ocean. If you're really lucky, you'll see whales or porpoises in the open sea. Over your Eggs Benedict or finnan haddie you may also see, on the other side, rainbows in Manoa Valley and fairy terns and frigate birds flying exceptionally close to the windows. These are special events that don't happen every day, of course. They may even happen rarely, but there aren't many places like this thirtieth-floor perch for a bird's-eye view of valley and sea.

Watching Surfers

The most intimate vantage point for viewing surfers is at Portlock Point. If the waves are churning on the south shoreline, they'll be a hair's width away from the ledge below you in what could be your most vicarious surfing thrill. This is admittedly a rare seasonal event because of the surf conditions required, but there's nothing like it on the island. To get there, take Kalanianaole Highway, heading east. Turn right on Lunalilo Home

Road, then turn left on Poipu and follow it, bearing right as it turns toward the sea. Make a right on Hanapepe Loop and a left on Hanapepe Place. Park and walk toward the ocean. There are obscure ledges toward the right. Watch your footing and stay as high as possible. The surf here is never as intimidating as the north shore winter surf, but if the waves are just right you'll have a front-row seat above surfers streaking by.

To watch the paipo-board (small surfboards for belly surfing or skimming the sand) surfers close up, the best view is from the Kapahulu Storm Drain, commonly called the wall, at the ocean end of Kapahulu Avenue, where Kalakaua Avenue splits to meet Monsarrat in Waikiki. This is an old-time favorite of Oahu's bodysurfers and paipo-board surfers, who ride perilously close to the stone wall to the breathless wonder of spectators. It's usually crowded here, with a festive, beach-going atmosphere as people gather to tackle the waves head-on, or to watch others doing it.

SHOPPING

I t takes vigilance to be a visitor shopping in Hawaii. The stores are full of things that look like they're made in Hawaii, but which were really made in the Philippines, Taiwan, or Hong Kong. Nominal labor costs in those countries make it cheaper to manufacture souvenirs there, so the prices are often lower. That may suit some people, but if you're looking for the genuine Hawaiian item, be sure to ask the sales clerk or check the label carefully.

The following stores have quality merchandise in a wide variety of areas. Although couture is alive and well in Hawaii, I have not included the Calvin Kleins, Lancels, Chanels, Guccis, Benettons, Ralph Laurens, and other well-known mainland and European boutiques that everyone knows about. I have compiled, instead, a very selective listing of shopping outlets that offer the best items in specialized areas, most notably items that reflect the best of Hawaii.

Apart from a couple of exceptions all of the following shops are in Honolulu and windward Oahu; the few shops located on the north shore will be in Haleiwa. For your convenience, the major shopping centers where most of the shops in Honolulu and windward Oahu are located are described as well.

Shopping Centers

THE ALA MOANA CENTER
Ala Moana

The 180 stores, restaurants, and services of this 50-acre shopping center make Ala Moana Center an unavoidable reality for everyone in Honolulu. Try as you might, you cannot escape it, and who wants to? With its central location and 7,000 free parking spots, it's one-stop shopping at its best.

You can find anything here, from amethyst geodes to designer cookies to custom-made kites and Vuitton luggage. There are ice cream and bicycle shops, health food stores and surf shops, photo processing and dry cleaning. Some things, such as groceries, can be more expensive here than at isolated markets in other areas, but most things are still more reasonable here than in Waikiki.

The shopping center recently opened the Makai Market Food Court with its twenty-one international restaurants, making this a dining stop as well. (See also Dining Out.)

There is a center stage area on the street level, mauka side of the center, where free programs are offered at least every weekend. Art shows and displays hang periodically in an exhibition area nearby.

The center is open daily, with most stores open from 9:30 A.M. until 9:00 P.M. except on weekends. Weekend hours are Saturday until 5:30 P.M., Sunday 10:00 A.M. until 5:00 P.M. These are the hours for most of the following stores that are in Ala Moana Center. Parking can be a problem during peak hours, but only on the first two floors. Top-level parking is usually available.

To get there from Waikiki, take the Number 5 bus marked Ala Moana/ Manoa, or the Number 8 marked Airport/Hickam or Ala Moana Center. The return to Waikiki is via the Number 8 marked Waikiki Beach/Hotels. If you're walking from Waikiki, head ewa on Kalakaua until Ala Moana Boulevard, turn left and pass the Ala Wai Boat Harbor and Ilikai Hotel. Ala Moana is about a twenty-minute walk from the edge of Waikiki.

ROYAL HAWAIIAN SHOPPING CENTER
2201 Kalakaua Avenue
Waikiki

There are three blocks to this shopping complex, three long blocks along Kalakaua Avenue in Waikiki. The 6½-acre complex includes three lei stands, several great restaurants, visitor services such as G.B.C. Packaging, a post office, and car rentals.

This is couture lane, with a string of upscale European boutiques such as Lancel, the Chanel Boutique, Louis Vuitton, and Les Must de Cartier lining the ground floor amid the kiosks and more touristy shops. Besides the designer shops, with their largely unaffordable merchandise, the Little Hawaiian Craft Shop (listed separately) is reommended.

The shopping center is owned by the Kamehameha Schools/Bishop Estate. Programs here range from free hula lessons to Hawaiian quilt making and fishnet making demonstrations. The center is open 9:00 A.M. to 10:00 P.M. Monday through Saturday, and 9:00 A.M. to 9:00 P.M. on Sunday.

WARD CENTRE
1200 Ala Moana Boulevard
Across from Ala Moana Park

Ward Centre is the newest and Yuppiest of the shopping malls. High-lighted with brass and natural woods, it's elegant and upscale, with shops to match. Except for its poorly designed parking lot, it has a pleasing design and a mood conducive to leisurely shopping and lunching. There are close to three dozen shops and restaurants in the complex, including Mary Catherine's (see Everyday Good Things), Il Fresco (see Dining Out), a deli, sushi bar, and numerous high-fashion apparel shops.

Ward Centre projects an image of success and taste that appeals to young professionals, like the Marin County of Honolulu. The center is open 10:00

A.M. to 9:00 P.M. Monday through Friday, 10:00 A.M. to 5:00 P.M. Saturday, and 11:00 A.M. to 4:00 P.M. on Sunday.

WARD WAREHOUSE
1050 Ala Moana Boulevard
Across Kewalo Basin

Ward Warehouse is the plain Jane of the Honolulu shopping malls, but it's precious. A low-rise of dark wood and manageable proportions, the Ward Warehouse houses some of this island's old favorites without the razzle-dazzle and "image" of its upscale cousin up the street, Ward Centre, that is. At this shopping center you won't have to dress up or walk a mile to move down your shopping list, and except for lacking a drugstore, groceries, and a few other specialties, the selection is fairly complete.

There are about seventy shops and eateries in the complex, ranging from gallery-type gift shops to a surf shop, a liquor store, coffee house, and camera shop. The center is open from 10:00 A.M. to 9:00 P.M. Monday through Friday, 10:00 A.M. to 5:00 P.M. Saturday and 11:00 A.M. to 4:00 P.M. Sunday. To get there from Waikiki, take the Number 8 Airport bus.

Shops

ACADEMY SHOP
Honolulu Academy of Arts
900 South Beretania Street
Across Thomas Square
Telephone: (808) 523-1493; 538-3693, ext. 250

Those who take the trouble to stop here will not be disappointed. The tiny shop is full of treasures, tastefully selected from a wide range of cultures, crafts, and media. While avant-garde, glittery earrings grace the counters, beautiful dark woods and baskets beckon from another corner. Many of the crafts, especially the carved woods, are made in Hawaii by excellent crafts people. There are silk scarves, baskets, beadwork, a wide selection of books, and wonderful fabrics such as silk saris from India and Guatemalan ikat. Batiks, woven purses, Shigra bags from Ecuador and Navajo Indian beads make this a multiethnic collection, and there are greeting cards as well.

Open 10:00 A.M. to 4:00 P.M. Tuesday through Saturday, 1:00 P.M. to 5:00 P.M. Sunday, and closed Monday. Major credit cards accepted for purchases over $15.

AILANA
930 Maunakea Street
Downtown
Telephone: (808) 536-5189

The selection of antique glassware, books, vases, crystal, and other tasteful art pieces and memorabilia is entertaining and enticing. Much of the selection is from private collections, including the owner's family, and from his years of prowling estate sales and attics for beautiful things of the past. There is Carnival Glass from Poland, genuine European Art Deco glassware, fluted crystal glasses and hand-painted plates. The books are rare and make great gifts for the friend who has everything. There's leather-bound Shakespeare here. Of course the merchandise changes because it's all one of a kind, so you must rely on serendipity. Open 9:30 A.M. to 4:30 P.M. Monday through Saturday. No credit cards.

ALTILLO
2117 Kuhio Avenue
Waikiki
Telephone: (808) 926-1680

They specialize in men's European sportswear here, which is extremely tasteful and expensive. Dwight Spacek always had conservative good taste; he's made it work in a selection that appeals to professional men and fashion plates, or just anyone who appreciates Italian silks, good cottons, and other natural fibers. They're ahead of the times here.

Open 11:00 A.M. to 8:00 P.M. Monday through Saturday. Closed Sunday. Major credit cards accepted.

ARTIST GUILD
Ward Warehouse
1050 Ala Moana Boulevard
Across from Kewalo Basin
Telephone: (808) 531-2933

If you don't come to the Artist Guild you may never see the state-of-the-art stained glass kaleidoscope they sometimes carry, or the most gorgeous silk scarves that flutter daintily in the wind. There are also beautiful native woods, in boxes, bowls, hair ornaments, and jewelry, as well as clothing, etchings, and ceramics. The shop reflects quality in every corner and represents dozens of the best island artists in all media. Highly recommended.

Open 10:00 A.M. to 9:00 P.M. Monday through Friday, 10:00 A.M. to 6:00 P.M.. Saturday, and 11:00 A.M. to 4:00 P.M. Sunday. Major credit cards accepted.

BANANA REPUBLIC
Ala Moana Center
Telephone: (808) 955-2602

Finally, the jungle brigade arrived and set up shop with its signature bags, outback pants, Egyptian cotton shirts, and well-ventilated cotton dresses and shorts. Banana Republic has its worldwide following, and Hawaii is no exception. The shop is entertaining, with a sense of humor, a theme, helpful sales clerks, and terrific clothing for life in the tropics. They make sure you walk out feeling like Alec Guinness or Meryl Streep. One day they even had an original orange flight suit from the Israeli army, made of Egyptian cotton.

Open 9:30 A.M. to 9:00 P.M. Monday through Friday, 9:30 A.M. to 6:00 P.M. on Saturday, and 10:00 A.M. to 5:00 P.M. on Sunday. Major credit cards accepted.

THE BIKE SHOP
1149 South King Street
Near Piikoi
Telephone: (808) 531-7071

This is the best camping store and bicycle store in the islands. It's also the only one in Hawaii listed in *Backpacking Hawaii*, which lends it considerable cachet among walkers and cyclists. The Fujis and Schwinns are here en masse, gleaming rows of them, and the camping equipment is awesome. North Face, Kelty, and all the best names are here in abundant choices—backpacks, sleeping bags, tents, accessories. You can also special order equipment, such as cold-weather gear. There is also a whole line of cycling outfits, with those odd-looking stretch pants and helmets to accompany the space-age look. Exercycles and wind trainers for the bicycles are here too. The shop also does bicycle repairs, and they are very reliable.

Open daily, 9:00 A.M. to 5:30 P.M. Monday through Saturday, Friday until 8:00 P.M., and Sunday 10:00 A.M. to 5:00 P.M. Major credit cards accepted.

BLUE GINGER DESIGNS
Ward Warehouse
1050 Ala Moana Boulevard
Across from Kewalo Basin
Telephone: (808) 526-0398

The crisp, handcrafted look of the made-in-Singapore batiks fills this shop with a wonderful flavor. There are hapi coats and dresses, children's wear and purses, potholders and totes. Just about anything you can make out of fabric is here. The Blue Ginger trademark is the fabrics, handmade and sewn in Singapore into fashions with a tropical island feel. They're appropriate for Hawaii and come in muumuulike designs that are cool, comfortable, and practical. Also recommended are the short-sleeved aloha shirt styles for men, made in the batik and so attractive.

Open 10:00 A.M. to 9:00 P.M. Monday through Friday, until 5:00 P.M. on Saturday, and from 11:00 A.M. to 5:00 P.M. Sunday. Major credit cards accepted.

BOX CLOTHING
404 Piikoi
Telephone: (808) 537-2988

Box Clothing is that rare breed, a shop with genuine bargains that make you come away glowing. Through some national marketing mechanism, Box gets name sportswear and sells it at incredible prices, for men and women. The Ala Moana store has menswear, the Piikoi store has men's and women's. You'll find rayon challis skirts, surf shirts, denim coats, jeans galore, and cotton sweaters for a fraction of what you'd find them for elsewhere. Gorgeous, soft, perfectly new rayon shirts may go for $10 or less; twill trousers that normally sell for $40 could be selling for half the amount.

All the garments are in boxes or in neat stacks, so you have to poke around on your own. You're bound to find a bargain and may end up spending a lot of money thinking of how much you're saving.

Open daily. Major credit cards accepted.

C. JUNE SHOES
Waikiki Trade Center
2255 Kuhio Avenue
Waikiki
Telephone: (808) 926-1574

The shoes here, and the handbags too, are the stuff of rock and roll and Hollywood stars; you have to be flamboyant and utterly confident to wear them. They are, however, tasteful. Lizard boots with snakeskin trim and high-grade leather shoes in all colors grace the windows of what is Hawaii's most astounding shoe store. Part Rodeo Drive, part New York, and partly C. June's personal footwear fantasies, the very expensive collection has all the names in the business: Weitzman, Bally, Charles Jourdan, Anne Klein, and Xavier Danaud. Crystal rhinestone-studded pumps, opalescent leathers, dark glasses, and leather dresses are the order of the day here. Although the merchandise is very upscale, there's a whole room next door devoted to sale shoes, which are plentiful and generously marked down.

Open 10:00 A.M. to 7:00 P.M. Monday through Friday, 10:00 A.M. to 6:00 P.M. Saturday, and noon to 6:00 P.M. Sunday. Major credit cards accepted.

CHAMPAGNE BY ZIA
2255 Kuhio Avenue
Waikiki Trade Center
Waikiki
Phone: (808) 926-8011

There are two shops in the center, one devoted mostly to men's wear and leather and the other to a sumptuous array of casual to formal wear in silks, cottons, linens, and exotic fabric blends that are mind-boggling in their beauty. Owner Mehdi Zia has exquisite taste and an eye for fine and unusual fabrics that drape beautifully and feel terrific. Most of the lines here are European, and there are earrings and accessories as well. The soft rayon blends are incomparable, as are the very *au courant* Swiss linens and fine Italian cotton shirts and slacks.

Open 10:00 A.M. to 11:00 P.M. daily. Major credit cards accepted.

CHOCOLATES FOR BREAKFAST
Ala Moana Center
Telephone: (808) 947-3434

Waikiki Shopping Plaza
2250 Kalakaua Avenue
Telephone: (808) 923-4426

Chocolates may look like any other designer store, but if you look close enough you'll see things here you won't find anywhere else. Owner Audrey Fu is notorious for discovering looks and designers, both internationally and in Hawaii. Local designers such as Dean Christopher have their work prominently displayed at Chocolates, as well as a healthy spectrum of sweaters, dresses, sportswear, and accessories from all over the world. Chocolates is also known for its outrageous belts and purses, for those expensive items women dream about but have to think twice about getting.

Open daily. Major credit cards accepted.

CREATIVE FIBERS
450 Piikoi Street
Near Ala Moana
Telephone: (808) 537-3674

Pearlridge Center
Telephone: (808) 488-0220

One of Honolulu's more enjoyable shops, Creative Fibers has a strong ethnic influence. There are natural fabrics from Holland and Indonesia, Japanese fabrics, cottons, yukatas, Guatemalan fabrics, and South Pacific specialties galore. The selection of local T-shirts can be found at the Pearlridge Center Shop, but the Ala Moana store has more than enough going for it. Woven coconut fiber bags from the Cook Islands have been found here, as well as some treasures from the Solomon Islands and other exotic treats. Not to be missed are the Polynesian silkscreened fabrics by Tutuvi. The 100-percent cotton yardage makes great pareus, tablecloths, wraparound dresses, even curtains. Made by local designer Colleen Kimura, Tutuvi is exceptional.

Open 11:00 A.M. to 6:00 P.M. daily except Sunday. Major credit cards accepted.

G. WILLIKER'S
Manoa Marketplace
2752 Woodlawn Drive
Manoa
Telephone: (808) 988-5506

A small, festive boutique, G. Williker's carries a unique assortment of body adornments. Forward-looking earrings by La Doux and other hard-to-find brands, unusually crafted handbags, belts, scarves, and other creative, colorful accessories are the order of the day here. The store is reliable for unique and whimsical gifts in all price ranges, or for that special piece of blown glass or Ira Ono Trashface jewelry. All prices.

Open 10:00 A.M. to 6:00 P.M. Monday through Saturday, 10:00 A.M. to 5:00 P.M. Sunday. Major credit cards accepted.

HARTLINE
135 Hekili Street
Kailua
Windward Oahu
Telephone: (808) 263-4698

Hartline does not buy locally, but it buys well. The shop carries some surprises, such as an occasional, pretty wide-brimmed straw hat that looks like it came from the Cook Islands but didn't, and some Laise Adzer belts and dresses, and go-everywhere ID sportswear. Some of the clothes are European, some are American, but all are eminently attractive.

Open 10 A.M. to 5:00 P.M. Monday through Saturday. Major credit cards accepted.

HAWAIIAN ISLAND CREATIONS

Ala Moana Center   Kailua (354 Hahani Street)
Telephone: (808) 941-4491   Telephone: (808) 262-7277

Pearlridge
Telephone: (808) 488-6700

Anyone twenty or under, and surfers or bicyclists of any age, must stop at this phenomenal shop. It began as a surf shop vending brightly printed "jams," body boards, and surfboards. Now it has a whole room of bicycles as well, many of them hanging from the ceiling and odd places. The shop has surf wear, bikinis, cotton sportswear, accessories for bicycling, helmets, cycling clothes, sunglasses, surfboard leashes, sun lotions, you name it. It's got loud music and bright lights, sort of like a Fiorucci for the bike and beach crowd.

Open daily. Major credit cards accepted.

HULA SUPPLY CENTER
2346 South King Street
Moiliili
Telephone: (808) 941-5379

Nestled between the Day-Glo cellophane skirts and Mylar hula skirts are some bamboo nose flutes, pahu drums and gourds, and the full range of hula implements. Raffia hula skirts, shell ornaments, Hawaiian and Tahitian wraps, and the red-and-yellow feathered gourds make exotic possibilities for gifts or souvenirs. (Check out the pareus, or Tahitian wraps—great for beach or pool!) If you're a dancer, better yet, but you don't have to be a hula pro to appreciate a good nose flute or drum for the spirit of Hawaii it expresses. There's a good dose of kitsch here, but you'll find some handsome natural specimens as well.

Open 9:00 A.M. to 5:30 P.M. Monday through Friday, 8:30 A.M. to 5:00 P.M. Saturday. Major credit cards accepted.

THE HONOLULU HAT COMPANY
1461 South King Street
Pawaa, close to Ala Moana
Telephone: (808) 945-2055

It's an out-of-the-way place with no profile at all, except among those who know and love Hawaiian crafts. Owner Rebecca Sullivan has been in the business twelve years and has cultivated invaluable sources on the Big Island for some hard-to-get hats made of the prestigious Kona lauhala. She started out with feather supplies and feather leis, and added hats. Today this is one of the few places where you can find a selection of hats without custom ordering, although you can do that here too. Men's and women's hats, Panama hats, wide-brimmed lauhala hats, narrow-brimmed lauhala hats, and many others are also available. Sullivan is a milliner and does her own blocking, so you can count on a good fit. The finer weaves are often available, as well as an occasional Cook Island launiu hat, very fine and hard to get. Honolulu Hats also has feather hatbands and leis. Prices for the feather leis range from $30 to $35 for the machine-stitched version and $85 and up for the hand-sewn ones. Lauhala hats go for $35 to $85.

Open everyday except Sunday. Validated parking behind the store. Major credit cards accepted.

IMAGO
Ward Centre
1200 Ala Moana Boulevard
Across from Ala Moana Park
Telephone: (808) 521-1112

Television anchorwomen shop here, and so do women who want to look like them. Imago customers are those who like linen suits, Nancy Heller easy knits, and designer clothing of natural fibers. Imago also has a great selection of elaborate belts and purses. A simple T-shirt can run high here, but it will be the best, as will the cotton slacks and crisp casual wear.

Open 10:00 A.M. to 9:00 P.M. Monday through Friday, until 5:00 P.M. Saturday, and from 11:00 A.M. to 4:00 P.M. Sunday. Major credit cards accepted.

LIBERTY HOUSE
Ala Moana Center and other locations
Telephone: (808) 941-2345

For years this huge department store has represented one-stop shopping at its best. Its four floors carry everything from designer chocolates (Godiva, Frangoes) to luggage, a bakery, contemporary sportswear, designer men's and women's wear, books, kitchen appliances, fabrics, shoes, jewelry, and all the usual and even not-so-usual department store items. It's the shop for odd things and ordinary things, for things you need and don't need.

The Young Islander department carries a healthy selection of made-in-Hawaii fashions, from elegant muumuus to contemporary silk dresses by Hawaii's known and unknown designers. The children's department is one of Hawaii's largest, and the shoe department is something no island woman can live without.

Open daily and nightly, with shorter hours on weekends. Major credit cards accepted.

THE LITTLE HAWAIIAN CRAFT SHOP
Royal Hawaiian Shopping Center
2233 Kalakaua Avenue
Waikiki
Telephone: (808) 926-2662

Anyone interested in native Hawaiian crafts must stop here. There are rare and wonderful Niihau shell leis, museum replicas of artifacts, an infinite array of shells, nuts, woods, coral, feather, and other works made by local artists. There are more than 200 kinds of Hawaiian seeds and woods sold here, plus hundreds more different shells from other areas of the Pacific. This is also one of the few places with good tapa from Tonga and Fiji. An occasional Solomon Island bag or Papua New Guinea mask or shield will join the other accoutrements, making this an exotic, exciting shop. Some seed and craft shops can be tacky, filled with items made in the Philippines or Taiwan, but the Little Hawaiian Craft Shop is in a class of its own, a quality, authentic representation of the best Hawaii has to offer.

Open 9:00 A.M. to 10:00 P.M. Monday through Saturday and until 9:00 P.M. on Sunday. Major credit cards accepted.

LOCAL MOTION
1714 Kapiolani Boulevard
Telephone: (808) 944-8515

Windward Mall
Telephone: (808) 247-8727

Koko Marina Shopping Center
Telephone: (808) 396-8373

Local Motion is of that ever-popular genre called "surf shop," which proliferates in Hawaii, Australia, and California, and whose look is being imitated by European companies hoping to ride the wave of its popularity. Local Motion is trendy, with surf couture, turbo body boards, surfboard wax, and Day-Glo zinc oxide. It sells surfboards, cotton short-sleeve shirts, bathing suits, tank tops, surf shorts, dark glasses, and the entire spectrum of paraphernalia to equip you for the sun and surf. There are some hand-painted T-shirts and all the names in surf wear, from its own Local Motion line to Gotcha, Maui and Sons, and Billabong. Along with Sony Walkmans and colored hair gel, shops like Local Motion rank way up there with the teens, who tend to blow their allowances on the look. While you're here, look into the Skinny Dip shop next door for swimwear and cotton T-shirts.

Open 9:00 A.M. to 9:00 P.M. Monday through Friday and until 5:00 P.M. weekends. Major credit cards accepted.

OOGENESIS
66-249 Kam Highway
Haleiwa, North Shore
Telephone: (808) 637-4580

Oogenesis has been here since the hippie era, when lacy, ethereal, Isadora Duncan dresses were quite the rage. Oogenesis has changed with the times, but it still has that offbeat flavor that makes its merchandise appealing. Stop here if you need a swimsuit or T-shirt. The swimwear and ocean wear selection is good, and if you don't find what you need you can always stop at RIX, its sister store down the street.

Open 10:00 A.M. to 6:00 P.M. daily. Major credit cards accepted.

PARISSI
444 Hobron Lane
Eaton Square
Waikiki, ewa end
Telephone: (808) 955-6885

Jacques Huaume flies to Europe several times a year and picks up accessories, leather clothing, Italian suits, silk and cotton shirts, and a marvelous array of wearables that, surprisingly, have a good island following. The leathers are exquisite, from soft lambskin to "glacé" red or metallic finish leathers in jackets and suits. The shirts are eminently tasteful, in short-sleeved cottons or silk, in soft, conservative stripes or splashier, surf-like pastels. Parissi's forte, however, is the leather clothing and the men's suits, which are expensive and well made. Some of the labels are well known, others less so, but all are of high quality. For men and women.

Open 10:00 A.M. to 8:00 P.M. Monday through Saturday, 11:00 A.M. to 6:00 P.M. Sunday. Major credit cards accepted.

POMEGRANATES IN THE SUN
Ward Warehouse
1050 Ala Moana Boulevard
Across Kewalo Basin
Telephone: (808) 531-1108

Anyone looking for a beautiful piece of clothing or jewelry made in Hawaii would do well to stop here. Pomegranates specializes in the quality garment of Hawaii, the elegant, well-constructed raw silk dresses or the hand-blocked skirt and top. Most of the clothes are locally designed and some have obscure labels. Yet the quality of the fabric, design, and workmanship of everything in this store is superior. Jewelry includes Guatemalan beads, Chinese porcelain beads, and imported ethnic looks in dramatic neck sculptures and earrings. There are handmade bags, fabrics galore, and a custom-design service too. Pomegranates is elegant without being stuffy, and chic without having to bypass the island market like so many European-oriented stores do.

Open 10:00 A.M. to 9:00 P.M. Monday through Friday, 10:00 A.M. to 6:00 P.M. Saturday, and 11:00 A.M. to 5:00 P.M. Sunday. Major credit cards accepted.

PRIVATE WORLD
Ward Warehouse
1050 Ala Moana Boulevard
Across from Kewalo Basin
Telephone: (808) 521-6250

This is the ultimate ethereal aerie, full of the finest cotton goods for bath, bed, and table. There are towels, bath sheets, and bath mats. There are 100 percent linen hemstitched napkins, placemats, and tablecloths. There are shams, pillows, wool throws, sheets, covers, white eyelet cushions, lace sachets, and upscale soaps. The sheets here are the finest you can get, 100 percent cotton in the best weaves and quality, with towels and household items to match. The whites are dazzling; you want to just lose yourself in those luxurious lace linens and embroidered coverlets with scented pillows. This is a surprisingly good place for out-of-the-ordinary gifts, and not all of them are expensive.

Open daily. Major credit cards accepted.

RAFAEL
Ward Centre
1200 Ala Moana Boulevard
Across Ala Moana Park
Telephone: (808) 521-7661

Rafael is frequented by fashion-conscious Yuppies who like natural fibers, the latest in linen suits, and the look of casual, easy elegance. The small shop is always full of possibilities in its characteristically neutral tones—grays, black, whites, tans, with an occasional splash of pastel or color. Rafael has a specific look that attracts discriminating shoppers, who do equally well with the few fine pieces of costume jewelry.

Open 10 A.M. to 9:00 P.M. Monday through Friday, Saturday 10:00 A.M. to 6:00 P.M., Sunday 10:00 A.M. to 5:00 P.M. Major credit cards accepted.

RIX
66-145 Kam Highway
Haleiwa
North Shore
Telephone: (808) 637-9260

Owner Inge Jausel has an eye for special things. Many of the items here are designed by her under her own label. Dresses, beachwear, T-shirts, thongs, purses, and the fabulous line of Paul M. Ropp clothing make RIX a good excuse for a stop anytime. You can outfit yourself completely, from a wide-brimmed straw hat for the beach to a risqué swimsuit, to the elegant coverup and the kicky, trendy jacket to top it off. Jausel buys from local designers, so you'll get a good dose of made-in-Hawaii clothes too. The swimsuit selection is large, so you have a good choice of bikinis or maillots, American labels or foreign.

Open 10:00 A.M. to 6:00 P.M. daily except Friday, 10:00 A.M. to 7:00 P.M..

SHARPER IMAGE
Ala Moana Center
Telephone: (808) 949-4100

This hi-tech, state-of-all-the-arts store has everything from the newest exercycles to rare watches and space-age telephones, survival kits, and massage chairs. The shop is crowded with gadgets, health aids, cutlery and jewelry, electronic toys, state-of-the art pocket knives, miniature billiards, you name it. There's a high turnover in the merchandise because their famous Sharper Image catalog lends a definite seasonal rhythm to things—so you must move fast. The leather briefcases are gorgeous, and so are those wonderful leather chairs with the moving massage rollers in the back.

Open 9:30 A.M. to 9:00 P.M. Monday through Friday, until 5:30 P.M. Saturday, and Sunday from 10:00 A.M. to 5:00 P.M. Major credit cards accepted.

SHIROKIYA
Ala Moana Center
Telephone: (808) 941-9111

The only thing lacking at Shirokiya is baby-sitters. Kids go nuts over the toy section and "Hello Kitty" wares while their parents slink next door to peruse the latest in Walkmans, stereos, tape recorders, and electronics. There are golf supplies, designer purses, pearl necklaces, kitchen wares, a bakery, furniture, and a thriving food department upstairs. Cotton hapi coats are popular here, as are the Japanese ceramics, lacquer ware, and hand-painted china. The food upstairs, however, is the star of Shirokiya. (See also Free for All.)

Open 9:00 A.M. to 9:00 P.M. Monday through Friday, until 7:00 P.M. on Saturday, and 10:00 A.M. to 5:00 P.M. on Sunday. Major credit cards accepted.

SHOP PACIFICA
Bishop Museum
1335 Kalihi Street
Kalihi
Telephone: (808) 848-4158

Certainly one of Hawaii's best resources in local crafts, the Bishop Museum gift shop is a browser's paradise. The books—the best collection of books on the Pacific—and the made-in-Hawaii gift items are wide-ranging, from carved native woods to silkscreened T-shirts and pressed island flowers. Occasionally you can find coconut sennit from Micronesia, sold in hardy bundles and hard to find elsewhere. Or you can find a robust selection of hand-carved bracelets, hand-carved wooden hair ornaments, and handmade jewelry and fabrics. Highly recommended for residents and visitors.

Open 9:00 A.M. to 5:00 P.M. Monday through Saturday. Major credit cards accepted.

SOMETHING SPECIAL
Kahala Mall
Kahala
Telephone: (808) 734-8504

Wayne and Jean Fukuda's eclectic, whimsical, and tasteful selection has had a huge local following for years. You can find inexpensive delights here, from T-shirts with a Hawaiian theme to exquisite baskets from all over the world. Something Special is known for its fabulous selection of blue-and-white porcelain ware from Japan and China, its T-shirts and Hawaiian-made things such as ceramic whistle necklaces and manapua paperweights, and fads such as yo-yos and wind-up toys that sell like hotcakes. You can have a great time browsing among the knickknacks in this thoroughly delightful store. Ask about their Mejiro products and T-shirts by Cane Haul Road and Taj.

Open 10:00 A.M. to 9:00 P.M. Monday through Saturday, 10:00 A.M. to 5:00 P.M. Sunday. Major credit cards accepted.

SPLASH
Ala Moana Center
Telephone: (808) 942-1010

New Otani Kaimana Beach Hotel
2863 Kalakaua Avenue
Waikiki
Telephone: (808) 923-6064

Splash is the leading swimwear shop in town, with a wide-ranging selection for all body shapes. The lines are made in Hawaii and elsewhere, from skimpy bikinis to maillots and the risqué Brazilian cuts. Some labels: SuHana, made in Hawaii by Splash's former owner; Sassafrass; Raisins, Soleil, made in Hawaii; Zanzara, made in Hawaii too; and the ever-popular Too Hot Brazil. Splash has a huge following among avid beach goers, who seem to have one suit for every day of the week, and who manage to keep their tan lines from crossing.

Open daily. Major credit cards accepted.

TAHITI ARTS
Hyatt Regency Waikiki
2424 Kalakaua Avenue
Waikiki
Telephone: (808) 923-2778

This shop deals in hand-blocked or hand-printed Tahitian prints. The fabrics are from France, and most of them are of polyester-cotton, which is regrettable but not unforgivable since they use the blend so it won't shrink or fade. There are shells by a Moorea artist, handmade Tahitian jewelry, a carved Marquesan bowl, hand-painted silks, and tropically printed pareus. A Tahitian seamstress will custom make anything out of the fabrics within 24 hours. There are Polynesian tapa and lauahala, men's aloha shirts, pendants, home decorations, and carvings. And there are the black pearls.

The pearls, a specialty of Tahiti, come in all sizes, are of high quality, and cost a pretty penny. The *nacre* glows in subtle greens, roses, and other tints over the prevailing black. Tahiti Arts has an extraordinary collection of these gems. Micronesian and Hawaiian artifacts, such as the coral poi pounder from Micronesia and the antique iron coconut grater, add a colorful, authentic flavor to the shop.

Open 9:00 A.M. to 11:00 P.M. daily. Major credit cards accepted.

VIS À VIS
Ala Moana Center
Telephone: (808) 945-3707

When the old favorite, McInerny, closed down, some of its enterprising buyers and executives pooled their talents and opened this shop. It hasn't taken the place of McInerny because nothing can, but Vis à Vis is at least a consolation. It sells men's and women's fashions of extraordinary taste and creativity, garnered from Europe and Japan and the world's fashion markets. You can go from a picnic to the symphony in the clothes and accessories here, and you can buy the pens, notebooks, and office paraphernalia to match. From its plain T-shirts to its linen skirts and silk shirts, Vis à Vis remains contemporary without looking trendy.

Open 9:30 A.M. to 9:00 P.M. Monday through Friday, until 5:30 P.M. on Saturday, and from 10:00 A.M. to 5:00 P.M. on Sundays. Major credit cards accepted.

EVERYDAY GOOD THINGS

Bakeries

BEA'S PIES AND DELI
1117 12th Avenue
Kaimuki
Telephone: (808) 734-4024

Bea leaves the fancy Bavarian baking to the other pastry chefs. She just keeps on making her own simple, home-style custard and pumpkin pies and they keep selling out. Not everything at Bea's is wonderful; some things are better than most. The best pies at Bea's are the custard pies and the custard-pumpkin, both of which have a following. The fillings are great and there are no soggy crusts, which adds to their appeal.

Open every day except Sunday. No credit cards accepted.

MARY CATHERINE'S BAKERY
Ward Centre
1200 Ala Moana Boulevard
Across from Ala Moana Park
Telephone: (808) 521-3525

Mary Catherine's represents the finest European baking traditions. A peek in the counter will tell you so, and a mere bite into one of the tortes, tarts, cookies, croissants, bars, scones, muffins, or cakes will show you they don't compromise on quality.

Specially ordered wedding cakes are assiduously made with the best ingredients, topped with real whipped cream or butter frosting, and decorated with live roses, baby's breath, and orchids. The pastries are beautiful to see and to taste. The chocolate chip cookies are notable as well; the double chocolate-chunk cookies are doubly good. You pay for the quality here, but no one's complaining. Croissants and eggs whipped and cooked in an espresso machine are offered for breakfast.

Open from 7:00 A.M. to 9:00 P.M. weekdays, 7:00 A.M. to 11:00 P.M.

Friday and Saturday, and 7:00 A.M. to 5:00 P.M. on Sunday. Major credit cards accepted.

SWEET THOUGHTS
1108 Twelfth Avenue
Kaimuki
Telephone: (808) 732-2579

2853 East Manoa Road
Manoa
Telephone: (808) 988-5788

Pastry Chef Mark Short has had a lot of influence in this town. He baked Chocolate Decadence for RoxSan's patisserie in its heyday, and he's baking it today for his own two bakeries. That means he has touched the lives of more than a few chocolate lovers, and he has proven to be unstoppable.

The selection of pastries is staggering, each one better than the next. You can find strawberry tarts and lemon bars and Ro Ros (round chocolate brownies), decadence cakes, and cheesecake. The decadence cake is made with real cream, chocolate, eggs, and butter—no flour. Like everything else at Sweet Thoughts, it's dangerously rich and satisfying and should not be approached with caution.

You can also order baskets of Sweet Thoughts pastries and have them delivered islandwide. They cost $18.95 to $70. Both Sweet Thoughts Bakeries are open daily. Major credit cards accepted.

Bookstores

HONOLULU BOOK SHOPS
Ala Moana Center
Telephone: (808) 941-2274

Honolulu Book Shops is Hawaii's top chain of bookstores, a reliable, helpful, and well-stocked purveyor of books that has been in Hawaii for more than thirty-five years. There are five branches on Oahu and more on the other islands, the most popular and complete of which is the store at Ala Moana Center. A staggering 35,000 titles are carried in Honolulu Book Shops. There's the usual general fiction here, along with extensive nonfiction and self-help books and the full range of periodicals. And if it's Hawaiiana you seek, it's the number-one seller here; Honolulu Book Shops has the most extensive selection in Hawaiiana around, except for the Bishop Museum shop. At any time of day the store is packed with bibliophiles and casual browsers who come for everything from maps and magazines to *The Wall Street Journal* or the latest John Updike.

Open daily at Ala Moana, with different hours at the other stores in Pearlridge Shopping Center, Windward Mall, Kailua Shopping Center, Kuapa Kai Center, and at 1001 Bishop Street downtown. Major credit cards accepted.

WALDENBOOKS
Kahala Mall
Telephone: (808) 737-9550

Royal Hawaiian Shopping Center
Waikiki
Telephone: (808) 926-3200

Waikiki Shopping Plaza
Waikiki
Telephone: (808) 922-4154

This giant national chain has fourteen stores throughout Hawaii, seven of them on Oahu. It is the biggest chain of bookstores in Hawaii with a selection of books for mainstream tastes in best-sellers and fiction. But there are Hawaiian videos as well—everything from travelogues to videos on music and volcano eruptions—and audio tapes, calendars, computer software, pens, postcards, games, and an extensive selection of hardcovers and children's books. Waldenbooks also offers discounts nationwide, through its book clubs for romance novels, mysteries, science fiction, and for children and senior citizens. With a minimum purchase, 10 to 15 percent discounts are offered on books only, with no membership charge to the buyer. Waldenbooks has branches in Windward Mall, Pearlridge, and on Kauai and Maui in addition to those listed above.

Hours vary with each store; the three listed above are open daily. Major credit cards accepted.

Coffeehouses

COFFEE MANOA
Manoa Marketplace
2752 Woodlawn Drive
Manoa
Telephone: (808) 988-5113

This is a very gregarious spot, *the* gathering place of the Manoa cognoscenti and folks who enjoy meeting over a good brew and a view that takes in the breathtaking Manoa Valley and the occasional waterfall that adorns its walls. Don't come here if you care to be anonymous; it's impossible to be here without seeing someone you know. They offer about thirty kinds of coffee, sold in bulk or brewed in a number of appealing versions, the espresso, cappuccino, and caffellattés that are so conducive to chatty tête-à-têtes and casual brainstorming in a relaxed and cordial atmosphere. There are croissants, cakes, pastries, and fresh juices (not freshly squeezed, but fresher than most) to appease the sweet tooth as well.

Open 7:00 A.M. to 9:00 P.M. Monday through Friday, and 8:00 A.M. to 4:00 P.M. Saturday and Sunday. Major credit cards accepted.

COFFEE WORKS
Ward Warehouse
1050 Ala Moana Boulevard
Across from Kewalo Basin
Telephone: (808) 545-1133

Follow the aroma of roasted coffee beans and you'll wind up at this pleasant café with its many appeasements for caffeine lovers. You can purchase your coffee in bulk here, or you can linger over a cup. Each day, three different coffees plus a Kona blend are served by the cup. The flavors rotate and are always good, encompassing everything from the very expensive Jamaican Blue Mountain ($32 a pound retail, no less) to the less exotic but equally respectable Guatemalan, Mocha Java, and other types. The decaf is water-processed, which is good news for purists, and the sandwich bar is satisfying. There are salads galore, from vegetable to pasta to potato and fruit, and a host of hefty sandwiches.

Open 7:30 A.M. to 5:30 P.M. Monday through Friday for food, until 7:00 P.M. for coffee service, and 9:00 P.M. for retail business; 8:00 A.M. to 5:00 P.M. Saturday for food, until 7:00 P.M. for coffee, and 8:30 P.M. for retail; 8:00 A.M. to 5:00 P.M. Sunday for food, and until 6:00 P.M. for coffee. Major credit cards accepted.

CROISSANTERIE
222 Merchant Street
Downtown
Telephone: (808) 533-3443

A downtown fixture for six years, this busy coffeehouse draws downtown professionals and artists who come to enjoy the changing art exhibits over sandwiches and croissants. Lion coffee is not served here in many versions (espresso, cappuccino, etc.), but there are enough to satisfy. And although the coffee is acceptable, it is not the rage of connoisseurs. In fact, it is merely adequate. Instead, we give the Croissanterie high marks for its commendable art exhibits that offer good exposure for local artists. Also notable are the croissants, which are baked on the premises and always delicious. Most important, the Croissanterie is the type of place in which you'd linger comfortably, reading a book or contemplating how nice it is to have a power lunch in such an unpretentious place. There is a wine bar here too.

Open 6:00 A.M. to 9:00 P.M. Monday through Friday, 7:00 A.M. to 4:00 P.M. Saturday, closed Sunday. Major credit cards are accepted.

Drugstore

LONGS DRUGS
Ala Moana Center, Nuuanu Pali, Kailua, and many other locations
Telephone: (808) 941-4433

Their slogan is "Make Longs a Part of Your Day," and it's easy to wind up doing that. Longs is the consummate drugstore, with everything from food items and cosmetics to those oddball appliances you can never find anywhere else. Watch for the sales, too, because when Longs puts those chocolate-covered macadamia nuts on sale, there's no better bargain.

Open daily. Major credit cards accepted.

Edibles and Groceries

ASIAN GROCERY
1319 South Beretania Street
Pawaa
Telephone: (808) 531-8371

When you marvel over the lemon grass and basil at a Thai restaurant next time, you could nod in the direction of the Asian Grocery. All the Thai restaurateurs shop here for their daily produce needs, most notably the parsley, lemon grass, and odds and ends such as ginko nuts, white lotus nuts, dried kumquats, chiles, curry powders, and spices. In short, all the things they need for tempting the palate are here. Pungent odors fill the shop, which has been an island institution ever since it opened years ago to serve the growing immigrant Asian community.

Open 10:00 A.M. to 6:30 P.M. Monday through Saturday. No credit cards accepted.

FORT RUGER MARKET
3585 Alohea Avenue
Ruger area
Telephone: (808) 737-4531

The Kamiya papayas are by the door, the poi is by the fish counter, and the lomi salmon and poke are probably selling out. That's how it is at Fort Ruger Market, where Peter Tamada and sons keep putting out the best lau lau, poke, fish, and Hawaiian dishes for their eager and loyal customers. Tamada is proud of his dried fish, called the aku jerky, that's being ordered swiftly from the mainland, and of his Korean spicy chicken wings. The poke and lomi salmon are mixed fresh for every order, and only Kula onions are used.

The warm, sweet aroma in the store comes from the boiled peanut pot, which dispenses hefty pounds of the steaming treats daily. Fort Ruger is famous for its boiled peanuts, which go for $1.50 a pound.

Open 6:45 A.M. to 6:00 P.M. Monday through Saturday and until 4:30 P.M. on Sunday. No credit cards.

MOM PRODUCE
2972 East Manoa Road
Manoa
Telephone: (808) 988-5588

There are several reasons for stopping here: One is the takeout food, the best-prepared food on the island; the second is the fresh-pressed juices; and the third is the fresh produce, certainly the best you'll find on the island.

Nedra Chung prepares the gado gado, the Indonesian salad with almond sauce, as well as the incomparable sweet potato salad and the tempeh and fresh ahi sandwiches. The selection may change, but you'll always have a few good choices. The fresh ahi is marinated with fines herbes, savory, cumin, garlic, tamari, and lots of fresh parsley, then cooked for the island-style sandwich. The tempeh is equally wonderful.

As for Daws Dawson, the man behind the counter, he's the expert on produce. MOM Produce gets fresh Kona oranges and tangelos, broccoli and cauliflower from Kula, an occasional shipment of air-flown English peas in pods, unsprayed Kamiya papayas (the best!), cooking bananas from Waiahole, Kahuku watermelons, Waianae corn, mangoes, and plump, vine-ripened, Beefsteak tomatoes touted by tomato connoisseurs as the best on the island by far. Daws is the only one selling these crimson volcanoes commercially.

The store is planning to expand its takeout business by installing a large, refrigerated gondola of these marvelous items to go. That will mean more people, but it will still be a mom 'n' pop store.

Open from 8:00 A.M. to 9:00 P.M. Monday through Saturday and until 8:00 P.M. on Sunday. No credit cards accepted.

PEOPLE'S OPEN MARKETS
Various sites around town
Telephone: (808) 523-4808

Local and mainland produce is featured at this traveling market, which moves from town to town throughout the week, sometimes stopping at several towns in one morning. You can still find home-baked goods, fresh eggs, fresh fish, occasionally, and the entire gamut of mangoes, papayas, bananas, lettuce, and fresh island produce, sometimes still wet with dew. A rare treat is fresh fiddleheads from the mountains, or that elusive white pirie mango, or lichees in season. The market was designed to support local farmers; there are twenty-one Open Markets throughout Oahu.

The biggest is on Saturday at Kalihi Kai Elementary School. The one closest to Waikiki is at Paki Playground near Diamond Head, open from 9:45 A.M. to 10:45 A.M. Wednesday, or try the one at McCully Recreation Center, 831 Pumehana Street, one hour before the one at Paki Playground on the same day. No credit cards accepted.

TANIGUCHI STORE
2065 South Beretania Street
McCully
Telephone: (808) 949-1489

Taniguchi's has mastered the takeout bento lunch, which it always carries in ample supply and variety. The shelves are lined with cooked eggplant, pumpkin, fried and broiled fish, pork and chicken cutlets, julienned burdock, and many more selections of already prepared, warm food wrapped in Styrofoam plates. Local foods are also displayed prominently in the fish section nearby, where an extensive selection of sweetened beans, lomi salmon, and other dishes is offered.

Open 7:30 A.M. to 7:00 P.M. Monday through Saturday, Sunday 9:00 A.M. to 5:00 P.M. No credit cards accepted.

TIMES SUPER MARKETS
Many locations on the island
Telephone: (808) 847-0811

For a large supermarket chain, Times does an exceptional job with local produce. Large, gleaming Kamiya papayas are always here, and you can usually find lotus root (hasu), burdock, fresh mountain yams, and all manner of exotic island produce nestled among mainland specimens. Times's specialty is ethnic and local produce, but it does well with the standards too.

Open daily. No credit cards accepted.

Fish Markets

TAMASHIRO MARKET
802 North King Street
Palama
Telephone: (808) 841-8047

What do you do when you need to whip up a bouillabaisse or paella? Head for Tamashiro's, where the lobsters and crab never sleep and the place is always bustling with the curious and the covetous. The local color is at its grandest here, with the Kalihi matrons shopping beside the Nuuanu lawyers and the downtown Chinatown fish brigade. The floors are wet and the pungent fish odors surround you, but you won't get a better view of better catch anywhere.

There are dozens of fresh fish to choose from; if you can't decide, they're very helpful on the other side of the counter. The papio, fresh lobster, king clam, Dungeness crab, and other crustaceans are always inviting.

Ethnic food, from steamed coconut pudding (kulolo) to prepared foods, such as lomi salmon and steamed lau lau, are offered here too, along with exotic fruit such as jack, starfruit, and soursop. Whatever it is you're looking for, you're likely to find it here. There are dozens of different prepared foods.

Open 9:15 A.M. to 6:00 P.M. Monday through Saturday and until 4:00 P.M. on Sunday. No credit cards accepted.

YAMA'S FISH MARKET
Manoa Marketplace
Manoa
Telephone: (808) 988-7618

Yama's makes its own lau lau, its own poke, its own lomi salmon, and its own delicious haupia, the white coconut pudding. Yama's is famous for its haupia, which is creamy and delicious beyond words, and which, auspiciously, often runs out.

What's also obvious about this fish market is that they have the best poke ever made, an excellent lau lau as well, and a range of offerings equally delicious. Yama's will also hold MSG upon request and is very accommodating on small taste-testing orders.

Open 8:30 A.M. to 7:00 P.M. Monday through Saturday, 9:00 A.M. to 5:00 P.M. Sunday. No credit cards accepted.

Health Food

CELESTIAL NATURAL FOODS
66-443 Kam Highway
Haleiwa, North Shore
Telephone: (808) 637-6729

The idea is to stop here to buy sandwiches and seltzer to go, and then take off for your picnic at Waimea Bay. Celestial is the old favorite, a health food store with a juice bar in the back and commendable brownies, banana nut-bread, fresh squeezed juices, avocado sandwiches, and vegetarian chili. The store carries produce, household items, books, herbs, essential oils, and, often, health food products new on the market.

Open 9:00 A.M. to 6:30 P.M. Monday through Saturday and 10 A.M. to 6:30 P.M. on Sunday. Major credit cards accepted.

DOWN TO EARTH NATURAL FOODS
2525 South King Street
Moiliili
Telephone: (808) 947-7678

Down to Earth redefined the term health food in Honolulu with its all-vegetarian products, organically grown vegetables, wholesome baked goods, and its up-to-the-minute vitamin and body-therapy products. You can tell it's a good store by its clientele: It's always busy, filled with everyone from grandparents to college kids, all stocking up on wholesome food. The prices are great too—you can always get a deal at Down to Earth, whether it's on Sunrise papayas or local avocados. Local fruits in season can be found here, as well as a superb collection of herbs and spices that can be bought in bulk, and at good prices. Right next door is Healthy's fast food, where vegetarian chili and tempeh burgers have their loyal followings.

Open 7:30 A.M. to 11:00 P.M. Monday through Saturday and until 9:00 P.M. on Sunday. No credit cards accepted.

HUCKLEBERRY FARMS NATURAL FOODS
1613 Nuuanu Avenue
Nuuanu
Telephone: (808) 524-7960

Huckleberry Farms is small, clean, and progressive in its selection of natural foods. You can find Ka'u Gold oranges from the Big Island, Kahuku papayas (the best), Hayden mangoes in season, and isolated caches of exotica such as starfruit, lichees, and soursop whenever they're available. The year-round selection is worthy, too, with such items as blue corn tortilla chips, a sizable assortment of vitamins, nuts, and grains in bulk, nonalcoholic wines and beers, and the store's forte, cheeses. Huckleberry Farms has one of the best and most reasonable cheese selections in town, and at good prices. You'll find dozens of imported and domestic cheeses, from the 99 percent fat-free, salt-free hoop cheese to the standard Brie, Parmesan, soft cheeses with vegetables and herbs, and mixtures such as salmon cream cheese. Herb teas, health breads, and the latest in healthy convenience foods abound here as well.

Open 9:00 A.M. to 8:00 P.M. Monday through Saturday, 10:00 A.M. to 7:00 P.M. Sunday. Major credit cards accepted.

Wine Shops

R. FIELD WINE COMPANY
Ward Centre
1200 Ala Moana Boulevard
Across from Ala Moana Park
Telephone: (808) 521-4043

Rick Field, Honolulu's oenophile, and partner Scott Shimamura run a very tasteful, very complete wine store with extra touches for the gourmet. There are the Cristal champagnes and the good buys on selected French wines, but the specialty is domestic wines. The wines from Burgundy and Bordeaux are carefully selected; there are some rare Domaine de la Romanee Contis and an occasional extravagance such as a double magnum of 1979 Mouton Rothschild. The shop is attractive and well-planned besides, and it carries gourmet chocolates, pâtés, flavored vinegars, cheeses, Petrossian caviar, and isolated spectaculars for those with odd cravings.

Open 10:00 A.M. to 9:00 P.M. Monday through Thursday, until 10:00 P.M. Friday and Saturday, and from 11:00 A.M. to 5:00 P.M. Sunday. Major credit cards accepted.

THE STILL LIQUORS
611 Kapahulu Avenue
Kapahulu
Telephone: (808) 737-0664

The specialty has always been California wines, a few hundred labels strong. The shop is owned and run by serious wine lovers active in benefit wine-tastings for good causes and public education. There are about 3,600 different products at this one store. The imported vintages have grown in recent years, and the selection is more varied than ever. The prices are good, too.

Open 9:30 A.M. to midnight daily. Major credit cards accepted.

THE BEST IN
HAWAIIANA

People skilled in the traditional Hawaiian crafts are a dwindling resource in Hawaii. Thankfully, there are a few dedicated souls left who have learned these skills, and who are teaching them to preserve the endangered traditions.

They are Hawaii's treasures, the bearers of tradition in a modern world. Although the teachers are, for the most part, elderly, their students may not be. Some are young and dedicated, learning from the kupuna (elders) or, if there's no one to teach them, from prowling the museums and arduously, painstakingly experimenting themselves. Weaving, featherwork, making leis—all are time-consuming arts requiring natural materials from the environment. Hawaiian artisans say the preparation of materials can be more laborious than making the object itself.

Hawaii's art scene is dynamic and diverse, an amalgam of media from Hawaiian and modern traditions. Oahu's galleries and artists reflect this mix. The following is a list of some of Honolulu's leading Hawaiian craftspeople, who are available to teach the skills or make things for you. There is one common thread binding them: a supreme love of the art, and a healthy respect for the ways of old.

Basketry

PAT HORIMOTO
45-1156 Makamae Street
Kaneohe, HI 96744

He can often be seen with a basket in his lap, weaving serenely at a Diamond Head beach. His technique is called *twining*, or *ka hana hinai*, which is traditional Hawaiian basketry using 'ie'ie, semierect vines that grow in the mountains. Not only must he pick these woody stems for his weaving, he must know where they grow in the wilderness, then he must dry the roots, strip them lengthwise, soak them until they become pliable. Only then can he weave. The preparation of the materials alone takes about a month.

Horimoto says there was no one to teach him, so he learned by peering through the cases at the Bishop Museum and through many years of dedicated, solitary pursuit. Today he is the only one doing traditional basketry, and he never deviates from traditional forms.

The weavings range from fish traps the size of breadfruit to small woven fish traps, large and small vessels, and traditional Hawaiian images used in religion by the ancients. His largest basket is about 24 inches high.

His work has been displayed at the Bishop Museum and is coveted by lovers of Hawaiiana. The baskets are evenly and expertly woven in various established Hawaiian patterns. They are strong, vital shapes with marvelous texture and an inescapable sense of antiquity.

Horimoto works on commission. Fees range from $40 for a small woven fish trap to thousands of dollars for a large religious image.

Featherwork

MARY LOUISE KEKUEWA
3779 Lurline Drive
Honolulu, HI 96818
Telephone: (808) 745-5411

So meticulous is this work that it could take hours to create 1 inch of a lei. The sewing of the feathers must be just so, enabling their patterns and colors to shine at their most brilliant. Mary Louise has taught this demanding and time-consuming art at the Bishop Museum for fifteen years. The craft evolved out of the flat feather leis worn by Hawaiian royalty and made from the feathers of native birds. Many of those birds are extinct, so contemporary artists (and there are few of them) use the feathers of pheasants, geese, and other game birds that are raised or hunted for other purposes, but whose skins are saved for leis.

Mary Lou has made kahilis (feather standards) and countless leis for hatbands and other items. Currently she is helping to make twenty kahilis for Kamehameha Schools' chapel, a momentous, years-long project using the feathers of Chinese golden pheasants, ring-necked pheasants, Canada geese, and blue peacocks. Besides teaching the art at the Bishop Museum (847-3511) three times a week, she makes feather leis on special order.

Hula Implements

HERMAN AND FREDA GOMES
84-239 Ikuone Place
Waianae, HI 96792
Telephone: (808) 695-9192

The making of hula implements would be a lost art were it not for people like the Gomes. Led into these ancient skills by their deep love of the hula, Herman and Freda Gomes make the gourds, rattles, flutes, and sticks used in the traditional dances of Hawaii. Many of the hula halau performing today are using implements they have made. Herman teaches at the Waianae Culture and Arts Center, and Freda, at the Bishop Museum. On weekends at their home, they work with students in fashioning nearly a dozen different kinds of traditional implements, including nose flutes; ulili, a triple rattler of three calabash gourds; uliuli, the gourd rattle containing seeds and colored feathers on top; and other mysterious, rhythmic sound makers made from plant material.

The materials, such as bamboo, coconut, and various seeds and pods, are gathered from the wilds of Oahu. Students are taught to identify them, collect them with care, and to grow their own plants when possible. Herman and Freda also make miniature implements out of kamani seeds and pods. The traditional gourds and rattlers, even the mahiole, or Hawaiian helmets, come now in miniatures as well as the real thing.

Lauhala Weaving

GLADYS GRACE
Telephone: (808) 737-4574

ANDREW OKADA
Telephone: (808) 988-4786

MARCIA OMURA
Telephone: (808) 377-5075

Gladys Grace, in her late sixties, is one of about a dozen lauhala weavers still weaving in Hawaii. She was a teenager when her grandmother in Kona, the Big Island, taught her to weave with the graceful, long leaves of the hala tree. When she moved to Honolulu in 1940, no one wore lauhala hats. She stopped weaving for forty years.

Upon retiring from her job in 1980, lauhala weaving was on her mind and the information of her childhood came flooding back. She began weaving again, making the classic hats with the ⅛-inch weave, including derbies, wide-brimmed cowboy hats, dainty ladies' hats, narrow brims, and many others.

You can imagine her delight when two eager students appeared and wanted to learn. Today Andrew Okada and Marcia Omura are the emerging young weavers in a craft perpetuated by the elders. The three of them work together, share materials, experiment together, and have exhibited together at the Honolulu Academy of Arts. Okada and Omura are already accomplished weavers, making hats out of hala strips an infinitesimal ¹⁄₁₆ inch wide.

Okada doesn't mind the hardness of Oahu hala leaves, so he collects them, dried, off the trees around the island. Gladys gets her materials from friends in Miloli'i on the Big Island. Honolulu lauhala is too hard on her hands; she likes the quality and softness of the Big Island fiber. The leaves are naturally thorny, so picking and preparing them is especially arduous. They must be softened, flattened, and then stripped of thorns and into even widths.

They will custom make hats for $35 to $50, an incredible price for such labor and quality. Soon there might be fans available. Okada is studying Gladys's fifty-year-old vintage fans, figuring out the complex weaves and coming out with some laudable fans of his own.

"We just enjoy it and want to be able to keep buying lauhala," says Gladys. "I have to bring the art out. I don't want to take it with me."

GALLERIES

CONTEMPORARY ARTS CENTER
News Building
605 Kapiolani Boulevard
Corner South Street
Telephone: (808) 526-1322

2411 Makiki Heights Drive
Makiki
Telephone: (808) 525-8047

At the time of this writing, the prestigious Contemporary Arts Center is planning to move to its new and hard-won location in Makiki, where it will be a full-blown art museum with a four-decade focus. This is a public, nonprofit foundation that collects and exhibits, and that deals with contemporary artists from Hawaii and the rest of the world. Seven exhibitions a year are scheduled, among them one from Japan and others on artists known nationally and internationally.

There are more than one thousand works of art in the collection here. When the move to Makiki is complete in October 1988, the collection will be housed in one of the most stunning architectural structures in the city. The historic 3½-acre estate is known for its extensive gardens, built in the 1920s by a Japanese master and encompassing pathways, bridges, and an abundance of indigenous and imported plants. The News Building location will be retained even after the Makiki museum opens.

GALLERY EAS
1426 Makaloa Street
Makaloa Square
Near Ala Moana Center
Telephone: (808) 947-1426

For years Gallery EAS has displayed the work of Hawaii's finest recognized and unrecognized artists. All media are represented here; ceramics, sculptures, paintings, fiber art, jewelry, and other items grace this attractive gallery. Japanese printmaking is prominently represented here, and a new department on wearable art offers the latest creations for ear, foot, and body. This is an attractive and pleasing gallery much loved by local art lovers, with well-attended monthly shows.

Open 10:00 A.M. to 5:00 P.M. Monday through Saturday. Major credit cards accepted.

HONOLULU ACADEMY OF ARTS
900 South Beretania Street
Across from Thomas Square
Telephone: (808) 538-3693

From its architecture and its collection to its programs, exhibits, and performances, the academy is one of Hawaii's top cultural resources. Founded in 1927 by Mrs. Charles Montague Cooke, it's grown into one of the finest Asian collections in the country. The American masters, Pissarro, Gauguin, van Gogh, Mayan sculptures, and ancient Hawaiian religious carvings are among the thousands of works of art displayed here. The building's Moorish architecture opens out to courtyards with sculptures and lily ponds. The academy gift shop is fine and the Garden Café's lunch is one of Honolulu's institutions.

Open Tuesday to Saturday 10:00 A.M. to 4:30 P.M., Sunday 1:00 P.M. to 5:00 P.M. Closed Mondays. Admission is free.

TENNENT ART FOUNDATION GALLERY
203 Prospect Street
Punchbowl
Telephone: (808) 531-1987

The work of Madge Tennent, internationally esteemed artist from Hawaii, is available for public viewing in this gallery. Some forty-five of her original pieces hang here, highlighting her work and development through-out most of her life. Tennent's work, *Local Color*, hangs in the National Museum of Women with the work of Georgia O'Keeffe. This Punchbowl facility gives a good look at her creative development and shows her broad, rich style of painting Hawaiians, a style that has been much imitated.

Open Tuesday through Saturday from 10:00 A.M. to noon, Sunday from 2:00 P.M. to 4:00 P.M., or by appointment. Closed Monday. Admission is free.

FLOWERS AND LEIS

You can always find good leis at low prices at the lei stands on Maunakea Street in Chinatown, where they generally open early and close late. The lei vendors line the streets side by side with their florals, some days with great new surprises. During graduation season and holidays, however, you must order ahead; they always run out. Here are the best places for leis in Honolulu.

CINDY'S LEI SHOPPE
1034 Maunakea Street
Chinatown
Telephone: (808) 536-6538

Cindy's is great for a good buy on an everyday lei, the walk-in or spontaneous purchase. Known for its budget prices, Cindy's has a loyal cadre of customers who have frequented the store for decades. It's nearly thirty years old, has a brisk, efficient owner, and occasionally has a rare colvillea or other special bloom among its everyday favorites. Good for ginger leis, pikake in season, and a host of strung leis, at low prices.

Open 6:30 A.M. to 9:00 P.M. Monday through Saturday, and until 7:00 P.M. Sundays. No credit cards accepted.

FLOWERS BY JR. AND LOU
2652 South King Street
Moiliili
Telephone: (808) 941-2022

The leis here are generally more elaborate than those in Chinatown. You can find haku leis already made, akulikuli leis occasionally, Hilo maile leis, and leis made of kukunoakala, the very Hawaiian, orange, spiny-looking flower that is quite the rage today. Pakalana in season and the usual ginger, pikake, rose, and ever-popular ilima are sold here as well. You won't always find the best prices, but you're sure to have a good selection.

Open 6:00 A.M. to 8:00 P.M. Sunday through Thursday and until 9:00 P.M. Friday and Saturday. Major credit cards accepted.

LITA'S LEIS
59 North Beretania Street
Near Chinatown
Telephone: (808) 521-9065

It's been here on Beretania Street for years, is very reliable, and carries leis of good quality. Lita Caneso doesn't skimp—her ilima leis are large and fluffy, her maile leis are from Hilo or Kauai, her rose haku leis come from the best lei makers in Kamuela. Her trademark is the fragrant puakenikeni, the creamy-white blossom that deepens in color by the day until it reaches the brilliant orange color of ilima. Micronesian-style ginger, the new twisted ti leaves, and haku leis and headbands are here as well, as well as a good supply of pakalana during spring and the most gorgeous rope pikake in season.

The puakenikeni costs about $6 to $7, depending on the supply, and all the other leis are fairly priced.

Open 7:00 A.M. to 9:00 P.M. daily. Major credit cards accepted.

NO KA OI FLORAL INC.
3046 Monsarrat Avenue
Diamond Head/Kapahulu
Telephone: (808) 735-3036

They have a good selection of flowers, but they excel in protea. During the winter months when these exotic, otherworldly blooms are in season, No Ka Oi carries the couture line, from the kings, queens, and duchesses to the minks and banksias and all other kinds. Private growers in Kula ship here, so you know there's a good supply. No Ka Oi also does special floral arrangements for such places as Michel's, so this is no garden-variety florist.

Proteas range from $1.50 to $10 a stem, with most of them in the $4.50 range. No Ka Oi will also box and stamp for shipping.

Open 8:00 A.M. to 5:00 P.M. Monday through Saturday and until 11:00 A.M. on Sunday. Major credit cards accepted.

RUDY'S FLOWERS
2722 South King Street
Moiliili
Telephone: (808) 944-8844

Rudy's has a large selection of flowers and leis, good prices, and friendly help. The haku leis here are beautifully made, and you'll be able to find those extra-special leis as well, such as the brilliant purple ola'a beauty, thousands of them strung into a thick garland several inches in diameter.

There are thick maile leis from the Cook Islands, Hawaiian maile leis, gingers, ilima, akulikuli, and other rare and regular types. The prices on flowers are good too, and you'll always find what you want here.

Open 7:00 A.M. to 8:00 P.M. Monday through Saturday, until 7:00 P.M. on Sunday. No credit cards accepted.

RAY WONG
769 Kalanipuu Street
Honolulu, HI 96825
Hawaii Kai
Telephone: (808) 395-3760

Ray Wong makes the couture haku lei. A six-time grand prize winner of the city's annual Lei Day lei-making contest, he is now a judge of the contest (something had to be done about his winning streak), with his own thriving business. He does not string or weave leis, he composes them. You must order ahead; he picks the flowers, vines, berries, and other materials from his prodigious yard, where lehua trees with red, yellow, and orange flowers grow bountifully along with other Hawaiian plants native to mountainous regions. And then he custom makes a lei for you. If the lei is going to the mainland, he'll select only those materials that can leave the island.

Wong's wreaths are becoming famous as well. Along with the leis, he makes floral arrangements for weddings and special events, but his wreaths steal the show. They're all custom-made, with local dried pods and leaves: lehua, achote, eucalyptus, hasu (lotus) pods, dried protea, milo seeds, and hau seed pods and leaves. Their colors, textures, design, and feel are special in every way.

There are no office hours; Wong works out of his home and you must order ahead. No credit cards.

SHIGERU UYEHARA
4156 Puu Panini Avenue
Kaimuki
Telephone: (808) 737-9082

The idea is to sit downwind from this pikake farm and inhale deeply. This is the most fragrant corridor of Honolulu. Imagine: one acre of pikake, rows and rows of it, all in one spot. For forty years the Uyehara family has been growing pikake at their farm, selling the flowers, and stringing leis. They also have pikake year-round, although in limited supply during the winter, while other florists are helplessly waiting for spring to roll around and this fragrant blossom to appear again.

You'll love Anna Uyehara; she is as sweet as the flower itself, selling single strands for $2.50 and thick, hearty rope pikake leis ("We use plenty flowers, and we make it long.") for $30.

Call during normal business hours to order ahead. No credit cards accepted.

GIFTS TO GO

U nlike the neighbor islands, which are known for specialties such as
Kula onions or potato chips, Honolulu does not have a particular
product it's identified with. However, there are many consummate gifts to
take with you.

Tutuvi is a fresh, crisp line of hand-painted pareus and T-shirts in
patterns and textures that are the best you'll find in Hawaii. Made by
Honolulu designer Colleen Kimura, Tutuvi is known for the quality of its
silk-screened designs, such as the popular monstera leaf, taro leaf, ginger,
and anthurium. Tutuvi is on 100 percent cotton and is the ideal gift; the
pareus can be worn, wrapped, hung, or sewn into clothing, and the T-shirts
can be worn by anyone, even children.

Crazy Shirts is the classic old favorite in T-shirts, with stores everywhere
vending hundreds of different kinds of T-shirts, sweatshirts, and special-
logo designs. Crazy Shirts is like the corner store; there's one on practically
every corner.

If you have the time, the best gift to go is something you've made. Temari
is Hawaii's best school in the Asian and Pacific fiber arts, offering classes in
everything from Japanese papermaking, using local fibers, to futon making
and dyeing fabric. It has a full roster of classes year-round, many of them
only a day or a weekend, taught by Hawaii's finest artists and crafts people,
who share their secrets in comfortable, pleasant classes at the Kaimuki
school. Contact Temari, Center for Asian and Pacific Arts. P.O. Box 7189,
Honolulu, HI 96821; telephone: (808) 735-1860.

Gallery EAS is a shopper's paradise as well as a gallery showcasing the
finest local talent. There are wearables made by island artists, everything
from hand-painted sneakers to clothing fashioned out of antique fabrics and
one-of-a-kind handmade purses and jewelry. Ask about their Ann Kimura
designs; they have a stylish ethnic flair to them and reflect a Pacific-Asian
influence perfect for island wear and gifts.

Out on the north shore, at the Turtle Bay Hilton, Sonya Hagemann offers
a rainbow-colored array of hand-painted cushion kits. Bird-of-paradise,
roses, morning glories, and other flora are hand painted onto 100 percent
muslin, then packaged into attractive kits for French knotting and quilting
as you choose.

In Waianae, noted potters Gail and Bunky Bakutis offer studio visits to their Pokai Bay hideaway. Written up in *Sunset* magazine and the like, the Bakutises are cordial and talented potters who put out stunning work. Contact: Bakutis' Pokai Pottery, 86098 Pokai Bay Street, Waianae, HI 96792; (808) 696-3878.

The ubiquitous macadamia nuts are not to be forgotten, either. They're everywhere, but it helps to check the local papers for sales at any of the popular Honolulu stores, such as Longs Drugs or ABC Drugs or Holiday Mart Daiei. The designer macadamia nuts—whole, elegant, and expensive—can be found at Morrow's in the Ala Moana Center. If you're sick of macadamia nuts, the Hawaiian Plantations jams and jellies are an expensive but feasible alternative. Poha, guava, lilikoi, and other tropical flavors are packed in dainty boxes with handsome packaging.

The Bishop Museum's Shop Pacifica, the Honolulu Academy of Arts gift shop, and Creative Fibers are among the most highly recommended stops for gift-shopping, as well as the Little Hawaiian Craft Shop for the lover of Hawaiian woods and crafts. For those into surfer chic, don't forget the plethora of state-of-the-art surf shops in Honolulu, namely Hawaiian Island Creations, Local Motion, and Town and Country Surf Shops.

MAUI

MAUI

Honolua Bay

Napili Bay

Kapalua

D.T. Fleming Beach Co. Pk.

Ka'anapali

W E S T   M A U I   M T N S.

Lahaina

Olowalu

Waikuku

KAHULUI AIRPORT

Ho'okipa Beach

Paia

KAHULUI

Huelo

HANA HWY.

Keanae

Wailua

Nahiku

Makawao

Olinda

Pukalani

HALEAKALA HWY.

KULA HWY.

Kula

HALEAKALA NAT'L PK.

Haleakala Crater

Hana

Seven Pools of Kipahulu (Oheo Gulch)

Kaupo

Ulupalakua Ranch

PIILANI HWY.

Wailea

Maalaea Harbor

Kihei

Makena

Makena Beach

Molokini Island

La Perouse Bay

0   2   4   6   8   10 Miles

A BRIEF HISTORY

Maui is the gilded lily of the Hawaiian islands, the glamorous seductress in whose clutches many are left powerless. It's no secret that the island of Maui has ensnared many in its web, from Charles Lindbergh, who lived out his final days in Hana and is buried there, to rock stars and jet-setters who are buying land in burgeoning numbers. For many newcomers, Maui is safe harbor from the encroachments of the modern world, yet tempered enough by urbanity to ward off boredom. On Maui you can hike for days in the wilderness or partake of a $25 gourmet brunch, swim at a nude beach or sip Sempe Armagnac with the oenophiles of the world.

The island is 728.8 square miles in size, larger than Oahu but less than a quarter the size of the Big Island. Dubbed the Valley Island, it is 25 by 40 miles in size and has more than 120 miles of coastline, more of it swimmable than on the other islands. The second largest of the Hawaiian Islands, Maui is home to 63,000 residents who live primarily in coastline towns, in the upcountry areas of Kula and Makawao, and in central Maui's Kahului and Wailuku towns with their combined populations of 23,000. Maui County, which encompasses the islands of Maui, Molokai, Lanai, and Kahoolawe, has its county seat in Wailuku.

The combined populations of these islands brings Maui County to 85,000 people, the third most populous in Hawaii. To give you an idea of scale, the land area they live on is roughly the size of Rhode Island.

With 2.2 million visitors in 1986 and close to 2 million the year before, there is caution in some corners about Maui's growth and "overdevelopment." Indeed, traffic slows during rush hour between Kaanapali and Kahului, and there are noticeably more businesses on the streets and more people in stores, on roads, on beaches, and on trails. On an island that has built its renown around wilderness, the growth can be disconcerting.

The Maui chapter of the Hawaii Visitors Bureau continues to claim that Maui's wilderness, its interior regions of Haleakala and the West Maui Mountains, is still intact. Maui Visitors Bureau director Frank Blackwell insists that according to his calculations, only 7 to 8 percent of Maui's actual land mass is inhabited.

That's because, golf courses, resorts, and hotels notwithstanding, nothing can touch the grandeur of Maui's major geological and esthetic presence, the 10,023-foot Haleakala. The world's largest dormant volcano, it encompasses all of eastern Maui, its ample crater and voluminous slopes spawning upcountry views, remote rain forests, volcanic soil for flower farms and ranches, sea caves, lava tubes, and time-worn cliffs that line the eastern Maui shoreline.

The 27,350-acre Haleakala National Park has drawn people to its summit for decades to witness the spectacle of its sunrise. From Mark Twain to Isabella Bird, they came, they experienced, and they put pen to paper in enraptured terms. Wrote Twain: "I felt like the Last Man, neglected of the judgment, and left pinnacled in mid-heaven, a forgotten relic of a vanished world . . . It was the sublimest spectacle I ever witnessed, and I think the memory of it will remain with me always."

After her view of the fabled sunrise, when "the familiar earth disappeared," Isabella Bird called Haleakala "a new world and without sympathy, a solitude which could be felt." Indeed, the crater remains a magnet for those who would touch the finer mysteries of its moonlike terrain, rarefied air, nene geese, silverswords, and other rare wildlife that live only here and on the Big Island. Some 1.2 million people—half of the visitors to Maui—visited Haleakala Park in 1985.

Haleakala means House of the Sun, and refers to one of the legends about Maui, the demigod and trickster of Polynesia whose lively exploits are chronicled in the ancient chants of Hawaii. In one of his better-known feats, Maui crept to the edge of Haleakala Crater and lassoed the sun at dawn, threatening it and securing its promise that it would slow its path across the crater. This timely ambush was successful and served to lengthen the day, giving Maui's mother, Hina, more time to dry her *tapa* (bark cloth).

In spite of its high profile, Haleakala is the kid brother of the two volcanoes that formed the island. It last erupted in 1790, much later than the western Maui volcanoes with their perpendicular canyons and sharply carved valleys. Eons before its later eruptions formed south and east Maui, Haleakala heaved lava from the sea to join with the already existing West Maui Mountains. The isthmus, the neck of plain between west Maui and the rest of the island, is central Maui.

The concept of two Mauis has always been a part of this island, not only in terms of geography but also in terms of history. It was not until the fifteenth century, under the reign of east Maui's Piilani, that the two separate kingdoms of Maui were united. In the years before, following the lengthy drought caused by the notorious Hua's sacrilegious killing of a priest, Maui was torn with strife among rulers competing for control.

Today the largest heiau in Hawaii is being restored in the hills of Hana. It was the heiau of Piilani, built around 1400, and it will soon be the site of an archaeological dig conducted by the Bishop Museum. Although some two dozen historical sites have been identified in Hana, Bishop Museum anthropologists say the actual number is more likely to be in the thousands.

That is not a shocking statement when you realize the depth and breadth of history that unfolded in the hinterlands of Hana. It is full of heiau, house sites and sea caves, ancient mounds, petroglyphs, and ruins. It was in Hana, too, that the famous Kahekili, Maui's last chief, won a battle at Kauiki Head, where he defeated a covetous Big Island ruler who desired to usurp him. Kauiki was also the birthplace of Ka'ahumanu, the woman who went on to become Kamehameha the Great's queen regent and favorite wife, and the one who broke the ancient *kapu*, prohibitions that included some discriminatory practices against women, after his death and became the foremost Hawaiian proponent of Christianity.

While the luminaries of the future were being born and groomed in the valleys of Hana, battles were raging in west Maui's Iao Valley. In 1790, the year of Haleakala's last eruption, Kamehameha arrived in Iao Valley and decimated his Maui rivals in a battle that dammed the stream with bodies and ran the waters red.

Meanwhile, Hawaiian villages thrived in Lahaina and Kaanapali, where historic sites remain today amid the hotel and resort development. In 1819, the year Kamehameha the Great died, the first whaling ships discovered Lahaina. Kamehameha's successor named Lahaina the capital of the kingdom, and the village thrived as a political center of Hawaii for the next three decades. By the mid-1800s the town was teeming as it served some 300 to 400 whaling ships that lay anchored in the bay. Census records show that Lahaina had 2,300 inhabitants in 1823; in 1846 there were 3,500 inhabitants and nearly 900 grass houses. Lahaina also had, and still does, Lahainaluna Seminary (now High School), the oldest American high school west of the Rockies. The two most prominent Hawaiian scholars and historians, David Malo and Samuel Kamakau, were students at this illustrious institution.

The missionaries arrived on Maui sometime after 1820. They established a strong Christian foothold in Lahaina, fueled partly by Ka'ahumanu's ardent conversion and her subsequent role as the religion's most powerful proponent. Within four years of the missionaries' arrival, Ka'ahumanu handed down Hawaii's first code of laws prohibiting boxing, fighting, murder, theft, and other crimes in an edict modeled after the Ten Commandments. Today several of Lahaina's historic sites are churches from this era. By the time the whaling industry in Lahaina waned in the 1870s, Lahaina had been changed forever.

In spite of its mixed reviews, Lahaina still has the distinction of being on the National Register of Historic Places and a town that stands out in west Maui. It is funky and raucous and touristy, but it is also the oldest-looking outpost with the least expensive hotel rooms in a coastline peppered with modern resorts. Kapalua, the northernmost of Maui's four resorts, has a glamorous, sleek sheen to it while Kaanapali, the first master-planned resort in Hawaii, is the mecca of dining and sophistication. The 1,500-acre Wailea in south Maui and its new neighbor, the Makena Resort, complete the 40-mile stretch of development along the leeward Maui coast.

But after all these years, it seems, there are still two Mauis. The smiling, cordial folks of Hana remain protected from the rest of the world by a virtually impassable road on the Kaupo side, and on the other side, a meandering, challenging, 54-mile route that is as long as it is stunning. While west Maui glimmers with its white-sand beaches and resort-tanned bodies dining on truffles and champagne, they're eating two-finger poi and fishing for lobster in Hana. For the visitor, that's a choice fit for kings.

GETTING AROUND

TRANSPORTATION

With the recent addition of the West Maui Airport in Kapalua, Maui now has three airports. The main airport is Kahului Airport in central Maui, where the interisland airlines of Aloha, Hawaiian, and Mid-Pacific land, along with United, Western, American, Air Canada, Total, Wardair, and other airlines. The other airport is Hana Airport in east Maui, served by Princeville Airways. At this writing, the only carriers serving Kapalua–West Maui Airport are Hawaiian Air and Princeville Airways, with aircraft seating fewer than fifty passengers.

There is no public transportation on Maui. However, Gray Line operates a shuttle service ([808] 877-5500) from Kahului Airport to Kaanapali hotels. For $8.30 one way you can ride in air-conditioned vans to Kaanapali, departing the airport between 10:15 A.M. and 4:15 P.M.

You can also approach Robert's Hawaii ([808] 871-6226) or Trans-Hawaiian Maui ([808] 877-7308), which generally handle prearranged groups but which may take others on a space-available basis for about $8.50. Trans-Hawaiian provides scheduled shuttle service from Kahului Airport to Kaanapali with 24-hour notice, between 10:15 A.M. and 4:15 P.M. If you need a ride beyond those hours, your choices are either a rental car (there are many at the airport and down the road toward Kahului) or a taxi, which will cost you about $34 to Kaanapali.

These three companies—Gray Line, Roberts, and Trans-Hawaiian Maui—are the major tour operators on the island and offer a wide variety of tours to all corners of Maui. Among the operators of small van tours, Ekahi Tours ([808] 572-9775) is a favorite.

If you're flying into the Kapalua–West Maui Airport, there are shuttles to Kaanapali hotels. There are also three car rental companies at Kapalua: Hertz ([800] 654-3131), Budget ([800] 527-0700), and Dollar ([808] 669-7400).

At the Hana Airport in east Maui, National Car Rental operates the Hana Rent-a-Car ([800] 227-7368).

If you land at Kahului Airport, you will be in the isthmus of central Maui, with Haleakala to the south of you and the West Maui Mountains to the northwest. Maui is generally divided into the following sections: upcountry (Kula, Makawao, Ulupalakua, and the flower farms up slope), central Maui (Kahului and Wailuku), east Maui (Hana), west Maui (Kaanapali, Lahaina, Kapalua), and south Maui (Wailea, Kihei, and Makena).

Although the road system is well maintained, there are several sections of the island, such as Kaupo and Kahakuloa, that are inaccessible except by four-wheel drive or high-clearance vehicles.

From Kahului to Kaanapali, the distance is 27 miles. From Kahului to Hana, it's 54 miles, and from Kahului to Ulupalakua, it's 24 miles. The distance from Kahului to Wailea is 17 miles, and it's 26 miles from Kahului to Haleakala. From Kaanapali in west Maui, it's 54 miles to Haleakala Crater and 80 miles to Hana. There is no one route that will take you entirely around the island in one neat circle, nor would you want to travel that way. A trip to Hana from west Maui, for example, is always a full-day affair, and so is Haleakala, if you plan to take day hikes into the crater. Except for the dirt roads past Makena and the rutted road past Hana, most of the highways are easily passable.

Helicopters

Maui's major helicopter companies are Maui Helicopters, operating out of Wailea ([808] 879-1601) or Kahului ([808] 877-4333); Kenai ([808] 871-6463); and Papillon ([808] 669-4884).

CAMPING

If you wish to camp or reserve a cabin in Haleakala National Park, write Haleakala National Park Headquarters, P.O. Box 369, Makawao, HI 96768; telephone (808) 572-7749. Camping is also possible in Hana's Waianapanapa State Park or the Poli Poli Springs Recreation Area (see Special Outings: On Land). Write the Division of State Parks, 54 High Street, Wailuku, HI 96793; telephone (808) 244-4354.

Hiking information and a state of Hawaii recreation map about Maui are available from the Division of Forestry and Wildlife, P.O. Box 1015, Wailuku, HI 96793; telephone (808) 244-4352.

HOTELS AND ALTERNATIVES

WEST AND SOUTH MAUI

West Maui encompasses Kapalua, Napili, Kaanapali, and Lahaina; the destinations in south Maui are Kihei, Wailea, and Makena. This stretch, which covers the majority of the western shoreline, does not include Maalaea and the isthmus of central Maui. Most of Maui's visitor accommodations are to be found here; the 45-minute drive from west Maui's Kapalua to Makena in the south will take you past 10,000 hotel and condominium units. This may seem to be a staggering figure, but compared to Waikiki's 1½-mile "strip" with 34,000 rooms, it is relatively small.

West Maui tends to be extremely touristy. The Kapalua Resort is an exception; with its posh Kapalua Bay Hotel, surrounded by the ocean on one side and mountainous heights and pine trees on the other, it is understated albeit expensive. Kaanapali is west Maui's hot spot with hotels, nightlife, and many shops. At the Kaanapali Beach Resort you will find three miles of white-sand beach with views of Molokai and Lanai. There are no budget accommodations here; those watching their purse strings had best look in Lahaina or Napili for accommodations.

Lahaina is a rowdy, salt-of-the-earth harbor town full of whaling history, with some excellent restaurants and boutique-laden streets. Loyalists love Lahaina in spite of its honky-tonk nature and lack of good beaches for swimming. Napili, a densely populated area, has condominiums available in all price ranges.

Kihei in south Maui is often referred to as the "mistake" in Maui's development, and I tend to agree. It is loaded with condominiums and is the least desirable of the south Maui destinations. Despite its location on the western shoreline, it is known for high-velocity winds. Its neighbor, Wailea, is more expensive, but the accommodations are worth the price. South Maui has two distinctive resorts: Wailea and Makena. Wailea is a well-planned resort with two championship golf courses and five clearly marked, accessible beaches. Makena Resort is the new kid on the block; it features one hotel, the Maui Prince, a golf club, and good stretches of beach.

Most Maui hotels will have rooms listed under the mountain-view and ocean-view categories. In west Maui you can have a stupendous view of the West Maui Mountains, the island's oldest and most sculpted. The ocean views from Kaanapali Beach offer Lanai and Molokai. From south Maui, Wailea and Makena in particular, you will gaze on the slopes of Haleakala. The ocean views here offer Lanai, Kahoolawe, and further south, Molokini Island.

The rates listed here do not include the 9.4 percent hotel room and excise tax. Also we recommend that you inquire about golf, tennis, diving, and honeymoon packages at the hotel of your choice. The larger hotels offer these packages, often at great savings.

Budget Hotel

PIONEER INN
658 Wharf Street
Lahaina, HI 96761
Telephone: (808) 661-3636

Noisy, old, and bawdy, the Pioneer Inn has a great following among budget travelers who want to be in the thick of the action and who stay up so late they don't mind the noise. It's a creaky walk-up with a courtyard, wooden railings, and rooms with a Tahitian motif. Rooms are on the second floor; the first floor of the building is taken up with a saloon, restaurants, and shops, which account for a lot of the activity. Across the road is the Lahaina Harbor, and a stone's throw away is a park with Lahaina's largest banyan tree, which takes up nearly a block. The mood is of swashbucklers toasting the sunset with a pint of grog. There's no pool, but there's daily maid service. Rooms are clean but with no frills, ranging from $18 for a single without bath in the original building to $27 for a room with bath, double occupancy. In the newer building, rooms are air-conditioned, have private bath and lanai, and range from $36, single occupancy, to $52 for a superior, in a quieter location with a better view.

Moderate Hotel

MAUI ISLANDER HOTEL
660 Wainee Street
Lahaina, HI 96761
Telephone: (800) 376-5226, (808) 667-9766

Surrounded by torch gingers, banana trees, very old palms, plumeria trees, papaya, and lush tropical greenery on 10 acres, the Maui Islander is an oasis in Lahaina. It's not on the waterfront, which doesn't detract because it's quieter, and it's a 5-minute walk from the sea wall. There are 372 rooms in nine two-story buildings, which are interconnected; a swimming pool, tennis court, and a barbecue and picnic area are part of the complex. Rooms have air-conditioning, ceiling fans, color TV, telephone, tub-shower combinations, and range from studios to two- and three-bedroom suites. Only the second floor, one-bedroom suites have lanais. The studios are large, with full kitchens and utensils, double beds and sofas. Upstairs rooms have high, open-beam ceilings. The one-bedroom suite sleeps up to four people at no extra charge. There's complimentary coffee in the morning, a friendly staff, and an activities desk that will set you up with anything. Rates begin at $82 and go up to $106 for a one-bedroom suite. Highly recommended.

Superior Hotels

HYATT REGENCY MAUI
Kaanapali Beach Resort
200 Nohea Kai Drive
Lahaina, HI 96761-1985
Telephone: (800) 228-9000, (808) 667-7474

The swingers, high fliers, oil magnates, and gold-chained occupants of the fast lane swarm to the Hyatt, the hot spot of west Maui with its 130-foot waterslide, ½-acre swimming pool, waterfalls, flamingos, $2-million art collection, 815 rooms, 55-foot catamaran, and other fantastic features. Developer Chris Hemmeter went to town on this $80-million extravaganza, filling its 18½ acres with flashy architectural feats such as an almost-underwater grotto bar where you can swim to your Sambuca and a rope bridge swinging over a lush garden area of swans, peacocks, macaws, and the like. Get the picture?

With an average occupancy rate of 90 to 95 percent, the Hyatt Regency Maui is one of the most successful hotels in the world. The size makes it impersonal, however, and it is a hotel of contrasts. While its standard guest rooms are mighty small, its 2,307-square-foot presidential suite is the size of a small island, with its own library, sauna, three baths, seven lanais, dining room, and second bedroom. And while its pool and waterways are generous, the beach it fronts is reefy and shallow, suitable for romantic sunset viewing but not for swimming.

Rates begin at $190 for the bottom-of-the-line terrace rooms, which are nothing special, with king-size or double beds and some with sofabeds. Terrace rooms could overlook the parking lot or garden; there are also golf course views, oceanfront rooms, and on up to the $2,000 presidential suite, with eleven categories all told. (There are several types of rooms in the $200 to $300 category.) Because there are three buildings at different angles to the ocean, there's a tremendous range in the views and types of room available; choose carefully. One of the deluxe categories here is the Regency Club, the top four floors of the central tower with an elaborate menu of amenities. Although the Hyatt is listed under the superior category, many of its rooms would fall under the deluxe category in terms of price. The Hyatt is a fun playground, but it's so obvious that it somehow lacks the elegance of what we think of as a truly deluxe hotel.

MAUI INTER-CONTINENTAL WAILEA
P.O. Box 779
Wailea, HI 96753
Telephone: (800) 367-2960, (808) 879-1922

It is large—600 rooms—and you may get lost or have to stand in line at the check-in. In terms of location, amenities, and overall level of comfort, however, the Inter-Con is a good value and is hard at work increasing it. A

$10-million refurbishment program is sprucing up the decor and adding, among other things, new artwork, refrigerators, minibars, remote controls for the TV sets, and marbled bathroom floors.

The 18-acre complex includes several buildings three to eight stories high, which curve around the lawn that slopes down to the sea. The shoreline fronting the hotel is jagged lava rock, but immediately to either side is a gorgeous white-sand crescent—Ulua Beach to the north and Wailea Beach to the south. A jogging trail along the ocean and well-tended, grassy areas invite you to take lingering strolls at sunrise or sunset. With the view of Kahoolawe and Molokini islands, it's dazzling. And 80 percent of the rooms have an ocean view.

Some of Maui's biggest visitor events occur here, from golf tournaments to windsurfing regattas and marine art shows. The size of the property and the extensive banquet and convention facilities make the Inter-Con popular for groups. Up to 700 people can be accommodated in the ballroom, and there are 13 meeting rooms. Of note are La Perouse, one of Maui's finest (if not the best) restaurants, and the Inu Inu lounge, a popular night spot with live music and dancing. All in all, they've found a lot for you to do at the Inter-Continental, and there will be a lot of you doing it—but the sensible layout and good planning make this a hotel worth looking into. Rates range from $175 for a garden-view room in a low-rise building to $350 for a honeymoon suite that's 50 yards from the ocean. Except for the suites, most of the rooms are the same size and layout and are priced according to view and location.

NAPILI KAI BEACH CLUB
5900 Honoapiilani Highway
Lahaina, HI 96761
(Hotel is in Napili)
Telephone: (800) 367-5030, (808) 669-6271

This is a very special hideaway on Napili Bay, favored by seasoned travelers seeking low-key luxury out of the mainstream. This is not a crowded high-rise, there are no large groups, it's quieter than most comparable hostelries. Seven two-story buildings house one hundred thirty-seven units, all with an ocean view and all with kitchens and lanais. All the amenities of a hotel are offered here except for room service for food. There are a restaurant and daily maid service. It's just south of the Kapalua Bay Hotel.

The Napili Kai Beach Club is not new but has aged gracefully enough. Its prime location on Napili Bay and its comfortable, understated style make it a favorite for those who can afford it. Rooms range from $130 double occupancy for a standard ocean-view studio to $180 to $225 for a one-bedroom suite and $275 to $335 for a two-bedroom suite. No credit cards accepted.

PLANTATION INN
174 Lahainaluna Road
Lahaina, HI 96761
Telephone: (800) 433-6815, (808) 667-9225

The Plantation Inn opened last September with a flourish. The only hotel of its kind in Lahaina, it has nine rooms and a separate cottage, each furnished differently in a turn-of-the-century motif. There are hardwood floors, brass beds and fixtures, canopied beds, stained glass, round windows, and other details that create the feeling of an old-fashioned country inn. The pool area is lushly landscaped, and there are three dining areas: indoors, a covered lanai, and an outdoor patio. Most exciting is the fact that noted restaurateur and chef Gerard Reversade, of Lahaina's famous Gerard's bistro, has relocated his eatery to this hotel. That means guests' meals—breakfast, lunch, and dinner—are created and provided by this talented chef.

The location, Lahainaluna Road, is not far from the main Front Street, but removed enough to be quieter.

There are three plans: with breakfast, a room is $95; with breakfast and dinner, $125; and with breakfast, dinner, and an air-conditioned car, $140. Dive packages are also offered.

SHERATON-MAUI HOTEL
Kaanapali Beach Resort
Lahaina, HI 96761-1991
Telephone: (800) 325-3535, (808) 661-0031

Its biggest asset is its location, on the best beach with the best snorkeling in Kaanapali. The spot is Black Rock promontory, from which the last chief of Maui, Kahekili, is said to have made his most awesome leaps. Black Rock, or Pu'u Keka'a, "turning point hill," was considered the spot at which souls of the deceased made their leap into the spirit land of their ancestors. Today the Sheraton wraps around this historic and gorgeous promontory; to its back are the West Maui Mountains, and in front lies a clear, turquoise ocean. The height of the promontory offers a vantage point for the restaurant located on its top and offers the best whale-watching views during winter.

The rooms are spread out in several buildings on a 23-acre property. Ignore the tacky boutiques and concentrate instead on the ocean and the mountains. A nice touch are the blankets of greenery covering some of the balconies. The Sheraton was the first hotel to be constructed in Kaanapali, and an ongoing renovation program is eliminating some signs of age.

There are 500 units of 4 types, all air-conditioned and without kitchens. There are cottages; the garden tower, the newest building; the cliff tower; and the Ocean Lanai. The garden tower is closest to the service area so some of the rooms there can be noisy. The Ocean Lanai, facing northwest around the corner from Black Rock, is the closest you can get to the ocean on Kaanapali, and it is breathtaking. The view is of the deep waters between Molokai and Lanai. You're about 20 yards from the edge of the cliff and when the whales are around, they look like they're at your fingertips. The cottages are also a different feature at the Sheraton. They're circular units on the lower floor, with balconies over the yard and walkways. Rates are from $150 for a standard, single occupancy, to $350 for a one-bedroom suite and $700 for the presidential suite.

Deluxe Hotels

KAPALUA BAY HOTEL
One Bay Drive
Kapalua, HI 96761
Telephone: (800) 367-8000, (808) 669-5656

The Kapalua is situated on a serene, classic white-sand bay with the best snorkeling in this part of Maui, a view of Molokai across the channel, and a feeling of serenity that eases away the urban madness. However, it is in northwest Maui, which makes it windier and cooler than the rest of west Maui. It's a hotel for the wealthy and discriminating, with a splendid golf course, pleasing architecture, and rooms that are not very spacious (420 square feet, excluding lanai), but quite tasteful. Surrounding the 750-acre development are 23,000 acres of pineapple land and three beaches overlooking Molokai and Lanai. You can imagine the sense of space and seclusion. The name means "arms embracing the sea," and it fits; two lava peninsulas cradle the bay and the hotel.

The vaulted lobby features high pillars, a sweeping, splendid view of the ocean, streamside dining, and generous greenery that invites the outdoors in. The rooms—there are 194 of them—are in low-rise structures that blend gracefully into the surroundings.

Like most hotels in Hawaii, the Kapalua is renovating all of its rooms. Tentative plans also call for adding new rooms and a spa facility. All rooms are the same size and configuration except for the suites, with price differences determined by view. There's a color TV, a supply of alcoholic beverages with Brie and caviar (for which your room is charged), a well-lit, well-mirrored bathroom with two sinks, and a lanai. Touches of natural wood and wicker add a tropical elegance to the decor.

More than the individual rooms, it's the overall feeling of Kapalua that impresses. Its sensible understatement and good taste appeal to a clientele of famous names, from Bjorn Borg to Kathleen Turner, but there are ordinary executives as well. Some come for the tennis, others for the golf at the Kapalua Golf Club (one of the top three in the state), and others for the shops, restaurants, and beach. The Kapalua shops provide some of Maui's most unusual and elegant shopping.

Rooms range from $195 for a garden view to $850 for the two-bedroom suites. Oceanfront rooms are $350, ocean-view prime, $295. Rates are for single or double occupancy.

MAUI PRINCE
5400 Makena Alanui
Kihei, HI 96753
(Hotel is in Makena)
Telephone: (800) 321-6284, (808) 874-1111

This newcomer to Maui has made an impact, and will no doubt mature with grace. Seibu, developer of the Prince hotels worldwide, has made its mark with its first Hawaii hotel. The Japanese esthetic prevails here, with spare, almost austere design and decor, which provide welcome relief from the rattan-wicker tropical ambience everywhere else in Hawaii. Everything here is expansive, crisp, pristine. The Prince made a bold statement, and we think it has succeeded.

The atrium-style lobby opens into a 30,000-square-foot courtyard with ponds and a Japanese garden in the middle. The V-shaped white building points to the beach in an arrowhead shape with a flat tip. The hotel is not directly on the beach, but is across a small road bordering the beach. Still close, but a difference. The design allows every room to have a view of the ocean (the mountains aren't bad either) and breaks the rooms down into those that are on the wings (ocean view) and those that are at the flat point of the V, the oceanfront. Because the Prince is the only hotel within miles and the first to be built in the spectacular Makena area (a sore point with conservationists), the views to all sides are unobstructed. The beach is a white-sand curve from which you can hop onto a catamaran for a snorkeling cruise to nearby Molokini.

There are 300 rooms on five floors, including twenty suites, each with double doors, a spacious lanai, a full-length mirror, separate dressing area, color TV, large desk, and the nicest carpet and decor you're likely to see in a hotel. Everything is in white, oyster, beiges, and tans; the overall effect feels extremely tasteful, uncluttered, and expansive. The floors are terraced, larger at the bottom and slowly narrowing, to give each lanai privacy. The telephone in the WC is a nice touch too.

Among its superior amenities are the Prince Court, one of Maui's best restaurants, and Hakone, an elegant, if overrated, Japanese restaurant. The lounge in the Molokini is a good after-dinner stop, and chamber music in the garden adds a tasteful diversion. The biggest failure at the Prince is its swimming pool, a sorry-looking outpost in a denuded landscape that, hopefully, will grow.

Rooms start at $175 for a garden-view room, $200 for an ocean-view room, and $230 for ocean-view deluxe; and go up to $250 for oceanfront and $270 for oceanfront deluxe. Suites are from $350 to $700. For those who can afford the quiet luxury of the Maui Prince, it will prove to be a departure from anything you've seen in a hotel. It's world class, exhibiting superb taste in everything from service to food and ambience.

STOUFFER WAILEA BEACH RESORT
3550 Wailea Alanui Drive
Wailea, HI 96753
Telephone: (800) 325-5000, (808) 879-4900

Until the Maui Prince moved in down the road, Stouffer's was the epitome of luxury and good taste in Wailea. One of Hawaii's top hotels, it's long been a favorite and has consistently won awards for excellence. There are 350 rooms in a lush garden landscape that covers 15 beachfront acres. The gardens are a big part of the hotel's appeal, for they are inordinately verdant and well maintained, with tropical and exotic plants, dainty footpaths and bridges, ponds, and cozy nooks in which some people like to get married.

The lobby—open, casual, and unpretentious—is on the fifth floor of a seven-story building. The rooms are in gray and raspberry, a cut above most hotels in quality and decor. More like a well-appointed living room than a hotel room, each room is highlighted with wicker and plush upholstery; there's color TV, a refrigerator, and the usual conveniences. The average size of the rooms is 500 square feet, including the lanais. The deluxe quarter of the hotel is the Mokapu Beach Club, with larger rooms, prime beachfront location, and high, open-beam ceilings in the upstairs rooms.

The beach in front offers excellent swimming and snorkeling and, to the south, a consummate view of Molokini and Kahoolawe islands. To the north is the imposing panorama of the West Maui Mountains, and straight ahead is the island of Lanai. Here and there are hammocks, cabanas, and palm trees dotting the lawn, all very picturesque.

Rooms range from $255 for a deluxe to $900 and $1,200 for the two-bedroom suite.

WESTIN MAUI
Kaanapali Beach Resort
Telephone: (800) 228-3000, (808) 667-7809

Chris Hemmeter, of the Hyatt Regency Maui and Hyatt Regency Waikiki, bought the old Maui Surf and plunked $155 million into renovating it. Close to the Hyatt and Marriott, in the center of Kaanapali Beach, it opened in the fall of 1987 with the same kind of opulence and lavishness that characterize the other Hyatts. To wit: 762 rooms, including 28 suites and 43 rooms of the Royal Beach Club, five swimming pools with waterfalls and slides, health club, and a $2 million fine art collection displayed throughout. Although it is not yet open at the time of this writing, earnest sybarites may want to check it out. Rooms begin at $185 for the courtyard, $235 for the golf-mountain view, and on up to the $450 to $1,500 suites. Ocean-view rooms are $235, and oceanfront, $275.

Alternatives

Keeping in mind that many of Maui's condos offer amenities similar to the hotels, here are some suggestions, listed alphabetically rather than by price range. Remember, most condo developments have offices with regular business hours, not twenty-four-hour service.

HOYOCHI NIKKO
3901 Lower Honoapiilani Highway
Lahaina, HI 96761
(Condo is in Kahana)
Telephone: (808) 669-8343

This moderately priced fourteen-year-old condo development is on the ocean, with an excellent view, and it's only two stories high. There are eighteen one-bedroom units in two sizes, each with complete kitchen, telephone, TV, bathroom with tub, and washer-dryer. There's a pool, outdoor gas grill by the seawall, and a view of the sun setting between Molokai and Lanai. For this price, it's hard to beat. The lawn area in front is a comfortable spot for sunbathing; because the bay fronting the property is not sandy, a stairway leads into the ocean from the seawall. Good swimming, snorkeling, and at some times of the year, surfing and boogie boarding can be had at Mahinahina just south, and the beach fronting the hotel is located about midway between Kaanapali and Kapalua.

The rooms have lanais facing the ocean; some have an Oriental decor, but mostly they're in rattan with tropical Hawaiian prints. There is no maid service, but the service is extremely friendly and the guests love to linger by the cocktail table at the seawall. Rates are $70 for a standard one-bedroom and $80 for the larger unit. No credit cards.

KAANAPALI ALII
50 Nohea Kai Drive
Lahaina, HI 96761
Telephone: (800) 642-6284, (808) 667-1400

The Alii is one of Kaanapali's newest properties and is also a terrific deal for groups or families who could benefit by the large one- or two-bedroom units that look and feel like an entire house in a wealthy neighborhood. Although the rooms are expensive, they give you a lot for your money. There are four buildings, each eleven stories high and interconnected. The units have mountain or ocean views and have all the amenities—maid service, porters, a beach good for swimming, pool, and tennis courts—except a restaurant. That's no problem because there are eateries aplenty in the surrounding hotels, just minutes away by foot.

The one- and two-bedroom units are immense, with fully equipped kitchens, utensils, dining room, washer-dryer, and are elaborately furnished with tables, kitchen counter with stools, extra beds and sofas, and so on. You won't lack anything here, not even a sauna, Jacuzzi, or exercise room. There are large picture windows looking from mountain to sea.

The Kaanapali Alii is lavish, well maintained, and professional. It's generous in its space and is highly recommended. Rates are $235 to $270 for the one-bedroom unit and $345 and up for the two-bedroom unit. The same rate applies for up to four people.

KAPALUA VILLAS
500 Bay Drive
Kapalua, HI 96761
(Located in Kapalua)
Telephone: (808) 669-0244

Located in the luxurious Kapalua Resort, the Villas offer an alternative—self-sufficient condominiums sprawled in attractive clusters across 80 acres. The Kapalua Bay Hotel manages 115 of these villas, some on seaside cliffs, others near the beaches, still others bordering the fairways of the golf course. All the villas have ocean views.

They come in singles, one and two bedrooms, and multilevel; all are impeccably decorated with rattan, artwork, carved mahogany tables, high-beamed ceilings, complete kitchens, sunken marble tubs, and touches of redwood. There is a consistency to the villas, even though they are condominiums, because of the overall level of the resort's taste. Daily maid service is provided and a shuttle bus will transport guests across the resort to the tennis courts, golf club, shops, and restaurants.

Each cluster of villas has its own recreation facilities such as pool, tennis courts, Jacuzzi, and such, which makes them moderately self-sufficient. That's part of the appeal among the golfers, tennis buffs, celebrities, and others who seek luxury accommodations with more privacy and self-sufficiency than the hotel. Rates begin at $215 for the one-bedroom with fairway view, double occupancy ($35 for each additional person, a bit steep), to $265 for the one-bedroom ocean-view villa, $335 for a one-bedroom oceanfront, and $315 and up for the two-bedroom villas.

MAKENA SURF
3750 Wailea Alanui Drive
Wailea, HI 96753
Telephone: (800) 367-5246, (808) 879-1595

The exquisite Makena Surf consists of all oceanfront apartments—$450,000-units—sprinkled across generously landscaped grounds with two swimming pools and four tennis courts. The wealthy and the reclusive would adore it. There are ten low-rise buildings, with rooms that maximize the ocean views and open spaces, decorated in splendid taste. Its location—at Makena, outside of the mainstream and activities of Wailea—offers privacy and anonymity for those who want to vacation in quiet isolation. Indeed, this deluxe oceanfront condo offers pricey surroundings with no fuss. Each unit has a private lanai that looks right over the ocean; some have sunken living rooms and two-person Jacuzzis. Needless to say, it's plush. Services include concierge, daily housekeeping, grocery delivery service if desired. Those favoring this low-key approach to luxury should expect to be on their own, with only the nearby beach and golf course. Other than that, the surroundings are raw and it's very, very quiet. Four-night minimum stay required. Rates are $300 for a two-bedroom oceanfront suite that sleeps four to $375 for a three-bedroom oceanfront suite that sleeps six.

MANA KAI MAUI
2960 South Kihei Road
Kihei, HI 96753
Telephone: (800) 525-2025, (808) 879-1561

The Mana Kai is a top value in the moderate category. Although it's in a typically windy corner of Kihei, it's on a mile-long white-sand beach and offers a car with every condo and free airport pickup. You have your choice of two-bedroom, two-bath, or one-bedroom, one-bath units with lanais that look over the ocean or Haleakala. There are telephones, color TV, laundry facilities on each floor, daily maid service, and a restaurant and sundry shop downstairs. The units sleep four to six people.

Some of them are very spacious, with full kitchens, L-shaped sofas, lanais running the entire width of the apartment, and queen-size beds. Below, you see coconut trees circling the white-sand beach and you have a view of Molokini and Kahoolawe. Furnishings are modest and the building is old, so there are some worn edges. But this is not the Maui Prince, and the prices reflect that. For those wishing to be close to the beach without paying luxury prices, the Mana Kai Maui is highly recommended. It's near the gorgeous Keawakapu beach, and Wailea is only minutes away.

Rates begin at $85 for two (no kitchen, but for room, car, and breakfast for two) to $163 for a two-bedroom, two-bath apartment with kitchen and car. It's $5 a day more for each extra person.

WAILEA CONDOMINIUMS
3750 Wailea Ala Nui Drive
Wailea, HI 96753
Telephone: (800) 367-5246, (808) 879-1595

Of the three Wailea condominium villages—Ekolu, Ekahi, Elua—Ekolu is farthest from the beach (about a two-minute drive), with views of Haleakala and the Wailea golf courses. However, the price differential is not that great, making Elua and Ekahi better values for those who wish to walk to the beach in no time. Ekahi, the oldest of the three condominium villages, is next to Stouffer's; Elua is between Stouffer's and the Maui Inter-Continental Wailea on the ocean; and the twelve-year-old Ekolu, the newest of the three, is further inland and next to the tennis club, with panoramic views of the golf course, mountains, or ocean. All are two-story wooden structures with lanais, and sprinkled around the grassy complex in well-managed clusters. Elua has mostly ocean views and is closest to the beach while most of Ekahi has a garden view.

Because only two hotels exist in the development, there's a sense of openness. And while the tennis club and golf courses offer something for the sports fans, the ocean is abundantly present and the hotel's restaurants and lounges take up the slack after dark.

Rates for Ekolu Village, which is farthest from the beach, are $150 for a one-bedroom and $200 for a two-bedroom. Rates for Ekahi range from $110 for a studio, double occupancy, to $165 for a one-bedroom, double occupancy. Elua's rates go from $180 ocean view, one bedroom, to $225 for a one-bedroom oceanfront and $350 for an oceanfront two-bedroom. Also offered are golf and honeymoon packages and car-condo packages. No credit cards accepted, only cash and checks.

If you wish more information on Maui's vast condominium offerings, you can write to any of these three top condo management companies in Hawaii:

Aston Hotels and Resorts
2255 Kuhio Avenue
18th Floor
Honolulu, HI 96815-2658
Telephone (800) 367-5124, 922-3368

Village Resorts
900 Fort Street Mall
Suite 1540
Honolulu, HI 96813
Telephone (800) 367-7052, 531-5323

Colony Hotels and Resorts
32 Merchant Street
Honolulu, HI 96815
Telephone (800) 367-6046, 523-0411

....

UPCOUNTRY AND EAST MAUI

Upcountry, which includes Makawao and Kula, and east Maui, which is Hana, are both extraordinary areas with distinctive features. They are not heavily developed and have much wilderness to explore. They also reflect different aspects of the great Haleakala, which dominates this side of the island. There is only one hotel in Hana, but there are many bed and breakfast and vacation rental possibilities. For information on bed and breakfasts, see A Note on Hotels at the beginning of this book.

Moderate Hotels

HEAVENLY HANA INN
P.O. Box 146
Hana, HI 96713
Telephone: (808) 248-8442

It looks like a Japanese inn, with its gate, pagoda structure, and stone lions guarding the entrance. The Heavenly Hana Inn is a longtime favorite of those wishing to explore Hana on a moderate budget. It is small and friendly, but a bit run-down. Most of the units are under one roof; these include the four garden suites, one on each corner of the building and each with two bedrooms, one bathroom, a kitchenette–dining porch, screened-in lanai, and private outside exit to the parking area. The units at the inn cost $70 for double occupancy. There's also a beach cottage on Hana Bay that rents for $75, double occupancy, and a family cottage that rents for $60 for two and $85 for four. The common areas at the inn are much like those in a home, with a reading room, dining room, utility area, and little niches for sitting. The entire inn has a Japanese motif, with large lacquer screens, antique furnishings, and old Japanese chests—not ideal and a little dark indoors, but acceptable.

KULA LODGE
R.R. 1, Box 475
Kula, HI 96790
Telephone: (808) 878-1535

There are five chalets for rent at the Kula Lodge, perched on the slopes of Haleakala and looking down vast sweeps to the West Maui Mountains in the distance. The cabins are charming and romantic and perfect for those wanting a headquarters in upcountry Maui, away from the madding crowds.

All the cabins are redwood A-frames and have carpeting and large glass sliding doors opening to a deck with chairs for watching the sunset. They're very basic, with no telephone, TV, or porters, with showers but no tubs in the bathrooms. You just check in at the lodge adjoining the restaurant and trundle off to your cabin carrying your bags. You're on your own.

The cabins range from a single-story room with double bed and twin bed in a loft for $80, to the more elaborate chalets with queen-size bed, Swedish fireplace, and stairs leading to a loft with twin beds, for $95. The premier attraction here is the view—each cabin has a lanai and there's nothing more invigorating than watching the day bloom down the mountain or wane with the west Maui sunset. Breakfast is included; prices based on double occupancy.

Deluxe Hotel

HOTEL HANA-MAUI
Hana, HI 96713
Telephone: (800) 321-4262, (808) 248-8211

The Hotel Hana-Maui is the ultimate hideaway in Hawaii. Undergoing a $24-million renovation, it has made a special effort to retain its authentically Hawaiian flavor while upgrading the property and amenities to the ultimate deluxe level. That's not easy to do, but director Carl Lindquist, a rare man, and the Hana-Maui staff, mostly Hawaiian residents who walk to work, have pulled it off with grace.

When the renovations are complete, there will be 105 rooms and suites, ranging from duplex cottages to one-bedroom suites and rooms with garden lanais, all sprawled generously over nearly 50 acres of splendidly landscaped lawns with towering heliconias, trees, and exotic palms. The porte cochere and ornate lobby are new. Once you check in, you find yourself on a jitney sailing over what looks and feels like a large, regal estate.

The buildings are low-rise, with rooms designed for maximum privacy and the most tasteful decor you'll see in a hotel. There are polished hardwood floors and large, neatly tiled showers, designed so you don't need a door or curtain. There's a telephone in the bathroom.

The motif here is elegant Hawaiian, with bedspreads like Hawaiian quilts (not hand-stitched, but effective) and mats of split bamboo covering the floor. The clean lines, the highlights of wicker, stone, and bamboo, and the colors—white, tan, blond, and oyster—give the decor authority. There are no televisions in any of the rooms, but there are activities galore.

The hotel has access to Hana's only white-sand beach 3 miles down the road, where the weekly luau is held. It's one of the best luaus in Hawaii, a time when the employees get together and put on a Hawaiian show, imu ceremony, and feast as if you were part of their families. If you choose, you can ride the hay wagon to the luau and sip wine to Hawaiian music while you gaze at the slopes of Haleakala.

The activities here include horseback riding, weekly cookouts, bicycle and tandem bike riding, botanical and historical tours, tennis, and, for interested parties, treks to Hawaii's largest heiau, a sacred spot otherwise inaccessible. New hiking and running trails for guests, an overnight cabin at the edge of the rain forest, and a European-style health spa are in the works. Rosewood, owner of the hotel, has grand plans to open up the outdoors for its guests.

Don't forget that the surrounding area, Hana, is considered "the most Hawaiian" place in Hawaii, with genuine, gracious people and lush surroundings peppered with waterfalls, wilderness, and historic heiaus and ancient sites. Those who discover Hana tap into the heart of Hawaii.

Rates range from $416 for a garden lanai room, double occupancy, to $531 and $556 for the Waikaloa Suites, which have indoor-outdoor lanais, separate sitting rooms, bedrooms, and lots of space. The newly opened oceanfront one-bedroom suites with Jacuzzis rent for $701. Meals for two are included in the charge.

Alternatives

Of course, not everyone can afford to stay at the Hotel Hana-Maui. Thankfully, this is one town where there are many vacation rentals and alternative accommodations. Here are the best, listed alphabetically.

HANA BAY VACATION RENTALS
P.O. Box 318
Hana, HI 96713
Telephone: (808) 248-7727

Suzanne Collins does a great job of managing a roster of about a dozen rentals in the Hana area, from exclusive homes with private Jacuzzis to simpler A-frames or pole houses in picturesque settings. All the homes listed with her are fully equipped with TVs, washing machines, and telephones. She and her husband personally handle the cleaning, so the house will be well maintained. Write and ask about Hale Kolohala, a three-bedroom redwood pole house on a secluded 5 acres of green, with a loft and fantastic view—$175, double occupancy. Another good one is Hale Honokalani on Waianapanapa Road, close to the beach on an acre of land. Hale Honokalani rents for $95, double occupancy, and is a five-minute walk from Waianapanapa State Park and beach. Rates range from $55 for two in a tiny cabin to $175 for the full three-bedroom. Weekly and monthly rates also available. No credit cards accepted.

HANA KAI CONDOMINIUMS
c/o Hana Kai Maui Resorts
P.O. Box 38
Hana, HI 96713
Telephone: (808) 248-8426

These apartments are right on a gorgeous beach and are the best deal in Hana. There's a pond on the property cradled in gingers and tropical plants, and all fourteen units have ocean views, full kitchens, and access to the beach only 40 yards away. They're individually owned condominium units, so each is furnished differently. The rooms on the ends of each floor are by far the most appealing, with large square lanais, windows to the ocean, sliding doors that close off the bedroom, hala trees outside. There are no porters, room service, or restaurant—just good rooms facing the ocean at prices that won't break the bank. Rates are $75 for the studio and $90 for the one-bedroom. Charming, quiet, and highly recommended.

DINING OUT

....

WEST AND SOUTH MAUI

From diners and coffeehouses to pricey continental palaces, they're all here, in all price ranges and types of cuisine. The eateries are listed alphabetically and cover the coastline from Kapalua down to Makena, the gold coast of cuisine where fine dining beckons from every corner. Many observers feel that Maui has the highest concentration of fine restaurants in Hawaii. It's a close call with Oahu, but see for yourself. Things change daily—and chefs do move around—so please call ahead to ensure they're still there, and to make reservations.

ALEX'S HOLE IN THE WALL
834 Front Street
Lahaina
Telephone: (808) 661-3197

Alex's Hole in the Wall is an old favorite with staying power. For many years it has occupied the same hole in the wall in Lahaina, purveying wonderful homemade pastas and cheesecake with a tropical twist. You walk upstairs to the dining room (the kitchen is at street level) and then proceed to dine in an intimate, comfortable setting of memorabilia. Everything here, from the pasta to its fillings, is homemade—even the sausage, which appears in various appetizers and entrées. Take your pick of lasagne, veal parmesan, spaghetti or pasta pomodoro, but be sure to leave room for dessert. Alex's is renowned for its Kahlua-banana-fudge cheesecake, a staple, and a rotating roster of flavors ranging from passion fruit to chocolate chip.

Moderately priced—full dinners range from $7 to $20. Open 6:00 P.M. to 10:00 P.M. nightly except Sunday. Major credit cards accepted.

THE BAY CLUB
Kapalua Bay Hotel
Kapalua
Telephone: (808) 669-5656

There's the view—of Molokai and Lanai—and there's the cuisine. Both are exceptional. The Bay Club opens for lunch and dinner with good choices. You might try the assorted seafood with angel hair pasta in creamy lobster sauce, nestled in fresh artichokes at lunch. The lobster sautéed with morels, fresh dill, Chardonnay, and cream; and the sautéed fresh ono with oysters and shrimp in a dill-flavored white wine sauce are among the many sophisticated dinner items. It's not an extensive menu but it's satisfying, with more than adequate seafood choices and a few meat selections, such as double spring lamb chops and veal scallopini with bay scallops and capers.

The mood is understated and elegant in the evenings, with the sort of cool clientele that doesn't ogle the movie stars and dignitaries frequently in their midst. The staff is knowledgeable and professional. All in all, the Bay Club is a safe, elegant choice for intimate dining over a continental menu, which doesn't dazzle with its innovation, but which is solid and sincere.

Expensive—dinner entrées range from $19 to $40 and all items are à la carte. Open 11:30 A.M. to 2:00 P.M. and 6:00 P.M. to 9:00 P.M. every day. Major credit cards accepted.

LA BRETAGNE
562-C Front Street
Lahaina
Telephone: (808) 661-8966

The French cuisine here is fine and the ambience has its charm. What was built to be the home of a sheriff in 1910 has been converted to a country French restaurant with classic touches: brocade wallpaper, touches of brass, stained glass, dark wooden beams, and classical paintings. When it comes to cuisine, however, it appears the reputation surpasses the meal. The seafood chowder was creamy, buttery, puréed, and in the end, unexceptional; the bouillabaisse, with gray snapper, barracuda, and clams, was served with rouille but its lobster was a little overdone. The menu, however, changes every six months to make room for such delights as mango duck in the summer, or opakapaka en papillote for winter. La Bretagne is known for its rack of lamb and seafood in puff pastry, which was acceptable but not stunning in spite of the freshness of the seafood. All told, La Bretagne is a good idea with a good reputation but is recommended with reservations.

Expensive—dinner for two costs about $70 to $80. Open 6:00 P.M. to 10:00 P.M. nightly. Major credit cards accepted.

CHEZ PAUL
Olowalu
Telephone: (808) 661-3843

Chez Paul has a huge following statewide and has established itself as a fine continental restaurant in the middle of, well, almost nowhere. Olowalu is where the petroglyphs are, but there is a welcome absence of Kaanapali high rises when you drive up to this ancient wooden storefront. The mood is in the now overworked category of "casually elegant," a phrase that originated on Maui to capture the essence of restaurants such as Chez Paul, where it is très chic to underdress over your St. Tropez or Kaanapali tan. However "in" it is, most people come for the food: poisson beurre blanc is Chez Paul's most famous dish, and the duck à l'orange is a close second. Scampi appetizers and delicate steaks are also favored, but it's the fish that is the rage.

Entrées are all $24.95 with soup or salad. There are two seatings nightly, at 6:30 P.M. and 8:30 P.M. Major credit cards accepted.

GERARD'S
174 Lahainaluna Road
Lahaina
Telephone: (808) 661-8939

Chef Gerard Reversade's French eatery is small, intimate, and much like an old café with cobbled floors and greenery galore, where you can walk in wearing anything from jeans to a silk suit. Open for lunch and dinner, it features classic Gallic offerings: Pâté Maison, Frog Legs Persillade, Poisson Cru, Tournedos with Truffles, etc. The chalkboard menu changes daily and is remarkably diverse. Examples: Ono au Beurre Blanc, Blanquette of Sweetbreads, Confit of Duck, Ahi à la Basquaise, Scallops à la Creme, and a seemingly endless repertoire tirelessly created by Reversade.

Informal, intimate, and moderately expensive.

At this writing, Gerard's is about to move to its new location in the new Plantation Inn Hotel, where it will serve breakfast, lunch, and dinner. Major credit cards accepted.

GREENTHUMS
839 Front Street
Lahaina
Telephone: (808) 667-6126

Abundant greenery and tables practically on the water mark this delight-ful Lahaina eatery. It opened in 1982 when an old fish market left the spot, and it has since carved a firm niche in the heart of the casual diner here. With its ocean view, great food, and the sound of the waves crashing close by, Greenthums is a breath of fresh air in frantic Lahaina. The triple-tiered arrangement offers splendid views over a menu of sandwiches, salads, fresh fish, kalua pig dinner, barbecue chicken, and Vegetables Delight—simple but satisfying fare, and all very good.

Inexpensive—two can dine for under $20. Open 7:30 A.M. to 9:30 P.M. every day. Major credit cards accepted.

HAPPY DAYS
Lahaina Market Place
Lahaina
Telephone: (808) 661-3235

It's like an old-fashioned diner from the fifties, with booths, hardwood floors, cane-backed chairs, and customers slurping malts and floats. In-formal and charming, it looks as if Archie, Veronica, and Jughead could walk in at any minute. The food is your basic hot dog–sandwich–soup–salad–fountain fare, with such items as the Happy Days Cheeseburger, stuffed avocado salad, tuna and patty melts. There's also homemade corn bread and homemade chili and beans, with an array of desserts: pecan pie, berry pie, Hot Fudge Saturday, malts, and ice cream in different forms.

Inexpensive; although a half papaya costs $2.50, other items are reasonable, and a big meal here could cost as little as $5 or $6. Open 7:00 A.M. to 9:00 P.M. daily. No credit cards accepted.

LAHAINA PROVISION COMPANY
Hyatt Regency Maui
Kaanapali Beach Resort
Telephone: (808) 667-7474

Although slightly overshadowed by its glamorous neighbor, the Swan Court, the LPC holds its own as a fine restaurant with a great hook: the yogurt bar, the chocoholic's bar, and, for the repentant, the salad bar. There are views from the restaurant, but there's no outdoor dining. At lunch a salad bar of local favorites competes with a menu of burgers and sandwiches, sweet and sour shrimp, and fresh island catch. The salad bar is enticing, with sashimi, fresh greens, and pasta and shrimp salads. At dinner, lobster tail; a Maui Clambake of lobster tail, clams, shrimps, fresh fish, and vegetables; steaks, brochettes, and salads round out a limited menu. The chocoholic bar is the finale, with ice cream and the tempestuous toppings.

Dinner entrées range from $16 to $28; the luncheon salad bar is $10.75. Open 11:30 A.M. to 3:00 P.M. for lunch daily and from 6:00 P.M. to 10:30 nightly for dinner. Major credit cards accepted.

LAHAINA TREEHOUSE BAR AND SEAFOOD RESTAURANT
Lahaina Market Place
126 Lahainaluna Road
Lahaina
Telephone: (808) 667-9224

The Lahaina Treehouse gives you the best of everything. It lets you dine in comfort in a casual Polynesian ambience. It offers you fine dishes, and a million of them. Best of all, it has transformed a large, venerable ohia tree into your dining quarters. Yes, it's a large, deluxe treehouse. There's a sense of humor here and a fine professional staff that makes you feel at home no matter what you order or what you're wearing.

There are three tiers to this operation, each drenched in greenery and plants. At night the mood deepens, with white tablecloths and linen napkins to add a dash of romance to the mood. And the menu—it's almost overwhelming. More than a hundred seafood items are printed on a large sheet, with check marks next to the items available for the day. (Somewhat like a long ballot with lots of choices.) The choices: shrimp cooked eighteen different ways, from beer batter to croquettes, gumbo, and tempura; mussels stuffed with marinara sauce or in sherry sauce with fettucine; smoked salmon fettucine; five different pasta preparations; and many others. For the fresh catch of the day, you can have your choice of fresh papio (jack trevally), mahimahi, or ahi (yellowfin tuna). Besides being good folks, these people know what they're doing and are able to offer you a level of professionalism to match their enthusiasm.

Highly recommended. Items in all price ranges, from $2.95 soups to a $16.95 fresh catch and $22.95 for lobster tail. Open 11:00 A.M. to 11:00 P.M. daily. No credit cards.

LOKELANI
Maui Marriott
Kaanapali Beach Resort
Telephone: (808) 667-1200

The specialty here is seafood, offered in a casual, inviting atmosphere in which you can dine to your heart's content without spending a fortune. They call their specialty "Maui cuisine," which means fresh Maui-grown vegetables, fresh herbs, fresh seafood from island waters, and a seasoned touch on the seafood chowders, pastas, and salads. To begin with, the dinners come with fresh homemade bread, seafood chowder (wonderful!) and a salad. The chef's special of poached opakapaka in champagne sauce with caviar is superb. The basic meats and steaks are here, so no one is neglected. For the most part, the preparations are simple and, although adventurous, they're not ostentatious. Seating is in discreet booths and tables in a pleasant, nostalgic ambience with old photos and tortoise shells on the walls—nothing special but very nice.

Overall, the Lokelani is highly recommended for those desiring good seafood at realistic prices. Entrées include broiled Pacific lobster for $16.95, seafood brochette for $15.95, fresh catch—wahoo, opakapaka, yellowfin tuna, red snapper, gray snapper—and filet mignon for $18.95, and many other generous dishes in the $20 range. A dinner for two without wine would run about $50 to $60. It's not inexpensive, but you get your money's worth. Open 6:00 P.M. to 10:00 P.M. nightly. Major credit cards accepted.

LONGHI'S
888 Front Street
Lahaina
Telephone: (808) 667-2288

Longhi's is a classic, arguably the most successful eatery on this island. Consistently popular and casually chic, it sits on Front Street like a magnet, always busy with celebrities, athletes, the hip, and the hungry. The black-and-white tiled floors add some panache; touches of koa and brass and many plants warm up the busy, sometimes frenetic ambience. Yet the fare, which changes constantly and is delivered verbally by the waiters and waitresses, never fails. One could dine at Longhi's for breakfast, lunch, and dinner for days and not tire of the menu.

Basically northern Italian, the menu features many homemade pasta dishes, which are consistently good—fresh seafood in various delectable herb preparations and imaginative vegetable dishes topped with herbs and cheeses. The menu differs every day, and only the freshest and finest ingredients are used. Longhi's is also famous for its home-baked breads and desserts, made with only the best ingredients and no shortcuts. Upstairs and downstairs dining has eased the crush some.

Moderately priced—about $40 for dinner for two. Open 7:30 A.M. to 10:00 P.M. daily. No reservations accepted. Major credit cards accepted.

LONGHI'S PIZZERIA AND DELICATESSEN
930 Wainee Street
Lahaina
Telephone: (808) 661-8128

Restaurateur Bob Longhi applied his magic touch to a pizza parlor, and it's attracting people from as far away as Wailea. Located next to the Kaiser Clinic on the main highway, it serves classic subs, hot Italian sausage and meatball sandwiches, plus custom sandwiches; the pizzas are winning favor among casual diners. There are also breads and the famous Longhi's pastries (devastating) and gourmet deli items, such as imported meats and cheeses. Imported and domestic wines and beers are available to accompany the pizza. Specialty pizzas include pesto pie, Longhi's ricotta pie, and an Italian sausage version that's quite popular.

Pizzas range from $7 for an individual size to $18 for the extra-large pizza. Open 8:30 A.M. to 11:00 P.M. daily. Major credit cards accepted.

MARCO'S RISTORANTE AND GELATERIA
844 Front Street
Lahaina
Telephone: (808) 661-8877

Marco's has emerged with a new look and rave reviews. Residents from all over Maui are actually braving Lahaina and ending up at the chic bistro, dividing their time between people watching in Mariner's Alley and pleasing their palates with pasta, pesto, calamari, homemade ravioli stuffed with crab, ono, and mahimahi and drenched in a wine cream sauce with tomato, cioppino of opakapaka, and many more temptations. The chef's allegiance to fresh and assertive herbs and his skill in preparation come through consistently. Desserts must not be overlooked, even by the most prudent. If you don't try the gelato or sorbetto of local fruits, you'll just have to return and face traffic again.

Informal and moderately priced, with entrées and specials from $7.95 to $18. Open 10:00 A.M. to 10:00 P.M. daily. Major credit cards accepted.

NIKKO
Maui Marriott
Kaanapali Beach Resort
Telephone: (808) 667-1200

The action-packed teppanyaki style of dining adds to the evening's entertainment as chefs wielding knives and poker faces descend artistically upon the prawns and scallops and beef. Nikko's well-rounded evening entails showbiz, sleight of hand, tongue-in-cheek, skill, and, of course, good food. Choices range from lobster and vegetables to sashimi and fresh shrimp, all delivered to your table from a teppanyaki grill that appears to eject the ingredients of your meal onto your plate with great gusto. Fresh vegetables are sautéed and served with the piquant Oriental sauces, and the meal is complete. Not quite complete, it turns out, until you experience the deep-fried ice cream. Ice cream is dipped into a tempura batter and then quickly fried so it's crisp outside, but still frozen on the inside. The Japanese decor all around you—the Nō masks, silk-screen paintings, and shoji doors—complete the dining experience.

About $20 to $30 per person for complete dinner of several courses. Open 6:00 P.M. to 10:00 P.M. nightly. Major credit cards accepted.

LA PEROUSE
Maui Inter-Continental Wailea
Wailea
Telephone: (808) 879-1922

La Perouse is one of the three best continental restaurants on Maui, if not the best. That may be a bold statement, but it is simply unavoidable. The chef has a ball with his creations: caviar with sour cream in a delicate pancake pouch; the famous Callaloo crabmeat soup, ambrosia with coconut milk and taro; Pacific snapper in romaine with champagne cream; peppered magret of duck with cassis; fresh island snapper with avocado, and so forth. There are many seafood specialties. The menu is imaginative, well executed, and diverse, blending enough of Hawaii's touches (taro, coconut milk, breadfruit vichyssoise, local seafood, Kula vegetables) with continental sophistication to make it a memorable meal. The room is plush and sensitively lit, with comfortable, hunter green booths and dark woods, oriental silk tapestries, and a horned candelabra from Africa. The service is efficient and cordial.

La Perouse is also consistent, having maintained an enviable reputation since its inception many years ago. Having won award after dining award, it has not rested on its laurels. The menu changes constantly and new creations keep winning favor among Maui diners. If we had to decide on a last meal on Maui, this would be it.

Expensive—entrées range from $19.50 to $29.75. Open 6:30 P.M. to 10:00 P.M. nightly except Monday. Major credit cards accepted.

PINEAPPLE HILL
Kapalua Drive, the top of the hill
Kapalua
Telephone: (808) 669-6129

The setting is a plantation home built in 1915 for D. T. Fleming, who helped bring commercial pineapple production to the island. After a glorious drive through Norfolk pines and ironwoods, you come across this picturesque home with its well-tended lawn and proceed to accept its hospitality. Recently remodeled, Pineapple Hill has new windows and paint but has lost none of its golden touches. It is still a charming, historic old home. The cocktail area has a big rock fireplace, and people love to gather on the patio near the waterfall. The Shrimp Tahitian is famous, prepared in lemon butter, garlic, and Parmesan cheese, with vegetables and salad—for $19.95. There are always two selections of the fresh catch, the most popular item on the menu. The rack of lamb, marinated in wine and herbs, has also received rave reviews, and the roasted chicken in a pineapple shell is also a winner. From the drive over there to the ambience and cuisine, Pineapple Hill is a well-rounded choice.

Casual and moderately expensive, with dinner for two at about $60. When you make reservations, be sure to ask for a window table. Open from 4:30 P.M. daily, dinner only. Major credit cards accepted.

THE PRINCE COURT
Maui Prince
5400 Makena Alanui
Makena
Telephone: (808) 874-1111

The Prince Court was the debutante of the year, arriving with much ado into the lofty heights of Maui's culinary realms. It didn't take long for this gourmet restaurant to ensconce itself at the top of the competitive heap. The cuisine is American, featuring a nouvelle touch on regional specialties, using Maui's freshest ingredients. The menu is a diner's fantasy.

First, the dining room. It's elegant and airy, with windows that look over the fabled Makena beach and the islands of Kahoolawe and Molokini. Located on the point of the V-shaped Maui Prince hotel, it is simply and tastefully decorated. Chamber music from the courtyard below wafts into the dining room as the meal unfolds in all its glory.

Consider these choices: Hawaiian prawns, lobster, and scallops in a saffron sauce with wild rice and pecans; roast wild duck breast with grained mustard and cranberry relish; steamed fresh salmon in vermouth with fettucine and fiddlehead ferns; buckwheat blinis with American caviar, chives, and sour cream. They take cuisine seriously here, and although obviously proud of their offerings, the staff does not bristle with self-importance the way they do at some of the lesser establishments.

The Sunday champagne brunch is a phenomenon, attracting visitors and local folks in growing numbers. You pay $25 for the startling choices gracing four buffet tables, accompanied by unlimited pours of Korbel. Consider these choices: marinated seaweed and ahi poke (raw tuna with seasonings); a table full of smoked, poached, and marinated seafoods; cheeses, salads, and hot fish and beef entrées artistically arranged by color, texture, and shape. Like dinner at the Prince Court, the brunch is lavish. Whether it's for dinner or brunch, the Prince Court will not disappoint. It has so much at stake and is obviously enjoying the limelight and accolades.

Expensive—entrées range from $22 to $32. Open for dinner from 6:00 P.M. to 10:00 P.M. nightly, and for Sunday brunch from 10:00 A.M. to 2:00 P.M. Major credit cards accepted.

SAM'S BEACHSIDE GRILL
505 Front Street
Lahaina
Telephone: (808) 667-4341

It's the newest mecca for the chic, a beachside restaurant that greets you with wood and wrought-iron doors, Italian marble floors, a winding koa stairway, and an immense suspended seashell, all leading up to an ocean view nonpareil and a daily changing menu of the best in American cuisine. Sam's is the Maui version of the highly successful Sam's Anchor Café in Tiburon, whose owners, Steve Sears and Brian Wilson, have taken a liking to the Valley Isle. Sam's is a big hit in Lahaina. You can drop in for anything, from deep-fried vegetables to duckling with papaya and lemon grass sauce. Only fresh ingredients are used; preparations include kiawe wood grilling, kiawe spit roasting, sautéing, and oven baking. It's a very special restaurant that appeals to all the senses.

If you'd like a black bean soup or smoked reef fish with cream cheese, it's here. If it's quail, suckling pig, or other types of game, they're here too. And if it's fish you desire, your choices are many—from lehi to striped marlin to onaga and opakapaka—whatever the fresh catch is for the day. The grills are set along the length of a wall, filling the air with olfactory pleasures.

The service matches the rest—solid, professional, and comfortable. And there's parking across the street by the baseball field—a major coup in impossible Lahaina. Casual attire. The prices: $3.50 to $7.50 for pupus (appetizers), $6.50 to $11.50 for lunch entrées, and $8.95 to $20.95 for dinner entrées. Open daily for lunch, happy hour, dinner, and for late-night drinks and appetizers; also open for Sunday brunch from 9:00 A.M. to 3:00 P.M. Major credit cards accepted.

SPATS II
Hyatt Regency Maui
Kaanapali Beach Resort
Telephone: (808) 667-7474

This Italian eatery is making a new impression on Maui diners. The word is that it's not as stuffy as it used to be. The pasta here is marvelous, from the pasta salad and pesto—the best—to a host of spicy classics. Spats is known for its veal. There are also appetizers galore, which make for excellent "grazing" before dancing, such as the warm Maine lobster salad served with warm balsamic vinegar dressing, calamari, or spinach ravioli with duck sausage. The angel hair pasta with clam sauce and the fettucine carbonara are delectable, and so is the jumbo shrimp with spicy pepper sauce. What's more, you can work it all off on the disco floor. Dine here before dancing (Spats is a popular disco too) and you'll save a $4.50 valet parking fee. Better check on their current dress code, just to be safe. Spats used to be quite rigid about that.

The price range: appetizers from $8.75; entrées $17.50 and up. Open 6:00 P.M. to 9:30 P.M. nightly for dinner, until 2:00 A.M. for cocktails, and for dancing 10:00 P.M. to 2:00 A.M. nightly except Monday. Major credit cards accepted.

SWAN COURT
Hyatt Regency Maui
Kaanapali Beach Resort
Telephone: (808) 667-7474

The setting is stunning. The fabled waterfalls of the Hyatt are framed by the ocean and highlighted with swans, flamingos, and live penguins in the Japanese gardens and ponds. There is lush landscaping; precious antiques and works of art are scattered here and there. The tables are set for fine al fresco dining, and the cuisine delivers the promise.

The tiered seating lends space and light to this arrangement. When the menu comes, it's difficult to decide what to order: smoked salmon and sturgeon on potato pancake, served with sour cream and golden caviar; escargots Swan Court, embellished with chicken, mushrooms, and zucchini in ginger-garlic butter; sautéed fresh island prawns with Mediterranean garlic sauce; curried seafood; the fresh catch with ginger butter; and the pièce de résistance, fresh island fish Eichenholz, filet of fish baked on an oakwood platter with lemon and capers. There are many, many more enticements, from roast duckling to medaillons of beef and fish and the popular grenadine of veal. If you don't overdo it, you can come back in the morning for a jogger's breakfast, an omelet, or any of dozens of selections to be savored amid the glorious gardens of the Swan Court.

Dinner is expensive, with entrées up to $28. Open for breakfast 6:30 A.M. to 11:00 A.M. Monday through Saturday and 6:30 A.M. to 1:30 P.M. on Sunday. Dinner hours are 6:00 P.M. to 10:00 P.M. nightly except Sunday. Major credit cards accepted.

....

CENTRAL, UPCOUNTRY, AND EAST MAUI

Covered here are the areas outside of west and south Maui—the central residential towns of Kahului and Wailuku, the upcountry towns of Makawao, Kula, and Paia, and on eastward to Hana, where the Hotel Hana-Maui and one village restaurant make up the town's eateries. This list contains coffee shops, delis, and fancy restaurants, arranged alphabetically. We strongly recommend that you call ahead or make reservations.

CASANOVA DELI
1188 Makawao Avenue
Makawao
Telephone: (808) 572-0220

The deli is the new kid on the block and already the darling of the upcountry set, a raging success with its homemade pastas, smoked mozzarella, Casanova pesto sauce, and other pleasures. Stefano Segre and his partners moved into town with great ideas, and soon the word was out. The deli has counters and minimal seating, but people gather there anyway for early-morning espresso and pastries. As the day wears on, the baguettes, cheeses, and pasta start moving. People love to drop by to see what's new and to stock up on premium Italian food.

Many of the best hotels on Maui use Casanova's pasta. The business has expanded into a busy, successful catering service that sells such specialties as pasta blackened with calamari ink, used with calamari and shrimp with great drama and panache. It's the in thing these days, and so is the imported Italian coffee. Whether it's a salami sandwich on the run or some pasta and pesto for later, or a party for 200 you want catered, you can't go wrong with this deli.

Inexpensive—sandwiches are about $3, lasagnas and pastas to go, $3 to $6 a pound. Open 9:00 A.M. to 8:30 P.M. Monday through Saturday, 9:30 A.M. to 7:00 P.M. Sunday. No credit cards accepted.

CHUMS FAMILY RESTAURANT
1900 Main Street
Wailuku
Telephone: (808) 244-1000

The diner concept—or revival—has taken hold in Wailuku, and Chums is a prime example. Sitting in a Naugahyde booth, you can listen to Elvis crooning "Blue Hawaii" while you dine on a varied menu of local and universal favorites. To wit: hot turkey sandwiches, teriyaki beef, saimin, burgers, oxtail soup, deep-fried seafood platter, and a winner—sea bass marinated in miso. You can find everything from Chinese noodles to chili here. The local items are "plate lunch" favorites in their fanciest form here—served on glass plates—and are part of a total package wrapped in an ersatz fifties image. It's delightful.

Casual and inexpensive, open for breakfast, lunch, dinner, and snacks with most dishes from $4 to $9. Open daily, from 5:30 A.M. to 11:00 P.M. Sunday through Thursday and until midnight Friday and Saturday. Major credit cards accepted.

HANA RANCH RESTAURANT
Across from Hana Post Office
Hana
Telephone: (808) 248-8255

Other than the restaurant at the Hotel Hana-Maui, this is the only restaurant in Hana. Thank goodness it's decent. In fact, even the takeout items at the counter outside are quite honorable, with honey-garlic chicken and the Hana Ranch burger the favorites. "Plate lunches" with macaroni salad and fried mahimahi are also available on the extensive takeout menu, and the recently introduced malasadas are a hit. Inside is an array of such things as barbecued chicken, beef short ribs, steamed vegetables, and a salad bar. The restaurant is run by the hotel, which puts a high priority on using locally grown food whenever possible, whether it's the Maui pork or fresh Hana vegetables. The restaurant is elevated, so you can see the ocean from the outdoor tables—a great way to start the day!

Buffet dinner about $15; à la carte items, $12 to $13. Take-out breakfast very inexpensive. Open from 6:30 A.M. to 10:00 A.M. for take-out breakfast daily and 11:00 A.M. to 3:00 P.M. for the luncheon buffet. The take-out service is also available 11:00 A.M. to 4:00 P.M. Dinner buffets are also offered Friday and Saturday. Major credit cards accepted for lunch and dinner buffet.

HAZEL'S CAFÉ
2080 Vineyard
Wailuku
Telephone: (808) 244-7278

Hazel's is Wailuku's best-kept secret. An oasis for local folks who start gathering there for breakfast, Hazel's is the classic local restaurant with Formica-topped tables, a jukebox, Hisashi Otsuka prints on the wall, and the best inexpensive local dishes in town. People love the daily fresh fish specials, marinated and grilled, and the beef stew and curry, or the roast chicken with its unobtrusive seasonings. (Even other restaurant owners frequent this place.)

You can have a fresh fish dinner for $5.75 or a $6 shrimp dinner, the most expensive items. Open 6:00 A.M. to 9:00 P.M. daily except Sunday. No credit cards.

HOTEL HANA-MAUI
Hana
Telephone: (800) 321-4262, (808) 248-8211

There's a story of how a hotel guest found a breadfruit in Hana and the chef here prepared it seven different ways for her. That would be just the beginning of a Hotel Hana-Maui experience, where the menu changes nightly and the freshest local ingredients are used in imaginative dishes blending Asian, Pacific, and Hawaiian traditions. That means poi pancakes for breakfast; sun-ripened Hana bananas; Hana pork sausage; curries, chutneys, and tropical fruit fillings all made from scratch; and only seafood that's selected from the catch of local fishermen who bring their bounty to the kitchen door. (No frozen fish served here.) It also means Hana slipper lobster in season, Molokai venison in season, Oahu chicken, and vegetables and herbs from the gardens planted in Hana by Rosewood, the hotel's owner. The surprises of the day combine the best of Hawaiian touches—taro, coconut, mango, banana—in untraditional ways, a very sophisticated cuisine. Expect to have a choice of fresh fish sautéed, baked, poached, steamed in bamboo, smoked over mango or guava wood, or grilled over kiawe. You could dine on quail from Texas or seaweed from Japan. What a delightful dilemma.

For hotel guests, meals are included in the hotel fee. For nonguests, breakfast is $11, lunch is à la carte, and the prix fixe dinner is $36. Reservations essential. Open 7:00 A.M. to 10:00 A.M. for breakfast, 11:30 A.M. to 2:00 P.M. for lunch, and 6:30 P.M. to 8:30 P.M. for dinner. Major credit cards accepted.

IDINI'S LIQUOR AND DELI
Kaahumanu Center
Kahului
Telephone: (808) 877-3978

It's always busy, and it offers a lot. The deli is a favorite hangout for casual rendezvous over French onion soup with Maui onions and four different types of cheeses, or lox and bagels. Sandwiches and soups are reliably good here, including the Boston clam chowder, the prosciutto sub, and croissants filled with cheeses. The salad bar features Maui vegetables. The art on the wall is by local artists. Carpeted, with cane-backed chairs and plastic utensils, it's casual and lively—a hub in Kahului where coffee lovers gather over excellent espresso. Idini's caters too.

Informal and inexpensive—prices are $3.25 to $8. Open 7:00 A.M. to 9:00 P.M. Monday through Saturday and 8:00 A.M. to 5:00 P.M. Sunday. Major credit cards accepted.

KITADA'S KAU KAU KORNER
Makawao
Telephone: (808) 572-7241

Famous for its saimin, Kitada's is a local favorite. For generations now, Kitada's has been serving what many argue is the best saimin on Maui, along with plate lunches and chicken hekka—a simpler version of sukiyaki—that regulars just adore. The star here is the elderly Mr. Kitada, who runs the show and has his own loyal fans, as he serves the dishes he's been making for generations.

Informal and very inexpensive. Open 6:00 A.M. to 1:30 P.M. daily except Sunday. No credit cards accepted.

KULA LODGE
Haleakala Highway
Kula
Telephone: (808) 878-1535

The view from the Kula Lodge takes in flower fields and a patchwork terrain. From the dining room you look out at the West Maui Mountains and feel as if you're on top of the world in your own chalet, with a fireplace behind you and the panoramic view ahead. The Kula Lodge is best for breakfast because of its view; dinner is okay but not exceptional. Eggs, French toast, pancakes, and the usual breakfast specials, including some vegetarian offerings, are the fare for early risers.

For many upcountry folks, it's a weekend ritual to stop at the lodge for Eggs Benedict with cottage fries, a great $6.75 start to the day. In the evenings, the menu changes to offer veal, steak, and fish dishes, including a $15.95 rack of lamb and a mahimahi amandine for $10.95. Open 7:00 A.M. to 3:00 P.M. Monday through Thursday and 5:30 P.M. to 9:00 P.M. Friday, Saturday, and Sunday. Major credit cards accepted.

MAMA'S FISH HOUSE
Kuau Cove
Telephone: (808) 579-9672

Watch for it just past Paia on the way to Hana. You can't miss the sign. Mama's opened in 1973 as Hawaii's first fresh fish restaurant, and it has maintained its reputation since. Set in a Polynesian decor with shells and carved woods, it looks over the ocean and is located next to the famed Ho'okipa windsurfing beach. The food here is consistently excellent, using only the freshest seafood and herbs. The choices: papio (jack trevally) in Hana ginger teriyaki, poached ono in champagne sauce, crab legs steamed in beer, Maui lobster salad, chicken in a papaya, poached moilua in lilikoi (passion fruit) hollandaise sauce, ono sautéed in mango butter, and so on. The stuffed fish Lani (baked and stuffed with shrimp) is a popular item, and the warm loaves of freshly baked bread are legendary. Mama's has achieved what many Maui eateries envy—enormous cachet in a competitive field, the perfect balance of casual and chic, and a menu that's one-of-a-kind.

Moderately expensive—dinner entrées are about $18.95 to $24.95. Open 11:00 A.M. to 4:30 P.M. and 5:00 P.M. to 9:30 P.M. daily. Major credit cards accepted.

PICNICS MAUI
30 Baldwin Avenue
Paia
Telephone: (808) 579-8021

Picnics has an enormous newsprint menu that folds out like a map to all the picnic pleasures possible. On the other side of the menu is the State's Maui Recreation Map. A Maui institution, Picnics is a popular stop for people heading to Hana, to the beach, back to Kaanapali, or even home. Many of the baskets at the polo games and crafts fairs contain picnics from Picnics. But in order to understand its popularity, it helps to have a look at its menu. First, they'll tell you, the vegetables are grown on Maui, from the Kula onions and potatoes to the Hana papayas and bananas and the tomatoes, avocados, and other greens used in its extensive menu. The choices: a picnic burger with Kula onion; the famous spinach nut burger of spinach, chopped nuts, Kula onions, sesame seeds, spices, and cheese for $3.35; the $6.95 Countryside Box Lunch of roast beef, turkey, fresh fruit, Maui potato chips, homemade chocolate chip cookie, and beverage; the $35 Executive Picnic of kiawe-broiled chicken, cheeses, wheat buns, Maui pota- to chips, papaya–macadamia nut bread, and macadamia nut chocolates; and many others. There are junior orders too, and side orders of the classics—French fries, dill pickles, cole slaw, and potato salad. Picnics takes its mission seriously—to provide the perfect accompaniment to the perfect Maui outing.

Inexpensive—burgers from $3.35 to $4.35, box lunches $6.95 and up. Open 7:30 A.M. to 3:30 P.M. daily. No credit cards accepted.

POLLI'S MEXICAN RESTAURANT
1202 Makawao Avenue
Makawao
Telephone: (808) 572-7808

101 North Kihei Road
Kihei
Telephone: (808) 879-5275

Polli's does not compromise on ingredients, a practice that has ensured quality Mexican food. A longtime favorite of vegetarian diners and Mexican food lovers, Polli's has delivered the best for years. (The Kihei restaurant is the newer one.) The nachos, smothered in melted cheese and homemade salsa; the chimichanga, a deep-fried burrito; and the usual enchiladas and chili rellenos are all very popular. So is the spicy Mexican pizza, called Sombrero Caliente. This is a haven for vegetarians who rely on healthy, lard-free ingredients. While the Makawao restaurant is warm and enclosed, the Kihei eatery takes advantage of the ocean view and whale watching at Maalaea Bay.

Moderately priced, with items from $3 to $15.95. Open 11:30 A.M. to 10:30 P.M. daily. Major credit cards accepted.

SIAM THAI
123 North Market Street
Wailuku
Telephone: (808) 244-3817

Robert Redford likes it, as do Alice Cooper, Jimmy Buffet, Bill Dana, Melveen Leed, and many others. They are among the celebrities who have found Siam Thai's fiery cuisine up to snuff. (Robert Redford's picture on the wall can't be bad for business.) In just four years, this Thai restaurant has established itself as Maui's best Thai eatery, specializing in curries that come in red, green, and yellow, and in the spring rolls and Evil Prince that are classic winners. Very popular is the massaman curry, a piquant stew with potato, onion, peanut, and Indian spices. The decor is simple, with carpets, plants, and white tablecloths covered with sheets of acrylic.

Dinner for two without liquor would cost about $20 to $25. Open 11:00 A.M. to 2:30 P.M. Monday through Friday and 5:00 P.M. to 9:00 P.M. daily. Major credit cards accepted.

SIR WILFRED'S
Maui Mall
Kahului
Telephone: (808) 877-3711

Coffee lovers go to Sir Wilfred's to stock up on Kona and Maui blends, the top-of-the-line Peabody Kona bean, and other gourmet coffee beans. And while they're wrapping them, the thing to do is to slip into the adjoining café for pesto pasta, Wailea pea salad, a bagel, perhaps, or quiche, or any one of the cheese plates or salads that make this such a sensible stop. A mecca for tired shoppers and light lunchers, Sir Wilfred's also serves croissants and other breakfast delights and spices them up with espresso, cappuccino, and other flavorful brews. Tea drinkers should try the exotic Hawaiian herb tea of mamaki and wapine, Lahaina spice, Makawao mint, and upcountry blend—pure Maui.

Inexpensive—a tuna sandwich is $4.30 and a pesto pasta salad, $3.50. Open weekdays 9:00 A.M. until 6:00 P.M., weekends until 4:30 P.M. Major credit cards accepted.

WAILUKU GRILL
2010 Main Street
Wailuku
Telephone: (808) 244-7505

It's straight from Melrose Avenue, very L.A., very Deco, in pink and gray with ceiling fans and gorgeous lamps. Yet it fits with Wailuku quite well, for Wailuku is an old, picturesque town. From its tasteful exterior to its wonderful food, the Wailuku Grill is one of the town's most pleasant stops.

You can find eggplant parmigiana, eggs Wailuku (local version of Eggs Benedict), quesadilla, ginger chicken, and grilled specials with a cross-cultural flavor. You can even find chili omelets, pizza, pesto pasta, and an occasional pasta with smoked salmon and dill cream. Basically it's an American-Italian menu with local touches, and it works. Prix fixe dinners can be arranged for groups of fifteen or more. Ice cream floats and near-beer, along with Chardonnay and Vouvray, ensure well-rounded drinks to accompany the delicious fare. Highly recommended—a star in the Wailuku dining scene.

Moderately priced, with a prix fixe dinner for $15, some pasta dishes at $9.50, and breakfast from $3 to $10. Open 7:30 A.M. to 3:00 P.M. weekdays, 8:00 A.M. to 2:00 P.M. Saturday and Sunday, and 4:30 P.M. to 8:30 P.M. Wednesday through Saturday. Major credit cards accepted.

YORI'S
309 North Market Street
Happy Valley, Wailuku
Telephone: (808) 244-3121

Yori's is a must. Only five minutes from the airport in adorable Happy Valley, it's a funky, eccentric, thoroughly charming restaurant serving American and Hawaiian food over vintage Hawaiian tunes from Yori's high-tech jukebox. Here you can dine on fried mackerel and poi while "Beyond the Reef" wafts nostalgically through the room and your eyes scan the walls for pictures of the familiar. Yori Uchida is a snapshot fanatic (he's gone through more than fifteen cameras and $11,000 in film and process-ing) and plasters every inch of wall space with pictures of customers and friends. And the food—the Hawaiian lau lau, pipikaula (braised beef), lomi salmon—is touted as Wailuku's best, prepared down-home style the way the locals love it.

Those who find Yori's inevitably return. And when they do, they make a game of finding their pictures among the jillions of the famous and the obscure covering the restaurant's walls.

Inexpensive and very casual. Open 1:00 P.M. to 10:30 P.M. daily except Monday. Major credit cards accepted.

THE BEST LUAU

OLD LAHAINA LUAU
505 Front Street
Number 118
Lahaina, HI 96761
Telephone: (808) 667-1998

This is the smallest luau in west Maui—guests always number fewer than 200—and it is the most Hawaiian of the commercial luaus. Held on a grassy area by the ocean near Whaler's Marketplace in Lahaina, it begins before sunset over views of Molokai, Lanai, and Kahoolawe. As the feast is un-veiled and the entertainment begins, guests gain a sense of what Hawaii used to be like.

The food, catered by a local Hawaiian family, includes the traditional favorites along with modern additions to the Hawaiian diet. On the side of tradition, there's kalua pig roasted in the imu, lomi salmon, poi, dried fish, opihi when available, poke (raw fish seasoned with onions and seaweed), breadfruit, sweet potato, and occasionally, crab or squid in coconut milk and other special touches. The more cautious palates will have barbecued ribs, barbecued chicken, and mahimahi to rely on. Liquor is not served, which means the tickets cost slightly less and you won't be served those watered-down Mai Tais that are the trademark of most luaus. However, guests are welcome to bring their own drinks.

The Hawaiian show begins with some Tahitian numbers acknowledging the Polynesian ancestors. Then it moves to the kahiko, ancient hula, and on to the missionary influence and the modern hula that resulted from it. The entertainers are accomplished, most of them Maui natives with a strong feel for the islands' dance and history. The evening begins at 5:30 and ends at 8:30, with a sixty-five-minute show. Luau nights are Tuesday, Thursday, and Saturday; tickets are $34 for adults and $15 for children. If you want to see the most genuine luau in west Maui, a luau of good food, entertainment, spirit, and hospitality, this is it.

NIGHTLIFE AND ENTERTAINMENT

Most of the after-dark action is concentrated in west and south Maui, primarily in Kaanapali and Wailea, the resort areas where, after the sun disappears behind Lanai and Kahoolawe, the dancers crawl out of the woodwork. Here are the clubs to watch for.

BANANA MOON
Maui Marriott
Kaanapali Beach Resort
Telephone: (808) 667-1200

The disco caters to a younger crowd that likes Top 40 contemporary music. On Tuesday, Friday, and Saturday, "teen disco," in which the under-twenty-one crowd can gather good-naturedly for sodas and dancing for a $3 admission fee, takes place from 5:30 to 8:30. Every night from 8:00 P.M. to 2:00 A.M. (except on Tuesday, Friday, and Saturday, when it starts at 9:00) the deejay turns on the mirrored lights and stacks those tapes for some serious disco dancing. There are two dance floors, lots of lights, and backgammon tables.

INU INU
Maui Inter-Continental Wailea
Wailea
Telephone: (808) 879-1922

The Inu Inu is the nicest nightclub on Maui. With its outdoor tables in the balmy sea breezes and a dance floor that jumps all night, it's a popular oasis for residents and visitors. The live band plays Top 40 dance music, some oldies, but mostly contemporary music; the small dance floor becomes jammed with enthusiastic dancers. Located just across from La Perouse restaurant, Inu Inu is comfortable even when it's packed. There are tables indoors and outdoors, and the music is usually good, pulsating at manageable decibel levels through the medium-size, well-ventilated room. Tables on the outdoor deck are the places to be on a clear night, and there are many of those in Wailea.

Open 9:00 P.M. to 1:00 A.M. nightly; no shorts or tank tops.

SPATS II
Hyatt Regency Maui
Kaanapali Beach Resort
Telephone: (808) 667-7474

People go to Spats for some serious eating or serious dancing. It's very straightforward, because there's no view or extraordinary decor. When the dining stops the nightclub opens up and, if you pass the dress code, you're on your own in a room full of music and a dressier-than-most crowd. It's a disco with a dress code: no shorts, beachwear, T-shirts, and no open-toed shoes for the men. Yet Spats is ever popular, and will probably become more so when they add Latin music to the repertoire.

Open nightly: 10:00 P.M. to 4:00 A.M. Thursday through Saturday, 10:00 P.M. to 2:00 A.M. Sunday through Wednesday.

Maui has great jazz musicians, great Hawaiian musicians, and an appreciative audience. Maui folks like to party and often think nothing of driving from Kahului to Kaanapali for an evening out. Two places to find good jazz are the Hyatt Regency and the Royal Lahaina's Ocean Terrace. Here are some of Maui's top entertainers and names to watch for when you're tripping the light fantastic.

Sal Godinez is a top musician who now plays solo on the grand piano at the new Westin Maui. With his expansive repertoire, Godinez fills the fine dining room with classical, jazz, and popular numbers spanning decades.

The Gene Argel Trio plays jazz on acoustic piano, acoustic bass, and drums. They play in the Kaanapali area and are suggested for jazz lovers.

Hawaiian music lovers must seek out the Ho'opi'i Brothers from Kahakuloa; you can't get more Maui than that. Richard and Sol sing in glorious falsetto and are absolutely adored by Maui folks. Also look for the Waiehu Sons, three popular musicians who play traditional and contemporary Hawaiian music.

Sam Ahia plays jazz on solo guitar when performing at clubs and lounges. When performing at private parties and boat cruises, his own versions of obscure Hawaiian classics come pouring out in an incredible stream of talent.

Other names to watch for are Jesse Nakooka, who does Hawaiian shows in Kihei; Buddy Fo, who plays Hawaiian music with a paniolo flair; and the group Hauula, which plays Top 40 dance music.

SPECIAL OUTINGS:
ON LAND

Bicycling

CRUISER BOB'S
505 Front Street
Lahaina, HI 96761
Telephone: (800) 654-7717, (808) 667-7717

Cruiser Bob's introduced the idea of bicycling 38 miles down from the summit of Haleakala to Paia at the coast. That was in 1983. It was a pretty daring concept, but it worked. Thousands of people have cruised down the slope, from children to seventy-year-olds who can say they've cycled down a volcano. Here's how it works: They pick you up at your hotel, outfit you in Paia, and take you on an hour-and-a-half van tour to the summit of Haleakala. You're served continental breakfast in Paia and at the summit. When the sun is up, you're matched to your bike and the cycling begins. There's a cruiser in front of the group and an escort van in the back. After hearing the wind rip through your helmet and watching the whole of Maui unfold beneath you, you arrive in Paia three hours later. Cost: just under $90, which includes a picnic lunch or a lunch break at a restaurant. You must be at least a novice bike rider, not pregnant, and at least 5 feet tall. Dress warmly, it gets cold up there.

LET'S RENT A BIKE
2580 Kekaa Drive
Kaanapali Beach Resort
Telephone: (808) 661-3037

Dollar Rent-a-Car decided that bicycles should have their day too. Before long the most complete line of bicycles to hit Kaanapali was lined up for rent. Fifteen-speed mountain bikes, twelve-speed racing bikes, bicycles for touring, cruisers, and tandems are the order of the day here, in eight different sizes for men and women and children over twelve. This is a sleek fleet; in racing bikes alone, there are six different choices. Accessories are offered too, such as bags, water bottles, and clips. Rental rates begin at about $5 an hour, with a two-hour minimum.

A suggested outing for the day, for hardy cyclists: Pack your swim gear, rent a bike, and bicycle up to Kapalua for the day. It's a 10-mile route with a spectacular view of the ocean and Molokai. When the road north meets Lower Honoapiilani Highway, traffic eases considerably and the bike lane on Highway 30, running above Lower Honoapiilani, widens to be about as roomy as a car lane. There's a catch, however; there's a substantial hill you must climb on Highway 30, with an elevation of several hundred feet. Forge on—most of the traffic will have gone on Lower Honoapiilani and you'll be left with a stupendous view on the upper road all the way to the Kapalua Bay Hotel, where you'll no doubt be ready for a swim and a hearty lunch.

MAUI DOWNHILL
333 Dairy Road
Suite 201 D
Kahului, HI 96732
Telephone: (808) 871-2155

Although Cruiser Bob's started it all, Maui Downhill has a big following too. They saw a good thing in Cruiser Bob's and started downhill cruising, providing a similar service for less. Hotel pickup, individually adjusted bikes, picture stops, continental breakfast and lunch, and windbreakers and safety gear are all included in the fee, which is $79 plus tax. It may not be as well known as Cruiser Bob's, but it's well liked for its personalized service and good guides.

Golf

KAPALUA GOLF CLUB
300 Kapalua Drive
Kapalua, HI 96761
Telephone: (808) 669-8044

There are two eighteen-hole championship courses here: the Bay Course and the Village Course. Designed by Arnold Palmer, both courses are touted for their dramatic vistas, views of the ocean, Molokai, and Lanai, and for the surrounding terrain of Cook pines, eucalyptus, and the famous Kapalua ironwoods.

The Village Course is the more challenging of the two, a par 71 course that measures 6,820 yards from the championship tees. Rising through the West Maui Mountains, it courses through two lakes and has three holes—the fifth, sixth, and seventh—that are notoriously unforgiving, passing a 40-foot drop-off, a fairway like a ski jump, and one fairway with seven sand traps.

The Bay Course is renowned for its fourth and fifth holes. The fourth doglegs past the site of a precontact Hawaiian village, to a lava peninsula cradled by white-sand beaches. The fifth hole, a par 3, requires a tee shot over one of the best snorkeling bays on the island. The $600,000 Isuzu Kapalua International, a huge nationally televised tournament, is held yearly at this stunning course.

Golfers love Kapalua for its elegance and views, but being further north than Wailea, Kapalua is windier, a big consideration for some golfers.

Fees are $50 for resort guests and $75 for nonguests, which includes green fees and the golfer's share of the cart.

WAILEA GOLF CLUB
120 Kaukahi Street
Wailea, HI 96753
Telephone: (808) 879-2966

The Orange and the Blue are Wailea's two eighteen-hole championship golf courses, sprawled across the sun-kissed south Maui resort with the slopes of Haleakala on one side and on the other, the five gorgeous white crescent beaches that border Wailea Resort. The par 72 Wailea Blue spans the upper slopes for more than 6,700 yards, with gentle inclines and four artificial lakes. Although considered the less challenging of the two, the Blue has seventy-two bunkers and is no piece of cake.

The Orange Course, also par 72, has greater texture, with slimmer fairways, more doglegs, greater inclines, forty bunkers, and one lake. It's received plenty of accolades, including being named one of the best-designed of the country's courses by *Executive Golfer* magazine. Inveterate golfers love Wailea for its ocean views, sunny weather, and kind, manageable wind conditions.

The fee is $30 for Wailea Resort guests, which includes a golf cart; for nonguests, there is a $35 green fee and a $15 fee for the golf cart. Those playing the second golf course on the same day pay only the golf cart fee the second time around.

Hiking

HIKE MAUI
Ken Schmitt
P.O. Box 10506
Lahaina, HI 96761
Telephone: (808) 879-5270

Maui's hiking possibilities are vast, even overwhelming. Haleakala is a lifetime project in itself, posing infinite options to the experienced or willing hiker. Not only do you have the crater, you have Poli Poli forest, the Kaupo Gap, and the waterfall-laden eastern flank with its myriad enticements.

Ken Schmitt's guided hikes are the Cadillac for the intrepid. An experienced and informed guide, he takes the guesswork and fuss out of planning and charts a course tailor-made for you. Some of the choices: Haleakala (of course), Oheo Gulch (Seven Pools of Kipahulu in Hana), Poli Poli Springs Recreation Area, La Perouse Bay (past Makena, south Maui) to Manawainui Gulch, Iao Valley, the Waihee Ridge Trail. These names may not mean much to you, but suffice it to say that Schmitt has access to Maui's most remote regions, knows them well, and chooses with you from about fifty trails. They're divided into eight categories: the canyons of west Maui, the coastal hikes (which sometimes include snorkeling), the ridges of west Maui, the Haleakala Crater, the waterfalls around Hana, the Waianapanapa coastal hike (in Hana), and Poli Poli. The treks last from five to twelve hours, overnight, or a week or longer with backpacks. Schmitt provides all gear and food; all you have to do is show up at his office with adequate clothing.

Important elements of Hike Maui are the detailed presentations of Hawaii's biology, geology, history, oceanography, legends, and ancient history given by a knowledgeable and earnest guide who can show you a side of Maui you could not find on your own. The five-hour hike is $50, the twelve-hour hike, $90. Fresh Maui fruit, organically grown produce, and sandwiches from a gourmet deli are the fare, except on nights when there's campfire cooking. On the overnight hikes, the cost is $300 for the first two people and $100 per person after that, all gear and supplies included. Children are welcome. If you want to jump from a waterfall into a clear pool and then relax in a hot tub in Hana, Schmitt will arrange that too.

IAO VALLEY STATE PARK
Wailuku

The 3-mile Iao Valley Road from Wailuku follows a stream into the park, passing the Kepaniwai Heritage gardens on the way. This is the valley in which Kamehameha the Great defeated the Maui forces in a bloody massacre that was said to have clogged Iao Stream with dead bodies. The name Kepaniwai means the "damming of the waters," a distant reference now overshadowed by the tranquility you feel in the valley.

As you enter the valley through its chiseled gorges, you approach the oldest part of the island, the heart of the West Maui Mountains with their 5,788-foot Pu'u Kukui. The sharp, green-covered cinder cone with its sky-reaching pinnacle is the Iao Needle, 1,200 feet from the valley floor and a sentinel to one of Maui's historic spots.

Clouds tend to drift in and out, clothing the perpendicular canyons in elusive mists and, frequently, with rain. At Pu'u Kukui, several miles inland from the Iao Valley State Park, rainfall is among the heaviest on earth— more than 400 inches a year.

This is one of Maui's most peaceful and special spots. If you drive to the end into the parking lot, you can park and follow the trail along the stream.

POLI POLI SPRINGS RECREATION AREA

This is an outing for hikers, explorers, nature lovers, and lovers of solitude. It will lead you to a remote area of Maui into the Kula Forest Reserve where, if you arrange it ahead of time, you can stay in a campground or cabin or take a 4-mile hike leading to Maui's most spectacular views. If you plan to stay overnight, we recommend that you get a cabin; it can be very cold.

The road to Poli Poli is best attempted on a four-wheel-drive or other high-clearance vehicle, but if the weather is clear, it'll be worth it. The dirt road is in poor condition, so be sure your vehicle can handle it. To get to Poli Poli, take Highway 377, also known as Kekaulike Avenue, to Waipoli Road and follow it. You will reach a 6,200-foot elevation in the Kula Forest Reserve, nearly 10 miles above Kula on Waipoli Road. You will enter a cold, majestic, remote wrinkle of Haleakala with a fertile trail system leading to the upper slopes of Ulupalakua, the mountains above the south Maui resorts.

The drive there takes you through dense thickets and planted stands of cedars, pines, cypress, redwoods, silver oak, sugi pine—towering trees that dapple the light and line the road as it curls around the park. The park embraces several trails, including the 1.7-mile Redwood Trail, the 1.7-mile Plum Trail, and the 4-mile boundary trail that crosses them. There's a three-bedroom cabin in the park that must be reserved beforehand, as well as a grassy area with picnic facilities and a campground.

It's cold for camping and even for the cabin—sometimes below freezing in the winter—but what a lovely spot for a picnic. The salutary air beats the blues away, and the wilderness surrounds like a protective cape of healing, generous green.

The cabin (without electricity) costs $10 a night for one person, with a sliding scale going down to $5 a night for six. For more information, write the Division of Parks, 54 High Street, Wailuku, HI 96793; telephone (808) 244-4354.

Horseback Riding

ADVENTURES ON HORSEBACK
P.O. Box 1771
Makawao, HI 96768
Telephone: (808) 242-7445

Frank Levinson's workaday world is the stuff of people's dreams. He takes groups of up to six people to remote waterfalls and rain forests in the mountains of Haiku. First he follows the coastline, then he leads you deep into an area where you can go swimming in a freshwater pool at the base of a waterfall. Experienced riders have an opportunity to canter; neophytes can meander at a comfortable pace. After traversing the hinterlands, you get to a pasture area where all of central Maui becomes visible and the breathtaking sweep from ocean to mountain is all that fills your view. There's one trip a day, from 10:00 A.M. to 4:00 P.M. and that includes lunch, the ride, swimming in the waterfall, and the accompanying pleasures of the ride. Cost is $95.

RAINBOW RANCH
P.O. Box 10066
Lahaina, HI 96761
Telephone: (808) 669-4991

Rainbow Ranch's riding domain is the West Maui Mountains and pineapple fields, with Molokai, Lanai, and the west Maui coastline in view. Depending on the weather and the plan, a ride to Fleming's Beach may be in store. Advanced riders may canter, but beginners may plod if they wish. Six plus the guide is the maximum number; there are four or five rides offered in the morning. Unlike the longer, more deluxe, scenic rides offered in Haiku and Haleakala, Rainbow is simpler, with shorter, more modest rides for those with less time and money. Cost is $20 to $60, depending on the length of the ride; picnic lunches may be ordered.

THOMPSON RIDING STABLE
R.R. 2, Box 203
Kula, HI 96790
Telephone: (808) 878-1910

From the 3,700-foot elevation you'll ride to, you'll look down upon central Maui and see four other islands in the distance. There's a lot of green on the slopes of Haleakala where you ride, patches of eucalyptus and pastureland. You'll ride on grassy paths that move up the mountain with panoramic views on all sides. Thompson's is the oldest horseback riding establishment on the island, having led riders around the mountain for more than twenty-five years. The rides vary, from a half-day trip to a full-day trip to overnight rides in Haleakala Crater. This is also the only stable on Maui that takes children under twelve. If there are enough people, a sunset ride can be planned too. Rides begin at $20 for an hour and a half.

Museums

MAUI HISTORICAL SOCIETY MUSEUM, OR HALE HOIKEIKE
2375-A Main Street
Wailuku
Telephone: (808) 244-3326

Nestled in the heart of Wailuku and cradled in the West Maui Mountains behind the Ka'ahumanu Church, the Maui Historical Society Museum is an excellent respository of Hawaiian tapa, quilts, and artifacts. The site is the old Bailey House, built in the mid-nineteenth century and named after Edward Bailey, a former manager of the Wailuku Sugar Company. He also painted, and it is here that his works are displayed along with the precontact artifacts sprinkled throughout this collection.

The museum houses the largest collection of Hawaiian artifacts on Maui, as well as missionary memorabilia and clothing, Hawaiian hats and woven crafts, and tapa, the bark cloth of Polynesia that reached its pinnacle of development in Hawaii. A dozen of the Hawaiian quilts from this museum were recently on display at the Great American Quilt Show in New York. The gift shop, too, is not to be missed, filled as it is with Hawaiian crafts and gift ideas not available anywhere else.

Not to be forgotten are the congenial guides and staff members, among them Maui's premier kumu hula, Hokulani Padilla. Just as she does when she performs the old and new hula of Hawaii, she will steal your heart with her warmth. The museum is open from 10:00 A.M. to 4:30 P.M. daily; suggested donation is $2.

HUI NOEAU VISUAL ARTS CENTER
2841 Baldwin Avenue
Makawao
Telephone: (808) 572-6560

Artists or would-be artists can check out this art center, located in an exquisite, tree-lined estate that now sponsors lectures and classes and contains studio space, potter's wheels, kilns, and other tools of the trade. The upcountry manse is a work of art in itself, an elegant haven for artists as well as a showcase for their work. You can attend free lectures by prominent visiting artists or take classes at reasonable rates. You can also rent studio space or a kiln, and when your artwork is done, you may even be able to display it. Ongoing exhibits at Hui Noeau are open to the public during the hours of 9:00 A.M. to 1:00 P.M. Visitors are welcome at all functions.

MAUI ART TOURS
P.O. Box 1058
Makawao, HI 96868
Telephone: (808) 878-2706

Art lovers Judy Ivec and Barbara Glassman will pick you up at your hotel in a Lincoln, greet you with a lei, and give you a copy of their book, *Maui Art*. That's the beginning of a tour that will take you into the studios of Maui's finest artists and to a nice restaurant for lunch—Mama's Fish House, perhaps. If the group has more than four people, a catered gourmet lunch with wine and caviar at one of Maui's best spots—Makena Beach, perhaps, or the Hui Noeau Visual Arts Center in Makawao—will be planned. The full-day adventure begins at 8:30 in the morning; you'll take in the studios of about four or five artists from Maui's prolific field. Some seventy artists in pottery, sculpture, raku, fabric design, wood sculpture, and other media participate in Maui Art Tours and open their homes to groups.

The day-long excursion, from pickup to lunch to the studio visits, costs $150. There's also a gallery tour, for the same price, which will take you on a swing through the art galleries of west Maui. Maui Art Tours is for those who like to see artists at work, and who don't mind shelling out for a first-class guided tour that provides an inside look at Maui's art scene.

Haleakala

No matter where you are on the large body of land called east Maui, you will be on, looking at, or touching Haleakala. This 10,023-foot mountain *is* east Maui. Its ample slopes form valleys, gulches, waterfalls, rain forests, and stark rolling deserts that cascade to the sea in all directions. With its circumference of 21 miles, its 3,000-foot-deep crater, and its land area of 19 square miles, the crater itself—the crown of Maui—is the prime spot for a view of the sunrise and the contemplation of nature's mysteries.

There are several ways to approach this mountain. You can hike through it or around it on various trails, drive around it by driving around the island, or sit at its summit viewing the cloud-tipped heights of its kingdom. Most visitors who choose the latter make the commitment of arising at 3:00 A.M., bundling up, and driving for two hours to the summit for sunrise. You can call (808) 572-7749 to get the time of sunrise. If the weather is cooperative (the sunrise can be obscured by clouds) and the light show is on, you will be treated to a kaleidoscope of pinks, golds, and reds as the crater catches fire with day. You can imagine how the demigod Maui hurled his lasso at the sun to slow its crossing and lengthen the hours of daylight. Powerful, too, is the presence of the volcano as you gaze at the cinder cones, vents, and fields of lava that make Haleakala an otherworldly place. Look for the silver-swords, the majestic plant that grows nowhere else but on Haleakala and in the Hawaii Volcanoes National Park. Even a short day hike on the Sliding Sands Trail offers the full splendor of Haleakala.

A suggested outing is to start with the sunrise—dress very, very warm-ly—and head for the actual summit a few hundred yards from the visitor center. On the way down, stop at the Kula Lodge for breakfast. The view from the lodge over the West Maui Mountains is a perfect complement to a Haleakala sunrise, for you can watch the light spread across Maui.

If you want to stay overnight in the crater you must do a lot of planning, for the three cabins on the crater floor are reserved months in advance and chosen by lottery. To reserve a cabin, write the Haleakala National Park, P.O. Box 368, Makawao, HI 96768. It takes two to three days to traverse the crater. For shorter day hikes, you might want to use the nearby Hosmer Grove as a campground. To get camping permits for Hosmer, go to the Park Headquarters from 7:30 A.M. to 4:30 P.M.

Hana

Hana is one grand special outing. If you're not staying there, you'll want to at least visit it, either by driving the full 54-mile, waterfall-laced scenic route from Kahului, or by flying in on Princeville Airways from Kahului (fifteen minutes) or from any of the neighbor islands. If you drive, be sure you go with a full day ahead of you and a full tank of gas; there are no service stations along the way.

Once you get to Hana, a new world will unfold before you and you will have your choice of quiet exploration, of horseback riding to beaches and rain forests, of hiking and swimming at Waianapanapa State Park, of picnicking, pool hopping, or seeing Hawaii's largest heiau. The following describes some of the best outings Hana has to offer.

Word has gotten out about Hana's Red Sand Beach. To get to this spectacular cove, go to the end of Uakea Road, past the Hana School and Hana Community Center. Past the intersection of Hauoli and Uakea streets is a small area where you can park your car. Follow the footpath toward the ocean, past the cemetery on the left. Watch your footing every inch of the way as you approach the cove. The narrow trail has been the demise of at least one person and has thwarted others. But when you see Red Sand Beach, you'll know why people brave the trail. The beach is the color of burnt sienna, a small inlet of red cinder ground into coarse sand. Around the cove in the nearby offshore waters, lava outcroppings shaped like a line of stalagmites form a protective barrier.

Although the beach has become a haven for nudists, it is also frequented by families, and suited sunbathers will also feel comfortable in the mixed crowd. In the sunlight, framed by red clay and black lava, the earth-red tones make the waves appear an incandescent white while they lend a dazzling, deep blue to the water. The water is clear, and in calm waters, safe for swimming. In the morning sun, as you loll and watch the turquoise of the ocean and the dramatic white of the waves against the rich redness of the sand, the beauty is unimaginable.

The Hotel Hana-Maui sponsors many activities—the weekly luau, horseback riding, and its fabled picnics—that are open to non–hotel guests as well. The horseback riding is a long-established offering that will take you across pastureland, to the uplands on the eastern flank of Haleakala, into areas where rare birds and rain forests abound. You can also ride along the shore or arrange for a special three-hour picnic ride, sunrise and moonlight rides, and a five-hour adventure of riding and swimming. During summer, the hotel also offers weekly overnight trail rides, all gear and tents provided. The hourly rates for the guided trail rides are $20 for nonguests, $17.50 for guests. For information, call the Hotel Hana-Maui, (808) 248-8211. Also offered are scuba diving and snorkeling with Hana Bay Divers, (808) 248-7289.

Also highly recommended is the ultimate cultural experience, a visit to Hawaii's largest heiau, called Piilanihale. The terraced stone platform, measuring 340 by 415 feet, was built in 1400 by Piilani, who had a forty-year reign as one of Maui's first chiefs. It was under Piilani that the Hana coast was united politically with the rest of the island after centuries of strife. The stone temple is surrounded by large breadfruit and hala trees. It is a stunning, powerful spot in which the echoes of the past still reverberate. Nearby is a cliff and a small sweep of the Hana coastline, with lava arches and a steep drop to the ocean. The heiau is inaccessible except by special arrangement through the Hotel Hana-Maui, (808) 248-8211, which can arrange a special picnic as well as a trip to the site.

The Hana Cultural Center on Uakea Road is also known as Hale O Waiwai 'O Hana, or House of Treasures. This small, single-room rural museum contains artifacts from the Hana area, from war implements to fish traps, gourds, and adzes. It is an intimate, quiet museum where you can get close to the objects: stone lamps, carved stone idols, shells, and the wood carvings and handiwork of Hana residents. There are also quilts, old photographs, and small displays in the one room, cared for by friendly volunteers. You can see how the Hawaiians made brooms out of coconut fronds and blankets and garments out of pounded mulberry bark, and you can get a feeling for the closeness of this ancient Hawaiian community. Because it's staffed by volunteers, hours may be irregular. Hours are normally 10:30 A.M. to 5:00 P.M. Monday through Saturday and 10 A.M. to noon Sunday, but it's highly recommended that you call before you go. Telephone (808) 248-8622.

The Waianapanapa State Park covers 120 acres of glorious coastline, but it's the stark black-against-blue coastline with its sea caves, dramatic lava sea arches, and black sand that really makes the magic. The volcanic coastline offers unsurpassed picnicking, fishing, hiking, and exploration. There are caves with spring-fed pools, an ancient Hawaiian coastal trail that leads to Hana, and a thriving seabird colony for nature lovers. A short hike from the parking area leads you to an ancient heiau.

Waianapanapa is one of east Maui's favorite campsites, offering a balance of wilderness and comfort in well-maintained picnic areas with a pavilion and showers, full cabins for rent, and an unforgettable beach of smooth black sand and pebbles. When conditions are right, the bodysurfing can be terrific, and the sound of the waves crackling over the pebbles adds another dimension to the surf. Offshore you may see turtles; the magic of this place is boundless.

There are housekeeping cabins for rent at $10 a person, $7 a person for two, and on down to $5 per person in a six-person group. For information on the cabins, write to the State Division of Parks, 54 High Street, Wailuku, HI 96793; telephone (808) 244-4354.

About twelve miles out of Hana heading south is the Oheo Gulch and its fabled Seven Pools, a part of the Haleakala National Park and one of the consummate stops on this coastline. Most visitors congregate at the pools below the bridge toward the ocean. The intrepid head for the hills, following the marked trail across the parking lot to the Makahiku Falls, half a mile up the hill, or to the Waimoku Falls a mile and a half up into the mountains. There are warning signs that should be heeded about flash floods and the dangers of following the stream. However, if the conditions are right (and you can ask the park ranger near the parking lot), a hike to the falls along the stream bed will rank among your top Hawaii experiences.

The Hawaiians made it a point to ask permission of the nature spirits before entering this or any other part of Hawaii's wilderness. Today many locals do the same, stopping briefly before intruding on the wilderness to offer a silent prayer.

The journey up the Oheo Stream is not for the fainthearted. You must be agile and fit to negotiate the smooth stream rocks. On the left bank heading upstream, you'll see some smooth, red, torchlike gingers growing in the shaded areas. This is awapuhi, the shampoo of the ancient Hawaiians and one of the best natural conditioners known. Squeeze the smooth, bulbous flower, and it will generously emit a clear, odorless gel. Slather it over your hair and leave it until you bathe under the waterfall. It will do wonders for your hair and soul to discover this ancient Hawaiian tradition.

Start early on your trip up the Oheo Stream, and, if you're lucky, you'll have the glorious mountain pools and the crowning glory—the Waimoku Falls and its crystalline basin—all to yourself.

Ulupalakua

All you need is a standard vehicle, a picnic lunch, and an adventurous spirit, and Ulupalakua will not let you down. Ulupalakua is on the southwestern flank of Haleakala, where the sheep and cattle of the 20,000-acre Ulupalakua Ranch graze next door to the pampered upcountry grapes. Hawaii's only vineyard, the 20-acre Tedeschi Vineyard, languishes on these slopes, cultivating the Carnelian for Blanc de Noirs champagne. Ulupalakua is upcountry Maui, with Maui's most magnificent views.

Decide whether you want a western lunch or a "strictly local" meal to go with the Tedeschi champagne. Then, depending on your decision, stop at Picnics in Paia for their Wayfarer or Executive picnic lunch (broiled chicken, sandwich, banana-nut bread, etc.), Makawao's Casanova Deli, or Wailuku's beloved Takamiya Market for the poke, fried calamari, shoyu eggplant, seaweed salad, and other gustatory adventures. Pack an ice chest and picnic blanket and head for Kula on the Kula Highway. Follow it past Kula, and about an hour and a half from the time you left Kaanapali, you should reach the Tedeschi Vineyard, where you will be greeted by a carved stone rain god dwelling quietly behind the tasting room. The rain god has been there for more than a century. Old-timers believe that when you put a maile lei and a jigger of whiskey in front of the statue, it invariably rains.

Whatever you do in the tasting room, spare yourself the pineapple wine and seek out the Blanc de Noirs. Take a look around the vineyard and then head for the road with your bottle and cooler in tow.

This is the raison d'être of this outing: the view from Piilani Highway, one of the least-traveled and most spectacular routes on the island. About three miles past the vineyard, where few people ever venture, are vast fields of Maui's most recent lava flows—young cinder cones carpeted with gentle green foliage, looking like sculptured breasts marching to the sea. All around are sweeping vistas of Molokini Island, Lanai, Kahoolawe, and the southern shoreline. The air is clean, the heights are grand. Pick a spot anywhere, and have a picnic.

SPECIAL OUTINGS:
IN AND ON THE WATER

Maui's water sports include snorkeling, scuba diving, and a mind-boggling selection of boat cruises, whale-watching cruises, sails, and fishing charters. Lahaina and Maalaea harbors are teeming with operations that will take you just about anywhere, for a price.

An activity that should not be missed is the snorkel sail to Molokini Island, a crescent-shaped crater visible from south Maui. Molokini is a marine preserve and is the prime snorkeling ground of Maui. There are dozens of boats that go out there, but the visibility and marine life are still astounding.

Another Maui specialty is whale watching; the waters off Lahaina and Maalaea are the premier spawning grounds for humpback whales in the winter months. Whale watching is a prominent activity from November through mid-April, when many year-round boat operations convert part of their business to whale-watching cruises. When the season is over, they simply reschedule their ocean activities and resume the usual dinner sails or cruises on the same boats. For this reason, the services listed under Whale Watching are reliable year-round because the operators maintain certain standards.

All whale-watching vessels are required to remain at least 100 yards from the whales. Because these sensitive creatures can be harmed, it's important to select a boat and crew who will look out for the whales' welfare while providing enlightened commentary.

Also worth remembering is the fact that you need not go out on a boat to watch whales. Often it's the closest you'll get, and the most thrilling view you'll find, but there are coastline spots on terra firma that will cost you nothing.

Just about every good beach or shoreline perch along west and south Maui can be a great whale-watching spot. Maalaea Harbor is considered especially fruitful because of the high incidence of sightings there of mothers and their calves. Along the drive from Kahului to Lahaina, there are numerous scenic overlooks along the highway that invite whale watching. A particularly good spot is Papawai Point lookout, where Maalaea Harbor ends and the long drive up the west Maui coast begins. As you're driving up Honoapiilani Highway just past Maalaea, the sign says SCENIC LOOKOUT. All along the coastline are overlooks and parks, a string of them, each with its own possibilities. Especially nice is the Launiupoko Wayside a few miles south of Lahaina.

To the north, the consummate whale-watching perch is at Black Rock promontory at the Sheraton-Maui Hotel in Kaanapali. The historic Pu'u Keka'a, as the point is called, is elevated hundreds of feet, affording a vantage point unsurpassed in Kaanapali. There's a restaurant and a lounge if you want to have a sunset drink, but what we recommend is a leisurely stroll around the gorgeous promontory.

Of course, underscoring this business of whale watching is the fact that just sitting with good intentions does not guarantee a sighting. With that in mind, you can enjoy the surroundings and the uninterrupted view of the neighboring islands simply for what they are—and if those friendly behemoths appear, so much the better.

A word of caution: Some Maui operations are called "six-pack" cruises, which means they don't take more than six people on a trip. Many of these six-packs limit the number of passengers just so they can be exempt from Coast Guard regulations, which require that any boat handling more than six people be subject to regular inspections. This is a safety feature that should be considered in your plans. Although a six-pack (such as Ed Robinson's Hawaiian Watercolors, for example), may be excellent, many of them are substandard.

Here is a list of operations that are reliable, reputable, and professional, maintaining high standards in the face of increasing competition.

Boat Cruises and Whale Watching

OCEAN ACTIVITIES CENTER
3750 Wailea Alanui
D-2
Wailea, HI 96753
Telephone: (808) 879-4485

A large, professional, and conscientious operation, the center can be relied on for Catamaran whale-watching tours, snorkel, scuba, and sunset sails, and sailing trips to Lanai. OAC operates six boats, offers hotel pick-up, has good skippers, and has been in the business for more than fifteen years.

The whale-watching tours feature one of Hawaii's top mammal researchers, Lou Herman, who comes over from Oahu annually during whale season to study their patterns. He also gives enlightened commentary on the cruises, injecting a lot of data, anecdotes, and experiences from his work on the other islands. The wide-beamed, 80-foot catamaran can carry up to eighty people with ample deck space. On a good day when the cat's at rest, the whales come to you. Whale watching costs $20 for two hours, $10 for children, with a portion of the revenues going to the Kewalo Marine Lab, a research facility of the University of Hawaii where Herman is a leading researcher.

OAC's new vessel, called the *Manute'a*, is receiving rave reviews for its excursions to the island of Lanai. Half-day, five-hour, and full-day trips are offered, departing from Lahaina Harbor daily at 8:00 A.M. The sail includes a stop on Lanai with a land tour and lunch at the Hotel Lanai. A prime feature of this trip is the noontime entertainment on Lanai, where beautiful Hawaiian dancer Lehua Pate and partner Sol Kaho'ohalahala perform the dances and chants of the island. Many visitors say they are the highlight of their trip. The half-day excursion to Lanai costs $55, with $85 for the full day.

Although OAC is known for its whale watching in the winter, it's also the top snorkeling outfit year-round, operating twelve-passenger, twin-diesel boats for snorkeling as well as a 46-foot catamaran, the *Kai Kanani*, that departs right from Makena Beach for Molokini Island. Snorkel tours cost $34.95 to $55; for a two-tank scuba dive with lunch, it's $85.

PACIFIC WHALE FOUNDATION
101 North Kihei Road
Kihei, HI 96753
Telephone: (808) 879-8811

The foundation is a nonprofit organization devoted to studying whales and educating the public. They operate a 53-foot twin diesel vessel, the *Whale I*, on daily two-hour cruises from November through the end of April. Naturalists and those who have studied whales are on board to answer questions and narrate. The tour costs $25.

PWF provides free lectures on whales at west and south Maui hotels, sometimes featuring guest speakers and prominent whale researchers. One of the organization's pet projects is the restoration and assembling of a humpback skeleton found off Kahoolawe, which will be on display in a shelter being built in Wailea. When it is assembled and displayed next to the recovered bones of a two-month-old calf that washed ashore, it will be the only humpback skeleton on display in Hawaii, and it will be free to the public.

The foundation is somewhat of a watchdog as well, setting its sights now on the preservation of Molokini Island, which now accommodates some 200 snorkel tours a week and as many anchorages. PWF is promoting efforts to minimize anchor damage or initiate some environmental controls on this beautiful marine preserve.

TRILOGY EXCURSIONS
P.O. Box 1121
Lahaina, HI 96767
Telephone: (808) 661-4743

Trilogy is the other reliable operator that offers trips to Lanai. Their Discover Lanai tours depart daily. There are three boats: a 40-foot trimaran, the *Trilogy III*; a 50-foot trimaran; and a 55-foot catamaran. The all-day cruise departs at 6:30 A.M. and begins with a continental breakfast. At Lanai, guests have a chance to snorkel in the marine sanctuary of Hulopoe Bay and have a teriyaki chicken picnic lunch. The largest vessel holds forty. The trip also includes a guided van tour of Lanai. Cost is $110 plus tax; $55 plus tax for a child.

WINDJAMMER CRUISES
P.O. Box 218
Lahaina, HI 96761
Telephone: (808) 667-6834

Whale watching is conducted from December through May on the *Coral See*, which guarantees that if you don't see a whale, you can go out again free. A naturalist and a marine biologist are on board as narrators, which lends infinite cachet to the cruise. The *Coral See* is a 53-foot power vessel that also conducts daily snorkel trips to Molokini. One nice touch about the whale-watching cruise is that part of the revenues go toward an internship program in whale research. Cost is $20 for the two-and-a-half hour trip.

Windjammer also operates a 65-foot, three-masted schooner for sunset dinner cruises. This is a tourist classic for west Maui visitors, a waterborne foray into the famous Lahaina sunset. The $39 dinner includes entertainment, an open bar, and a prime rib or teriyaki chicken dinner.

Fishing

THE EXCEL
P.O. Box 146
Makawao, HI 96768
Telephone: (808) 661-5559

The Excel specializes in bottom and sportfishing and has an excellent record among fishermen. There are two large boats, 43 feet and 50 feet, plus a 35-footer that handles sportfishing exclusively. The charters are personalized; you can arrange for food, pick your course, and throw a party while you troll for ahi.

All bait and tackle are provided, including Penn International tackle (top of the line) and live bait as well. A maximum of twelve people are allowed on a fishing trip. To avoid tangled lines, trolling is rotated, with six people active at a time.

There are four-, six-, and eight-hour fishing trips, on a share or private basis. The least expensive, a four-hour bottom-fishing combination boat, costs $65 on a share basis. An eight-hour, exclusively sportfishing day costs $125 on a share basis. Private charters range from $325 for a smaller boat for four hours to $1,200 for the 43-foot or 50-foot Deltas. You could choose to fish, snorkel, or go to Lanai if you wish. Excel is known for its professionalism, and for its crew, which knows the island waters well.

Scuba Diving

CENTRAL PACIFIC DIVERS
780 Front Street
Lahaina, HI 96761
Telephone: (808) 661-8718

Central Pacific Divers has been in business since 1971 and is the oldest and most established dive operation on Maui, highly regarded in the scuba community. Their two boats, including the 50-foot *Alaskan*, are twin diesels, the best for scuba diving.

Nearly all the dive masters are instructors in a staff that averages fifteen years of diving, eight years of teaching, and five years with the company. They love the Maui waters and will take good care of you.

There are two trips daily, to Lanai or Molokini Island, departing from Lahaina Harbor. The Molokini dive, usually a two-tank dive, costs $69. The three-tank dive costs $82, which includes continental breakfast, lunch, and cold drinks. A $3 charge is also levied for rental of regulator and wet suit.

LAHAINA DIVERS
710 Front Street
Lahaina, HI 96761
Telephone: (808) 667-7496

The other top outfit is Lahaina Divers, which has been in business for ten years. Their dive trips go to Lanai and Molokini as well. They operate a 43-foot twin-diesel Delta and charge $69 for the trip to either island, with a $3.50 rental fee for wet suits and other gear. (Tanks and weights are included in the fee.) The boat departs at 7:00 A.M. and is back by 12:30.

The afternoon trip usually explores west Maui, and it's popular for introductory dives. A $57.50 fee will cover two dives for certified divers in the shallow reefs off the western coastline. Night dives are also offered on Monday and Thursday, when the intrepid can be seen gathering at the local reef. Cost is $57.70.

Snorkeling

SNORKEL MAUI
Ann Fielding
P.O. Box 1107
Makawao, HI 96768
Telephone: (808) 244-7572

Marine biologist Ann Fielding will give you briefings on marine and coral life, provide refreshments, pick a spot, and snorkel with you. Formerly with the Waikiki Aquarium and the Bishop Museum, she's well trained in tropical marine life, knows Maui's waters very well, and leads the most educational snorkeling trips on the island.

No more than seven people are allowed on an outing, so there's always personalized service. The snorkeling site is determined by the weather that day, but the sites are always rewarding. During summer, when the northern waters are calm, she may take you to Honolua, a marine preserve on the northern coastline. During winter, the southern shore—Ulua, the Ahihi Kinau Marine Preserve—beckons with its myriad tropical reef fish.

The biggest advantage, however, is the orientation Fielding gives to tropical marine life in Hawaii. She'll tell you what you can expect to see, what can hurt the marine life, what their patterns are. She'll also take you to places you might not get to otherwise. The trip is either one long snorkel or two shorter ones of about forty-five minutes each. All gear is provided, even air mattresses and vests for beginners. And she's the only one on Maui who will snorkel closely with you. Cost is $30.

Windsurfing

Maui's Ho'okipa Beach is regarded as the best windsurfing spot in the world. Around it has emerged a growing community of windsurfing businesses, rentals, shops, and instructors to cater to the growing market. Herewith, the best:

HAWAIIAN ISLAND WINDSURFING
460 Dairy Road
Kahului, HI 96732
Telephone: (808) 871-4981

They have the biggest rental fleet for windsurfers, and the most complete line of accessories. They have a little of everything—rentals, custom boards, sails, and accessories galore.

HAWAIIAN SAILBOARDING TECHNIQUES
Alan Cadiz
P.O. Box 1199
Paia, HI 96779
Telephone: (808) 579-9267

Cadiz is one of the top-ranking sailboarders in the country, a leading competitor, who is now offering advanced instruction in windsurfing at Kanaha Beach on Maui's north side. Kanaha generally has flat water and good wind, making it ideal for windsurfing and teaching.

Cadiz prefers to teach the advanced sailors in water starting, wave sailing, slalom sailing, and his personal specialty, jibing. He's also the only instructor on Maui using color video as an instructional aid. He'll tape you, then set up his color monitor on the beach so all can see what you're doing. He's got a huge word-of-mouth reputation and gives private lessons while most of the other operations give group instruction. Cost of a lesson ranges from $35 an hour to $80 for one three-hour lesson that includes the videotape feedback.

HI-TECH SAILBOARDS
51 Baldwin Avenue
Paia
Telephone: (808) 579-9297

230 Hana Highway
Kahului
Telephone: (808) 877-2111

The best, newest, fanciest, state-of-the-art boards are available at Hi-Tech Sailboards, one of the big names in the international windsurfing scene. The fancy stores are brimming with the latest new boards to buy or rent—the Sharper Image of the sailboarding set.

MAUI WINDSURF CO.
520 Keolani Place
Kahului, HI 96732
Telephone: (808) 872-0999

They teach, rent sailboards, sell sails, boards, equipment, and accessories. One of Maui's better known operations, it has a large fleet of boards for rent and offers windsurfing instruction (mostly group instruction) to beginning and advanced sailors.

BEACHES

These are Maui's best beaches, listed from north to south along the west and south shores of the island. If you wish more information on Maui beaches, John Clark's *The Beaches of Maui County* is the definitive book on Valley Isle beaches.

Honolua Bay

You're on your own here, there are no comforts. Honolua has no parking or restrooms, but the waters offshore are a marine preserve with some of the best snorkeling on the island. The boulder-and-sand beach is a few miles north of Kapalua on the Honoapiilani Highway. You can often see the surfers' cars lining the road; there are some trails leading to the beach. In spite of its rockiness and the occasional murkiness caused by stiff north shore winds, Honolua is popular for swimming, surfing, snorkeling, and bodysurfing when the conditions are right.

Mokoleia

Also known as Slaughterhouse, Mokoleia is a gorgeous white-sand bay popular in the summer months. It adjoins Honolua Bay and forms a part of the conservation district; you cannot fish or remove any marine life. There's swimming, snorkeling, and bodysurfing here, but as with all north-shore beaches, the shoreline is subject to extreme seasonal shifts because of sand erosion. Watch for the line of cars on Honoapiilani Highway about a mile past Fleming Beach Park; here the trails lead down to Slaughterhouse. As with Honolua, there are no restroom facilities.

Fleming Beach Park

This is not to be mistaken for Fleming Beach, which is what some folks call Kapalua. Fleming Beach Park, at the base of the Kapalua Golf Club's sixteenth hole, is a wide beach with waters that are popular for surfing, bodysurfing, swimming, and snorkeling. There are public access, parking, restroom, and picnic facilities. Fleming Beach Park is one of west Maui's favorites, but you must exercise caution because of occasional riptides.

Kapalua

The beach at Kapalua has the best near-shore snorkeling on the island. The protective arms of lava that reach out to the sea on both sides make this the safest of west Maui's beaches. This is the beach often called "Fleming" by local residents, but it should not be confused with the beach park. The clear, mostly calm waters and the protective reef barrier make this a wonderful spot to swim and snorkel. To get there, drive north on Honoapiilani Highway to the Kapalua Resort. A parking lot and right of way are not far from the hotel.

Black Rock Promontory

Pu'u Keka'a, or the Black Rock Promontory on which the Sheraton-Maui sits, has the best swimming and snorkeling on the 3-mile Kaanapali Beach. The waters are brilliant and clean, protected by the protruding promontory and swept clean by the currents. Many snorkelers can be seen exploring the waters beneath and around the cliff, known to the ancients as the jumping off point for souls of the deceased. You can rent snorkeling gear at the Sheraton, but public parking is about a five- or ten-minute walk away from the hotel.

Keawakapu

This is a beautiful, half-mile-long white-sand beach between Kihei and Wailea. Popular for swimming and snorkeling, Keawakapu has a sandy bottom, with lava outcroppings at each end of the beach. Although there's parking and a public right-of-way, there are no restroom facilities. Maui residents love Keawakapu, but even though it is stunning, the famous Kihei winds can blow here too. An artificial reef made of car tires and concrete was planted offshore of Keawakapu, which enhanced marine life in the area. The state built this underwater habitat to fortify the declining reef life, which resulted in dramatic increases in fish and marine life, according to the state's latest survey of the area.

The Wailea Beaches

Of all Maui's beaches, Wailea's five offer the best facilities, access, and broad, white-sand crescents popular for all types of beach goers. You can find good snorkeling, bodysurfing, and swimming here. And you'll discover a good mix of Maui residents and visitors. On weekends, many Kahului and Wailuku residents drive over to partake of the sunny pleasures. Of the five Wailea beaches, Ulua is said to have the best snorkeling. It's rumored that Lloyd Bridges (remember "Sea Hunt"?) once declared Ulua the best snorkeling spot on the coast. It is also busy, however, and sometimes crowded. The other four—Wailea, Mokapu, Polo, and Keawakapu—are great beaches as well. The beaches are clearly marked, with paved parking, access, and well-kept bathroom facilities.

Makena

Makena's real name is Oneloa Beach, but you never hear it referred to as anything but Makena. The long, graceful, white-sand curve was immortalized in the hippie days, when the gentle environment of the area invited paradise seekers to squat. Today there are only kiawe groves and white sand, and two beaches still loved by Mauians: Big Beach and Little Beach. Little Beach is Maui's nude beach, a petite curve a short hike over the hill from Big Beach. Big Beach is wide, expansive, and remote enough to offer a degree of privacy. There's neither paved parking nor restrooms, but the swimming, snorkeling, and bodysurfing are good. To get there, follow Makena Alanui past the Maui Prince and follow the narrowing dirt road to the sea. Big Beach is wide, and there are many places to park near the kiawe grove.

Waianapanapa

The black-sand beach at the Hana's Waianapanapa State Park is called Pailoa. It's not ideal for swimming, but it is a beautiful beach in Hana, where beaches do not abound. The shoreline of the park is volcanic and rugged, but there are sea caves, lava tubes, ancient trails, and an old coastal trail to explore.

Ho'okipa

The world-famous windsurfing beach, Ho'okipa, is located off the Hana Highway near Paia. Ho'okipa is on Maui's northern shore and is the best spectator beach on the island. Waves reach 10 feet in the winter; with the typically strong wind conditions in the area, all the makings of spectacular windsurfing, including the best surfers, are here. There's a white-sand beach and full restroom facilities, paved parking, and picnic facilities. When a windsurfing contest is on, colorful sails dot the beach like a handful of confetti.

SHOPPING

....

WEST AND SOUTH MAUI

Maui is a shopper's paradise. You can shop till you drop here, whether it's for Kula onions or Maui potato chips or designer art-to-wear at exorbitant prices. But shopping on Maui has its regional qualities, and it helps to know what's good where. As a rule, you'll pay more for a purchase in a resort area than in a residential mall where local folks shop. You pay for convenience too. Understandably, most people wouldn't dream of driving from Kaanapali to Kahului to save a few dollars on a beach towel.

These are the west and south Maui shops in all categories, listed alphabetically. Some of them are one of a kind and dazzling, with prices to match. The truth be known, we like shopping in Kahului, where a few good boutiques and shops (except in shoes) provide satisfying items for most needs. See also Shopping: Central, Upcountry, and East Maui, which follows this section.

THE BIKINI COMPANY OF LAHAINA
858 Front Street
Lahaina
Telephone: (808) 667-2142

A division of the Hobie Company, The Bikini Company attracts a young, hip surfing crowd that buys Day-Glo zinc oxide to go with their surfer jams or mix-and-match bikinis. Tops and bottoms are sold separately here too, in a selection of colorful tropical lines of swimwear for men and women.

Open 10:00 A.M. to 6:00 P.M. daily. Major credit cards accepted.

BLUE GINGER DESIGNS
658 Front Street
Lahaina
Telephone: (808) 667-7007

Lahaina Cannery
Lahaina
Telephone: (808) 667-5433

Whaler's Village
Kaanapali
Telephone: (808) 667-5793

Distinctive tropical batiks from Singapore fill this shop with dresses, muumuus, aloha shirts, children's clothing, handbags, hapi coats, and the like. Although they're not made in Hawaii, there's a tropical feel to the well-made, all-cotton, handmade clothing. Women will find sundresses and jumpsuits along with potholders, place mats, napkins, visors, and belts, which appear in the distinctive Blue Ginger motifs.

Open 9:00 A.M. to 9:30 P.M. daily. Major credit cards accepted.

COLLECTIONS LIBERTY HOUSE
Hyatt Regency Maui
Kaanapali Beach Resort
Telephone: (808) 667-7785

This is a large, cavernous store filled with clothes and accessories for the adventurous. It's much more tasteful than the typical resort shop, with international labels in swimwear, sportswear, handbags, and jewelry. The clothes go from casual to dressy, from silk dresses to avant-garde, futuristic earrings and handbags that cost more than most dresses. Clothes for men and women.

Open 9:00 A.M. to 10:00 P.M. daily. Major credit cards accepted.

DISTANT DRUMS
The Kapalua Shops
Kapalua
Telephone: (808) 669-5522

One of the more interesting shops in west Maui, Distant Drums is an exotic amalgam of artifacts and gift items from Bali, Asia, and the Pacific Basin. Spears, spirit masks, and shields from New Guinea mingle with the carved wooden Balinese frogs and intricate baskets made with fine workmanship. If you're looking for Balinese shadow puppets or fine silver handcrafted earrings, you'll find them here too, in all price ranges.

Open 9:00 A.M. to 6:00 P.M. daily. Major credit cards accepted.

FOR YOUR EYES ONLY
The Wharf   **Wailea Shopping Village**
Lahaina   **Telephone: (808) 879-0545**
Telephone: (808) 667-9188

Lahaina Market Place
Telephone: (808) 661-8167

They specialize in sunglasses and eyewear, and they take their job seriously. State-of-the art sunglasses line the counters, with a full array of patented lenses to protect the eyes from harmful rays. This shop is recommended for those seeking protective eyewear for the powerful Maui sun. You'll pay more here than at the drugstore, but you're sure to have better protection. Vuarnet, Revo, Bollé, Pro, Rayban, Suncloud—all the name lines are here.

Open 9:00 A.M. to 9:30 P.M. daily. Major credit cards accepted.

LAHAINA PRINTSELLERS
Whaler's Village
Kaanapali
Telephone: (808) 667-7617

The Wharf,
Lahaina
Telephone: (808) 661-3579

Rare maps, rare map originals, exquisite prints and paintings of Hawaii's endangered wildlife, and the largest collection of engravings and antique maps in Hawaii are only some of this gallery's offerings. The shop is bathed in a sepia tone reflecting off its hangings of wood-framed, antiquated maps from the eighteenth and nineteenth centuries. There's a map of Hawaii by William Bligh from the historic journey he took with Captain Cook in 1778. Items are in all price ranges, and you don't have to be a cartographer to enjoy this journey across oceans and time. The larger gallery is in Lahaina.

Open 8:30 A.M. to 10:30 P.M. daily in Kaanapali, 9:00 A.M. to 5:00 P.M. in Lahaina. Major credit cards accepted.

LONGHI FINE CLOTHING
The Kapalua Shops
Kapalua
Phone: (808) 669-5000

Longhi's is high fashion for the high rollers: clothes for movie stars and those who like to be seen. More Rodeo Drive than Maui, Longhi's brims with art to wear and the more obscure and adventurous couture labels of the world. A pair of shoes here could pay for a semester of college, but you can be sure no one else on the block would have them. Italian silks and leathers, Japanese couture, Willie Von Rooy triangle sweaters, beaded leather handbags, fantasy dresses and day wear can be found among this mind-boggling array. The buyers travel the world for out-of-the-ordinary pieces that fit their bold fashion statement. There is no other shop like it in Hawaii.

Open 9:00 A.M. to 6:00 P.M. Saturday through Tuesday, to 8:30 P.M. Wednesday through Friday. Major credit cards accepted.

MAUI'S BEST
Wailea Shopping Village
Telephone: (808) 879-4734

Maui Marriott
Kaanapali
Telephone: (808) 661-7678

If you go to only one shop on Maui, this should be it. Maui's Best ingeniously honed in on Maui's multifarious specialties, from Kula onions to protea wreaths to Hawaiian quilt pillowcases and gorgeous hand-painted silk scarves. Everything, from the Makawao teas to the handwoven baskets, is made on Maui. There are books, candies (Island Princess, the store's own label, and not to be missed), bamboo nose flutes, Maui potato chips, and koa cutting boards. The shop is discriminating yet thorough, embracing the many crafts, comestibles, and arts that abound on the Valley Isle.

Open 9:30 A.M. to 5:30 P.M. Monday through Saturday and 11:00 A.M. to 5:30 P.M. Sunday in Wailea; 9:00 A.M. to 10:00 P.M. daily at the Maui Marriott. Major credit cards accepted. (See also Shopping: Central, Upcountry, and East Maui, for their other branch.)

SANDAL TREE
Hyatt Regency Maui
Kaanapali
Telephone: (808) 661-3495

As far as we know, this is one of the few places on Maui, if not the only, where one can enjoy fashionable footwear without paying platinum card prices. A refreshing selection of attractive and affordable shoes, sandals, and thongs for men and women can be found here, from made-in-Brazil versions to handmade Italian leathers.

Open 9:00 A.M. to 10:00 P.M. daily. Major credit cards accepted.

SILKS KAANAPALI
Whaler's Village
Kaanapali
Telephone: (808) 667-7133

Nowhere are hand-painted garments more tired than on Maui, the former hippie haven in which the hand-painted look took hold and then set in like a pit bull, never to let go. At Silks Kaanapali, you can forget your aversion to hand-painted fabrics and relax in a world of fluttering colors and gentle beauty. Local artists such as Gaye Pope imbue scarves, dresses, shirts, and accessories with the pristine colors of Hawaii by hand-painting silks. There are raw silks, Japanese silks, silks in handbags and tunics, with primitive patterns and ethereal patterns—the whole gamut of looks for elegant women of good taste. The quality is matched by the costume jewelry, a collection of embellishments in avant-garde looks and techniques.

Open 9:30 A.M. to 9:30 P.M. daily. Major credit cards accepted.

SUITS ME
Maui Marriott
Kaanapali
Telephone: (808) 667-6132

The selection of swimwear is broad enough to include the average figure, not just the reed-thin, nubile bodies that frequent the surf shops. The selection, then, is ample, with bikinis and maillots for all types of bodies and all ages. Some labels: Too Hot Brazil, Gottex for Women, Sassafrass, Raisins. For men there are sedate swim trunks and wild-printed surf shorts, and for the unprepared, beach towels.

Open 9:00 A.M. to 9:00 P.M. daily. Major credit cards accepted.

WOW SWIMWEAR
Azeka Place
Kihei
Telephone: (808) 879-1448

WOW is known for its large selection of swimwear—the largest on the island—and for its thoughtful gesture of selling tops and bottoms separately. That way, if you have a size 4 top and a size 12 bottom, you can still outfit yourself in a bikini and make a splash at Ulua Beach. SuHana, Zanzara, and other local designs can be found in a dizzying selection of prints, sizes, and styles for men, women, and children. Sunglasses and visors are here too, and for the amply endowed, D-cup swimwear and cuts that reach the navel.

Open 8:30 A.M. to 9:00 P.M. weekdays, 10:00 A.M. to 7:00 P.M. Saturday and Sunday. Major credit cards accepted.

....

CENTRAL, UPCOUNTRY, AND EAST MAUI

Central Maui is where local residents shop. Here you can find a great selection of most things at nontouristy prices. Stores are listed alphabetically.

ARTFUL DODGERS FEED 'N READ
55 Kaahumanu
Kahului
Telephone: (808) 871-2677

The counter serves coffee, sandwiches, desserts, and baked goods. The shelves hold used books, new books, and records. A good selection of Hawaiian books and new releases can be found among the more than 30,000 used books and records that grace the shop. It's funky, eccentric, and wonderful. You can read *Yoga of the Vacuum Tube* or old Audubon Society and *Geo* magazines over carrot cake and coffee, or you can peruse the U.S. Department of Interior Geological Survey maps. Art by local artists hangs in displays that change monthly, which is only part of why people love to hang out here.

Open 7:30 A.M. to 8:00 P.M. weekdays, 9:30 A.M. to 8:00 P.M. Saturday, 11:00 A.M. to 7:00 P.M. Sunday. Major credit cards accepted.

COLLECTIONS
3677 Baldwin Avenue
Makawao
Telephone: (808) 572-0781

The shop is a delightful conglomeration of soaps, sportswear, costume jewelry, baskets, candies, and miscellaneous items of good taste. Not affiliated with the Liberty House Collections resort shops, this one has been in Makawao for over ten years and has a loyal following among Maui residents. Reasonably priced knit dresses, Caswell-Massey soaps (where else can you find them in Hawaii?), hats, fins, sweatshirts, Putamayo cotton dresses, dolls, clothes made in Cyprus, bamboo tables, Chinese embroidered slippers, Maui sachets, and Noa Noa dresses made in Guam make this a browser's paradise. It's small and manageable, with a friendly staff that delights in the merchandise.

Open 9:00 A.M. to 6:00 P.M. Monday through Saturday. Major credit cards accepted.

HALE HOIKEIKE GIFT SHOP
2375-A Main Street
Wailuku
Telephone: (808) 244-3326

Also called the Maui Historical Society Museum or the Bailey House, the museum is a worthy stop for anyone interested in Hawaiian history and artifacts. (See Special Outings: On Land.) It also has a gift shop that's the best place to find a good cross-section of Hawaiian crafts, from Maui lauhala to Maui teas and sandalwood. Hawaiian tapa purses are rare in Hawaii today, but you can find some here. Wesley Sen, who gets Hawaiian *wauke* (paper mulberry) from Maui, beats the bark into tapa, dyes it with Hawaiian dyes, and makes his crafts available at this shop, the only one on Maui to carry them. This is not a large gift shop, but it fairly sings with the spirit of Hawaii.

Open daily from 10:00 A.M. until 4:30 P.M.. Major credit cards accepted.

HASEGAWA GENERAL STORE
Hana
Telephone: (808) 248-8231

Immortalized in a song made famous by Don Ho, Hasegawa's is a Maui institution. A dusty, cluttered general store, it boggles the mind with its wares—plates, old fishhooks, books, snorkels, Maui potato chips, T-shirts, pickled vegetables, horseshoes, screws, wheel barrows, and a million other items—all jammed into this friendly chaotic store. Aside from the Seven Pools and the Hotel Hana-Maui, Hasegawa's is Hana's most famous landmark.

Open 7:30 A.M. to 6:00 P.M. Monday through Saturday, 8:30 A.M. to 3:00 P.M. Sunday. Major credit cards accepted.

LIGHTNING BOLT
55 Kaahumanu
Kahului
Telephone: (808) 877-3484

Casual active wear is the genre here—everything you'd need for a day of boogie boarding, surfing, swimming, or just going to lunch at Marco's. Walking shorts, tank tops, T-shirts, dress shirts, and aloha shirts—they're all here for men and women, in local and mainland designs. Swimwear includes SuHana, Raisins, Too Hot Brazil; and for the men, Patagonia shirts and Quicksilver surf shorts. A colorful array of surfboards adds even more dimension.

Open 10:00 A.M. to 5:00 P.M. Monday through Thursday and Saturday, until 6:00 P.M. Friday, and 11:00 A.M. to 3:00 P.M. Sunday. Major credit cards accepted.

MAUI CRAFTS GUILD
43 Hana Highway
Paia
Telephone: (808) 579-9697

The quality arts and crafts of Maui are displayed here, from raku pieces to handwoven belts and accessories, to beautiful handmade boxes of sugi pine and other woods from Maui. Koa mirrors, bamboo vases, coconut frond weavings, and basketry mingle sweetly with the ethereal silk scarves by Lady Di. Ask about their silk-screened pareus, exotic and useful for beach, picnics, and housewear. The old wooden storefront has been transformed into an attractive two-floor gallery brimming with quality gifts. All items are by Maui artists who are selectively screened. And they'll ship anywhere.

Open 9:00 A.M. to 6:00 P.M. daily. Major credit cards accepted.

MAUI'S BEST
Kaahumanu Shopping Center
Kahului
Telephone: (808) 877-2665

This is the original of the highly successful chain specializing in Maui's best. To begin with, you can't get past the door without smelling and coveting some Island Princess candies made at the front window: macadamia nut brittle, caramel corn, white chocolate–coated Kona coffee beans, and a sinful assortment of toothsome sweets. And the fudge, made only sporadically, could cause a minor revolution. Inside is a distinctive selection of woven baskets, handwoven shawls, hand-carved woods, batiks, hand-painted silks, teas, barbecue sauces, and myriad other items—all made on Maui. There are two other shops in west Maui, but this was the first. The quality consistently shows good taste and discrimination.

Open 9:00 A.M. to 5:30 P.M. Monday through Wednesday and on Saturday, until 9:00 P.M. Thursday and Friday, and 10:00 A.M. to 3:00 P.M. Sunday. Major credit cards accepted.

MAUI SWAP MEET
Kahului Fairgrounds
Puunene Avenue
Kahului

Every Saturday from 8:00 A.M. on, Maui residents engage in the weekly ritual of the Swap Meet. The fairground teems with shoppers picking up local vegetables and fruit, leis and flowers, handmade crafts, and second-hand goods. The swap meet is a local institution. The favorite shopping spot of those in the know, it's also for sensible bargain hunters in hot pursuit of the freshest, best, and most reasonably priced produce.

No credit cards.

MIRACLES UNLIMITED
12 Market Street
Wailuku
Telephone: (808) 244-5307

Crystal balls, crystal wands with gemstones, crystal-tipped kaleidoscopes, wands tipped in crystal with rose quartz and agate—you get the picture, this is fairyland. Give yourself some time here. It's a healing environment with astoundingly beautiful gems, high-quality crystals, and crystal-embellished objects. Tourmaline, amethyst, topaz, lapis, and other gems are in abundance, trimmed in gold and silver and illuminating the counters. Don't let the airy-fairy environment intimidate you. Miracles is a shop worth exploring, with friendly help and a positive feeling to accompany the healing stones.

Open 10:00 A.M. to 5:30 P.M. Monday through Saturday. Major credit cards accepted.

TIGER LILY
55 Kaahumanu Avenue
Kahului
Telephone: (808) 871-2465

Tiger Lily is where the local cognoscenti, the well-dressed women of Maui's social set, shop to their heart's content. These are the women who wear designer clothes and go to polo meets, who have good taste and pocketbooks to match. The offerings: Michele Lamy, Bis, Nicole Miller, Laise Adzer designs for women; handbags and accessories; made-on-Maui potpourris and gift items; delicate soaps and sachets. There are upscale sweaters, silk dresses, the latest in bejeweled belts. Clothing ranges from shorts to fine dresses, and prices range from about $50 to $300.

A tasteful, elegant shop, open 10:00 A.M. to 6:00 P.M. daily except Sunday. Major credit cards accepted.

UPCOUNTRY DOWN UNDER
3647 Baldwin Avenue
Makawao
Telephone: (808) 572-7103

The selection here is of fine cold-weather clothes from New Zealand, ranging from sheepskin slippers to sweatshirts and gorgeous hand-knit sweaters. It seems like an odd concept for Hawaii, except when you realize it gets cold on Haleakala, Mauna Kea, Kokee, and all the upcountry slopes in the state. So Peter Marshall decided to open up shop in a colder area, and Makawao was it. Very popular are items from the Australian Outback collection, including miners' workshirts out of silk, handsome drovers' men's coats in oilskin and denim, and those sweaters that can go anywhere.

Open 9:00 A.M. to 5:00 P.M. daily except Sunday. Major credit cards accepted.

EVERYDAY GOOD THINGS

WEST AND SOUTH MAUI

LONGS DRUGS
Lahaina Cannery Shopping Center
Lahaina
Telephone: (808) 667-4384

Longs has everything you could possibly need in the realm of everyday things—prescription drugs, household detergents, stationery, cosmetics, liquor, calculators, suntan lotion, and so forth. There's also a photo processing department that handles the work quickly, efficiently, and at a reasonable price. Whether it's rubber zoris (flip-flops) for the beach or a can of macadamia nuts, Longs won't let you down.

Open 8:30 A.M. to 9:00 P.M. Monday through Saturday and until 5:00 P.M. Sunday. Major credit cards accepted.

DOWN TO EARTH
136 Dickenson Street
Lahaina
Telephone: (808) 667-2855

Down To Earth, the grandfather of successful health food stores, has opened a Lahaina branch. Local produce, baked goods, vitamins, organically grown vegetables, and other healthful vegetarian items can be found in the store section of this establishment. Outside, under a canopy, you can dine on smoothies, sandwiches, salads, and vegetarian burgers from the juice bar.

Open 7:00 A.M. to 9:00 P.M. Monday through Saturday and 9:00 A.M. to 7:00 P.M. Sunday. No credit cards accepted.

PARADISE FRUIT MAUI
1 Keala Place
(Across from McDonald's)
Kihei
Telephone: (808) 879-1723

Open twenty-four hours a day, Paradise Fruit offers everything from healthy sandwiches and salads to freshly baked cookies and fruit breads. It's a great stop for a picnic lunch to go. You can get everything from fresh carrot juice to a pita melt or a shrimp and avocado sandwich—the choices are varied. They've also designed elaborate fruit basket combinations— everything from Maui potato chips with macadamia nuts, papaya, and pineapple to Kona coffee gift packs, Maui onions, and Maui potato chip packs for mailing. Ask about their mail-order gift packs. They'll make it supremely convenient for you to take home those strawberry papayas and Kula onions.

Open daily. Major credit cards accepted.

TAKE HOME MAUI
143 Luakini Street
Lahaina
Telephone: (808) 661-6185

Although you can find fresh Maui produce in any market or local food store, some people prefer to pay a higher price at specialty shops to ensure agricultural clearance for out-of-state transport. This is a convenience; without an agricultural stamp you risk confiscation at the airport. Shops such as Take Home Maui make it easy to take produce home because everything is prepacked, preinspected, and stamped for clearance. Kula onions are sold in 5-pound bundles for $12.95, in 10-pound bundles for $24.95, and on up. They also deliver to your hotel or arrange to have you pick up the goods at the airport.

Open 8:30 A.M. to 5:30 P.M. daily. No credit cards accepted.

CENTRAL, UPCOUNTRY, AND EAST MAUI

LONGS DRUGS
Maui Mall
Kahului
Telephone: (808) 877-0041

Hawaii's old standby is here for your basic needs. Whether it's de-odorant, straw beach mats, toys, or Scotch tape, Longs will have it. Watch for their sales on macadamia nuts and chocolate-covered macadamia nuts; they're the best deal you can find on these expensive Hawaiian snacks. They also carry film and camera supplies and offer a film-processing service.

Open 8:30 A.M. to 9:00 P.M. Monday through Saturday and until 5:00 P.M. Sunday. Major credit cards accepted.

UNCLE HARRY'S HAWAIIAN CRAFTS AND FRESH FRUITS
On the Hana Highway
Keanae
Telephone: (808) 248-7019

Don't miss Uncle Harry's. If you're lucky, you'll meet Uncle Harry Mitchell too. He may be outside carving a poi pounder or pig board, or he may be opening a coconut and "talking story." Uncle Harry is a Maui treasure, a respected Hawaiian kupuna (elder) and Hawaiian activist who does everything from write songs to travel to Vanuatu representing Hawaiians for a nuclear-free Pacific. The shop, run by his son, Harry Jr., is a bastion of aloha, with local crafts made by Maui artists, shells from Keanae, and papaya, avocado, passion fruit, coconut, and other fruits grown on the island. The bowls are made of koa, milo, hau, and other woods from Maui. There are snacks and food items for the rest of the drive to Hana. Most important, they're good people here—Hawaiians who live close to the land, who plant and fish in the old ways, and whose door is open to share their culture with those who might wander by. Airport pickup or fruit orders to go can also be arranged. The stand is about halfway to Hana, in beautiful Keanae.

Open 9:30 A.M. to 4:00 P.M. daily. Major credit cards accepted.

DOWN TO EARTH
1910 Vineyard Street
Wailuku
Telephone: (808) 242-6821

Very fresh local produce such as Kula onions and strawberry papayas are sold here, and at good prices. There are baked goods of whole wheat flour, vegetarian vitamins, a wide selection of natural things for the healthy eater. The outdoor section has been expanded to include a juice and sandwich bar that dispenses burritos, smoothies, and vegetarian sandwiches made of wholesome ingredients.

Open 8:00 A.M. to 7:00 P.M. weekdays, until 6:00 P.M. Saturday, and 10:00 A.M. to 5:00 P.M. Sunday. No credit cards accepted.

KOMODA STORE AND BAKERY
Makawao
Telephone: (808) 572-7261

It's been here for more than sixty years, with a wooden floor that creaks more loudly and a new generation behind the counter. Makawao's most famous store, Komoda's has one thing that doesn't change—its famous cream puffs and pastries. Long before sophisticated Bavarian pastries made their way to Hawaii's shores, Komoda's was putting out simple baked pleasures that gained an interisland following: cinnamon donuts, rolls, German chocolate cake, pies, breads, and the crème de la crème, the cream puffs. They also carry Maui potato chips and local bananas and even poi—simple products resting in modest bins while the aroma of fresh baking wafts through. Nice elderly Japanese ladies putter behind the scenes as they have for three generations; they're the secret behind those tantalizing cream puffs that always sell out.

Open 6:30 A.M. to 6:00 P.M. Monday through Saturday, 7:00 A.M. to noon Sunday. No credit cards.

SHIROKIYA
Kaahumanu Shopping Center
Kahului
Telephone: (808) 877-5551

Although much smaller than the landmark Honolulu store, Maui's Shirokiya has similar offerings and the same touch. You can find Japanese food items here, from Maui manju to bento lunches, and you can check out their toys and hardware as well. People like Shirokiya for its delicate samplings of Japanese food, packed and ready to go.

Open 9:00 A.M. to 5:30 P.M. Monday through Wednesday and on Saturday, until 9:00 P.M. Thursday and Friday, and 10:00 A.M. to 3:00 P.M. Sunday. Major credit cards accepted.

TAKAMIYA MARKET
359 North Market
Wailuku
Telephone: (808) 244-3404

You should not leave Maui without poking around among the mounds of potato salad, fried squid, Chinese noodles, lau lau, fried fish, kalua pork, sushi, seaweed salad, and the unrelenting medley of local delicacies at Takamiya's. In fact, gourmet food notwithstanding, Takamiya's should be christened "the first stop for any picnic" for those with an adventurous palate. The food is home-cooked, freshly prepared, and ready to go in wrapped Styrofoam plates. There's a fish counter with sashimi and poke (Hawaiian-style raw fish, seasoned with onions), and immediately in front is the fabled assortment of morsels from east and west: corn bread, rice balls, mochi, roast pork, shoyu chicken, fiddleheads, macaroni salad, you name it. If you're lucky, there'll be fresh oyster mushrooms from a Haiku farm. The tiny store is full of surprises and is a delight for visitors and residents.

Open 6:00 A.M. to 6:30 P.M. Monday through Saturday. No credit cards accepted.

TASAKA GURI GURI
Maui Mall
Kahului
Telephone: (808) 871-4513

Like shave ice on Oahu, Tasaka Guri Guri is the saving grace for a hot day. Guri Guri, the invention of the Tasaka family, has been one of Maui's most celebrated delights ever since Gunji Tasaka invented the sensation sixty years ago. It's neither ice cream nor sherbet, but something in between. It melts like ice cream but isn't as creamy, and it comes in two flavors—pineapple and strawberry. They're served in dainty scoops with sweetened azuki beans, a concoction that is so good the *Los Angeles Times* has requested its recipe. The Tasakas sell about 50 gallons a day; that's a lot of small scoops. Follow the lines on the Maui Mall and see for yourself. There are even insulated bags and a precisely timed protocol for getting these treats to the neighbor islands before they melt.

Open 9:00 A.M. to 6:00 P.M. Monday through Thursday, until 9:00 P.M. Friday, until 5:00 P.M. Saturday, and 10:00 A.M. to 3:00 P.M. Sunday. No credit cards accepted.

FLOWERS AND LEIS

In west Maui, the best place to buy leis is on the front lawn of the Baldwin home on Thursday, 9:00 A.M. until noon. That's where the Lahaina senior citizens gather weekly for their lei-making demonstrations and to socialize. This is a chance to get to see Hawaii's beautiful kupuna at work, stringing fragrant leis as they did in the old days. The leis are for sale after the demonstration. The Baldwin home is to the right of The Wharf, corner of Front and Dickenson streets in Lahaina.

Other than that, Safeway in Lahaina at the Lahaina Cannery (661-3787) has a florist with a good, steady supply of leis and flowers. The usual strung leis, from pikake to roses and ilima, can be found here, as well as Maui protea. Open 8:00 A.M. to 10:00 P.M. daily.

As a last resort you can always check the other local flower shops— Lahaina Florist (Lahaina Shopping Center, 661-0509) and The Wharf Florist (658 Front Street, 661-0655).

In upcountry, east, and central Maui, you will find the larger and better-known protea farms. Among the best are Sunrise Protea (878-2119). Upcountry Protea (878-2544), and Hawaii Protea Cooperative (878-6273). All are located on the slopes of Haleakala in upcountry Maui, where the flowers proliferate on the rich volcanic soil. These flower farms have large selections and walk-through gardens where you can observe the flowers growing. They also have gift shops where you can select cut flowers, dried flowers, and other gift items. Be sure to ask which days they pick the blooms, so you can get them as fresh as possible. The farms are open daily and have mail order and shipping available as well. The following shops also have flowers and leis for sale as well as other items.

AH FOOK'S SUPER MARKET
Kahului Shopping Center
Kahului
Telephone: (808) 877-3308

This old-time family supermarket has shelves of protea, poinsettias, anthuriums, roses, orchids, and other flowers, cut or growing in brilliant profusion. The selection is ample but not vast, and the prices are fantastic.

This is one of three family-run supermarkets in Kahului that provide beautiful Maui blooms at untouristy prices.

Open 8:00 A.M. to 8:00 P.M. weekdays, until 7:00 P.M. Saturday, and until 4:00 P.M. Sunday. No credit cards accepted.

NODA MARKET
Kahului Shopping Center
Kahului
Telephone: (808) 877-3395

Noda's selection of local flowers may be small, but there will always be some on the shelves. Torch gingers, red gingers, and a decent selection of protea can be found in the flower section at the front of the store. Once you get past the flowers you can always explore the dried fish, Kitchen Cook'd Potato Chips, and the famous Kula onions.

Open 6:00 A.M. to 6:00 P.M. Monday through Thursday and on Saturday, until 8:00 P.M. Friday, and until noon Sunday. No credit cards accepted.

OOKA SUPER MARKET
1870 Main Street
Wailuku
Telephone: (808) 244-3931

This supermarket is loved by local residents, who shop here for everything from futons to beer to Ka'u Gold navel oranges. This is also where you can get protea and other local flowers at the best prices in town, including protea kings, queens, needles, and other types of the noble bloom. Anthuriums, roses, and leis are always available. And the shop bustles with local residents buying maile and pikake leis for their sweethearts. There's also a good selection of red and pink ginger from Hana. Most local people look here for flowers before venturing anywhere else.

Open 7:30 A.M. to 8:00 P.M. Monday through Wednesday and on Saturday, until 9:00 P.M. Thursday and Friday, and until 6:00 P.M. Sunday. No credit cards accepted.

GIFTS TO GO

Maui is the queen of regional specialties, from its world-famous Kula onions to Maui's own Kitchen Cook'd Potato Chips, the original, much-imitated-but-never-duplicated best. Maui prides itself on its specialties and even has a contest going with Texas on which state grows the sweeter onion.

Kula onions are more expensive than plain "Maui onions"—a sort of inferior generic—because they're grown on the upcountry slopes of Haleakala, where the altitude, sun, and soil conditions foster the characteristic sweetness of this otherwise pungent bulb. You can find Kula onions in any Maui market, but if you plan to leave the island with them, they should be stamped and approved or you risk confiscation at the airport.

Maui potato chips are easier to carry, but they do crush. You can find Kitchen Cook'd packed for traveling at some specialty stores, but only you can decide whether it's worth the expense. Or you can pack them yourself. Many potato chips proclaim themselves "Maui" or "Maui-style" potato chips, but no one has come close to Kitchen Cook'd.

Along with protea, these are the obvious, most commonly selected products that leave the island. But there are many, many more products that aren't promoted, aren't as well known, and make excellent gifts to go.

Definitely top drawer are Chocolate Chips of Maui by Discriminating Taste, Inc. These are the ne plus ultra of the snack pack: hefty Maui potato chips (made in Kahului) hand-dipped in rich dark chocolate and then packaged in a luxurious red box labeled with the dippers' name. Very deluxe, delicious, and chic—very Maui. They cost about $2.95 for 2 ounces and $4.95 for 4 ounces. They're being called the "yuppie chips" and are already being ordered by the likes of Ralph Lauren.

And then there are the crafts. Weavers Susan Kilmer and Mika McCann use native materials in their work, which is featured in galleries around Maui. Each gathers her own vines, grasses, roots, and fibers and weaves them into distinctively styled, gorgeous baskets and nonfunctional fiber sculptures. Judy Bisgard and Akemi Daniels are also prodigious weavers using local materials.

Quala-Lynn Bancroft makes pressed-flower wall hangings of hibiscus hybrids and frames them in koa for sensational island pieces. She grows her own hibiscus—the state flower—in firecracker red, white, purple, and all colors, and she picks and grows angel's-trumpets, water lilies, and goldcups for pressing in her special laminating process. The colors are well preserved, and the composition and work are elegant. Prices range from $45 to $300; the work is displayed at the Maui Crafts Guild in Paia, and personal studio visits can be arranged. Telephone (808) 879-6772.

Cloud Rock La Belle makes high-quality leis out of ornmamental seeds. He's been collecting seeds for the eighteen years he's been on Maui, combing the valleys, mountains, and shorelines. There are kukui, wiliwili, and about two dozen different varieties, which are husked, sorted, drilled, treated, and strung into leis in four lengths. Prices are $25 to $65.

Maui is also rich in works made out of native Hawaiian woods. Ask about Val Diehl's handmade boxes of sugi pine or milo. He leaves part of the bark raw, textured, and frayed, then polishes the rest into a refined container of mixed textures.

The bamboo flute is another hot item from Maui, made by artist Jim Green of Island Bamboo. It comes with a printed tag giving precise playing instructions. The bamboo flute is textured and earthy, a piece for the mantel if not for the lips.

Hand-turned bowls of milo, mango, koa, sandalwood, and other native woods make great gifts too. Wayne Omura and Takeo Omuro are leaders in this field, with high-quality gallery pieces at various outlets.

Other ideas: an antique map or engraving from Lahaina Printsellers, Makawao mint and other upcountry teas, Maui sachets and potpourris. There's also a Maui Lager now, and the Tedeschi champagne, and various first-class candies made on Maui, such as Island Princess macadamia nut brittle. (See also Shopping, Maui's Best.)

For something different in silver jewelry, you might be interested in Noreen Quick's whimsical flowers, plants, birds, and animals of Maui.

Most of the crafts mentioned above can be found at the Maui Crafts Guild in Paia, one of the best places for local gifts. (See also Shopping, Central, Upcountry, and East Maui.) Maui's Best is also brimming with made-on-Maui offerings these days, from edibles to silks, books, and fibers. What a relief from those hand-painted T-shirts and marine paintings!

MOLOKAI

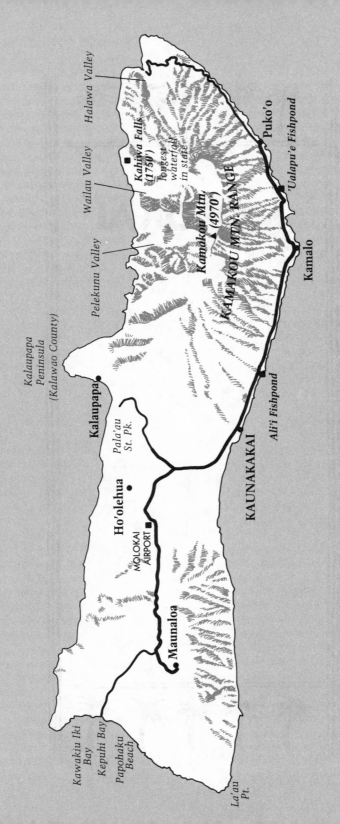

MOLOKAI

Halawa Valley

Wailau Valley

Pelekunu Valley

Kalaupapa
Peninsula
(Kalawao County)

Kahiwa Falls
(1750')
longest
waterfall
in state

Kamakou Mtn.
(4970')

KAMAKOU MTN. RANGE

Puko'o

'Ualapu'e Fishpond

Kamalo

Kalaupapa

Pala'au
St. Pk.

Ho'olehua

MOLOKAI
AIRPORT

Maunaloa

KAUNAKAKAI

Ali'i Fishpond

Kawakiu Iki
Bay
Kepuhi Bay
Papohaku
Beach

La'au
Pt.

0 1 2 3 4 5 Miles

A BRIEF HISTORY

Molokai is known as the Friendly Isle, which tells you a lot about its people. A smile comes readily here and the "aloha" is genuine, touched by an innocence that comes from living on a pristine, under-developed island.

Except for a small part of the island known as Kalaupapa, which encompasses Kalawao County and a national park, Molokai is a part of Maui County. It's the fifth largest and least developed of the major Hawaiian islands, home to 6,000 residents who are scattered across the island's 261 square miles. Shaped like a wide-tailed fish with its belly up, Molokai is 38 miles long and 10 miles wide and sits surrounded by islands on all but its northern shore, where waterfalls and cliffs languish in primordial isolation. A mere 22 miles away from its western tip, across the turbulent Kaiwi Channel, lies Oahu. Western Molokai residents can see the twinkling of Oahu's lights in the distance while 1,381 feet high atop the town of Maunaloa, an antiquated service station with an enviable vantage point claims it's the only one in the world with a view of Diamond Head. Indeed, on a clear day you can see Diamond Head across the ocean and even an occasional twinkling of Oahu high rises. Meanwhile, on Molokai's south shore, the whalelike shape of Lanai dominates the horizon, while from the east end near Halawa Valley, west Maui's sophisticated resorts glimmer an 8-mile galaxy away.

Molokai residents are proud of their island's idiosyncrasies. They'll be the first to tell you that there are no traffic lights on the island, no air conditioners, elevators, movie theaters, bowling alleys, discotheques, no golden arches or fast-food franchises, no building taller than three stories. What Molokai does have are heiau and shrines aplenty, the highest sea cliffs in the world, the longest stretch of white-sand beach in the islands, and the longest waterfall in the state. Molokai also boasts the highest percentage of Hawaiians of all the major inhabited Hawaiian Islands (Niihau is the exception) and proudly bears the moniker "the most Hawaiian island of all."

These features bear remembering as you approach the island. You must be careful not to be fooled by its apparent simplicity and modest, humble charm. Petite as Molokai is, it is a powerful and diverse island, a destination that has long lived in the shadow of Maui but which is rapidly coming into its own, and on its own terms.

To begin with, this island is not for everyone. It's not for the high-flying, fast-living visitor who wants to dance the night away, shop in expensive boutiques, or dine in fancy restaurants. This island is for those willing to peel off their watches and urban expectations to enter another time, a distant, tranquil time before high rises and pollution and prepackaged entertainment.

Although it's poor in nightlife, Molokai is rich in history. Signs of a settlement in Halawa Valley have been dated to 650, and there are fish ponds along the southern shore said to have been built around the fifteenth century. It is said that 10,500 people once lived on Molokai, in communities from Halawa, rich in fishing and taro farming, to the west end, where a quarry of natural basalt rock furnished materials for ancient Hawaiian adzes and implements.

In the latter part of the sixteenth century one of Hawaii's most revered prophets, Lanikaula, lived on Molokai and is said to be buried under a large grove of kukui trees still visible on the east end and considered one of the most sacred spots on the island. From its earliest years the island was rich in religious culture and shrouded in mystery—even feared for its rituals in sorcery. This reputation for mystery, combined with its other label the "Lonely Isle," resulting from its later affiliation with Hansen's disease at Kalaupapa, contributed to Molokai's early isolation.

Even contact with westerners came to Molokai later than to the other islands. While Captain Cook discovered Hawaii in 1778, it was not until 1786 that Molokai got its first glimpse of foreigners, when British Captain George Dixon dropped anchor offshore. But that must not have been nearly as intimidating as Kamehameha the Great's visit six years later, when he conquered the island with a showy, 4-mile line of canoes along the southern shore. In Ho'olehua, on the land where the Molokai Airport now stands, Kamehameha trained his warriors and prepared to attack Oahu.

His descendant, Kamehameha V, is even more closely identified with Molokai. He lived there as Prince Lot Kapuaiwa before becoming king in 1863. It was for him—and some say by him—that the famous Kapuaiwa Coconut Grove on the south shore was planted, all 1,000 trees, hundreds of which still stand. He also spent his summers at Malama, his vacation complex near Kaunakakai Wharf, where a stone foundation behind the thatched canoe club is all that remains of the home today.

There are fifty-eight ancient fish ponds on Molokai's southern shore, fringing a tranquil coastline with waters that are silty and brown. The discoloration is caused by the runoff from years of erosion in the pasturelands above, where imported sheep and cattle grazed wantonly for more than a century.

Sheep and cattle arrived on the island in the 1830s, and three decades later Molokai's first axis deer made their debut, a gift from the emperor of Japan to Kamehameha V. Molokai's penchant for animals continues today with the Molokai Wildlife Preserve in the west end's Kaluakoi Resort, where deer, ibex, greater kudu, oryx, ostrich, and other creatures of the plains roam 1,500 Serengeti-like island acres. The much-publicized giraffes have all died and have not been replaced.

Of greatest renown on this island is the work of Father Damien Joseph De Veuster, a Belgian priest who arrived in 1873 to unify and care for a settlement of lepers in the isolated northern peninsula of Makanalua, better known as Kalaupapa. He made the settlement his home and died there sixteen years later, a victim of the disease. Today the Catholic Church seeks to have him canonized and Kalaupapa is a national park with a close-knit community of one hundred residents, still isolated on a peninsula inaccessible by car. Visitors, who cannot roam unattended, must hike in, take a mule ride down a steep trail, fly in, or arrive by boat.

Perhaps least visible on Molokai are its native birds and endemic plants, fragile and endangered as they are throughout Hawaii. The Molokai thrush—'olomao—and the kakawahie, the Molokai creeper, live only on Molokai and are very rare, living in what is today the protected environment of the Kamakou Preserve, managed by the Nature Conservancy of Hawaii. Of 250 kinds of Hawaiian plants existing in the preserve, 219 are endemic to Hawaii. One notable native plant is maile, its fragrant leaves entwined into leis and offered to the goddess of the hula, Laka, by hula dancers old and new. Still used in Hawaiian ceremonies, it grows in small clusters in the forest reserve near the Waikolu Lookout, not far from where the historic sandalwood pit still lies. The boat-shaped pit was dug into the ground so sandalwood loggers could measure their harvest to fit the hold of the traders' boats. From 1810 to 1830 the sandalwood business flourished, only to die when unhappy workers destroyed new trees so they and their children would not be called away to work in the mountains for such long periods.

In later years the people of this island became more familiar with the struggles of commerce. The 60,000-acre Molokai Ranch, originally the land of Kamehameha V and comprising 38 percent of the island, changed hands several times and eventually became a major producer of beef, the second largest cattle ranch in the state, and one of the largest producers of honey in the world. Molokai's agrarian rise continued through the 1920s, when Del Monte began raising pineapples and importing Filipino and Japanese laborers to work the fields.

Fifty years later Dole ended its Molokai operation and in 1988 Del Monte, too, is pulling out, signaling with finality pineapple's demise on the island. Diversified agriculture may take up some of the slack and tourism—amid protest by a group of activists—is an alternative most Molokaians seem to want confined to Kaluakoi, the only master-planned resort on the island.

A smattering of hotels and condominiums, some small farmers, and small businesses make up the fragile economic base of this island. Residents hunt as well as fish, for there are wild turkey, deer, pheasant, quail, francolin, and a plethora of game roaming the acres of scrub. Unemployment is high and electricity costs are among the highest in the country. But it's worth remembering that on this undeveloped island you are given access to the social fabric of everyday life. When you shop in Kaunakakai, you're shopping where many generations of Molokai residents have always gathered and continue to. Local foods and many accents greet you on the streets and in stores. Molokai is as you see it, with residents going about their daily business and a raw integrity that can intimidate as well as embrace. And remember, too, that because Molokai has lagged behind the other islands in tourism and urban development, its natural treasures are that much greater. Approach this unspoiled island with respect and sensitivity and you will reap great rewards, for Hawaii's complex past is vitally present here.

GETTING AROUND

A twenty-minute flight from Oahu or Maui will land you at Ho'ole-hua's Molokai airport, one of two landing strips on the island. The other is at Kalaupapa on the northern coast, a popular visitor attraction also accessible by mule ride and a steep hike.

Three airlines fly to Molokai: Hawaiian Airlines, Princeville Airways, and Air Molokai. Round-trip fares from Oahu are about $30 to $40 on the smaller airlines and more on Hawaiian's DASH-7 turboprops. Flights from Ho'olehua, called "topside," also fly into Kalaupapa peninsula at prices ranging from $20 to $25.

There are four car rental companies on the island: Tropical ([800] 352-3923), Avis ([800] 331-1212), Dollar ([808] 567-6156), and Budget ([800] 527-0700). The car rentals have small counters at Molokai Airport.

The Kaluakoi Hotel and Golf Club is getting ready to open a moped rental service through Molokai Trails ([808] 552-2555, ext. 510). Fully automatic Suzuki F2-50s go for $5 an hour to $25 for a full day, and there are also fins, snorkel equipment, and boogie boards for rent.

There is neither public transportation nor taxi service on the island. A few of the hotels offer shuttle service to the airport, but sightseeing is usually done by tours or in rented cars. Although some of Molokai's sights are best approached in a car with four-wheel drive, there are no four-wheel-drive vehicles for rent on the island. (Avis rents Jeeps, but not with four-wheel drive.)

As you drive from the airport you will be on the plains of Ho'olehua between the eastern and western volcanic masses that form the island. The third major geologic feature of Molokai, the Makanalua Peninsula where Kalaupapa is located, was formed most recently when lava from the Kauha-ko Volcano created the peninsular dab of land on the northern coastline about 2 million years ago, during the late Pleistocene period.

Here on Molokai the words *mauka* and *makai* are used no differently from the way they are anywhere else in Hawaii, meaning toward the mountain and toward the sea. But on this horizontally shaped island, the term *west end* refers to the town of Maunaloa and the 7,000-acre Kaluakoi Resort and the miles of sandy coastline it flanks. There are six public accesses to beaches on the west end; one of them, the Papohaku Beach park, has restroom and shower facilities.

The term *mana'e*, on the other hand, is Molokai's way of referring to the east end, particularly the long stretch of reefy shoreline beginning at Kamalo on the south shore and ending at Halawa Valley. Dominating eastern Molokai are the Kamakou mountain range with its 4,970-foot summit, the dense upland forests of the Kamakou Preserve, and a series of chiseled valleys, homes, and historic sites that roll to water's edge. Halawa Valley is the last valley accessible by car before the mysterious and remote north-shore valleys begin. Ubiquitous on the road to Halawa are the shoreline fish ponds, still standing as they did centuries ago.

Molokai Airport is eight miles from Kaunakakai. The hotels and condos of Kaluakoi are about 13 miles from the airport.

TOURS

Tour operators on Molokai include Gray Line Molokai ([808] 567-6177), Robert's Hawaii, Inc. ([808] 552-2751), and Damien Molokai Tours ([808] 567-6171). Damien Tours offers guided tours of Kalaupapa and is known for its informative and congenial guide, Richard Marks.

CAMPING

County permits are required for camping at both Papohaku Beach park on the west end and O Ne Alii Beach Park on the south shore. O Ne Alii is tranquil and historic, but the south shore is not known for terrific swimming because of its silt and rocks. Although Papohaku is not always safe, it's a far more attractive beach with restroom and picnic facilities on acres of well-kept grounds. County camping permits cost $3 a night for adults and $.50 a night for those under eighteen, and are available for a maximum of three consecutive nights. Special waivers can be arranged for larger groups. For more information contact the County Office, P.O. Box 526, Kaunakakai, HI 96748; telephone (808) 553-3221.

You may also want to camp amid the ironwoods of the 234-acre Pala'au State Park on the northern coast overlooking Kalaupapa, or in a forested area near the Waikolu Valley lookout. Both are spectacular sites, but as with any mountainous area you run the risk of rain. Both sites have restroom facilities and free camping. Permits, with a seven-day limit, can be obtained by contacting the Department of Land and Natural Resources, 1151 Punchbowl Street, Room 325, Honolulu, HI 96813; telephone (808) 567-6083. Other camping spots in Pala'au are on Molokai Ranch lands. To camp there, contact the Molokai Ranch and request a pass. Passes cost $5 a night per adult, up to five people in the party. Contact: Molokai Ranch, P.O. Box 37, Maunaloa, HI 96770; telephone (808) 552-2767.

Molokai has many other potential camping spots, but they are on private ranchlands or in areas with private access. Highly recommended is Kawakiu Beach at the top of the string of west end beaches. It is secluded, with a shady kiawe grove for picnicking, but there are no facilities. Although

swimming may be safe there during the summer, winter waters are dangerous and caution is always advised. The beach is fringed with white sand,
lava coastline, and a crescent bay and is considered the most beautiful on
the island. There is no charge for camping there, but you do need a pass
from Molokai Ranch (see address above). Ask them for directions to Kawakiu via the dirt road.

In all camping and beach areas, beware of drinking the water unless
boiled or treated.

HOTELS AND ALTERNATIVES

Budget Hotel

PAU HANA INN
P.O. Box 546
Kaunakakai, HI 96748
Telephone: (800) 367-8047, (808) 553-5342

A sentimental favorite among budget travelers, Molokai's oldest hotel is undergoing a facelift. Recently purchased by the Hotel Molokai, the Pau Hana Inn is a small, bare-bones hotel on the south shore with ground floor units and rates beginning at $35. There are thirty-six guest units, which are in both the original structure and the newer concrete building, where rooms are bigger and have two queen-size beds. The deluxe oceanfront suites can be had for $72 and feature lanais and bigger beds. The rooms are spare, but the studios have kitchenettes and the oceanfront units at least have a view. There are no telephones or television sets. A pool and chairs under a hau tree make the courtyard a favorite spot for reading and lingering.

The restaurant and bar area is dominated by a concrete stage by the ocean and a large banyan tree planted in the late 1800s. This is where local folks gather on the weekends to enjoy Molokai's only late-night entertainment—live music and dancing. It can get rowdy. Adjoining the lounge is the restaurant—informal and plain but noted for some of its dishes, such as its roast beef.

The Pau Hana Inn is popular because of its low rates, but as with any good deal you get what you pay for. Be prepared for noise, a barrackslike room, and no-frills accommodations, and you'll be just fine.

Moderate Hotel

HOTEL MOLOKAI
P.O. Box 546
Kaunakakai, HI 96748
Telephone: (800) 367-8047; (808) 531-4004, 553-5347

From its seaside bar to its two-story wooden bungalows, the Hotel Molokai oozes charm. There is a Polynesian flavor throughout, from the longhouselike lobby with its high ceiling and suspended canoe to the plumeria, ti, and hala trees peppering the well-groomed grounds. And the pace is slow, unhurried, definitely country.

You'll have to carry your own bags and make your phone calls from the pay phone near the lobby. The upper units have high, high ceilings and all rooms have ceiling fans. There are no television sets, clocks, or radios in the rooms, but instead you can spend your time on the swinging bench on the balcony, listening to the wind in the coconut trees or the laughter from the bar by the pool.

What may be the world's tiniest refrigerator hides near the dressing area, and the melange of wicker and dark painted wood is far from new or fancy. The mottled mirror and can of Raid prove there is no pretension, adding a perverse charm to the clean and entirely acceptable room. Prices range from $45 for a ground-floor standard with twin beds to $65 for a family unit. Some of the second-floor units have lofts with beds and ample room to sleep several. The south-shore beach on which the hotel sits is not very good for swimming, but it's a great backdrop for dinner, drinks, or a morning stroll.

A favorite hangout for Molokai residents is the small bar by the pool, overlooking the ocean and next to the Holo Holo Kai restaurant, the best on the island.

Superior Hotel

THE KALUAKOI HOTEL AND GOLF CLUB
P.O. Box 1977
Maunaloa, HI 96770
Telephone: (800) 367-6046, (808) 552-2555

It is, as they say, the only game in town—at least if you're looking for a hotel on the beach with telephones in the rooms and a full range of amenities. If it were in any other location it would be mediocre, but its spectacular location on Kepuhi beach puts it in a different league. The Kaluakoi Hotel opened as the Sheraton Molokai in 1977, a brown, unobtrusive, low-rise cluster of 292 units on a 219-acre complex. The new management, Colony Resorts, is renovating and says it intends to inject new life in the form of more organized recreational activities and, perhaps, such features as Zodiac and outrigger canoe rides to appeal to the grown-up Club Med set.

Rates range from $95 for a garden-view unit to $125 for an ocean-view cottage. All units have lanais, ceiling fans, rattan furniture, color televisions, and refrigerators. The cottages and second-floor guest rooms have high, open-beam ceilings and, depending on the price and location, breathtaking views of the ocean and the golf course. The one- and two-story structures have a Polynesian ambience, a feeling enhanced by their proximity to the beach and the relentless, hypnotic crash of waves that add immeasurably to the hotel's appeal.

No matter where you are on the grounds, the beach—although not always good for swimming—will be only a short walk away and the open expanse of beach and golf course is everywhere around you. The freshwater pool is painted black to retain heat, and there is a Jacuzzi on the grounds.

No room service, though, and the sundry shop opens at 9:00 A.M. and will run out of the daily newspaper unless you sign up ahead of time.

You can, however, get room service from the bar, and the snack shop is a popular alternative to the much more expensive Ohia Lodge, the island's only fancy restaurant and the only eatery for miles. (The Paniolo Broiler opens only when necessary.) There are four regulation-size Laykold tennis courts with night lighting, and for golfers, there is one of Hawaii's favorite—albeit windy—eighteen-hole golf courses. Demonstrations in Hawaiian crafts are also popular, especially long-time employee Sam Rawlins's coconut weaving–storytelling sessions in the gazebo. The only night life on the grounds consists of Hawaiian and contemporary music in the bar.

The hotel is far from perfect, but its flaws are largely forgivable because of its setting, its feeling of open space, and especially its people. Service here is exceptionally friendly, Molokai-style.

Alternative

KE NANI KAI
Hawaiiana Resorts
1100 Ward Avenue, Suite 1100
Honolulu, HI 96814
Telephone: (800) 367-7040, (808) 523-7785

Ke Nani Kai is nearly indistinguishable from the Kaluakoi Hotel from the outside, so close is it to the hotel and so similar in design and appearance. Although it has phone service, a swimming pool, daily maid service, and other amenities, it is a condominium with a two-night minimum. Because there's no restaurant on the property, most guests go to the neighboring Kaluakoi Hotel's Ohia Lodge.

The two-story brown buildings contain spacious one- and two-bedroom units with balconies, high ceilings, sofabeds, full kitchens, color TV, telephones, and, for the most part, pleasant views of rolling lawn or golf course, with the ocean in the distance. It is part of the Kaluakoi Resort but unlike the Kaluakoi Hotel, it is not an oceanfront hotel.

During peak season, rates range from $85 a night for a maximum of four to $115 for maximum of six in a large two-bedroom ocean-view unit. And they are large. With sofabeds and lots of space, there is ample room for families, two couples, or small groups who want to pool resources and keep costs down. All the units are modern, clean, and spacious, fully equipped with kitchen, full-size refrigerator, kitchen utensils and linens, dishwashers, and clothes washers and dryers. A one-bedroom unit will hold up to four guests, a two-bedroom, six guests.

Easy access to the spectacular west end beaches adds to the appeal here. A spa, tennis courts, and 15 acres of manicured grounds enhance the package. If you have a family or small group and cooking is not an issue, this will be a terrific value for you.

DINING OUT

A word on Molokai restaurants: Fine dining does not exist on Molokai. The eateries of this small island are casual, ranging from drive-ins to diners to coffee shops with good food. This is not the place for nouvelle cuisine or fancy china, but you'll find some good home-style cooking and honest, inexpensive meals.

HOLO HOLO KAI
Hotel Molokai
Kaunakakai
Telephone: (808) 553-5347

From breakfast to dinner, it's a find. Perched as close to the water as possible, with Lanai in the distance and birds on the shoreline, it has much more going for it than good food. But yes, the food is great.

The breakfast musts are the French toast, made with the famous Molokai bread, and the papaya batter pancakes. There are also Hawaiian crêpes filled with fresh tropical fruit preserves, and mahimahi, meats, and the usual breakfast eggs.

For lunch there are sandwiches, salads, and seafood. And for dinner fresh fish, pasta primavera, Hawaiian beef stew, and homemade soups made daily. The fresh seafood is usually very good, served grilled, poached, or with a variety of simple sauces. The service is spotty, but remember, this is Molokai, sauntering through the day on its own slow rhythm.

Moderately priced—dinner for two is about $25. Open 7:00 to 10:30 A.M., 11:30 A.M. to 1:30 P.M., and 6:00 to 9:00 P.M. daily. Major credit cards accepted.

JOJO'S CAFÉ
Maunaloa
Telephone: (808) 552-2803

Jojo's Café is in a building that was an old hospital, then an Italian restaurant, then a tavern. Now it's a wholesome café with old booths, an antique bar made in the 1800s, and good food. Fresh fish and local dishes, such as Korean ribs and rib steak, are the specialty here. Proprietor Perry

Buchalter and his mother-in-law, Josephine Espaniola (for whom the restaurant is named), concoct all kinds of specialties, such as homemade passion fruit toppings for ice cream and a black-eyed bean dish with pork and potato shoots. There's also the very popular chicken with green papaya.

Two people can dine heartily here for less than $20. Open 11:00 A.M. to 7:30 P.M. daily except Saturday. Cash only.

KANEMITSU BAKERY
Kaunakakai
Telephone: (808) 553-5855

Kanemitsu's is a bakery, not a restaurant, but it does serve food and has a small seating area. This local favorite has been a Molokai fixture since 1942 and still puts out the best pastries on the island. Cinnamon rolls and sweet buns start pouring out of the oven for breakfast and are served to those who congregate at the few Formica-topped tables. The restaurant section opens at 5:30 in the morning and serves until 11:00 A.M., but the bakery is open until 6:00 P.M.

The Kanemitsus bake about 2,500 loaves a day—5,000 on holidays and busy days—and distribute their famous breads to hotels on the island and fancy restaurants on Oahu, the Big Island, and Kauai. The old family recipe has barely changed in more than forty-five years. The choices: whole wheat bread, cinnamon bread, sweet bread, onion-cheese, raisin-nut, coconut-pineapple, the famous Molokai bread (a soft French loaf), and many others that are carted off the island as favorite gifts for people on jaunts from the neighbor islands.

Inexpensive. Open 5:30 A.M. to 6:00 P.M. daily except Tuesday. Cash or checks only.

MID NITE INN
Kaunakakai
Telephone: (808) 553-5302

No one comes to Molokai without dining at the Mid Nite Inn. It's fifty years old, the most popular hangout on the island, and one of two social centers in Kaunakakai (the other one is the baseball park). It's said that U.S. Senator Daniel Inouye phones ahead from Honolulu to reserve their beef stew.

The room is large, with ceiling fans, linoleum floors, Naugahyde booths, Formica-topped tables—sort of an upgraded diner with a lot of character. Locals start gathering here at 5:00 in the morning for coffee, half an hour before the restaurant opens, and for the rest of the day it's jumping. Philip and John Kikukawa are the family's third generation to run the restaurant, which was founded by their dressmaker grandmother as a noodle shop with good beef stew. In the days when the steamers and passenger ships frequented Kaunakakai Harbor, the Mid Nite Inn stayed open to feed them. The name stuck even though they now close at 9:00 P.M.

The rage here are the fried akule and other fresh fish dishes at good prices. The Kikukawas are the last to buy from the Molokai fishermen and thus buy at low prices they pass on to customers. The oxtail soup, pancakes, and fried opakapaka are also honorable, and there's catering and a banquet room as well. Ask about the diesel grill—it's World War II vintage and the secret of their fabulous grilled fare.

Inexpensive—two can dine well for $15. Open 6:00 A.M. to 1:30 P.M. and 5:00 to 9:00 P.M. Monday and Saturday; 5:30 A.M. to 1 P.M. and 5:00 to 9:00 P.M. Tuesday through Friday; and 7:00 A.M. to 12:30 P.M. Sunday. No credit cards.

MOLOKAI DRIVE-INN
Kaunakakai
Telephone: (808) 553-5655

It's not a restaurant, it's a fast-food counter. But it has the best plate lunches on the island: fresh mahimahi when available, fresh ahi at other times, served with the classic carbohydrate—two scoops of rice. The saimin and fried saimin are also popular, and so are the hamburgers, not your garden variety version but something a little more, well, crafted. Fresh fish burgers and sandwiches round out the menu, which is itself a visual treat. "Par Fay," "French Frys," and other imaginative misspellings are endearing features of this down-home drive-in.

Inexpensive—plate lunches are $3.50. Open 7:00 A.M. to 10:00 P.M. Sunday through Thursday and until 10:30 P.M. Friday and Saturday. Cash and traveler's checks accepted; no credit cards.

OHIA LODGE
Kaluakoi Hotel and Golf Club
Kepuhi Beach
Telephone: (808) 552-2555

This is your only choice for anything nearing fine dining. The Kaluakoi Hotel's restaurant has a vaguely Polynesian motif and the standard hotel restaurant menu that tries hard to be something it isn't. However, with a new chef coming in, changes may be in store.

You'll find breakfast, lunch, and dinner here, but expect to pay more than anywhere else on the island. Dinner fare features the usual chicken, fish, and beef dishes, including salad bar and a catch-of-the-day that, if they haven't yet run out, may surprise you by being delicious. Fresh ahi in a wine and butter sauce and the barbecued chicken are among the better dinner items. Whatever you do, don't order the prawns macadamia unless they've stopped heaping them with mounds of bread crumbs that look like a plateful of mice. Take heart, however; it's been promised that the new chef will enhance the cuisine in this, the only restaurant for miles.

Expensive, with $18 to $25 entrées. Open 6:30 to 11:00 A.M., noon to 2:30 P.M., and 6:30 to 9:00 P.M., with cocktails served until midnight. Major credit cards accepted.

NIGHTLIFE AND
ENTERTAINMENT

Molokai has its share of great Hawaiian musicians, and it's never hard to find them. Chances are they're playing at either the Pau Hana Inn, the Kaluakoi Hotel, or the Hotel Molokai. Some names to watch for: Zachary Helm, who plays guitar, Hawaiian and contemporary, and who sings in the classic Hawaiian falsetto; Kimo Paleka, who bills himself as "Molokai's own"; and the group FIBRE, the Friendly Isle Band Rhythmic Experience, who play contemporary music that people love to dance to.

SPECIAL OUTINGS:
ON LAND

Golf

THE KALUAKOI HOTEL AND GOLF CLUB
P.O. Box 1977
Maunaloa, HI 96770
Telephone: (800) 367-6046, (808) 523-0411

Hawaii's avid golfers often wax poetic about the Kaluakoi Golf Club, largely because it is such a sleeper in such a splendid environment. The championship par 72 course was designed by Ted Robinson and features five holes flush against dramatic, rocky oceanside cliffs. The most difficult short hole, number 11, is along the ocean close to Pohaku Mauliuli Beach and is heavily trapped, with strong winds. In fact, heavy winds are the biggest liability of this course. Although it is one of Hawaii's best courses, it often gets overlooked because of its winds and because it's on less-traveled Molokai. However, Kaluakoi's fans rate this as one of the top five courses in the state, not only because of its layout and condition, but because its people are singularly warm and cordial. Golf rates are about $40 for cart and green fees for a non–resort guest and about $6 less for resort guests, with special rates available for groups. For reservations: (808) 552-2739, 521-1625.

Historical Sights

'ILI'ILI'OPAE HEIAU
Mapulehu

This is Molokai's largest heiau—ancient Hawaiian stone temple—and also the island's oldest. Part of a complex that's a National Historic Landmark, the heiau is a stone platform 286 by 87 feet and 11 to 22 feet high. It is awesome and powerful—a long plain of moss-covered rock, centuries old, used by the ancients for human sacrifice and the worship of their highest gods. Originally three times its present size, it was the center for a large group of *kahuna* (Hawaiian priests), who trained aspirants and then sent them to work in other areas. Legend has it that the mythological *menehune*, leprechaun-like beings who worked only at night, built the heiau with stones brought from Wailau Valley on the other side of the island. The hike from the road to the heiau is pleasant, through mango trees and a stream bed. Walk cautiously, especially as you climb the terrace. To get there, drive east on Kam V Highway, past the Mapulehu Mango Grove on the right. After you cross the bridge, look for a green gate on the left. Park and follow the trail. Someone at the caretaker's cottage will direct you. The heiau is on private property and all they ask is a call to let them know you're coming: Pearl Petro, (808) 558-8113.

KALAUPAPA

One of Molokai's two National Historic Landmarks, Kalaupapa National Park is the island's foremost visitor attraction. It is also Molokai's most famous idiosyncrasy. Isolated by ocean on one side and 1,600-foot cliffs on the other, it is its own separate county, administered by the State Department of Health and populated by a community of one hundred or so linked to a tragic episode in Molokai's history. Kalaupapa is a former leper colony immortalized by the martyrdom of Father Damien, who cared for the patients and died of leprosy in 1889. Kalaupapa residents are free to live elsewhere but have chosen to remain among the old wooden homes, churches, general store, and rugged terrain so heavily imbued with Father Damien's love. Looking along the northern coast from the peninsula, you can see the steepest and highest sea cliffs in the world and the unforgettable splendor of Pelekunu and Wailau valleys, all the way east to Halawa. You must be at least sixteen to visit, and you must have a guide once you reach Kalaupapa by mule, hike, or small plane. If you do not take the mule ride or any tour, you must have permission from the Department of Health in Molokai or Honolulu. The hike is steep—1,600 feet—and be prepared to dodge mule chips while you share breathtaking views and a partially paved trail. Damien Tours charges $15 for a tour of the peninsula, which lasts three to four hours.

Horseback Riding

HAWAIIAN HORSEMANSHIP UNLIMITED
P.O. Box 94
Kualapu'u, HI 96757
Telephone: (808) 567-6635

You cannot imagine the beauty of Sarah Selnick's playground. To begin with, her thirteen horses—thoroughbreds, quarter horses, an Appaloosa, an Arabian, and a Morgan—live in a meadow called Horse Heaven, a 200-acre mountain paradise in which no man-made object is visible. It's the most exquisite riding terrain imaginable: rolling hills like Irish moors, grassland and trees as far as the eye can see, natural hillsides with cushy grass for free riding on spirited, healthy horses. Selnick teaches English riding and offers horseback riding in Molokai's hinterlands only to accomplished equestrians, preferably with referrals from equestrian organizations. This is not a rent-a-horse; Claremont sends riders to her. (One of her horses is a descendant of Secretariat.)

There are five different rides: one deep into Molokai's mountains through grassy mounds and meadows; one to Kalaupapa Cliffs; a forest ride to Waikolu Valley Lookout in the Molokai Forest Reserve; a ride to a west-end beach; and one to Kaunakakai, stopping for lunch at the Pau Hana Inn. They last four to six hours except for Waikolu, which is the longest ride, silent and soft on pine needles and amid wild plums, freshwater pools, waterfalls, fern grottos, and rare native flora. Rides can be customized too, and Selnick goes all out to prepare gourmet lunches or, for the adventurous, the best of local Hawaiian dishes.

Prices vary, but one $850 package includes hotel, rides, all the lunches, first and last night's meal, and a rent-a-car—for seven days. Independent riders pay $50 for half a day and $75 for a full day, including lunch. For experienced riders, a dream come true; for nonriders, a reason to learn.

MOLOKAI MULE RIDE
P.O. Box 200
Kualapu'u, HI 96757
Telephone: (800) 843-5978, (808) 567-6088

Close to 7,500 people a year descend into Kalaupapa by mule, traversing two dozen switchbacks on a 1,600-foot descent along a 3-mile trail once traveled by Father Damien and Jack London. It's not a bridle path, but you don't have to watch your footing; the mules do all the work. The Molokai Mule Ride by Rare Adventures has experienced muleskinners guiding you from topside to the peninsula for lunch, a tour, and an effortless trip back up. The youngest visitor has been sixteen, the oldest eighty-eight—the adventurers come from Keokuk to Sweden and points beyond. The exhilarating descent into Molokai's historic landmark offers breathtaking views and a limitless vista of the northern terrain. Started by a wheelchair-bound entrepreneur in 1973, the mule ride changed hands in 1983 and is run by reliable operators who know their mules and the territory. You must be sixteen years and older and no more than 225 pounds. Wear jeans or comfortable slacks, bring wind and sun protection, and don't forget camera and film. The cost is $65.

Special Excursions

HALAWA VALLEY

A trip to the east end and Halawa Valley is a must for any visitor. The main highway ends at Halawa, making it the last point on the island accessible by car before the north-shore valleys begin. There are signs that Halawa was populated as early as 650, making it the site of the earliest Hawaiian community on Molokai. Taro farmers and fishermen thrived in this fertile valley until the 1946 tsunami hit. Today stone remnants of house sites and temples remain in the valley, bearing testament to the halcyon days of Halawa.

It's a 28-mile trip one way from Kaunakai to Halawa, so expect an all-day outing and depart with mosquito repellent, a full gas tank, and a picnic lunch. After you leave Kaunakakai, you pass miles of ancient Hawaiian fish ponds and a series of coves and beaches along Kamehameha V Highway along the south shore. You'll come to the overlook spanning Lamaloa Head, the mouth of Halawa Valley, and the bay and flat river mouth below. Mauka (toward the mountain) you will see the two majestic waterfalls: 250-foot Moa'ula Falls to the left and the 500-feet Hipuapua Falls to the right.

Follow the road past the green church and take a left-hand road to the trail head for Moa'ula Falls, consisting of upper and lower sections cascading into a large mountain pool. You must hike in about 2½ miles. It is an idyllic, paradisiacal spot said to be guarded by a *mo'o*, a mythological lizard celebrated in many of Molokai's ancient chants and dances.

MOLOKAI RANCH WILDLIFE PARK

It looks like the Serengeti: antelope, Indian black buck, axis deer, rhea, greater kudu, oryx, eland, and some 500 animals usually seen only on an African safari. They roam 1,500 acres of Molokai Ranch land and are easily seen close up as your van traverses dirt roads, ravines, plains, and kiawe thickets in an environment remarkably unlike the tropics and considered one of the finest natural game preserves in the world. Some animals will even approach your van and are eminently cooperative with photographers. The wildlife safari is educational and entertaining, especially for children.

Tours, at $12 for adults and juniors and $6 for children twelve and under, can be arranged from the activity desk of any hotel or by calling Rare Adventures, (808) 567-6088, or the Molokai Ranch, (808) 553-5115. The daily tours last an hour and a half and are given in air-conditioned, 15-passenger vans.

KAMAKOU PRESERVE
The Nature Conservancy of Hawaii
1116 Smith Street
Suite 201
Honolulu, HI 96817
Telephone: (808) 537-4508

Environmentalists, conservationists, nature lovers, and those with more than a passing interest in Hawaii's endangered wildlife will clearly love the

Conservancy's natural history tours of Maui and Molokai. Limited to eight participants, the trips give you access to the most remote regions of Molokai's Kamakou Preserve while a knowledgeable Nature Conservancy guide fills you in on the rare birds, plants, and endangered life in the area. The Conservancy plans to offer eight trips a year, but that could change. What won't change is the insight, education, and rare opportunity the trips give you to explore otherwise inaccessible regions of Hawaii. You will see dense, ancient bogs with miniature flora, birds that exist nowhere else, and fossil deposits and archaeological sites on pristine coastal dunes. The eight-day package begins at the New Otani Kaimana Beach Hotel on Diamond Head and swings over to Maui's Stouffer Wailea Beach Resort, then to the Kaluakoi Hotel on Molokai for the foray into Kamakou Preserve. The trips are not for everyone, surely not for the fainthearted. Bring your field glasses, mosquito repellent, and bird-calling repertoire. Costs for 1988 are $1,850 double occupancy and $2,100 single occupancy, $250 of which goes to The Nature Conservancy as a tax-deductible donation. The Conservancy acquires and manages critical natural habitats in Hawaii and other parts of the United States.

You can also hike in the Kamakou Preserve, but you need a four-wheel-drive vehicle to get to the preserve entrance at Waikolu Lookout. For directions and weather conditions, contact the preserve manager, (808) 567-6680.

PALA'AU STATE PARK

You can camp there, hike there, or just drive up, peer into Kalaupapa, and pay your respects to the phallic rock. Whatever your reasons for coming here, once you arrive you will want to linger. The Pala'au State Park is nearly at the center of the island, at an elevation of 1,000 feet. At 233.7 acres in size and with full facilities, it's the best campsite on Molokai. It can be reached by driving to the northern end of Kalae Highway, where the northern coastline looms beneath you and trails among ironwoods beckon. There are restrooms, picnic tables, water, and easy access to the Kalaupapa trailhead. There are also thickly forested areas and an arboretum of Hawaiian trees, and there is the Kalaupapa Overlook with the fabled view described by many writers, such as Jack London and James Michener. The Kaule o Nanahoa, a 6-foot phallic rock, casts long shadows among the ironwoods, harking back to the days when Hawaiian women sought its power as a cure for infertility.

PURDY'S NUTS
Ho'olehua
Telephone: (808) 567-6495, 567-6601

Tuddie Purdy has demystified the macadamia nut, presenting it in its simple, unadorned splendor under the shade of his nut trees with their flowers like bottle brushes and miraculous, rock-hard shells. The beauty of his operation is its small size and intimacy. Purdy, his cats, and his mother, Theo, greet you on their 1-acre spread and give you a brief tour that explains such things as the growth cycle of the trees, the volume of nuts yielded from a single tree (25 to 30 pounds in the shell), and, most interesting, how to extract their fleshy morsels from their impossible encasements. The shelling will delight you because of its high-calorie rewards. It is accomplished with a Purdy original, a rubber holding device that prevents the unseemly bashing of fingers. You can wash it down with fresh coconut water and coconut, another Purdy offering. The real treat is Purdy himself, an eager, amiable sort, and his mother, who also makes maile, rare pink-and-white akulikuli, and other exotic flower leis to order. Macadamia nut honey is sold here as well, and as for the nuts, they're sold in the shell or shelled and lightly roasted with Hawaiian salt. The roasted nuts go for $11 a pound—Purdy gets them from the Big Island because he doesn't have processing equipment, but they're fresh as can be and well worth the price. Tours are given at noon daily, but call ahead to confirm and get directions.

WAIKOLU VALLEY LOOKOUT

Molokai is deceiving. Its lush, verdant areas are largely hidden or inaccessible, as if concealed behind a veil of ubiquitous scrub and kiawe. To get to the higher elevations with their fern grottos, waterfalls, and white tropic birds against sheer purple cliffs, you must rely on a couple of things: good weather for manageable road conditions, and a four-wheel drive vehicle. The Waikolu Valley lookout, 13½ miles from Kaunakakai and a 45-minute drive upland, requires a car with four-wheel drive except in the driest of weather conditions, when a conventional vehicle may succeed but is risky. The Waikolu Valley lookout is in the Molokai Forest Reserve, a dense wonderland of ginger, ferns, ohia, and waterfalls galore. The road to the lookout takes you past a famous pit used by the Hawaiians to measure their sandalwood harvest. When you get to the lookout you confront a steep-sided valley with ribbons of waterfalls and to the left, a part of Kalaupapa. Waikolu, meaning "three waters," is a source of water for central and west Molokai. Across the road from the lookout is a pavilion with water and restrooms, and walks in any direction will lead you through dense thickets of Hawaiian flora. Waikolu Valley's view and moist mountain air are pleasures earned and not easily forgotten.

SPECIAL OUTINGS:
IN AND ON THE WATER

HOKUPA'A OCEAN ADVENTURES
Halawa Valley
Telephone: (808) 558-8195

Glenn and Mahealani Davis are rare finds for travelers or residents: dedicated Hawaiians with a love of the land, a firm grasp of Hawaii's history, and a commitment to maintain the old traditions of taro farming, tapa making, lauhala weaving, fishing, planting, and living by the old ways. Because they live in Halawa Valley, Molokai's isolated northern coastline is their own backyard. Its valleys, waterfalls, the highest sea cliffs in the world—3,300 feet—and its dazzling sea caves and isolated inlets are the treasures of Molokai they will share with you. Weather permitting, they'll take you to Molokai's most remote spots on their 25-foot twin-engine vessel, *Mahealani*, the only boat tour out of Halawa Valley. Glenn Davis is a licensed Coast Guard captain with years of experience, and he knows the best spots for snorkeling, bottom fishing, or just learning the legends of the land. He'll show you that each bay has a waterfall and a special name that captures its features. The boat carries a maximum of six. It's $200 to charter the whole boat or $50 a person for fewer than six. Cruises can be customized, but the standard cruise lasts four hours. If you're lucky enough to meet the Davises, you'll come away feeling enriched.

RODONIS
Molokai Shores
Unit 132
Kaunakakai, HI 96748
Telephone: (808) 553-3311

Since owner and skipper Randy Dennan (it's a she) moved over from Alaska to take over this operation, guests on the 50-foot yacht *Rodonis* have never been happier. The word is out that the *Rodonis* has been reinvigorated. The charters will take you to neighboring Lanai for an all-day snorkel sail or for something as simple as two hours on a sunset champagne cruise off the east end of Molokai. Because it's owner operated, there's the benefit of flexibility, personalized service, and special touches such as home-cooked meals and spontaneous guitar sing-alongs. If you'd like vegetarian meals, they'll prepare them for you; if you want a short excursion or an extended sail to a special corner of the islands, they'll do that too. A minimum of six people is required. Rodonis Sailing Charters also offers sail training and extended interisland cruises by special arrangement. Rates range from $69 for the sunset cruise to $89 for the all-day snorkel tour and more for the three-island and extended cruises.

BEACHES

Molokai's finest beaches are concentrated on the west side, where six public accesses have been established by the Kaluakoi Resort. On the southern shore of the island, however, there are beaches galore with easy access—it's just that they're reefy, not good for swimming and because of their abundant fish ponds, they are known more for their historic value than for recreation. As you drive further east toward Halawa, however, the beaches become more attractive. Keep an eye out for Murphy Beach Park, across and slightly past an old sugar mill; Rock Point, a popular surfing spot slightly past Honouli Wai Bay; and a beautiful white crescent called Small Bay at Kumimi, with gentle waves and rock-filled waters that are, in spite of this, good for swimming. With picturesque Maui across the channel, these beaches make great picnic spots but are entirely different in nature from the west end beaches listed below. For more information on Molokai beaches, consult John Clark's *Beaches of Maui County*.

Dixie Maru

Kapukahehu is popularly known as Dixie Maru, named after a Japanese fishing boat that wrecked offshore in the 1920s. Dixie Maru is one of the southern crescents on the spectacular western coastline of Molokai, known for its white-sand beaches and frequently turbulent surf. Access is through the Kaluakoi Resort; there is parking, a small dirt path, and kiawe trees lining a salt and pepper (more salt than pepper) bay bordered on each side by banks of black lava. Dixie Maru is a favorite with locals and although caution is advised year-round, the safer summer months are marked by good body and board surfing in the protected inlet of the cove.

Kawakiu Beach

Kawakiu is one of the northernmost accessible beaches on Molokai's western shoreline, a magnificent white-sand bay flanked by a cliff and lava outcroppings. In between is a perfect crescent that is safe for swimming, but only when the waters are calm. Nevertheless, this is Molokai's most beautiful beach. Public access was won only after protesting Hawaiian activists demanded it from the Molokai Ranch, but even today you must persevere to find it. You can get there via a dirt road or a long hike from Kepuhi Beach. The dirt road, beginning at Maunaloa Highway, turns off about 2½ miles north of the road to the Kaluakoi Hotel. Kawakiu has revealed more signs of ancient habitation than any of the other beaches, such as house platforms, a burial cave, and a heiau. Camping is allowed here with special permit from the Molokai Ranch. Kawakiu is a rare entity today: an unspoiled, isolated, gorgeous piece of shoreline that captures the essence of a bygone Hawaii.

Kepuhi Beach

Flanked on its southern point by historic Kaiaka Rock, Kepuhi is the beach on which the Kaluakoi Hotel sits. It's an easily accessible beach with a curve of white sand and changeable waters that offer safe swimming only under the calmest of conditions. Undertow and deceptive currents make this a beach requiring caution. It is, however, popular among accomplished board surfers who frequent an offshore spot called Boiler's, so named because of the roiling, cauldronlike foam circles in a specific part of each wave. Although the waters are intimidating, the beach is ideal for long, romantic sunset strolls or simple picnics by the shore. Highly recommended is a special foray to the tee of the twelfth hole of the surrounding golf course, where a shady spot under kiawe trees before a wide, pristine beach offers the picnic spot of your dreams. During summer months children frolic in the tidal pools and jump off a protruding rock into the water. You can drive up to and park in a dirt area across the twelfth fairway, but be on the lookout for wayward golf balls as you head for the beach.

To the left of Kepuhi Beach is an imposing lava promontory called Kaiaka Rock. It's the site of an ancient heiau 39 by 18 feet, which was tragically bulldozed and covered by the U.S. Army in the late 1960s. Nevertheless, native Hawaiians still revere Pu'u O Kaiaka as a historic and valuable site. Old bricks are still visible on Kaiaka, from the days when the first pineapples were shipped off the island from this point. You can follow an old Hawaiian trail to the top and the other side of Kaiaka.

Papohaku Beach

It's known as the longest white-sand beach in Hawaii, quite a distinction. It's nearly 3 miles long, a majestic, straight line of white sand that during calm summer months is inviting and irresistible. It is, however, rarely ever safe for swimming. Nearly 100 yards wide during some parts of the year, it's flanked on the north by Kaiaka Rock, a historic cinder cone, and to the south by prominent lava outcroppings. There are several ways of approaching Papohaku, but the easiest way is through Papohaku Beach Park, a well-kept facility with restrooms, showers, and campgrounds. The many ancient structures found around Papohaku indicate that an unusually large Hawaiian settlement must have existed there in the old days.

Pohaku Mauliuli

Most people call it Make (*Mah*-kay) Horse Beach. It's also called the Eleventh Hole Beach and is not easily accessible. However, hardy hikers can approach it by following the coastline from Kepuhi Beach to the south.

Pohaku Mauliuli consists of a large black rock and two white-sand coves with tidal pools along a shoreline that changes considerably with the seasons. If you hike here, beware of loose cinder on the paths and use utmost discretion in swimming, for the waters have strong currents. In spite of all the caveats, Pohaku Mauliuli is a splendid, isolated beach much loved by Molokaians.

SHOPPING

Aside from a few neighborhood stores along Kamehameha V High-way, groceries are available at the Friendly Isle Market Center in Maunaloa and at either Misaki's or Friendly's on Kaunakakai's main drag. Most people from around the island, including residents from as far away as Halawa Valley, plan their grocery shopping around Misaki's or Friendly's, which carry the essentials but have far more than a supermarket selection. There is also a health food co-op, Molokai Buyers, Inc., around the corner from the Molokai Dive Shop in Kaunakakai, with a small selection of takeout sandwiches, produce, and health food items. Whenever you can, treat yourself to local Molokai produce, such as tomatoes, sweet potatoes, and herbs. They're Molokai's specialty, especially the young, sweet onions that rival their famous Maui cousins. As for gifts and other items, read on.

BIG WIND KITE SHOP
Maunaloa
Telephone: (808) 552-2364

Maunaloa is windy, which makes it perfect for Hawaii's only kite factory. Jonathan Socher, kite designer nonpareil, takes his craft seriously and produces everything from airborne hula dancers—a classic—to Molokai kites with palm trees and clouds. Everything from unicorns and Moorish idols to Diamond Head are immortalized in his nylon fantasies, and each is made right there in Maunaloa. His wife, Daphne, is an artist and his partner. While Jonathan gives free kite-flying lessons on the windy slopes of Mauna-loa, Daphne devises new ways of coloring the skies with their dreams. Big Wind distributes throughout Hawaii but only here do you get the factory tour.

Open 8:00 A.M. to 5:00 P.M. daily except Sunday. During some of the winter months, they open Sunday at 11:00 A.M. to 2:00 P.M. Personal checks and all major credit cards accepted.

JO'S OF MOLOKAI
Hotel Molokai
Kaunakakai
Telephone: (808) 553-3444

There are two things worth noting here. The first is the lauhala bags and purses in the front counter, made lovingly by a woman who collects the hala leaves from 40 feet away on the hotel grounds and then weaves them into fine, smooth, impeccably crafted works with a personal touch. The lauhala, as the fiber is called, is not only from Molokai, it's a fine example of a Hawaiian craft originating from a venerable and familiar tree. The second notable is the shop owner's husband, Bob Johnson, a salt-of-the-earth guy who uprooted himself from the fast lane of Hollywood to languish in the hills of Molokai. He's in the shop most days, speaking in the unmistakable baritone you heard in "Mission Impossible": "This tape will self-destruct in five minutes. Good luck, Jim."

Hours vary. Major credit cards accepted.

MOLOKAI FISH AND DIVE
Kaunakakai
Telephone: (808) 553-5926

If you're looking for fishing gear, snorkels, suntanning lotions, beach towels, wooden postcards, tennis balls, or swimming trunks, this is the place to go. The best selection of original Molokai T-shirts can be found here, including a marvelous array of swimming trunks and suits. A cross between an old-fashioned country store and a sports and souvenir shop, it offers just about everything you need. Jim Brocker, artist and owner, will happily advise on fishing spots, charters, and other marine activities.

Open 9 A.M. to 6:00 P.M. Monday through Friday; Saturday, 8:00 A.M. to 6:00 P.M.; Sunday, 8:00 A.M. to 2:00 P.M. Major credit cards accepted.

EVERYDAY GOOD THINGS

MOLOKAI DRUGS INC.
Kaunakakai
Telephone: (808) 553-5790

The island's first pharmacist is still on Molokai, and so is the drugstore he started half a century ago. Today it's run by his son-in-law and his son-in-law's brother, the only two pharmacists on this tiny island. There are full prescription services at Molokai Drugs, plus all manner of miscellany, from rubber zoris and suntan lotions for beach goers to snacks, cards, and books about Molokai. It's a drugstore, yes, but it's also a bit of an old-fashioned general store.

It's open 8:45 A.M. to 5:45 P.M. daily except Sunday. Major credit cards accepted.

MOLOKAI PHOTO CONNECTION
Davis Building
Puali Place
Kaunakakai
Telephone: (808) 553-9913

Joe and Kathy Morawski run a dependable, efficient camera and film service that provides overnight color print processing by Fuji and Kodak, the most complete line of camera batteries on the island, minor camera repairs, usual and unusual types of film, and a wedding and portrait photography service. What's more, they are a generous, hardworking couple eager to please their customers. They have about a dozen photo drop-off counters, from the Kaluakoi Hotel to the little towns scattered over the island. There is a one-hour film processing lab on the island (Island Photo Processing), but Molokai Photo Connection prefers to spend the time to fly its film to Fuji and Kodak for the best quality in prints and slides. The overnight service is a small part of what they do here. Molokai Photo Connection also has the only commercial darkroom on the island for black-and-white processing, and they sell film wholesale as well.

The Kaunakakai store opens from 10:00 A.M. to 5:30 P.M. Monday through Friday, 8:00 A.M. to noon on Saturday, and is closed Sunday. The other stores have their own hours. Major credit cards accepted.

FLOWERS AND LEIS

KUUALOHA FLOWERS AND LEIS
Kaunakakai
Telephone: (808) 553-5652

Cynthia and Donald Gutierres give you more than you bargained for. There are leis and flowers here, yes, but also lots of Molokai generosity that has them working late, adjusting work hours, and bending over backward for those who find them. These are good-hearted people who offer an imaginative, splendid selection of flowers and leis. Besides the roses and spring flowers, you'll find protea here during winter months and maile, pikake, ginger, gardenia, tuberose, and the full gamut of leis, wound and strung. The breathtaking, doubly thick rope pikake lei may be wound with brilliant purple straw flowers, or a single strand may be combined with the magenta akulikuli. The haku, or woven, leis are made to order; the deluxe version has the featherlike, pink petals of the king and queen protea individually woven, petal for petal, and combined with seeds. Cigar leis, leis made of the bright orange fruit of the hala (pandanus) tree, and other exotica are also the fare here. If you order the hala lei, you get its Hawaiian history as well; they'll tell you the dried fruit was used to brush dye onto Hawaiian tapa, the traditional bark cloth. Special touches abound here.

Open 8:00 A.M. to 3:00 P.M. Monday through Thursday, 8:00 A.M. to 4:30 P.M. Friday and Saturday, and closed Sunday. No credit cards.

GIFTS TO GO

SYLVIA ADAMS
P.O. Box 202
Kualapu'u, HI 96757
Telephone: (808) 567-6435

One of the few weavers on the island, Adams maintains the painstaking art of lauhala weaving by gathering and preparing the prickly coils of the hala tree, then weaving and plaiting the dried strips into baskets, bracelets, and purses. Her work is museum quality and functional, like the traditional work of the Hawaiians. Adams learned from master lauhala weaver Louise Kekahuna and has had her work exhibited in the Honolulu Academy of Arts and the Kauai Museum. When you see and feel her work, you touch the living presence of Molokai, from hala tree to completed craft. Adams will weave items to order, but she needs time to complete them—at least a week for purses and longer for the bigger pieces. She also makes wili and haku leis in classic Hawaiian fashion, using the maile, ferns, and native flora of Molokai.

ALAPA'I HANAPI
Star Route 295
Molokai, HI 96748
Telephone: (808) 558-8378

Working out of his east end home, Hanapi fashions native woods into traditional Hawaiian shapes: poi boards, paddles, bowls, platters, and more. Following only Hawaiian or Polynesian motifs, he crafts his work meticulously and is generally only accessible through art exhibits and shows throughout Hawaii. A current commission of his is a series of wooden carvings for the state, depicting the Kumulipo, the Hawaiian creation chant. He is a revered wood sculptor with a fierce allegiance to Hawaiian materials and themes, and his work is for the serious collector: He works only on commission, with a $1,000 minimum. His woods—koa, milo, and occasionally hau—are from Molokai and the Big Island.

LANAI

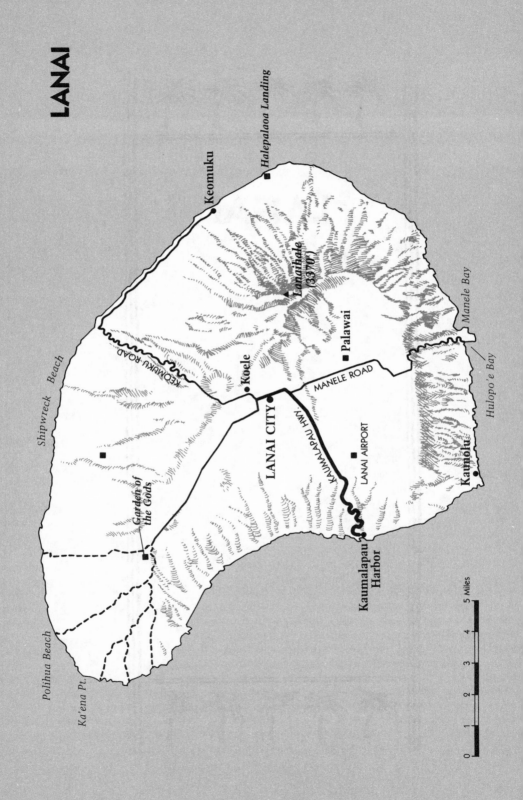

LANAI

Polihua Beach

Ka'ena Pt.

Garden of the Gods

Shipwreck Beach

KEOMUKU ROAD

Keomuku

Halepalaoa Landing

Lanaihale (3370)

Koele

LANAI CITY

KAUMALAPAU HWY.

Palawai

MANELE ROAD

Manele Bay

Hulopo'e Bay

Kaumolu

LANAI AIRPORT

Kaumalapau Harbor

0   1   2   3   4   5 Miles

A BRIEF HISTORY

It's said that Lanai was the first Hawaiian island to be inhabited by the gods and the last to be populated by people. In between, the legend goes, Lanai was inhabited by questionable spirits.

It was well into the fifteenth century that the island's spirits finally cleared out and it was safe to come aboard and live. Even back then Lanai was a latecomer to the ways of the world, and, ironically, the same can be said today.

All eyes in Hawaii are fixed on this tiny island as it prepares to toss its hat into the tourism arena. While the rest of Hawaii has been grooming its shorelines and greeting tourists for the past eighty-five years, Lanai has put all its efforts, land, and people into the production and cultivation of pineapples. Although neighbor island hunters and outdoorsmen have long stayed at Lanai's only hotel, it was thought that tourism was for the other islands and not for this laid-back outpost, with its dirt roads and pineapple fields.

Lanai is owned by Castle and Cooke, one of Hawaii's "Big Five" corporations that recently came under the control of businessman David Murdock. Murdock has made no secret of his personal interest in Lanai. Not long after making headlines for suggesting that Castle and Cooke employees switch from aloha shirts to business suits, he became visible on Lanai, flying into the tiny and predominantly red-dirt island in his white Learjet with his personal mechanic. It is this scenario, then—the picture of a small, backwoods, privately owned island cautiously, and for the first time, flinging wide its doors—that we approach when we come to this island.

Lying 8 miles to the west of Maui, 7 miles south of Molokai, and 15 miles northeast of Kahoolawe, Lanai is a small, 17-by-12-mile, pear-shaped mound. The name means "swelling" or a "hump," and when seen from neighboring Maui and Molokai, it's a comforting whale on the horizon.

For generations the people of Lanai have roamed the slopes of this island, swimming, hunting, hiking, and camping wherever they pleased. With its population of 2,178 living on a mere 141.2 square miles of land, there is a comfortable intimacy here. Everyone on Lanai knows everyone else; there are two service stations, one school, one park, one cemetery, one airport, one hotel, three stores, and not a single bridge or traffic light. At five every morning the plantation whistle goes off to announce the start of the work-day. It has always been that way. There is one town, Lanai City, where all the people live, go to school, and shop.

Two new, upscale hotels are being built—one on Hulopoe Bay at Manele Harbor, the island's only accessible white-sand beach, and the other in Koele, a charming, tree-lined bluff 1,900 feet above sea level, bordering Lanai City and the golf course. Koele is expected to open in the fall of 1988 and Manele one year later. Understandably, many Lanaians feel a mixture of trepidation and anticipation as they look at the jobs, traffic, population growth, and tremendous changes in life-style they know are now inevitable.

Lanai activists say they spent thirty years fighting development and are still being vigilant. There's no denying that the decline of the pineapple industry and a critical economic void fueled arguments in favor of develop-ment. Residents also point to the young, who are exiting the island in droves, driven by the lack of jobs and leaving a sizable population of Lanai's senior citizens with no one to take care of them.

Indeed, a walk around the park in Lanai City reveals the poignant dilemma. There are children, grandparents, and high school students, but young adults are a rarity. A trip to Lanai City's cemetery, one of the most interesting in the world, reveals a riot of colorful plants, weathervanes, piles of stones, sculptures, and plain wooden crosses neatly and proudly tended. The community gathers every so often for a town-wide cemetery cleanup, and there are always two empty graves at the ready.

Visitors to the island have much to see, beginning with the highest ridge on the island, the 3,370-foot Lanaihale. The road to the top of Lanaihale takes you to vistas where all the other Hawaiian islands may be visible. Ohia, mountain naupaka, pili grass, and other native plants flourish among thick stands of Norfolk pine that blanket the central ridge of the island. The pines are a dominant feature of Lanai and this mountain, and were planted by George Munro, a New Zealander hired to manage the Lanai Ranch in 1910. It was hoped the trees would add coolness to the barren plains while they helped to increase the water supply on the island.

Lanaihale descends to the west into the Palawai Basin, a flatland where Hawaiian villagers of old somehow managed to grow yams. Today it is covered with rows and rows of pineapples that eventually drop to the southern coast, where the village of Kaunolu is located. Kaunolu is one of the Lanai's richest archaeological treasures, a network of house sites and terraces remaining from a once-thriving fishing village. Kamehameha loved Kaunolu so much that he returned twenty years after fighting on this island and made it his summer home.

Kaunolu was one of several prominent fishing villages with remains that were studied and documented by the Bishop Museum's illustrious Kenneth Emory, former chairman of the museum's anthropology department. The other villages he studied were Naha and Keomuku, which mark the eastern point of the island. Even Manele, where the harbor stands today, was a village in ancient times.

The drive to Keomuku is via Keomuku Road, the main thoroughfare that crosses the northern flank of Lanaihale heading northeast. After a long drive through flying wild turkeys and Jeep trails on wet sand, you'll come across the most prominent point of present-day Keomuku, the Kalanakila o Ka Malamalama Church. This ancient roadside church is undergoing restoration through an effort led by community members. In 1921, when Emory arrived to conduct his anthropological research, forty of the island's 185 people lived in Keomuku. "Auntie" Elaine Kaopuiki, the island's *kumu hula*, or hula master, and one of its respected elders, says her husband's family was the last to move out of the village.

Emory discovered that nearly 3,000 Hawaiians had lived in the coast, toplands, and valleys of the Maunalei Gulch on this sector of the island. He found hundreds of house sites and eleven heiaus, old stone game boards for the Hawaiian game *konane*, and trails meandering up Lanaihale. He also found petroglyphs, still visible today.

Like the rest of the Hawaiian Islands, Lanai had its years of embattlement and suffered its share of slaughter at the hands of warring kings. In 1778, the year Captain James Cook "discovered" the islands, a Big Island chief and his nephew, Kamehameha, ambushed Lanai and slaughtered every opposing warrior. The king, Kalaniopuu, then went on a violent rampage that destroyed every living thing in his path.

Through the late 1700s and 1800s, foreigners discovered Lanai—first the explorers (a captain sailing with Cook), then the missionaries, and finally the Mormons. One of its most colorful members took control of much of Lanai's lands—Walter Murray Gibson, who, accused of using the Mormon Church for his personal gain, was summarily excommunicated from the church but continued to live many years on the island he loved. He eventually became a prominent public official and King David Kalakaua's prime minister. When he died, the land went to his daughter and her husband, who attempted an abortive sugar venture in Maunalei. Three years after it opened, the sugar plantation closed, broke. In 1903, when only about 130 people lived on Lanai—partly the result of emigration to Lahaina—the entire island was bought by Charles Gay, whose family owned the island of Niihau. Financial problems forced him to give up the island before long, and it was soon snatched up by a group of investors from Oahu who formed the Lanai Company, a ranching operation. After another change of ownership, the island was bought by Jim Dole, who had already established Hawaii's pineapple industry with his agricultural achievements on Oahu. He decided on pineapple as the industry for the island and in 1924 began bringing in foreign laborers for his pineapple fields, establishing Lanai City as the island's residential and industrial center and launching the multiracial plantation that has continued to this day. Castle and Cooke, the parent company of Dole Company, today owns 98 percent of Lanai.

No doubt the advent of tourism in 1988 will add new activities to the already growing roster of diving, hunting, sailing, and sightseeing possibilities on the island. Lanai is considered a consummate hunting ground, and its waters are said to have the greatest abundance of scuba diving spots of all the islands of Hawaii. That bodes well for visitors—they'll have a gorgeous beach, an underdeveloped island, an isolated playground in which to explore the ocean, land, and secrets of old Hawaii. As for the good people of this island, they'll be watching carefully and hoping that their barefoot days haven't gone forever.

GETTING AROUND

It's impossible to get lost in Lanai. The airport consists of a small room with a chain-link fence separating the runway from the rest of the airport. Air Molokai ([808] 839-4040) and Hawaiian Air ([808] 537-5100) are the only carriers serving this airport.

There are two service stations that rent cars on the island: Oshiro Service and U-Drive, 850 Fraser Avenue, Lanai City, HI 96763; telephone (808) 565-6952; and Lanai City Service, 1036 Lanai Avenue, Lanai City, HI 96763; telephone (808) 565-6780.

Although it's more expensive, it's recommended that you rent a four-wheel-drive vehicle so you can get to areas not served by the limited paved road. Many of Lanai's most exciting areas are only accessible by four-wheel-drive vehicles.

When you arrive on this island, you'll be just minutes away from Lanai City, the picturesque social center where Norfolk pines line the streets and hillsides, at a 1,600-foot elevation. The one paved road goes through the center of the island, from Hulopoe Bay to Lanai City and from Lanai City to the northeastern shoreline via Keomuku Road.

Some of the island's best sights are hard to get to and require long, patient, well-navigated travels through pineapple fields thick with red dirt.

CAMPING

There are six campsites available for campers at Hulopoe Bay. Permits must be acquired from Castle and Cooke's Keole Company, at P.O. Box L, Lanai City, HI 96763; telephone (808) 565-6661.

HUNTING

There are abundant pheasant, deer, and mouflon sheep on this island. For information on hunting permits, contact the Keole Company at the address given above.

HOTELS AND ALTERNATIVES

HOTEL LANAI
P.O. Box A-119
Lanai, HI 96763
Telephone: (800) 624-8849, (808) 565-7211

For years this has been Lanai's sole hotel, much loved by guests and residents. Built in the 1920s, it was where visitors to Castle and Cooke's Dole Company stayed when they visited. It has the only bar on the island and the only restaurant that's not a coffee-shop/diner. Its charming lodge atmosphere, with fireplace and friendly people, makes it a hotel you immediately love. There are ten rooms on the less than 2-acre property at an elevation of 1,600 feet. The air is cool and crisp and a blanket of Norfolk pines surrounds it.

Hotel Lanai used to be leased out to Ocean Activities Center by the island's owner, Castle and Cooke. Castle and Cooke recently took over operation of the hotel, however, and is planning to upgrade it and use it partly as a training center for new hotel workers. It's an old-fashioned lodge that has long been used by hunters and is now seeing its share of visitors.

There are knotty pine walls, a fireplace in the lobby, wood floors, and lauhala mats: Nothing fancy here; everything is very inviting and pleasant. The rooms have a shower but no tub. They're modest but clean, with twin beds, a chair by the window, a dresser, and a small bathroom.

The meals are respectable, with fresh fish dinners that are reliably good. The dearth of restaurants on Lanai makes this the place for breakfast, lunch, and dinner, for local folks and visitors.

Rates, including the 9.4 percent tax, are $55.59 for single occupancy, $63.22 for double occupancy, and $70.85 for triple.

Coming Attractions

THE LODGE AT KOELE
Lanai City

Now being built, this will be Lanai's first new hotel. It's due to be completed in the fall of 1988 with 102 rooms in two stories at the foot of

Lanaihale, the mountain just outside of Lanai City. It's being touted as an upscale lodge for the hunter, the fisherman, and the outdoorsman-sportsman. There will be botanical gardens and footpaths through the adjacent, pine-covered hillside. The hotel site is a property of 21 acres.

THE MANELE BAY HOTEL
Hulopoe Bay

Planners describe this two-story, 250-room hostelry as an "old kamaaina estate." The roof line will have the look of an estate, and the hotel will be situated on a hillside presiding over the lovely Hulopoe Bay. The hotel will be surrounded by a large canopy of trees. The road leading to the hotel, which also leads to Hulopoe and Manele Bay today, will be heavily land-scaped.

It will be a luxury resort, with an eighteen-hole golf course nearby. The hotel will be set back from a ledge that looks directly over the ocean, on a hill; nonetheless, the rooms will have ocean views and the beach will be accessible. As for the existing Hulopoe Bay and all its facilities, Castle and Cooke says a park facility next to the bay and the hotel will be maintained by the company, and open to the public.

There are more people opening up their homes as bed and breakfast operations on Lanai. To find them, contact B and B Hawaii, Box 449, Kapaa, Kauai, HI 96746; telephone (808) 822-7771.

DINING OUT

L anai City has a very uncomplicated dining scene. The one bar and dinner restaurant is at the Hotel Lanai ([808] 565-7211), where you can get everything from great breakfasts to a surprisingly good fresh fish dinner. The lodge serves a limited lunch and can be quite a beehive of activity as local residents drop in after work for happy hour.

The other two eateries are Dahang's Pastry Shop (409 Seventh Street; telephone [808] 565-6363), which, with its out-of-this-world cream puffs, is the locals' breakfast gathering place, and Jerry Tanigawa's tiny storefront, which serves the island's best hamburgers. Tanigawa's landmark diner has a sign reading s.t. properties, inc. (419 Seventh; telephone [808] 565-6537).

Between these three, one can eat quite well in Lanai City, and if that's not enough, there are three stores where you can buy your own groceries. (See Everyday Good Things.)

SPECIAL OUTINGS:
ON LAND

Hiking

For an island of this size, Lanai offers more than its share of good hiking. The island's premier hiking trail is the Munro Trail that traverses the 3,370-foot Lanaihale with its astounding views of at least three, and sometimes all five, of the other islands. Its pines and eucalyptus stands flourish among native plants—ohia, mountain naupaka, palapalae ferns, and pili grass. The trail was named after the man who planted the Norfolk pines on the island, a New Zealander named George Munro.

This hike is considered difficult, with a considerable elevation gain and a long, steadily ascending 8½-mile route. You don't have to go the whole way, however. The trail takes you across razorback cliffs and deep, sudden gulches you wouldn't imagine existed on Lanai. From this vantage point you can see a large portion of this small island.

You can also hike the Kaiholena Gulch Loop, which also leads to Lanaihale. It's a four-hour hike that's not as strenuous as the Munro trail and passes through areas reforested with native plants.

Special Excursions

HULOPOE BAY
South Lanai

Hulopoe is one of the calmest, prettiest bays in all of Hawaii. Fortunate sailors, whales, fish, and porpoises have long frequented this naturally protected bay while generations of Lanaians have fished its waters and played along its shores.

For some years now, the water has been a marine life conservation area. That means you can't spearfish, drop anchor, or lay a net anymore, but unlike other similar areas, you can cast from the shore here.

Along with the park and shopping area in Lanai City, this is the social center of the island. Lanaians love to congregate at the beach for picnics and lazy days. The beach, a broad, white-sand bay with full and well-maintained facilities, has gentle waves that can be ideal for bodysurfing. Best of all, Hulopoe has always had warm showers. The pipes are heated in the mountains and end up serving warm, luxurious water for sun-kissed, salty bodies.

To the left, around the bend on the rocky shoreline, are some large tidal pools in which school children love to play. A sharp turn around the corner reveals Sweetheart Rock and a cove that's gorgeous but hard to reach.

To get there, take Manele Road from Lanai City. It's the main paved road on the island and leads straight to Hulopoe Bay and neighboring Manele.

KAUNOLU
South Lanai

High on a rocky ledge overlooking the ocean, Kaunolu still has a haunting majesty that must have accounted somewhat for its popularity in ancient times. House sites, terraces, petroglyphs, and a tremendous network of archaeological remains bear testament to the thriving fishing village that was once here.

The area is a registered National Historic Landmark and somewhere bears a shrine to Kamehameha's fishing god, said to have been secretly placed there upon Kamehameha's orders. The area underwent extensive archaeological research in the 1920s by the Bishop Museum's Kenneth Emory, who painstakingly documented every finding in this area, and others. What you see today is a tranquil bluff next to Lanai's highest steep cliffs—over 1,000 feet—with a pebble cove in between. On land are stone terraces, a heiau, and even a cave, and in the valley that opens into the bay, a complex series of petroglyphs remains.

Lovers of history and nature could spend long hours here, even without a beach to swim from or the usual ocean activities. The sheer power of this spot is sustaining, inviting exploration and short walks among the sites. A great place to picnic is the bluff overlooking the pebble beach, with the sea cliffs just beyond it. To get there, take Manele Road south for about 3 miles from Lanai City. When the road veers to a sharp left, continue on Kaupili Road, which goes straight ahead through the pineapple fields. The fourth dirt road toward the ocean leads to Kaunolu.

POLIHUA BEACH
North Lanai

If you can handle an hour-long drive over a bumpy, rutted, and totally precarious road, you will have earned a look at Polihua. This north-shore beach is a magnificent reward for the hardy few who have braved the road to its remote northern shores. On the way you pass an eerie, haunting patch of red and purple dirt with moonlike shapes, the fabled Garden of the Gods, Lanai's most unusual and stunning sight.

The beach, when you finally arrive there (especially if you get lost in the pineapple fields, as many do) is like a distant fantasy: totally secluded, with a wide, white-sand beach, turquoise waters, and long, rolling sand dunes. The shoreline is peppered with kiawe trees. The beach is over a mile and a half long, the longest and widest on the island. You can see Molokai in the near distance. The beach is not recommended for swimming; there are no facilities, no lifeguard, and the waters are considered unpredictable and dangerous. It can also be windy at Polihua.

The area is known as the breeding grounds for sea turtles. It is not unusual to see them here. A Pele chant from Lanai talks about Pele's love for the area because of her love of the turtle eggs. Many a visitor to Polihua sees large, dark green shadows in the water near the surface as turtles come up for air and then swim merrily along. If you are lucky enough to be close to them, you can even hear them take a breath.

Before heading to Polihua, be sure the roads are dry. And get detailed directions from someone at the service station or hotel because it's *very* tricky getting through the unmarked dirt roads to the Awalua Highway that leads to it.

SPECIAL OUTINGS:
IN AND ON THE WATER

CLUB LANAI
Kahalepalaoa
East Lanai
Telephone: (808) 871-1144

A Hollywood producer bought 8.4 acres of east Lanai, developed and landscaped it, and began bringing boatloads of Maui visitors to its shores. They spend the day at Club Lanai eating, playing volleyball, and touring the area by bike or van. The beach isn't the most attractive, but it is a beach, and it's private.

Lahaina is 7 miles across the channel, not a long way on a clear day. If conditions are right the snorkeling at Club Lanai can be marvelous. You must bring sun protection, however, because the newly planted trees do not provide much shade and are not yet very lush. In fact, the area looks as if it needs time to mature.

The biggest drawback to Club Lanai is its dependence on good weather on its one route. Unlike other charters that can take alternate routes to calmer waters and clearer weather, Club Lanai is stuck with this route, come hell or high water. In addition, service here can be appalling.

Once they get to the landing, guests are totally isolated from the rest of Lanai, which is an hour away in Lanai City. Except for a tour to the nearby Keomuku area, their entire experience of Lanai is confined to the developed club area. Some Lanaians, however, consider having that many fewer cars or vans in Lanai City a plus.

The best thing about Club Lanai is Elaine Kaopuiki, Lanai's revered kumu hula and a person anyone would be fortunate to know. A fourth-generation Hawaiian from this historic area, Elaine has stories, history, legends, and the Hawaiian arts to share. She and her students answer questions, demonstrate Hawaiian crafts, make leis, weave, and best of all, they do the hula. And what hula it is!

Cost for the whole day at Club Lanai is $80. You can make a reservation through your hotel activities desk or by contacting Club Lanai, 333 Dairy Road, Suite 201-A, Kahului, HI 96732; telephone (808) 871-1144.

LANAI SEA CHARTERS
P.O. Box 401
Lanai City, HI 96763
Telephone: (808) 565-6958

This is the class act of Lanai's sailing world. Captain Bob Moon is Lanai's old-time sailor; he's been giving tours out of Lanai for over ten years. Lanai Sea Charters was the first sailing charter available on Lanai, and it has grown into a popular multiday sailing adventure to which people keep returning.

Moon is an air force captain with wide experience piloting C-130s and other vessels across many oceans. The boat, *The Stacked Deck*, takes up to six people in a private charter. On share-boat trips, a minimum of two is required.

Moon knows all the best snorkeling and dive spots: Sheraton's Black Rock on Maui, Honolua Bay on Maui, the north shore of Molokai during summer months, and all the spots around Lanai, Molokai, and Maui.

Guests are met at the airport and transferred to the boat at Manele Harbor, where the cruise begins immediately. Rates range from $125 a day on a share-boat charter to $2,590 for a seven-day crewed charter, with many options in between.

TRILOGY EXCURSIONS
Lanai City Service
1036 Lanai Avenue
Lanai, HI 96763
Telephone: (808) 565-6780

Lanai City Service, one of two on the island, is owned by Trilogy Excursions and handles some free and independent travelers'(FITs) bookings from Lanai with advance notice. For the most part, however, they handle the excursions for Trilogy's Lanai trips originating on Maui. Most of their tours are boat tours, arranged in about four programs that show you Lanai from the ocean and Lanai on land. Trilogy's excursion from Maui sails into the Hulopoe area, where guests picnic and have lunch before climbing aboard a van for a land tour of the island. (See also Maui, Special Outings: In and on the Water.)

EVERYDAY GOOD THINGS

There are no dry cleaners or florists on Lanai, there is a health clinic but no drugstore, and the town folds up for siesta between noon and 1:30 P.M. daily. There are no traffic lights, and a little corner of the town square is daintily stacked with pieces of cardboard for the senior citizens to sit down on. That's how Lanai is—comfortable, intimate, and full of endearing eccentricities.

If you happen to be at Hulopoe, the island's only accessible white-sand beach, and you overhear someone say she's going to "town," that usually means Honolulu, and more likely than not it's to shop. If someone is going to the "city," that usually means the sedate Lanai City, the hub of the island. In fact, Lanai folks say the surest way to see someone you know is to go to Ala Moana Center on Oahu, where you're bound to see a neighbor buying all those things he or she couldn't get on Lanai. There just aren't many stores or conveniences on the island. Here are the two main stores, which you wouldn't miss anyway.

PINE ISLE MARKET
Lanai City
Telephone: (808) 565-6488

Pine Isle has everything from wine to clothing to film and fresh fish. In fact, on an island where no one even looks at day-old fish, Pine Isle is known for its supply of fresh fish from local fishermen. The general store also offers a 48-hour film processing service whereby film is flown off the island to be processed at Fuji or Kodak. Service may take less than 48 hours, depending on the flight schedules of the airlines. Although limited in its selection, this is a charming, wonderful store where local residents shop, so there's nothing touristy about it. Like all other stores on the island, Pine Isle opens daily except Sunday and closes from noon to 1:30 weekdays for the traditional Lanai-style siesta. Major credit cards accepted.

RICHARD'S SHOPPING CENTER
Lanai City
Telephone: (808) 565-6047

Richard's is the other big store in Lanai City—big according to Lanai standards, of course. Richard's is full of clothes, sewing notions, fishing supplies, stationery, food, and miscellany you wouldn't dream of, such as old kitchen appliances no longer made or available anywhere else. The store opened in 1946 and has dusty corners with great potential for collectors of memorabilia. The usual food items can be found here, among them fresh vegetables and produce shipped from Honolulu. It's open Monday through Saturday and closed weekdays from noon to 1:30 P.M. No credit cards are accepted.

KAUAI

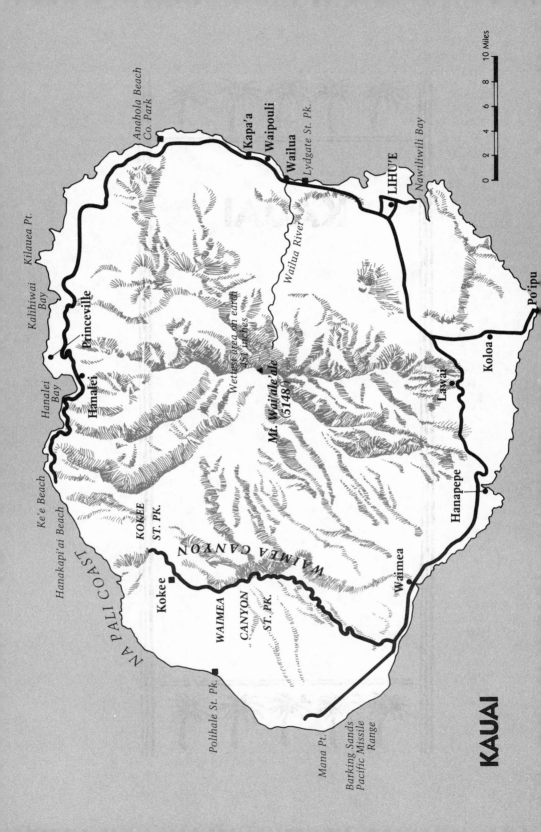

KAUAI

NA PALI COAST

Polihale St. Pk.

Mana Pt.

Barking Sands
Pacific Missile
Range

Waimea

WAIMEA
CANYON
ST. PK.

Kokee

KOKEE
ST. PK.

WAIMEA CANYON

Hanakapi'ai Beach

Ke'e Beach

Hanalei
Bay

Hanalei

Princeville

Kalihiwai
Bay

Kilauea Pt.

Anahola Beach
Co. Park

Wettest area on earth
451 inches

Mt. Wai'ale'ale
(5148')

Hanapepe

Lawai

Koloa

Kapa'a

Waipouli

Wailua

Lydgate St. Pk.

Wailua River

LIHUE

Nawiliwili Bay

Po'ipu

0   2   4   6   8   10 Miles

A BRIEF HISTORY

An elderly Hawaiian woman, a wise and knowledgeable kupuna, once compared the Hawaiian island chain to a human body. In a remarkable analogy, she said the islands are like chakras, the seven spiritual centers referred to in Hindu teachings. The chakras are subtle energy centers that go from the base of the spine up the center of the body, culminating in the crown chakra at the very center of the top of the head. "Kauai is the crown chakra of the Hawaiian islands," the kupuna said decisively.

It is a haunting thought. Kauai is certainly the oldest of the islands, the northernmost of the islands, and, many say, the most hauntingly beautiful of the islands. It is where the wettest spot on earth, the 5,148-foot Waialeale, reigns supreme with its twin, the 5,243-foot Kawaikini. While 450 inches of rain fall yearly upon Waialeale, its daunting crater hides in the clouds, and ribbons of waterfalls stream down its sides to feed and nourish the whole island.

Waialeale, poised at the center of an island shaped like the human heart, could well be the crown of Hawaii. It was in the plateau of Waialeale's center that the ancient Hawaiians built an alter to Kane, the most important of their four gods. It is said they climbed for days to reach it, up the river, up the slopes, clutching at vines and roots through oozing bogs and precipitous ridgelines, on their journey to honor their god.

According to Ed Joesting in his book *Kauai, The Separate Kingdom*, the altar—2 feet high, 5 feet wide, and 7 feet long—was made of lava rock and still stands today at the summit, near a phallic stone.

From this center of Kauai flows a series of streams, canyons, waterfalls, mountains, ponds, and rivers that spawn some of the world's most unusual habitats and wildlife. In the Alakai Swamp on Waialeale's northwest flank, dwarfed indigenous plants persist in the shadow of the *o'o a'a*, a bird that was thought to be extinct, while other endangered species live delicately in their final refuge.

The island is 558.2 square miles in size, the fourth largest of the Hawaiian islands. The dense, mountainous heights descend to the sea in a dramatic cascade, forming 90 miles of coastline and, some estimate, more than forty beaches. Waialeale and Kawaikini are the twin peaks of the single shield volcano that formed the island.

Nearly 45,000 people live on the island, in communities stretching from Hanalei on the north shore to Waimea on the west side, in primarily coastal towns that curl around Kauai's one main highway. Some residential areas crawl up the lower regions of Waialeale's flanks, such as the historic Wailua that faithfully follows the Wailua River. It was this waterway that the ancients followed on their arduous journey to Kane's altar.

Most visitors to Kauai are stunned by the majesty of the Na Pali Coast, its sheer sea cliffs and pillars plunging to the sea from great heights. It is a shoreline of sudden, sharp turns and razor-clean edges, where stone ruins of ancient villages still pay homage to the past. Coupled with its beauty and mystery, the abundance of wild fruit growing in Kalalau Valley made it the hippie paradise of the 1960s and 1970s and, today continues to attract campers seeking the ultimate wilderness experience. In these hills and valleys are mysterious stone walls and structures attributed to the legendary *menehune*, the leprechaun-like race of workers who were never seen but who were said to have performed prodigious deeds at night.

From one side of the island to the other, it is said, the menehune built ponds, walls, roads, and even entire villages, hauling stones across great distances in the darkness of night. It was said that when a menehune was seen or if he committed a crime, he was turned into stone. Some of these boulders, like Pohakinapua'a on the way to the Waimea Canyon, actually have names and are credited in local folklore as the stone remnants of menehune who met their demise. Also in Waimea is Kiki-a Ola, a stream and watercourse called Menehune Ditch, said to have been built in one night by the king, Ola, and his cadre of menehune. It is the most notable of their achievements, cited for its esoteric stonework and anomalous design, unlike any other in Hawaii.

Waimea in west Kauai, where menehune legends abound, is full of folklore and history and is the perfect town to undergo a communitywide restoration program. Part of a federal program called Main Street, Waimea is one of several historic towns in Hawaii working to revitalize business, architecture, and historical awareness with programs, planning, and aggressive marketing.

After all, it was in humble Waimea that the era known as post-contact Hawaii was born. While searching for the Northwest Passage linking Asia to Europe, Captain James Cook sighted the tranquil Waimea Bay on January 19, 1778. That day was to go down in history as the "discovery" of the Hawaiian islands, a somewhat annoying claim because of its presumption that these long-existent islands with their thriving culture were "discovered," and therefore legitimized, by Cook. The ships *Resolution* and *Discovery* came into view, and in no time canoes laden with food and pigs were paddling out to the ships. As the valley was ignited with excitement, some wondered what was afoot in the "trees moving on the sea." In the days he was there, Cook traded iron, nails, and metal items for food, and when he eventually came ashore, the natives bowed before him.

In the exchanges between Hawaiians and the westerners in Waimea, and later in neighboring Niihau, western flora arrived in Hawaii along with syphilis and other diseases. Joesting's *Kauai, The Separate Kingdom* reports that 66 of 112 members of Cook's crew had VD. Although Cook was aware of the problem and sought to prevent its spread, by the time he returned to Hawaii a year later the disease had spread throughout the islands. Venereal disease was a major factor in the rapid decline of the Hawaiian population.

War contributed its fair share, too. The Hawaiians battled vigorously on all the islands, chief against chief and island against island, each out to conquer the next. By the time Kamehameha had conquered first the Big Island, then Maui, Molokai, and Lanai, it was obvious that Oahu was next, and after it, Kauai. One year after the famous battle of 1795, in which Kamehameha's forces drove their Oahu enemies off the Nuuanu Pali, the sixteen-year-old Kaumuali'i became king of Kauai. Soon after conquering Oahu, Kamehameha set his sights on Kauai and gathered thousands of canoes and armed soldiers. But Kauai, in spite of its own internal disharmony under its youthful ruler at the time, was simply not to be conquered.

Due to an uncanny natural phenomenon, Kauai became the only island in Hawaii not to be invaded—or conquered—by the ambitious Kamehameha. A vicious storm in the channel between Oahu and Kauai swamped Kamehameha's oncoming canoes and forced the fleet to retreat. Kauai and Niihau joined the rest of the Hawaiian kingdom by agreement, not war, in 1810.

Some observers lend great importance to this fact—the imperviousness of Kauai to Kamehameha and his momentous forces. Some people cite it as yet another testament to this island's remote, untouchable nature. After all, Kauai is 80 miles away from the rest of Hawaii, separated by the tempestuous Kauai Channel, which has foiled many an attempted crossing. Standing apart with its neighbor, Niihau, Kauai has always had a separate history.

While islands like Molokai and Lanai were late to be discovered and populated, archaeological evidence suggests that Kauai was the first. It's reported that Polynesian seafarers lived on Kauai some five centuries before the rest of Hawaii was settled. It is also known that at least two heiaus, one in Waimea and one in Wailua, bear uncanny resemblances to heiaus in Central Polynesia, and that even the Hawaiian language was pronounced slightly differently on this island.

Once Kauai was discovered by foreigners, it was coveted by them as well. After Kamehameha, the most notorious among its would-be usurpers was a man named George Scheffer, a former physician with the Russian army who weaseled his way into a partnership with Kaumuali'i and attempted to seize control of the island. With the support of Kaumuali'i, he gave Russian names to places on Kauai, planted grapes, cotton, and melons, and built a fort at Waimea, hoping to turn it into a Russian trading post. Scheffer soon lost his power and fled to South America, when his efforts to annex Hawaii to Russia came to naught. A sign in Waimea today points to "Russian Fort," a reminder of this era in the mid-1800s when the Russian flag was flown in Waimea.

In ensuing years Kauai was exploited for its sandalwood. The most serious exploiter was Kaumuali'i himself, whose profligate trading was devastating for the forests and the workers. Efforts to produce silk were also made on Kauai, where, in the late 1830s, mulberry trees were planted and great hopes were aroused for silkworm culture. A drought decimated the mulberry trees in 1840 and hopes then turned to sugar production, coffee, tobacco, cloth, and whaling.

Sugar and pineapple production were the only large-scale commercial ventures that could be sustained for years. When pineapple canneries began closing, eyes turned to tourism, but only with caution and, among many, dread.

Hurricane Iwa in 1982 devastated west Kauai, where the Poipu Resort is located, and swept through the island in a fierce, destructive sweep that stunned the entire state. But the island set out to rebuild itself and today takes pride in its success.

Indeed, visitors to Kauai today will hear stories about the hurricane but see few, if any, signs of its destruction. Hotels have been refurbished with better standards, and people's attitudes have changed markedly. The depression that followed the hurricane, they say, caused many to rethink the position of tourism in the island's economy.

Still, there is caution in some corners. The infrastructure of the island is feeling the weight of growth—roads are more crowded, the main highway can be jammed, there is really a rush hour on Kuhio Highway. After all, people still remember the days when residents and visitors would make special trips to a cane field road in Kekaha to ogle and be awestruck by the island's only traffic light.

Those days are gone, but similar charms remain. Buildings on the island, for example, must be no higher than the height of a coconut tree. The standard, officially in the city's ordinances, means that hotels and resorts must limit their heights to about three or four stories. It is an ordinance that enhances the island, for much can be said about its Bali-Hai mystique, its feeling of remoteness that would be ill-served by modern high rises. On Kauai, Waikiki is a lesson to be avoided, and many feel that even Maui's level of development is too extensive for this island.

That is not to say that Kauai doesn't like visitors. You should feel welcome here. People would like the island to hang on to those qualities that attracted folks in the first place. But here, a subtle element prevails. Maui and Molokai will embrace you warmly, but Kauai will watch you watching her. From the sheer cliffs of the Na Pali Coast to the impenetrable bogs of the Alakai Swamp, this is a formidable island. It dares you to penetrate its secrets. However much you may enjoy its majesty and partake of its many pleasures, you may come away knowing little about it. For, no matter how long and how devotedly one lives and learns on this island, boundless questions remain. This is a powerful and beautiful island but, ultimately, distant and unknowable.

GETTING AROUND

Kauai is a 20-minute flight from Oahu. It has a brand-new airport, the Lihue Airport, which is five times larger than its old one.

The three interisland airlines—Aloha, Hawaiian, and Mid-Pacific—fly into the Lihue Airport, as well as United Airlines. There is also a small private airstrip in Princeville in Hanalei, serviced by Princeville Airways.

There's no public transportation on Kauai, but there are taxis and car rentals at the airport. Gray Line ([808] 245-3344) offers prearranged shuttle service to Poipu and the Kapaa-Wailua hotels. They recommend that you book a shuttle ahead of time. They may still take you at the airport without a reservation, but only on a space-available basis. The Shoppe Hoppers, Inc. ([808] 332-7272) offers transportation from Poipu resorts to the airport for $6 one-way, with reservations.

When you land in Lihue you'll be in east Kauai, 14 miles from Poipu and 10 miles from Kapaa. Lihue is 43 miles from Kokee State Park on the west side and 32 miles from Hanalei. There's one road that curls around the perimeter of the island, Route 50, also called Kuhio Highway. As it nears the north shore, Route 50 turns into Route 56. Heading west, Route 50 meets another major throughway, Route 550, which leads up to the Waimea Canyon and Kokee State Park. The road around Kauai is notable because it ends at Kokee on the west side and at Haena on the north shore; the two areas are hours away by car but a mere corner away in distance, separated by the Na Pali Cliffs.

TOURS

There are several tour companies on Kauai. The largest are Robert's Hawaii ([808] 245-9558), Gray Line ([808] 245-3344), and Trans Hawaiian Kauai ([808] 245-5108). Trans Hawaiian also offers personalized van tours of Kauai's major attractions plus motorcoach transportation through its affiliation with Kauai Island Tours.

CAMPING

Kauai has several state parks that are good for camping: Polihale, the Kokee State Park (cabins also available through Kokee Lodge), and the Na Pali Coast State Park. Kokee is by far the most diverse, with housekeeping cabins, developed campgrounds, and picnic areas. It's extremely cold in Kokee, though, so be sure you're prepared if you choose to camp.

Polihale is a broad white-sand beach on the west side, the last beach before the Na Pali Coast begins. There are no cabins here, but there are facilities for picnicking, tents, and trailers.

The Na Pali Coast is by far the most rugged. Campers must backpack in on an 11-mile trail, or they can have their gear shuttled in by Zodiac while they hike in during the summer months. There are primitive campgrounds in the Kalalau Valley, one of Hawaii's most distinctive wilderness areas.

For information on all three camping areas, write the Division of State Parks, P.O. Box 1671, Lihue, HI 96766; telephone (808) 245-4444.

HOTELS AND ALTERNATIVES

....

WEST, SOUTH, AND EAST KAUAI

With the exception of Kokee, which is a state park with cabins, there are no hotels or condominiums in west Kauai. Most of Kauai's visitor accommodations are in Poipu on the south shore, in Wailua and Kapaa on the east shore, and in Hanalei on the north shore. Please keep in mind, too, that Bed and Breakfast Hawaii is based on Kauai and has an active roster of homes. (See A Note on Hotels at the beginning of the book.)

Most of the accommodations in the lower-priced categories are condominiums. They'll be listed under Alternatives after the hotel listings. Hanalei hotels are in the North Shore section.

Budget Hotel

CORAL REEF
1516 Kuhio Highway
Kapaa, HI 96746
Telephone: (800) 843-4659, (808) 822-4481

The old Coral Reef got a much-needed facelift when the new owners took over at the end of 1985. They immediately set about renovating, painting, planting, landscaping, and installing new furniture and drapes. The hotel is on a lackluster beach in Kapaa, next to a bridge and close to the softball field and the town's public library. It's a convenient enough location, about midway between the north and south shores, and the prices make all the flaws forgivable.

There are twenty-six units all together, with some in the main building and others in the oceanfront wing. The rates are $25 to $40 for rooms in the main building (with most of the rooms in the $30 range) and $45 for oceanfront. There are lanais in some of the upstairs units and the grounds are lush and pleasant—overall, a welcome bargain in an inflated market.

Superior Hotels

COCO PALMS RESORT
P.O. Box 631
Lihue, HI 96766
Telephone: (800) 542-2626, (808) 822-4921

With the Coco Palms, you must look at the big picture instead of the details. The lagoon, the thatched structures, the coconut grove, the memory of Elvis in *Blue Hawaii*, the torchlighting ceremony that originated here—nostalgia prompts us to list it. That, plus the $7-million renovation it's undergoing, somewhat mitigates the outlandishness of some of its details. Just close your eyes when you see the lily-pad and frog-motif tiles, and appreciate the large clamshell basins instead.

The 46-acre, thirty-four-year-old resort contains a large lagoon, three swimming pools, and thatched-roof cottages. There are also 390 rooms and suites altogether, all of them undergoing a much-needed facelift. The best visual elements of the property are the tall coconut trees, the generous use of lava rock, and the lily-covered waterways. No doubt they contribute to the fact that some 600 weddings occur here a year.

The closest beach is across the street, so the best view you can have is of the lagoon or the ocean from a distance. There are nine clay tennis courts, a small zoo, and a Polynesian touch that's the most pleasing factor of the Coco Palms.

The rooms range from $105 for a standard to $370 for a two-bedroom suite, with many categories in between. Ask about their wedding packages—they're very popular.

SHERATON COCONUT BEACH HOTEL
Coconut Plantation
P.O. Box 803
Kapaa, HI 96746
Telephone: (800) 325-3535, (808) 922-3455

There are 309 units at the Sheraton, 70 percent of which have ocean views. It's not a dazzler but it is the nicest hotel in this east Kauai neighborhood situated midway between the north shore and Poipu. The hotel itself stands between an enormous coconut grove on one side and the ocean on the other. Don't get your hopes up, though; the beach is not good for swimming—it's reefy and shallow. You'll have to be content with wading, using the pool, or heading for the Wailua Beach down the road.

The lobby area is bright and airy, with a prominent stained-glass window dominating the decor. The views from the rooms could be over the ironwoods, tennis courts, ocean, or walkways because the four-story structure has four divergent wings connected by walkways. Each room has color TV, air-conditioning, king-size or double beds, and a lanai, and all are attractively furnished in rattan.

Two big pluses for the hotel are its very popular luau and, in the evenings, entertainment by Na Kaholokula, among the best singers in Hawaii. Not a plus is the fact that room rates here are comparable to those at the Sheraton Kauai in Poipu, where you have a better beach and better weather.

Rates start at $110 for a grove view or a garden view, $125 for a partial ocean view, and on up to a $275 VIP suite.

SHERATON KAUAI
R.R. 1, Box 303
Koloa, HI 96756
Telephone: (800) 325-3535, (808) 822-3455

The choice here is whether you want to face the garden or the ocean, but you really can't go wrong. There are 114 rooms in a two-story structure on the oceanfront (and more than 100 additional units currently being built), and 230 rooms across the street, in a four-story building set amid lush gardens and landscaping. It's nice to be close to the ocean, but the garden rooms aren't bad at all, especially those on the higher floors.

The beachfront part of the Sheraton is splendid, with a small grassy area looking out to the lava shoreline and surfers beyond. There's a cocktail lounge that's so close to the ocean you can almost feel its spray. The restaurants look over the same dramatic view as the oceanfront rooms, which are well-designed and placed close to the ocean. Plans call for adding tennis courts and a fitness center; when the new oceanfront rooms are in, the Sheraton Kauai should be booming.

Rooms run from $95 for a standard room to $120 for a garden room, $180 for an oceanfront room, and $245 to $305 for the suites.

Deluxe Hotels

STOUFFER WAIOHAI BEACH RESORT
R.R. 1, Box 174
Koloa, HI 96756
Telephone: (800) 227-4700, (808) 742-9511

The Waiohai in Poipu has many rooms in the superior category, but it's listed under deluxe because it's in a class of its own on Kauai. It is expensive, and it's simply the most elegant hotel on the island.

The building is open and generous, fanning out toward the sea in a three-pronged structure shaped like a **w**. There are abundant maile-scented ferns, spider lilies, sago palms, and exotics brimming over in the nicely landscaped grounds. In the lobby, the Hawaiian exhibits of pheasant hatbands, Niihau shell leis, and artifacts are effective.

The rooms are spacious and tasteful, with large potted palms and, in some of them, a love seat and living area. The usual amenities are here, including a large dressing area with sit-down vanity and lanai overlooking ocean or garden.

There are 434 rooms in the four-story building and the categories range from standard to superior, deluxe, and suites. The rate for 1987 (new rates aren't ready) for the standard room, double occupancy, is $125; superior, $160; deluxe garden view, $190; one-bedroom with ocean view, $350; and on up to the $900 two-bedroom oceanfront suite.

THE WESTIN KAUAI
Lihue, HI 96766
Telephone: (800) 228-3000, (808) 245-5050

Wunderkind Chris Hemmeter, the darling of the sybarites, bought out the old Kauai Surf Hotel and converted it to the most elaborate hotel Kauai has ever seen. Situated on beautiful Kalapaki Beach near Nawiliwili Harbor, the 847-room behemoth sits on 580 acres along the beach and on the cliffs. Imagine this: Hemmeter put $350 million into creating his super-resort, adding such things as thirteen restaurants and lounges; a 26,000-square-foot pool with an island, fountains, rivers, slides, and waterfalls; lawns and botanical gardens; and a beachside promenade of crushed marble and mosaic tile. That's the mild stuff. There are dozens of horse-drawn carriages as well, and a 2.1-acre reflecting pool. Add a boathouse, European health spa, and golf and racket club and you have Hemmeter's idea of fun.

Although it's too new to say whether it's succeeding (the hotel opened in fall 1987), the hotel is out to draw the traveler who wants fun on the Disneyland scale and has a big pocketbook and flashy, outrageous taste.

There are twenty-nine luxury suites, six split-level penthouse suites, and forty-nine rooms in the Royal Beach Club. The rest of the rooms are in the courtyard, ocean-view, oceanfront (higher floors on the ocean), and beachfront (lower floors on the ocean) categories, with rates ranging from $180, single or double occupancy, to $245 for the oceanfront and $285 for beachfront. The suites rent for $450 to $1,500.

Alternatives

GARDEN ISLE COTTAGES
2666 Puuholo Road
Koloa, HI 96756
Telephone: (808) 742-6717

You can't get better than this on Kauai. These are cottages, not high rises, and they lean over a cliff on the sun-kissed south shore of Poipu. Owners Sharon and Robert Flynn add a personal touch to the place and have created a pleasing tropical ambience of bananas, hibiscus, palm trees, and heavy foliage to blanket the cliffside. The cottages sit overlooking a small, rocky bay. The white-sand shores of Poipu are not far away. Inside, the Flynns have decorated with their own sculptures and crafts, such as batik, to warm up the decor.

There are sea-cliff cottages and cottages farther from the ocean. The sea-cliff cottages have one bedroom, kitchen, bath, and two lanais, and cost $55 (1987 rates). The cottages farther from the ocean are also one bedrooms, with kitchen, patio, living-dining area, and cost $50. The best deal is the $34 small studio and the $38 large studio, with bath and lanai. All prices are for double occupancy.

KAHILI MOUNTAIN PARK
P.O. Box 298
Koloa, HI 96756
Telephone: (808) 742-9921

There are cabins for rent at the foot of the Kahili mountains not far from Poipu, where the Seventh Day Adventists own 200 glorious acres with trails, a pond, and welcome isolation from Kauai's touristy areas. These are not posh cabins, but they're a very attractive alternative, and very conveniently located about midway between Hanalei and Kokee. You drive through the cane fields off the main highway to get there and the main pavilion appears out of nowhere, with a pond in front where people can fish.

It's not a dry area, so that's a consideration. But the price is attractive. There are seven wooden cabins that rent for $33.28 for two, with linens, a shower outside, a bathroom, refrigerator, two-burner stove, dishes, and the basics. The cabinettes are the same, except that the bathroom and shower are shared. There are ten cabinettes for rent at $19.24 for two. They have concrete floors and are rougher than the cabins, but remember, you're paying about $10 a person to stay there.

There are no amenities, of course, For most of the people who stay here it doesn't matter, because they're out hiking and exploring the island anyway.

KAPAA SANDS
380 Papaloa Road
Kapaa, HI 96746
Telephone: (808) 822-4901, 822-4902

The landscaping is gorgeous; the lush walkways are lined with torch gingers, red ti leaves, tiare gardenias, palms, and tropical plants galore. It's obvious the gardens are tended with care, and they add immeasurable charm and space to a tiny, adorable operation on an out-of-the-mainstream beach in Wailua. There are only twenty-three units, but the Kapaa Sands' beachside location, prices, and cordial management make this a deal we recommend most highly.

The area was an old Japanese Shinto temple and the beach was a feeding ground for sea turtles. A venerable, important-looking boulder has been retained from those days. It's inscribed with Japanese characters and was used to mark the pathway to the temple. Today it sits by the office door, in front of the gardens.

There are eight two-story buildings on the property. There's daily maid service, and accommodations range from studios to two-bedrooms. Views are of the garden or ocean; the garden views face the road, but beyond that you have a marvelous view of the Sleeping Giant mountain as well.

Rooms are equipped with telephone, TV, and full kitchen. These are small quarters, but sparkling clean and quite complete. The wooden buildings are attractive, and the oceanfront rooms with their lanais looking out to sea are hard to beat. Although the beach is not very good for swimming, it is a lovely stretch of white sand bordered by beach naupaka and highlighted with a piece of driftwood that looks like it should be in a museum. The tiny swimming pool is located where the Japanese temple's sumo ring used to be.

Prices range from $49 a day for a garden studio to $59 for an oceanfront studio (an unbeatable deal), $69 for a two-bedroom with garden view, and $79 for a two-bedroom with oceanfront view. All the units are comfortable, and some even have dishwashers and disposals. A three-night minimum is required; during winter months, the minimum is seven days. Reserve ahead; they're booked far in advance by regulars.

KIAHUNA PLANTATION
R.R. 1, Box 73
Koloa, HI 96756
Telephone: (800) 367-7052, (808) 742-6411

With its white wooden verandas and exceptional landscaping, the 35-acre Kiahuna looks like a plantation villa on the beach. In fact, it used to be the plantation home of the Moir family, whose Moir Garden with 3,000 varieties of cactus still occupies the eastern slice of the property.

The operation is run exactly as a hotel, with all the amenities except for twenty-four-hour office hours. There's a fine restaurant (the Plantation Gardens), maid service, bell service, and an efficient, well-run operation to complement the physical beauty of the grounds and rooms.

The lobby area and dining room have the charm of an elegant turn-of-the-century manse, with white wicker and hardwoods on a terrace that overlooks a lawn of lily ponds, flowers, and willow and plumeria trees.

The buildings, which go no higher than three stories, are spread out among the generous lagoons and charming white wooden bridges. The well-groomed kiawe trees and sago palms grow in stately, graceful arrangements. All the green against the white wood is stunning. When the ocean appears before it all, you get the full impact of the Kiahuna charm.

The views vary, but each room is equipped with full kitchen and kitchen utensils. There is no air-conditioning available here, which can be a problem when there is no ocean breeze. Some units are very close to the ocean. You get a great view but some beach noises, too. Room rates for the one-bedrooms begin at $125 for up to four people in a garden superior, $210 for an ocean view, and up to $280 for an oceanfront view. There are five one-bedroom categories altogether. For the two-bedrooms, which are two-story units, the rates range from $210 to $375.

KOKEE LODGE
P.O. BOX 819
Waimea, HI 96796
Telephone: (808) 335-6061

If you like to spend your days walking in unspoiled wilderness with rare wildlife, sitting by a fireplace and reading, and being at a 3,600-foot elevation with little traffic and only the sound of wild chickens, this is your place. Writers and artists dream of spending months in seclusion here, writing the great American novel while the rest of the world carries on. This is not the tropical Hawaii most people think of, it's upcountry Hawaii at its best. Trouble is, there are only twelve state cabins here so you have to plan ahead, especially during holidays. And the cabins rent for only $25 a night. More than a few people reserve for the next year when they leave.

The cabins, lodge, and museum are part of the Kokee State Park bordering the Waimea Canyon. At the end of the road, a lookout allows you to peer 4,000 feet down into the Kalalau Valley on the Na Pali Coast. The island's best trail system traverses the 4,345-acre park. (See also Special

Outings: On Land) Every summer at the start of the Kokee plum season, residents from all over the island line up in their cars and haul away armloads of the black, juicy fruit. Anglers love the fact that the state's only rainbow trout season opens here each August.

The cabins are rustic, with hardwood floors, fireplaces, full kitchens, and linens. You purchase firewood from the lodge and bring your own food up the hill from Waimea, or you can dine at the Kokee Lodge restaurant. The lodge has terrific breakfasts, the best corn bread on the island, the standard burgers, and fish dinners. Kokee is about 40 miles from Lihue, the county seat and site of the airport, and about a 90-minute drive from there.

Kokee is an unequivocal favorite on Kauai, heartily recommended for the adventurous and imaginative. If it's the hot, tropical sun you crave, Polihale Beach is down the hill about a 25-minute drive away.

POIPU SHORES
R.R. 1, Box 95
Koloa, HI 96756
Telephone: (800) 367-5686, (808) 742-6522

Poipu Shores, located on a cliffside past Brennecke Beach, is a dramatic shoreline perch with waves pounding very close to your room. It's a find. Thirty-nine units, all oceanfront, are in a three-story and a four-story building, which literally cling to the cliffs. You can breakfast on your lanai watching whales and dolphins, or you can watch the sunset from a swimming pool so close to the ocean it gets splashed now and then with salt water.

There are townhouses and five one-bedroom units, the rest are two-bedrooms; all have fully equipped kitchen, color TV, lanai, wicker furniture, linens, books on shelves, and other comforts. The two-bedroom units have huge picture windows the length of a room, looking over the well-manicured lawn in front and the black lava cliffs. A small path along the coastline is great for sunset strolls. The townhouses have two stories; they are narrow but gorgeous, and the bottom floor opens on to the front lawn and the lava rock wall over the sea.

Rates are $100 for two people if you're staying three to six nights and $90 a night if you're staying a week or more. The two-bedroom units go for $130 for up to six people for three to six nights and $117 for a week or more. The three-bedrooms go for $150 for three to six nights and $135 for a week or more, for up to six people.

Obviously, the longer you stay the better the deal. With the good management and efficient service, this is worth looking into.

WAIKOMO STREAM VILLAS
Grantham Resorts
P.O. Box 983
Koloa, HI 96756
Telephone: (800) 325-5701, (808) 742-7220

This is an utterly charming complex of white wooden buildings set amid streams, willow trees and palms, and green lawn surrounding ponds. Waikomo Stream Villas is a beautiful escape from the norm.

There are one- and two-bedroom units in three-story structures, which are barely nine years old. Each of the sixty-units are individually furnished according to the condo owner's taste. All one-bedroom apartments are on the ground or second floor; all two-bedroom units are on the third floor and contain a loft. Some have partial ocean views in spite of the fact that Waikomo Stream Villas is not on the ocean. It is, however, close to the Poipu beaches on the south shore and all the restaurants in the surrounding area.

All apartments have fully equipped kitchens and lanais that look over the lawn and the stream and have garden views primarily. Dishwashers, linens, full refrigerators, and other comforts ensure you'll be self-sufficient here. And the apartments are huge: 1,100 square feet for the one-bedrooms, 1,800 square feet in the two-bedrooms.

Although the apartments are nice, it's the grounds that are most impressive. Dainty white wooden bridges cross the stream, which meanders through the property in fields of laua'e ferns, bamboo, palms, willows, ti leaves, gingers, and other tropical delights. The closest safe swimming beach is at the Sheraton Kauai, about a ten-minute walk away.

Waikomo Stream Villas has several different rate schedules, depending on the time of year. Rates range from $100 for a one-bedroom to $115 for the two-bedroom. All have garden views, and weekly and monthly rates are also available. No credit cards accepted.

YMCA IN POIPU
P.O. Box 1786
Lihue, HI 96766
Telephone: (808) 742-1200

Again, the YMCA saves the day with inexpensive rentals in a prime area, Poipu, where they practically charge you for the salt air. Just across the Poipu Beach Park, the Y has a 3-acre property with dorm rooms for rent. There are beds inside the dorms and a camping area outside. There's a communal kitchen and across the street is the nicest picnic ground around, the Poipu beach.

It costs $8 for a room in the dorm (very basic, just shelter) and $6 to camp outside. About twenty people can fit indoors and there's lots of space for campers. The men's and women's dorms are separate, each with its own bathroom facilities.

The Y in Poipu is very close to Brennecke Beach and a popular restaurant, the Brennecke's Beach Broiler. You have a great restaurant close by and one of the best bodysurfing beaches merely yards away. If you don't mind roughing it, and you don't mind being in an area that can be noisy, you'll save some good bucks here.

NORTH SHORE

Visitor accommodations in Hanalei and the north shore are centered in the 10,000-acre Princeville Resort, dominated by the Sheraton Princeville, its only hotel, and condominiums. Those who choose to stay in north Kauai usually pay rates that are on the expensive side; there are no budget accommodations in the area.

Deluxe Hotel

SHERATON PRINCEVILLE HOTEL
P.O. Box 3069
Princeville, HI 96722-3069
Telephone: (808) 826-9644

They have tried very hard to make this a smashing, dashing hotel, and it almost succeeds. The views from the building are stupendous, everything is new, the service is enthusiastic—it's just that it's all so overdone and effusive they almost stifle you in cuteness. (We'll get to that later with the Teddy bears.)

There are beautiful Hawaiian quilts and stone and wood artifacts in the lobby, which add a nice touch. The rose tree quilt from 1850 is impressive, and such items as a stone herb pounder from Polihale add some historical cachet. The shops and restaurants surrounding the complicated lobby complex don't capitalize on the views as the rooms do, which is puzzling.

There are close to 500 employees serving 300 rooms, which is a high ratio of service. The 23-acre property is situated high on a bluff overlooking the unforgettable Hanalei Bay and the taro-laden Hanalei Valley. The hotel is built in three terraces that crawl down the hillside toward the Hanalei River. Even from the elevator foyers, the view looms below you through mitered, floor-to-ceiling glass corners and glass windows that open out. It's all very generous—you can see the Hanalei Pier, the beach where *South Pacific* was filmed, and the mountains beyond.

The hallways to the rooms are outdoors; the lobby is on the ninth floor of the eleven-story building, with the restaurants on the eighth. The pool and Jacuzzi may be the most picturesque in the world, next to the beach where you can loll and watch the sunset or the mountains.

The rooms are decorated in a colonial motif: hunter green with touches of beige and natural wood. A nice touch is the jar of homemade brownies, which are delicious (they charge you after you empty the jar), but which seem to attract more ants than people. The artwork, nineteenth-century Emile Bayard engravings of old Hawaiian scenes, is beautiful. Regrettably, the room becomes overly busy with the Hawaiian quilt pattern on the bedspread and the pineapple pattern punched into the copper on the TV console. There is a sense of contrived cheerfulness here, none of it helped by the Teddy bear sitting on the bed.

The rooms rent for $175 to $265, and the suites, $500 to $1,100.

Alternatives

CAMP NAUE
P.O. Box 1786
Lihue, HI 96766
Telephone: (808) 742-1200

It's hard to imagine such a deal could exist so quietly in Haena. Haena is on the north shore at the end of Route 56, where the trails to the Na Pali Coast begin. It's a gorgeous stretch of beach, mountain, and streams, and has wet and dry caves for exploring, and offers an infinite variety of outdoor adventures.

Camp Naue is less than 2 miles from the end of Route 56 and Ke'e Beach, on 4½ acres of beachfront land. It's owned and managed by the YMCA, which rents two bunkhouses right on the beach. You bring your own bedding, but there are bunk beds and very basic shelter. Kitchen facilities are available only for larger groups. In addition, 2 acres of the property make up a grassy, pleasant area for tents, with hot showers, toilets, and a large covered pavilion. The cost is $10 per person for the bunkhouse and $8 per person for camping. Trekkers and scuba divers from the other islands love to stay here because it's so close to Tunnels, a famous area for snorkeling and diving.

ALOHA RENTAL MANAGEMENT
P.O. Box 1109
Hanalei, HI 96714
Telephone: (800) 367-8047, (808) 826-9833

HAWAIIAN ISLANDS RESORTS INC.
P.O. Box 212
606 Coral Street
Honolulu, HI 96810
Telephone: (800) 367-7042, (808) 531-7595

These are not condominiums but rather the management companies for the two best condominium units in the area: Pali Ke Kua and Pu'u Poa. If you're interested in these apartments, which are described below, you'll want to contact either Aloha Rental Management or Hawaiian Islands Resorts, both professional and reliable operations. Because both companies handle the same types of units in the same buildings, the major variable between them is price. Both Pali Ke Kua and Pu'u Poa have spacious units; those facing the ocean have sensational panoramas of Hanalei Bay, the Pacific Ocean, or, in the distance, the purple and green Bali Hai mountains.

Pali Ke Kua condos are valued at about $225,000; the Pu'u Poa condos, $400,000. Yet Pu'u Poa rental rates are only slightly higher than Pali Ke Kua's, making Pu'u Poa even more attractive.

Keep in mind that these management companies handle other properties as well, so you have other choices and personalized service.

PALI KE KUA

There are one- and two-bedroom apartments here, all with full kitchens, washer-dryers, and lanais. The two-story building offers mountain-garden, ocean-view, and oceanfront units. Like most condos, the units are individually furnished according to the owner's taste. All the apartments are spacious, and because the building is on a cliff, the ocean and mountain views are breathtaking. The one-bedroom units sleep about four, the two-bedroom units, six.

Hawaiian Islands Resorts rents its one-bedroom mountain-garden units in Pali Ke Kua for $90, the one-bedroom ocean views for $105, the one-bedroom oceanfronts for $120; the two-bedroom mountain-garden units go for $115, the two-bedroom ocean views for $125, and the two-bedroom oceanfronts, $135.

All of Aloha Rental Management's one-bedroom condos in Pali Ke Kua are oceanfront; there are no garden-view apartments in this size. The one-bedroom oceanfront units rent for $120, which includes a standard economy car with no air-conditioning. Aloha Rental's two-bedroom units rent for $140 for ocean view or oceanfront, with car. There are some garden-view apartments in the two-bedroom category.

PU'U POA

This is widely known as the best condo property in Princeville. When two couples travel together and share an apartment, as many do at Pu'u Poa, the biggest problem is deciding who gets the master bedroom. All condos in this four-story building have two bedrooms and two baths, with a master bedroom that has a dazzling view and a luxurious bathroom that includes a large, deep Japanese soaking tub. What's more, the condos are huge—2,600 square feet—and each has a full dining room, kitchen, two vanities, and two lanais. All units have an ocean view because the building is located on a 150-foot bluff.

There are telephones, washer-dryers, dishwashers, all kitchen utensils, and ceiling fans. The view from Pu'u Poa could be of the Bali Hai mountains, Hanalei Bay, the golf course, or the open ocean. You can hardly go wrong.

Hawaiian Island Resorts rents the two-bedroom apartments for $135 to $150. Aloha Rental Management rents its units for $160, which includes a rental car.

SEALODGE
c/o Aloha Rental Management
P.O. Box 1109
Hanalei, HI 96714
Telephone: (800) 367-8047, ext. 251; (808) 826-6751

Sealodge condos are smaller but a great value: 500 square feet in size, on the same bluff that Pali Ke Kua is on, with a view of the ocean from every unit. The reason Sealodge doesn't get as much attention as the other condos is that it faces the Kilauea Lighthouse (east) instead of the Bali Hai mountains (west), which is what most people know about and request when they come to Princeville. But Sealodge's ocean view is stunning, and the condos are one of the best values in Princeville.

The one-bedroom, one-bath units have a small lanai, cable TV, and telephone. Those without their own washer-dryers can use the laundry facilities available throughout Sealodge.

The rate is $95 for a room and car.

DINING OUT

WEST, SOUTH, AND EAST KAUAI

Kauai's culinary offerings have proliferated in recent years. No longer are the choices limited to a saimin stand or steak house; now there are sushi bars, pizza houses, grill-your-owns, and a festive sprinkling of haute cuisine.

Here are the best on the whole island (a section on the north shore follows), listed alphabetically.

Restaurants

ALOHA DINER
971-F Kuhio Highway
Waipouli
Telephone: (808) 822-3851

One of Kauai's more modest treasures, the diner is a haven for Hawaiian food and saimin lovers. It's tiny, crowded, with electric fans in the corners, Formica-topped tables, and the aroma of cooking fish. All the favorites are here—lomi salmon, chicken luau (chicken in coconut milk and taro leaves), fresh fried mackerel, and other pleasures, served with poi. The real aficionados go for the special seaweed with garlic and crushed kukui nuts, ordered a day in advance. Aloha's has the best Hawaiian food on the island.

Inexpensive—a meal for two would run about $12. Open 10:30 A.M. to 3:00 P.M. and 5:30 to 9:00 P.M. daily except Sunday. No credit cards accepted.

THE BEACH HOUSE RESTAURANT
5022 Lawai Beach Road
Poipu
Telephone: (808) 742-7575

The Beach House has such a large following that diners from Hanalei will make special trips to partake of its fresh catch, lobster, or steak and seafood, prepared grilled, poached, and in a number of delicate ways. Located on the beach at Poipu, it resurrected itself with great panache after suffering the blows of Hurricane Iwa. Although the food can be inconsistent, the view is unrivaled: you sit close to the ocean, with a front-row seat to the sunset, which appears through the large glass doors. The ambience is casually chic, and the menu has something for everyone who loves seafood, steak, and appetizers for those who like grazing.

Moderately expensive, with entrées from $13 to $23. Open Monday through Sunday 5:30 P.M. to 10:00 P.M. Major credit cards accepted.

BRENNECKE'S BEACH BROILER
Across from Poipu Beach Park
Poipu
Telephone: (808) 742-7588

This delightful restaurant is perched on the second floor across from the beach park, offering a fine ocean view without being on the beach. It serves the best simple seafood preparations on the island and has a perfect ambience for casual dining. There are hardwood floors, high ceilings, lanai furniture, and large windows lined with nasturtiums. The chef has fun preparing fresh seafood in local styles as well as the classic favorites. Try their combination seafood appetizer plate (sashimi, octopus, poke) for a real adventure, or the ceviche. Their pasta comes in any form and is good in the evening. For lunch, the fresh fish burger is superb. Their house specials include their "mocktails," such as the "brown nipple" with banana, vodka, kahlua, coconut, banana, and cream—oy vey. Overall, a favorite stop any time of day.

Moderately priced, with entrées from $5 to $8 at lunch and $6 to $15 at dinner. Open 11:30 A.M. to 3:00 P.M. for lunch and 5:00 P.M. to 10:30 P.M. for dinner daily. Major credit cards accepted.

THE BULL SHED
Menehune Shopping Village
Lihue
Telephone: (808) 245-4551

796 Kuhio Highway
Kapaa
Telephone: (808) 822-3791

In spite of their inauspicious name, the restaurants have carved a firm niche in the dining scene on Kauai. They're immensely popular, particularly the original one in Kapaa with its great ocean view. Particularly good are the rack of lamb, the prime rib, and, of course, the seafood, from the fresh catch to the lobster. The new Lihue restaurant lacks the view of the Kapaa original, but the quality of the cuisine is reported to be consistent. The menu is unpretentious and straightforward; there are no surprises here.

No reservations accepted, casual. Moderately expensive, with entrées from $8.95 to $18.95. Open 5:30 P.M. to 10:00 P.M. daily. Major credit cards accepted.

CLUB JETTY RESTAURANT
Nawiliwili
Telephone: (808) 245-4970

Jutting out over the water as it has for nearly forty years, the Club Jetty looks like a pier with windows. It's charming, funky, and appealing, and is known more for its family feeling and character than for its cuisine. It serves standard Cantonese food in a large room with windows overlooking Nawiliwili Harbor, where it's spent decades watching the ships come in. Mama Ouye, the grande dame of the operation, is a classic hostess. Habitués remember the old days, when the underwater lights illuminated manta rays in the water, circling gracefully while diners above them demolished the chow fun and spareribs. At night the lounge next door becomes a nightclub that jumps with dancing until the wee hours.

Informal and moderately priced, with entrées from $4.95 to $21.95. Open from 4:30 P.M. to 9:30 P.M. Monday through Thursday and the lounge next door is open until 3:30 A.M. on the weekends. Major credit cards accepted.

EGGBERT'S
4483 Rice Street
Lihue
Telephone: (808) 245-6325

The split-level restaurant has a widespread reputation and a huge menu that includes the best Eggs Benedict on the island, banana hotcakes, and make-your-own omelets. Eggbert's also prides itself on being the earliest-serving bar on the island. Along with Kountry Kitchen, Eggbert's is one of the best breakfast spots on the island, the ideal starting point to the day. You can choose a chili salsa omelet served with sour cream and chives, Portuguese sausage, and any one of a variety of combinations—they're all good. Dinner includes stuffed mushrooms, sashimi when available, and a variety of sautéed, charbroiled, and baked fish dishes. And for dessert, what else—a Belgian waffle.

Informal, with omelets beginning at $3.95 and complete dinners at $7.95. Open 5:30 P.M. to 9:30 P.M. Wednesday through Saturday for dinner, 7:00 A.M. to 3:00 P.M. Monday through Saturday for breakfast and lunch, and 7:00 A.M. to 2:00 P.M. Sunday. Major credit cards accepted.

GAYLORD'S
Kilohana
Puhi
Telephone: (808) 245-9593

Everyone watched as Kilohana opened its aristocratic doors and hoped to become a hot new attraction. A historic plantation home, it was restored to its full splendor, with its original Gump's furniture and the beveled glass from eons ago. The restaurant in this shopping and museum complex, Gaylord's, had a lot to live up to—and it has.

It offers truly elegant al fresco dining. You sit in the marvelous courtyard of a spacious Hawaiian manse, surrounded by flowers and Hawaiian plants. You peruse a menu with luncheon offerings such as broiled Alaskan salmon, various pastas and salads, and fresh fish in subtle and attractive preparations. For dinner, the choices include baked Brie in phyllo, fresh New Zealand scallop roe au gratin, lobster Normandie, scampi Provençale, Alaskan silver salmon sautéed and finished with caviar-lime butter. The choices aren't smashingly daring, but the dining experience succeeds. With the shops and museum open during the day and the dry Puhi air at night, Gaylord's is pleasant night or day.

Dinner entrées range from $16.95 to $22.95, with appetizers in the $6 to $7 range. Lunch, about $20 for two without wine. Lunch, casual; dinner on the dressy side. Open 11:00 A.M. to 4:00 P.M. for lunch and 5:30 P.M. to 9:30 P.M. for dinner Monday through Saturday, and 10:00 A.M. to 3:00 P.M. for Sunday brunch. Major credit cards accepted.

GREEN GARDEN
Hanapepe
Telephone: (808) 335-5422

It's a large room loaded with plants, fishing paraphernalia, and happy diners. You can always count on getting great fresh fish here, whether it's kiawe-broiled ono or the fresh island papio. The restaurant is like an oasis, serving everyone from starving hikers from Kokee, who straggle down the hill for a good meal, to neighbor islanders in the know who come straight here for lunch. At lunch, the ono sandwiches are remarkable; at dinner, the fresh catch is always good. Equally inviting is the ambience—strictly local, very informal, and pleasantly cluttered like a comfortable room.

Moderately priced, with entrées from $5.95 to $21. Open 7:00 A.M. to 2:00 P.M. daily and from 5:00 P.M. to 9:00 P.M. nightly except Tuesday. Major credit cards accepted.

HAMURA SAIMIN STAND
2956 Kress Street
Lihue
Telphone: (808) 245-3271

Every kid on Kauai has been raised on Hamura saimin—if not after a football game, then surely after a movie. In fact, just about everyone on the island has eaten at Hamura, because not to do so is heresy. Steaming vats filled with broth contain homemade noodles, which are plunked into large bowls along with eggs, vegetables, and various garnishes. The soup and noodles march across the tiny counters countless times every day. Hamura's homemade noodles, neatly packed in pink cartons, are often carted interisland as well, as coveted gifts from local families. You'll be glad you tried Hamura's, because you will have tried the best of a local ritual, saimin.

Informal and very inexpensive, with prices from $1.16 to $4.30. Open daily from 10:00 A.M. to 2:00 A.M. and until 4:00 A.M. Friday and Saturday. Cash only.

J J'S BROILER
2971 Haleko Road
Lihue
Telephone: (808) 245-3841

The Slavonic steak here is legendary; steak and garlic lovers rave about the way J J's slathers on the butter, garlic, and herbs. But J J's is also popular for its New York steak served on a sizzling platter. Although some seafood dishes are offered, this is largely for hearty meat eaters. The restaurant is an old converted plantation home.

Moderately priced, with entrées from $11.95 to $19.95. Open 5:00 P.M. to 9:00 P.M. every day. Major credit cards accepted.

KAKO'S SAIMIN STAND
Next to Nishimura Store
Hanapepe
Telephone: (808) 335-5401

The real truth about saimin is that the best is found in Hanapepe. This is a competitive field; Kauai folks discuss who's got the best saimin like some people discuss the stock market. Kako's is not very well known—certainly not as well known as Hamura's—but the saimin, homemade daily, and the soup—made from scratch from an old family recipe, make this unequivocally the best in the field. Her kiawe-broiled teriyaki beef sticks and the barbecued chicken have a loyal following, too.

"Kako" is Dorothea Hayashi, who took the tiny shop over from friends who ran it for over twenty years. Hayashi uses their broth recipe, an old family secret that sent their friends' children through college. She makes 10 pounds of noodles a day—when she runs out, that's it. Everything is homemade here; it's a six-table restaurant that you'll never forget.

Very inexpensive—a meal can cost under $4. Hours are changeable, so please call ahead. No credit cards accepted.

KAPAA FISH AND CHOWDER HOUSE
1639 Kuhio Highway
Kapaa
Telephone: (808) 822-7488

KOLOA FISH AND CHOWDER HOUSE
5402 Koloa Road
Koloa
Telephone: (808) 742-7377

A meal that begins with passion fruit margaritas can hardly go wrong. The seafood here is fresh and good, from the daily fresh catch to the seafood fettucine and shrimp in coconut. The menu is creative enough to satisfy, yet safe enough for the unadventurous—everything from prime rib to meals with a hint of Tahitian flavorings served in a comfortable, airy, nautical ambience. The kiawe-broiled fish and the seafood chowders are excellent, and so are the fresh fish sandwiches for lunch. Although the Koloa restaurant gets all the glory, the Kapaa one is terrific too.

Moderately priced, with entrées from $9 to $17 at the Kapaa restaurant, and up to $24 at the Koloa restaurant. Open 5:30 P.M. to 9:30 P.M. in Kapaa and Koloa, and also from 11:30 A.M. to 3:00 P.M. in Koloa. Major credit cards accepted.

KAUAI CHOP SUEY
Harbor Village
Lihue
Telephone: (808) 245-8790

There's nothing spectacular about the menu—it's standard Chinese food—but the light touch and fresh vegetables make the food here special. You know it's good because the restaurant is always crowded with local families and lunchtime diners who work in Lihue and think nothing of schlepping down the hill to Nawiliwili for a heaping plate of Kauai Chop Suey's Cantonese shrimp.

No reservations accepted. Informal and inexpensive—lunch for two can cost $13. Open 11:00 A.M. to 2:00 P.M. Tuesday through Saturday and 4:30 P.M. to 9:00 P.M. Tuesday through Sunday. No credit cards accepted.

KIIBO RESTAURANT
2991 Umi Street
Lihue
Telephone: (808) 245-2650

Kiibo has inexpensive and informal Japanese country food, which is served in a pleasant room dotted with folk art while Japanese music plays. Sashimi, fried mahimahi, sushi, ramen noodles, and other delights come in neat, unpretentious servings on ersatz lacquer trays. The oyako donburi, a rice dish with steamed eggs and vegetables, is delicious, as is the sukiyaki. The green-tea ice cream is an appropriate end to the meal.

Informal and inexpensive—two can dine here for $12. Open 11:00 A.M. to 1:30 P.M. and 5:30 P.M. to 9:00 P.M. Monday through Saturday. Cash only.

KOUNTRY KITCHEN
1485 Kuhio Avenue
Kapaa
Telephone: (808) 822-3511

One of two best breakfast houses on the island, Kountry Kitchen torments you with its choices. Omelets in many forms are the fare here, from kim chee (fiery Korean pickled cabbage) with sour cream to sprouts, sausages, vegetables, and a myriad mix-and-match possibilities. The home fries are grand, too, and so is the corn bread.

Dinners feature inexpensive seafood and steaks, from a $6.95 mahimahi to catch of the day for $11.95—a bargain by all means. Informal. Open 6:00 A.M. to 2:30 P.M. and 5:00 P.M. to 9:00 P.M. daily. Major credit cards accepted.

THE MIDORI
Kauai Hilton and Beach Villas
Lihue
Telephone: (808) 245-1955

The Midori has created an environment that resembles a Japanese gallery, with artifacts on the walls, an antique bamboo table, Imari plates, a granite column in the center, lacquer screens, and a bonsai plant on every table. The environment is enclosed, with no windows, but you don't notice it at all because there's so much visual stimulation around.

Midori is a new restaurant in a new hotel, with an impressive menu that blends Asian, continental, and Pacific cuisines. Highly recommended is the cream of taro soup with smoked ahi, a bold idea that's a resounding success. The "seafood experience" comes with buttered seaweed, another winner. Other temptations: Molokai shrimp with truffle and Cognac sauce; grilled duck breast with shiitake mushrooms; boneless quail salad with oyster mushrooms, baked in phyllo; broiled lobster, clams, and other seafood with gourmet sauces. The accompaniment of rosemary rolls with goat cheese is ingenious and delicious. We compliment the chef.

The dessert tray is full of rainbow-colored fruit tarts and a chocolate mousse layer cake, but it was the pecan pie, simple and true, that was the best.

Highly recommended. Expensive, with entrées from $17 to $23. Open 6:00 P.M. to 9:45 P.M. nightly except Sunday. Major credit cards accepted.

PLANTATION GARDENS
Kiahuna Plantation
Poipu
Telephone: (808) 742-1695

Touches of white wicker on hardwood, graceful cactus and willows outside the open veranda, old plantation photographs—such is the dining ambience. For atmosphere and good seafood, Plantation Gardens is a winner.

There are appetizers, light suppers, and dinners that range from fresh fish to Alaskan king crab legs, crab Florentine, fish stuffed with crab. When they're in season, the fish will be uku (gray snapper), ahi (tuna), ulua (trevally), catfish, ono (wahoo), and many others. There's also an international theme, with preparations scanning the globe from Japan (teriyaki), Italy (scampi), to Australia (lobster). The naughty hula pie for dessert is hazardous, but the environment is so soothing you won't have a care.

Moderately expensive, with entrées from $10.95 to $24.95. Open 5:30 P.M. to 10:00 P.M. daily. Major credit cards accepted.

TAMARIND
Stouffer Waiohai Beach Resort
Poipu
Telephone: (808) 742-9511

Tamarind offers a superb, sophisticated dining experience. Banquettes, mirrors, brass, formal service, and formally clad waiters express serious intentions here, and it's not all show. The menu is imaginative, offering unlikely combinations that work: lobster salad with papaya and fresh ginger; the legendary Tamarind salad of mushrooms with walnuts, artichoke hearts, snow peas in a creamy dill dressing; lobster and scallops in puff pastry. The vegetables, very nouvelle, are the perfect accompaniment, and the lobster with black bean sauce is the best of the Orient with a light continental touch. The silver chopsticks served with the oriental dishes are an endearing detail. When it's time for dessert, you must be persuaded to have the strawberry soufflé with Grand Marnier cream sauce. It's unthinkable that you should live without it.

It would be sacrilege to have service that doesn't live up to this cuisine, and thankfully that's not the case here. The waiters are entirely professional, attentive without being distracting.

Expensive, with entrées from $17.50 to $25. Open 6:00 P.M. to 10:00 P.M. nightly for dinner. Major credit cards accepted.

Pizzerias

THE BRICK OVEN
Kukui Grove Center
2488-A Kaumualii Highway
Lihue
Telephone: (808) 245-1895

Route 50
Kalaheo
Telephone: (808) 332-8561

The Brick Oven already had a large following after ten years in Kalaheo, where people would march in expectantly after being referred from friends in Germany or New Jersey. Word has indeed been spread about this tiny family operation, and now there's a second Brick Oven to rave about. This is thin-crust pizza, the sauce is homemade from a family recipe, and the toppings are fairly standard, except for the Canadian bacon and pineapple pizza or the "super" with everything on it. The dough is from another family recipe, and is slathered with garlic butter before baking. They're very modest about their pizza here, but east side Kauaians used to drive all the way to Kalaheo for it. Now they only need go as far as Lihue.

There are tables, but no booths, and no video games. This is strictly a quiet, pleasant family business that takes great pride in its pizza and the fact that everything is made from scratch—and the family's not even Italian.

Pizzas range from under $10 to $18 for a top-of-the-line, everything-on-it pizza. Open 11:00 A.M. to 10:00 P.M. Monday through Thursday and on Saturday, to 11:00 P.M. on Friday, and to 5:00 P.M. Sunday. Major credit cards accepted.

....

NORTH SHORE

BEAMREACH
Pali Ke Kua
Princeville
Telephone: (808) 826-9131

The Beamreach has a minimal view but wonderful cuisine. Steak and seafood are the fare here; the Beamreach has a way of coming through on simple dishes, such as the kiawe-grilled teriyaki chicken. There are home-made liver pâté, Scallops Bourguignonne, and a scampi that is quite popular. Only about a dozen entrées grace the menu, but what is there is done well.

Expensive, with entrées from $8.95 to $35. Open 6:00 to 10:00 P.M. every night. Major credit cards accepted.

CHARRO'S
Kuhio Highway (15 min. past Princeville)
Haena
Telephone: (808) 826-6422

Las Vegas entertainer Charro came to Hanalei on her honeymoon, fell in love with the place, returned, and opened a restaurant. It's the hottest new restaurant on the north shore, with high ceilings, rattan furnishings, and a light, pleasant ambience. The showstopper here is the view: the north and east sides of the restaurant have enormous glass windows that look out to the ocean. It's located not far from where Kuhio Highway ends at Ke'e Beach; you can't miss the big sign on the ocean side of the road.

The cuisine holds its own too. Paella is a favorite here, and so is the veal marsala. The chefs, from Reno nightclubs, can get showy at times, but they are successful. There is always fresh ahi, with fresh fish in at least four preparations that change daily. One day the offering may be sesame-ginger sauce, another, papaya-lime.

Expensive—lunch entrées range from $5.95 to $8.95, dinner, $15.95 to $23.95. Open 11:30 A.M. to 3 P.M. and 5:30 P.M. to 10 P.M. daily. Major credit cards accepted.

DUANE'S ONO-CHAR BURGER
Anahola
Telephone: (808) 822-9181

Standing by the roadside on the way to Hanalei, Ono-Burger, as it's called, is a mecca for ravenous passersby. Luring them with its succulent sandwiches, Ono-Burger is a takeout stand and a picnicker's paradise, with tables under the tree for lingering. The sandwiches are excellent, from the vegetarian special to the tuna salad, but it's the burgers that are famous. Ono-burgers are charbroiled and superior; rumor has it that some popular Hawaiian entertainers from Oahu make special trips to Ono-Burger.

Inexpensive, from $3.40 to $5.50 for sandwiches. Open 10 A.M. to 6:00 P.M. Monday through Saturday. No credit cards accepted.

THE HANALEI DOLPHIN
Hanalei
Telephone: (808) 826-6113

The Dolphin rests by the Hanalei River, serving seafood in a cozy, rustic ambience and enjoying its longstanding reputation as Hanalei's favored seafood restaurant. The Dolphin's preparations are different enough to make you want to return. The broccoli casserole light dinner is a wonderful invitation to graze and is a nice change from the sea of seafood dishes you'll encounter on Kauai. The Haole Chicken is breaded with seasonings and Parmesan, and the Hawaiian chicken is marinated in soy sauce and ginger.

The shrimp, scallops, calamari, fresh catch, and mahimahi (not necessarily fresh) comprise a well-rounded seafood selection. For meat eaters, the New York cut tenderloin and seafood-steak combinations offer a choice.

Moderately expensive, with entrées from $7 to $35. Open 6:00 P.M. to 10:00 P.M. daily. Major credit cards accepted.

THE SHELL HOUSE
Hanalei
Telephone: (808) 826-7977

The Shell House is terribly overshadowed by its high-profile neighbor, Tahiti Nui, but its food is excellent and the restaurant is a find. This is a sleeper of a restaurant, which may look seedy from the outside but which offers terrific seafood, elegantly prepared. The fresh catch comes in a variety of preparations—poached, grilled, sautéed—and you can be confident it'll be good, especially the fresh sea bass with hollandaise sauce, macadamia nuts, and bananas.

Moderately expensive, with entrées from $6.95 to $18.95. Open 8:00 A.M. to 10:30 P.M. daily. Major credit cards accepted.

....

THE BEST LUAU

SHERATON COCONUT BEACH
Coconut Plantation
Waipouli
Telephone: (808) 822-3455

As commercial luaus go, the Sheraton does an adequate job. The imu ceremony is pleasantly arranged in a coconut grove, which adds an air of authority to the whole affair. There's a torch-lighting ceremony and each guest is greeted with the obligatory shell lei.

The luau is set in an open-air pavilion with a stage—that's a plus, because it's always nicer to have a luau outdoors. The other elements of a luau—food and entertainment—add up, well, adequately, with the food being the stronger factor.

The unveiling of the pig from its earthen oven is always a thrill, and it's hard work too. As the pig is removed from its imu, the narrator explains the tedious process—out come the taro, sweet potatoes, bananas, and other things that have been cooking in the imu along with the pig.

The food is buffet style, like all commercial luaus, except that the Sheraton's food is better than most. The menu includes the roast pig, sweet potatoes, fried rice, chicken long rice, mahimahi, poi, lomi salmon, teriyaki beef, and other inviting items. Of special note is the delicious rice pudding that also comes out of the imu. The entertainment, alas, is nothing you'd write home about.

Cost is $33 adults, $22 children; $14 for the show only. The luau is held nightly except Monday.

NIGHTLIFE AND
ENTERTAINMENT

The only certain thing about nightlife on Kauai is that the Hawaiian group Na Kaholokula is the best. Led by Robbie Kaholokula, his brother Kimo, and with the excellent dancer Pua Vidhina, they put on a show that will take you on a journey into the legends, customs, and everyday life of Hawaii. Their voices are clear, pure, inspired—you will not hear anything better in Hawaii. Vidhina's hula (ancient and modern) is flawless, and the group's tender harmonies leave not a dry eye in the house as they sing songs inspired by their father, Jimmy Kaholokula. They usually perform at the Sheraton Coconut Beach's Paddle Room ([808] 822-3455).

Coco Palms Resort ([808] 822-4921) has Larry Rivera, who's been singing there for more than three decades, strumming his guitar with soft night music in the lagoon-side dining room. Not far away is Smith's Tropical Paradise ([808] 822-4654) above the Wailua Marina by the Wailua River, where there's a nightly Polynesian show featuring some of the liveliest Tahitian dancing on the island. Other names to watch for: Jack Wilhelm and his Polynesian Revue, and Glenn Medeiros, the boy wonder whose record has hit the national charts.

Those in a more raucous mood usually head for Club Jetty ([808] 245-4970), the wharfside institution where the joint starts jumping with live music and you don't know which visiting celebrity will join the party. Scarcely anyone visits Kauai without visiting Club Jetty, and it's loved by locals too.

Most of the resorts have their own lounges with piano music or shows. Gilligan's at the Kauai Hilton is a popular disco with contemporary and Top 40s music, and the Westin Kauai, which opened last fall, has a medley of entertainment choices. By far the most picturesque lounge is the Sheraton Kauai's Drum Lounge ([808] 742-1661) in Poipu, which looks right over the water (although you can only see it when there's a moon) and features live music and dancing nightly.

SPECIAL OUTINGS:
ON LAND

Bicycling

NORTH SHORE BIKE AND SNORKEL CRUISE
P.O. Box 1192
Kapaa, HI 96746
Telephone: (808) 822-1582

It's easy pedaling for about 6 miles on the north shore, where you get those heady ocean views, and then you snorkel in a wonderland of tropical fish that will actually eat out of your hands. At some point, just so you don't miss out on anything, you even swim in a freshwater pool near a waterfall in Haena. A beach barbecue of hamburgers, fresh Kauai fruits, chips, marshmallows, etc. follows. It's all festive and well planned. North Shore Bike Cruise will pick you up in a van and drive you out to the north shore where all this activity begins. Baby carriers and small bicycles are also provided, as well as life jackets for beginning swimmers. You're picked up at 7:00 or 8:00 A.M. and returned at 3:00 or 4:00 P.M.; all snorkel gear, bicycles, helmets, and equipment provided. Children three to seven, $32.50 (under three years, free); seven years and older, $65. Swimsuit, camera, and towel are about all you'll need to bring.

Golf

PRINCEVILLE GOLF COURSE
P.O. Box 3069
Princeville, HI 96722
Telephone: (800) 334-8484, (808) 826-9644

Rated one of the top one hundred golf courses in the United States, Princeville astounds golfers with its scenic beauty. The twenty-seven-hole course (nine additional holes are newly opened as a separate course) meanders over cliffs, near the ocean, and always with the famous Hanalei hills, the northern flank of Waialeale, as the backdrop. Princeville's ocean, lakes, and woods courses have enchanted golfers for years with their even movement through contrasting environments. It overlooks Hanalei Bay, the jewel of the north shore. It's also where the LPGA's Kemper Open is held every year for a star-studded gallery. Fees are $40 to $50.

WAILUA GOLF COURSE
Lihue, HI 96746
Telephone: (808) 245-2163

Wailua Golf Course is the pride of the island. Regulars who have golfed here for thirty-five years still wax poetic about its beauty. The eighteen-hole course was designed by a local pro, Toyo Shirai, and is ranked today among the top twenty-five public courses in the United States. There are abundant ironwoods and Norfolk pines; palms; ocean views; deep, gaping traps; and gentle slopes that maximize play on all fronts. And it is challenging. The course is laid out so you have to think about your shots; you can't play recklessly. Wailua was Bing Crosby's favorite hangout whenever he came to Kauai. It's rumored he once proclaimed the seventeenth hole the most beautiful golf hole he'd ever seen. For a world-class public course, the fees are unbelievable: $15 monthly green fees for residents ($8 for seniors!), $10 a day for nonresidents, plus just under $12 for carts.

Helicopter Tours

Helicopter tours are booming on this island. More than any other island, Kauai is noted for its aerial views of the interior, where Waialeale, the wettest spot on earth, presides with strings of waterfalls streaming down its crater sides like tears. Were it not for the boat and helicopter tours, the Na Pali Coast would escape our view; and were it not for the helicopters, Waialeale's majesty would be hidden from all. Last summer, even the privately owned Niihau was cautiously opened up to helicopters.

Although many hikers and sightseers complain about them buzzing over valleys (and they are an intrusion to hikers), those who see Kauai by air say it's a valuable and unforgettable experience. Once you're in the air the island sells itself, but it helps to have a competent pilot and an informed narration. Here are Kauai's best.

JACK HARTER HELICOPTERS
P.O. Box 306
Lihue, HI 96766
Telephone: (808) 245-3774

Jack Harter is the original, the man who twenty-five years ago began the first aerial tours of the Na Pali Coast. Today there are dozens of helicopter companies doing what he started, but Harter is in a league by himself. Considered the senior pilot of Kauai's skies, he's done everything from helping in rescue missions to charting the sightings of Kalalau's elusive golden eagle. He has refused to expand, choosing to fly and narrate every flight. Harter knows Kauai as few do, and his narration reflects that.

The tour, which takes in most of the island, including Waialeale and the Na Pali Coast, lasts an hour and a half and is $125 per person. It's the longest tour available and what a good price! Cash and traveler's checks only; three flights daily on weekdays, closed weekends. Because he's the best-known and most popular of the helicopter operators, he's always booked in advance. It's recommended you book at least one week ahead, earlier if possible.

OHANA HELICOPTERS
3222 Kuhio Highway
Suite 4
Lihue, HI 96766
Telephone: (808) 245-3996

People love Ohana because it's small, owner-operated, and personal. Two pilots who are natives of Kauai own the business, fly the helicopters, and give enlightening narrations. They know the island well, and it shows. The Mokihana Tour is fifty minutes for $104; the Maile is a sixty-five-minute tour for $140.40.

SOUTH SEA HELICOPTERS
P.O. Box 1445
Lihue, HI 96766
Telephone: (808) 245-7781

Another very reputable operation is South Sea, a two-helicopter company known for its professionalism. There are four pilots, all military trained and well versed in island geography, history, and legends. The Ultimate Splendor (the names sound like honeymoon suites) is a longer tour of the Waimea Canyon, Na Pali Coast, the Hanalei Valley, and the pièce de résistance, the crater of Waialeale. The fifty-minute Golden Eagle tour costs $115, the sixty-five-minute Ultimate Splendor, $135. Major credit cards accepted.

WILL SQUYRES HELICOPTER SERVICE
3222 Kuhio Highway
Lihue, HI 96766
Telephone: (808) 245-7541

Will Squyres runs another owner-operated helicopter business that keeps receiving accolades. Except for some complaints about the sound system, the tour is expremely popular, and so is Squyres. His sixty-minute tour costs $110 and takes you over the island's interior and the Na Pali Coast, including the awesome Waialeale crater.

Hiking

LOCAL BOY TOURS
P.O. Box 3324
Lihue, HI 96766
Telephone: (808) 245-8899

Although the wilderness is free and you could always hike on your own, there are certain reasons for guided hikes. One of them is the quality of information the guide provides on such things as wildlife, history, legends, indigenous plants and their uses, medicinal plants and how to identify them, and other details that could make the difference between a great hiking experience and a once-in-a-lifetime one. Another reason is knowledge of the area. A good guide has access to, and will take you to, places you'd have to work very hard to find on your own. Another point worth mentioning is safety. Marijuana growers have planted their illegal crops in large tracts of Hawaii's wilderness, which they often guard menacingly, making some wilderness areas hazardous for explorers.

Lloyd Pratt grew up on Kauai and has been hiking the island all his life. Part Hawaiian, he is also a serious student of Hawaiiana and shares everything he knows. At Ke'e Beach he'll show you the hula heiau, Hawaii's most important, and explain its legends and history. On the Na Pali Coast hikes, he'll explain who lived in each valley, what they grew, how they ate, how they made rope and sandals out of such things as ti leaves and hau tree vines. Wearing *malo* (traditional Hawaiian loincloth) and pareus, with ti leaves, ferns, and vines draped about neck and forehead, Pratt and his guides will demonstrate everything from haku lei making to coconut basket weaving. By the time you return you may be similarly draped with the fragrant maile and ginger, nibbling on wild mountain watercress, guava, mountain apple, banana, and other gatherings from the wilds.

The choices are vast, from short day hikes to three-day camp-outs deep in Kalalau Valley. The trails cover the whole island, from the Sleeping Giant to Kokee trails to the remote Na Pali Coast valleys. There are snorkel side trips and swimming in waterfalls and pools. All food and gear are provided, and for the extended camp-outs in the summer months the supplies are taken in to Kalalau Valley by Zodiac. The rest of the time, hikers are expected to do their share in carrying the gear. Hikes range from easy to advanced and cost anywhere from $40 for the short day hikes to $250 for the camp-outs, with reduced rates for children. Pratt will happily answer questions about Kauai hiking in general, even if you wish to hike on your own. Ask him how to get to the Ho'opi'i lava tube in Kapahi, with its freshwater pool and dainty waterfalls. He'll show you how to get there so you can soak yourself in the water-filled tube.

KAUAI MOUNTAIN TOURS
P.O. Box 3069
Lihue, HI 96766
Telephone: (800) 331-8071, (808) 245-7224

Not everyone can hike the mountain trails of Kokee, but most people would like to. After all, they are among the best in the world. Doug Fu of Kauai Mountain Tours is the only tour operator authorized to take small van tours into forest reserve areas, on the dirt roads and backwoods of the Kokee State Park bordering the fabled Na Pali Coast. From the air-conditioned comfort of an eight-passenger station wagon, you can view waterfalls, rare honeycreepers, Waimea Canyon from its other side, and sugi pine forests and stream areas looking over Kauai's most isolated valleys. It's strictly sightseeing, with only short walks, but the seeing is unbelievable.

You'll see areas few people see: natural glens of koa, kukui, medicinal plants, ferns, waterfalls, ohia trees, streams, and, if you're lucky, some wild boar or black-tail deer. Fu, a native of Kauai, knows Kauai well, and he makes sure he and his guides don't stop at the usual places.

There's a long tour, which includes a box lunch from Green Garden restaurant (a favorite), and a short tour of fewer stops and no lunch. Cost is $52 for the short tour and $72.80 for the long tour of 6½ to 7 hours. Hotel pickup is offered. If roads become impassable because of the weather, Alternate routes will be selected.

Horseback Riding

CJM COUNTRY STABLE
5598 Tapa Street
Koloa, HI 96756
Telephone: (808) 245-6666

They mix in Hawaiian legend, some good information on birds and wildlife, and oceanside trails rich in history where the salt air blows free and clean. You can ride to a secluded beach where sea turtles come out of the water, or past an ancient Hawaiian fishing ground, or to a clear, reefy cove for snorkeling. The area is Poipu, with gorgeous beachside trails (natural, not man-made) leading to deserted beaches beneath cliffs full of legend, such as the sacrifice ledge at Haupu mountain. The rides range from a scenic one-hour ocean ride to a two-hour trip to Pu'u Pihakapu, more commonly called Black Mountain, and a three-hour "Tropical Beach Trail Delight" that takes in swimming, snorkeling, lunch, and a leisurely ride between mountain and ocean. The one-hour ride is $18.50, the two-hour ride is $30, and the three-hour ride with lunch is $48. You can also get a special ride with a guide for $40, where you can gallop and explore as you choose. Maximum per ride is ten people, which makes it a more personalized experience than most. There've been many satisfied customers at CJM. Closed Sundays.

PO'OKU STABLES
P.O. Box 888
Hanalei, HI 96714
Telephone: (808) 826-6777, 826-6484, 826-7473

You have a choice of a beach ride, valley ride, or a waterfall picnic ride in the unforgettable wilds of Hanalei. The 10,000-acre Princeville Ranch allows a lot of space for roaming and some unequalled vantage points for viewing Waialeale, the crown of the island. From open cattle land to the cliffside vistas of the ocean, Po'oku leads good rides. Up to twenty can go on a ride. The one-hour Hanalei Valley ride is $15; the beach ride, $30; the three-hour waterfall, picnic, and swimming ride, $55. Lunch includes European cheeses; Kauai's special, Jacques' Bread; sweet sausage; vegetables; and other nibbles. Closed Sundays.

Museums and Historical Sights

GROVE FARM
P.O. Box 1631
Lihue, HI 96766
Telephone: (808) 245-3202

This is for history buffs and those interested in Kauai's sugar plantation era and the long, abiding influence of one of its most significant families. The home of George Wilcox, the founder of Grove Farm, is maintained today as a museum on stately, scenic grounds. Much of the 80-acre site is in a valley, with the Hoary Head mountain range in the distance and the town of Lihue in front. It's a historic site museum, built in 1864 and open today for guided tours offering a glimpse into the sugar plantation and Hawaii's politics from the monarchy until it became a state. The large, old building has a tin roof, two libraries, dining area, and memorabilia from the turn of the century. The 2½-hour tour is limited to six people per guide. Reservations are required, and some people book months ahead. Cost is $3 per person.

KAMOKILA HAWAIIAN VILLAGE
6060 Kuamoo Road
Wailua
Telephone: (808) 822-1192

Kamokila is a low-key, educational, and no-nonsense tour of a restored Hawaiian village that still sits serenely amid breadfruit trees and petroglyphs. In a quiet and beautiful setting above the Wailua River, the restored thatched homes, taro patches, poi-pounding demonstrations, and ancient implements tell a story of times past. It is not a fancy, slick operation, but rather homegrown and professional enough, with an earnest staff and a rustic feeling that adds enormously to its appeal. There's nothing plastic here, not a plastic lei or a plastic credit card or a Mai Tai.

The guide takes you around the grounds and shows you the sleeping house, the eating house with its coconut and carved wood utensils, the herbalist's house with its stone mortar and pestle and medicinal plants, and the oracle tower where food was offered to the gods by the kahuna (priest) or chief. Peacocks and chickens are roaming around freely, with a wild pig on display behind wire. At scheduled times, hula dancing and Hawaiian entertainment fill the drum house with festivity. At other times, there are demonstrations in such things as the preparation of medicinal plants. It's so informal you just follow the guide around and can ask questions to your heart's content. Open 9:00 A.M. to 4:00 P.M. daily except Sunday; $5 admission. No credit cards.

KAUAI MUSEUM
4428 Rice Street
Lihue
Telephone: (808) 245-6931

If you love small, well-planned, and manageable museums, museums that enlighten without overwhelming, you'll love the Kauai Museum.

Housed in a lava rock structure in Lihue, it sensitively tells the story of Hawaii, with rare and beautiful artifacts in sensible displays.

Included are displays of Kauai's geology, wildlife, and ethnic history, with artifacts from Oriental cultures as well as the Hawaiians' and missionaries'. Well-preserved furnishings of missionaries' homes and priceless native bowls, stone implements, featherwork, and photographs line the walls of this tiny museum.

You won't have to spend hours to get the story of Hawaii, but you could if you wanted to. Just leave time for the gift shop, which has a glorious selection of books and gift items, some of them sold exclusively here. Open 9:00 A.M. to 4:30 P.M. Monday through Friday, 9:00 A.M. to 1:00 P.M. Saturday. Admission is $3 for adults, children under eighteen free.

PACIFIC TROPICAL BOTANICAL GARDENS
P.O. Box 340
Lawai, HI 96765
Telephone: (808) 332-7361

Daily tours will take you through the most highly respected botanical research facility in Hawaii, the Pacific Tropical Botanical Gardens. If you can get a reservation—and it can be difficult—try not to miss this. They've expanded their tours of the nearby Allerton Garden, also a must.

The 186-acre Pacific Tropical Gardens have excellent displays and a magnificent setting, but it is primarily a scientific, research, and educational facility in botany. The Allerton Garden is known the world over for its landscaping, design, and setting. Rare tropical plants are set in a lush 125-acre valley, a private estate, with statues, waterfalls, mountains, and streams that have been featured in *Life* magazine and a host of other publications. The tour takes you from the center of Lawai Valley down to the ocean—unforgettable.

Monday through Friday there are 1½-hour tours going twice a day through the Allerton Garden and the Pacific Tropical Botanical Gardens; on the weekends, an exclusive walking tour of the Pacific Tropical Botanical Gardens is offered. Cost is $10 per person. Reservations are a must, for they take only fourteen people at a time and they're booked far in advance.

Special Hikes and Special Places

KEAHUA ARBORETUM
Wailua Homesteads

If you've always wanted to picnic on a grassy lawn by a stream and then heave yourself on a rope swing into a pool of clear mountain water, consider this your spot. There aren't many places where you don't have to hike for miles to find what you find here.

The Keahua Stream flows generously down from the eastern flank of Waialeale, the volcanic mass of the island. Beautifully worn stream rocks border the healthy stream (no mere trickle, this) and the park of orange-barked eucalyptus, kukui nut, ohia, guava trees, and native and introduced species. There's plenty of parking, and an easy walk along the stream will lead you to the shaded area with tall trees and the much-loved rope swing where children pretend they're Tarzan. Be careful, the swing is not as easy as it looks, but you don't have to jump, you can always ease in. Take mosquito repellent just in case, and a romantic picnic lunch would be nice. After the swim, you can walk upstream and explore the area or wander through the arboretum, which includes several easy trails. The Kuilau Ridge Trail leads to a picnic area; if you hike to the second shelter, you'll pass waterfalls and exquisite scenery.

To get to Keahua, turn mauka from Route 56 onto Route 580 next to Coco Palms Resort, a few feet north of the Wailua Bridge. Drive through the Wailua Homestead to the end, where the road veers left into the park.

The Moalepe trail is part of the Keahua Arboretum trail system located on the other side of the Sleeping Giant, deep in the mountains above Wailua. It's an easy hike of 2.5 miles with a 500-foot elevation gain, offering a view of half the island, sweeping along the eastern shoreline to the south in a breathtaking panorama. For such a gentle hike, it offers intimate peeks into the prolific environs of the Waialeale crater and the waterfalls, streams, and abundant vegetation it spawns on all sides. Weather can be very wet and the trail could be muddy, so be careful. Near the intersection of the Moalepe Trail and the Kuilau Trail, there's a picnic spot, and further north, a lookout that will reward your labors.

The Kuilau Ridge Trail also deserves your attention. It's slightly over 2 miles and is laden with fruit trees, well maintained and dramatic. Strategically placed picnic sites overlook dense canyons while a ridgeline section puts you above streams, valleys, and waterfalls. You can start on the Kuilau Ridge Trail from the Keahua Arboretum, or you can hook up with it from the Moalepe Trail. To get to the Moalepe Trail, take Route 581 (a right turn from 580) and go north to Olohena Road.

KOKEE STATE PARK
Division of State Parks
P.O. Box 1671
Lihue, HI 96766
Telephone: (808) 245-4444

You must have expectations when you go to Kokee. It deserves them. Presiding over the northeast flank of Waialeale, it borders the fabled Na Pali Coast and offers views of the most distant, mysterious, and historic valleys of the island, the valleys of the Na Pali Coast. Past the Waimea Canyon on the drive north, Kokee is at the 4,000-foot elevation, with crisp air, wild boar and deer, seasonal plum picking and trout fishing, and a rich and varied habitat for some of Hawaii's most rare and endangered wildlife. The island's most extensive system of hiking trails exists in this 4,345-acre park, where you can walk through sugi pine groves and distant streams or hike to vistas thousands of feet above inaccessible valleys where Hawaiians once thrived and grew taro.

There's a museum—a must to help you get oriented—a lodge that serves three meals a day, state cabins, and, in its innermost regions, the Alakai Swamp, which contains one of the most fragile ecosystems on earth. Waialeale, with its average annual rainfall of 450 inches, feeds the Alakai Swamp. Microscopic ferns, miniature maile, and what scientists think are some of the last species of rare birds in the world exist in this strange habitat where only the most intrepid hikers go. It is so wet and boggy that plants are stunted; their roots remain on the surface because the bogs are too deep for them.

Most hikers stick to the Waimea Canyon trails or the many stream, canyon, and lookout trails: the easy, 1-mile Berry Flat Trail; the 2.5-mile Kawaikoi Stream Trail; the strenuous, 3.3-mile Pihea Trail; or the breathtaking, 3.3-mile Awaawapuhi Trail. There are many, many more trails for all capabilities and preferences, all of them stunning.

The best thing about Kokee is that you don't have to do anything if you don't want to. The meadow in front of the lodge is picturesque, with passing clouds that make it look like a Chinese painting. There are numerous spots in the area for just reading and lolling. Chances are, however, that once you get to Kokee you will be unstoppable. There are new worlds to explore and the air is invigorating; you will be nourished and replenished here.

For information on camping and hiking in the park, write the Division of State Parks, whose address is listed above. For more on the cabins at the Kokee Lodge, see Hotels and Alternatives, West, South, and East Kauai. As the trails are so extensive, it's helpful to consult Robert Smith's *Hiking Kauai* or Craig Chisolm's *Hawaiian Hiking Trails*.

NA PALI COAST
Division of State Parks
P.O. Box 1671
Lihue, HI 96766
Telephone: (808) 245-4444

The Na Pali Coast is the other hiking mecca of Kauai. Ranging from the 2-mile hike from Ke'e Beach to Hanakapiai Beach, to the rugged 11-mile backpacking hike that continues to Kalalau Valley, the Na Pali Coast offers challenge, waterfalls, and vistas of sea cliffs like nowhere else in the world. (It's also Hollywood's favorite "set," having been the backdrop for everything from King Kong's jungle scene to *Raiders of the Lost Ark*.)

The trailhead is at Ke'e Beach, where you can sign in at the register. The first leg to Hanakapiai is manageable, taking you to cliff's edge where you can see whales and tropic birds and the ribboned cliffs of Na Pali. Pick wild guavas and watercress on the way, and don't miss the side trip to the waterfall from Hanakapiai Valley Loop. Just take the Hanakapiai Falls Trail and head mauka—it's strenuous and will take one to two hours to get there. If that's too much, you'll have to settle for Hanakapiai Beach, a wide, sandy plain with tiny caves on the side and a stream that meets it. Swimming is hazardous, especially in the winter—there have been many rescues here. But Hanakapiai Beach is a beach lover's fantasy, where sun-drenched skin meets white sand. All around are steep cliffs and the tangible embrace of a valley that was home to the ancient Hawaiians.

Those who forge on past Hanakapiai—and *don't*, without preparation— will encounter waterfalls plunging into the ocean, sea caves, and lush stream valleys with hidden delights.

SPECIAL OUTINGS:
IN AND ON THE WATER

Water activities on this island are just beginning to take off. Boat cruises and Na Pali Coast trips on inflatable rafts are very popular, as are scuba dives to underwater caverns on the north and south shores of Kauai. The following are the best in their areas, listed alphabetically.

AQUATICS KAUAI
733 Kuhio Highway
Kapaa, HI 96746
Telephone: (800) 822-9422, (808) 822-9213

They have the largest boat on the island, have never had an incident in eleven years in the business, and are professional and highly regarded. The 43-foot *Odysseus* is a twin diesel that takes divers and snorkelers out to the Mana Crack, a north shore site with the only coral reef near the island, which is an Aquatics Kauai exclusive. The first dive is 85 to 95 feet, with a 100- to 150-foot visibility. The Na Pali Coast dive at Mana Crack is $75 without gear, $90 with gear, and that includes lunch.

There are local dives, too, launching out of the south shore for underwater forays into lava shelves, lava tubes, pinnacles, and horseshoe-shaped ledges. These local tours are $60 without gear, $75 with.

BLUEWATER SAILING
P.O. Box 1318
Hanalei, HI 96714
Telephone: (808) 822-0525, 826-7471

Those who've taken these cruises rave about the family feeling and quality service that Rick Marvin and crew provide. The 42-foot *Pearson* is a ketch rig yacht that sails from the north shore's Hanalei in the summer and from Port Allen on the south shore in the winter. Most popular is the half-day sail that includes snorkeling and sports fishing. There's also the panoramic Beamreach and Bali Hai sunset sail, a two-hour romantic cruise; and the all-day, seven-hour Na Pali sail that stops and lets you snorkel before the most beautiful sea cliffs in the world. Snacks or lunch are provided.

The boat is large and luxurious, but only six are allowed on a tour. That makes for a lot of space, personalized service, and the luxurious feeling you're on your own private yacht in a remote island paradise. The half-day tour is $60, the Sunset and Beamreach $35, and the all-day cruise, $100.

KAUAI BY KAYAK
Adventure Kayaking International
P.O. Box 3370
Lihue, HI 96766
Telephone: (800) 331-8044, (808) 245-9662

They are synonymous with kayaking in the islands, a large and growing company that specializes in adventure. That means different things on each island, depending on the ocean's offerings. On Kauai you can kayak up the Huleia Stream to a wildlife refuge where lush growth surrounds a tranquil waterway. The area was filmed in *Raiders of the Lost Ark, Uncommon Valor,* and other adventure movies, adding an aura of glamour to your own trip. The guides love what they're doing and have so much fun you can't help but enjoy yourself. The river is easy to maneuver and the boats are stable, safe for nonswimmers and children.

If the river is too tame for you, the same company leads custom-designed expeditions to wilderness areas on all the islands as well as to South Pacific Islands. They take it very seriously, this business of adventure, and they'll make sure you're not bored or underchallenged.

The river adventure is $30; sea kayaking and camping on all the other islands is $225.

LADY ANN CRUISES
P.O. Box 3422
Lihue, HI 96766
Telephone: (800) 367-8047, ext. 446; (808) 245-8538

Lady Ann Cruises is one of the two leading operations on the island (the other is Na Pali Zodiac), not only because of its boats, tours, and service, but also because it has the rare privilege of being allowed to make landings on the Na Pali Coast. Lady Ann can now make day trips to the Na Pali Coast's most remote and exotic valleys, Miloli'i and Nualolo, four valleys over from Kalalau and the Valley of the Lost Tribe. In this business, access is paramount and these new permits are a coup. Not only must you have the equipment and means, you must be highly reputable to get the go-ahead from the state. In Kauai's mushrooming world of ocean sports, the credo is the more remote and exotic, the better.

On Kauai, Nualolo and Miloli'i are part of a conservation district. The five-hour excursions to Nualolo and Miloli'i offer views and vistas you'll never forget. The trip is on either a 38- or 34-foot Radon that leaves Hanalei Bay in the morning. Following a 17-mile coastline, you enter some stunning sea caves and pass waterfalls and jagged canyons where there are heiaus from civilizations long gone. After anchoring at Nualolo, guests snorkel ashore through a channel and tour the ruins of an ancient Hawaiian village on the east section of the beach. The $90 deluxe tour of Nualolo includes lunch, beverages, snorkeling gear, and instruction. Similar trips are offered to Miloli'i one valley over, on weekdays only. These valleys are often seen by helicopter, but to actually touch the sand, swim among the abundant fish, and be in the cradle of antiquity is a thrill you cannot imagine.

The Na Pali tours are offered in the summer, when weather conditions are calm. During the winter months Lady Ann Cruises offers 2½-hour whale-watching cruises on Kauai's south shore and snorkeling tours of Kipu Kai, a gorgeous, privately owned valley with a protected white-sand bay. No matter which Lady Ann cruise you select, you will be with a quality outfit.

NA PALI ZODIAC
P.O. Box 456
Hanalei, HI 96714
Telephone: (808) 826-9772, 826-9371

Captain Zodiac, as he's called, started it all. He began exploring the Na Pali Coast more than a decade ago. Soon he had a fleet of Zodiac rafts shuttling others in to gasp and swoon at the beauty of it all. Today Na Pali Zodiac is the undisputed leader in the inflatable raft tour business that's so popular on Kauai.

The rafts are just like those used by Jacques Cousteau—heavy-duty 23-footers with twin Mercury, 80-horsepower engines. The ride is low on the water, offering a thrill to passengers as they skim the waves and watch the porpoises, tropic birds, and the sea crashing into the towering cliffs.

Until Lady Ann Cruises got its new permits recently, Na Pali Zodiac was the only one permitted to land at remote Nualolo Valley. The company also offers a Zodiac drop-off service in the summer months in which campers and their gear can be shuttled in, dropped off, and picked up from Kalalau valley. Besides all this, Captain Zodiac has earned some community goodwill by helping in rescues and in hauling trash out from the valleys. The company is also noted for its excellent crew and up-to-date narration, which has earned the respect of even the most discriminating.

Tours go to Kipu Kai during winter months, and to the Na Pali Coast only when weather permits. The cost is $45 for a three-hour snorkeling cruise. Summer excursions on Na Pali Zodiac include a sunrise tour of the Na Pali Coast for $40 ($35 for children); a morning excursion for $55; a 5-hour expedition for $90; and the ultimate expedition, a 6½-hour foray into sea caves, valleys, beaches, and ancient ruins, with snorkeling, shell hunting, and swimming on the Na Pali Coast that costs $125. The Na Pali Coast is a must on your visit to Kauai, and this is one great way to see it.

SEA SAGE DIVING CENTER
4-1378 Kuhio Highway
Kapaa, HI 96746
Telephone: (808) 822-3841

Sea Sage was the first dive store to open on Kauai and is one of the two top operators on the island. Snorkel and scuba tours from shore or from a custom-built Radon are the offerings here, including a snorkeling picnic with detailed lessons on water safety and marine life.

They'll take you to Tunnels Reef on the north shore, the Ahukini Landing on the east shore, and to the many popular dive sites off Poipu on the south shore. Rates range from $45 for a snorkeling picnic to $75, including gear, for a 4-hour, two-tank shore dive. If you have your own gear, it's $60.

Ask about their photography service too. Nikonos and other underwater camera equipment are available for rent; the crew will willingly snap a picture of you swimming among the moray eels and humuhumunukunukuapua'a, the abundant and colorful state fish.

BEACHES

Kauai has 90 miles of shoreline and many beautiful beaches. Going around the island, we have listed the best, beginning from the west and moving south, east, and north.

As with all the beaches of Hawaii, you're advised not to swim on the west and north shores during the winter months.

Polihale State Park

Kauai's longest stretch of white-sand beach continues for 15 miles on the west coast, beginning from Waimea and ending at Polihale.

For those who know Kauai, Polihale is a magic word. A 5-mile drive through the cane fields will take you through a dusty stretch where owls can sometimes be seen swooping through the air. The tall, purple, sphinxlike cliffs command the area like sentinels, until suddenly the wide, white beach unfolds before you. In the distance looms the island of Niihau.

Polihale is a state park with facilities for camping and picnicking, but you need nothing more than its beach to grasp its full power. Bordered on one side by sea cliffs that begin the Na Pali Coast, it is a wide, elegant stretch of sand that matches the straight horizon. When the light of sunset gleams purple on the backwash and Niihau nods in the distance, it evokes a feeling of solitude, of being at the outer edge of an old island.

Swimming, however, can be very dangerous. Polihale is known for its powerful undertow, especially in the winter months.

To get there, take Route 50 past Barking Sands Missile Range and follow the signs to Polihale.

Salt Pond Beach Park

Local families have been coming here for generations, to fish and swim and collect salt at the nearby salt ponds. The reddish Hanapepe salt, available here, is considered by Hawaiians to be the best there is. The beach is a comfortable curve with a protective reef, tidal pools, and gentle, turquoise waters that are enthusiastically explored by everyone from snorkelers to children. Salt Pond Beach is a lovely surprise, easily accessible and amply supplied with picnic and shower facilities. An added bonus is the famous west side weather—always hot and sunny. To get there, take Lokokai Road in Hanapepe. It's just off Route 50 past Hanapepe Park.

Poipu Beach Park

Poipu is crowded and mainstream, so don't expect Bali Hai. It is still a lovely beach, however, so don't write it off until you check it out. There is plenty of room for walking along the long white stretch, and there is plenty to do as well. A south shore jewel with a small, protected bay, it's great for swimming, bodysurfing, surf watching, snorkeling, and tidal-pool exploration. Children love it, and it's safe. There are bathroom, shower, and picnic facilities, and a grassy lawn for everything from sunbathing to volleyball. To get there, drive to Poipu on Poipu Road and take a right on Hoowili Road.

Shipwreck

This is a unmarked, gorgeous beach at the far end of Poipu, flanked on one side by a cliff that is sometimes dotted with fishermen as they cast into the sea from the heights. The beach is a generous curve of white sand, a part of Keoniloa Bay at the southern tip of the island. Shipwreck is past the last condominium development in Poipu. You're on your own here; there are no facilities or water and no grassy parks—just a lovely place to sunbathe or explore. On calm days you'll see people snorkeling, bodysurfing, and boogie boarding close to shore. However, Shipwreck is said to have a fierce undertow, so be aware and be careful. Also beware of that algae-covered piece of wreckage visible from the shore.

Shipwreck is popular among local folks who plant themselves for long hours of serious sunbathing—be generous with that SPF!—and close-to-the-shoreline swimming. It's a nice change from the more crowded beaches such as Poipu. To get there, take Poipu Road to the end, past Poipu Kai apartments. After the paved road ends you'll be on a dirt cane road. Follow the cane haul road a few hundred yards until you hit a turn off to the right. Follow that to the dirt parking lot.

Mahaulepu

Mahaulepu is the reward at the end of a long road. Carved into the south shore beyond Shipwreck, it has something for everyone, from tidal pools to a soft crescent beach where you can linger to your heart's content. The area is pristine and full of surprises. If you explore along the coastline, you'll come across reefy areas with tidal pools that teem with life. Behind and before you, the view is fantastic. Swimming is recommended only during summer months and on days when the seas are calm. Mahaulepu is actually the name of a large area with several different beach sites, the most popular of which is a beach called "Pine Trees" by the locals. There are no facilities in the area, so come prepared.

To get there, take Poipu Road to the end and continue on the unpaved portion, past the right turnoff to Shipwreck. You'll drive several miles past various turnoffs. Stay on this main road; it will make a gradual turn to the left and head inland. At the intersection (there won't be a stop sign), turn right and continue past a coral quarry. The road will take you to Pine Trees, the only point where the road is a few feet from the ocean's edge. There are ironwood trees in the area, and the beach is shaped like a fishhook. At the tip of the fishhook are rugged limestone cliffs; the long, sandy beach is along the shank of the hook.

Kalapaki Beach

Great for novice surfers and outrigger canoes, Kalapaki Beach is the front lawn of the newly rebuilt Westin Kauai, Kauai's most extravagant hotel. No doubt the new hotel will mean more people on this lovely beach, but Kalapaki holds its own anyway. Kalapaki is the best beach in Lihue, bordered by Nawiliwili Harbor on one side and sharp cliffs on the other, with a view of the stunning Hoary Head Ridge in the distance. Surfers have been riding the waves here for generations, and in the old Kauai Surf days, outrigger canoes gave thrilling rides. To get there, head for Nawiliwili Harbor and park near the seawall. There's plenty of space.

Lydgate

It's easy to take Lydgate for granted because it's so accessible and convenient. A nicely paved road leads there from behind the Kauai Resort, and there's parking aplenty amid picnic tables and ironwood glens. There's even a great view from the parking lot. Families love this beach because it's protected by boulder breakwaters, with a lagoonlike bay ideal for children's swimming. It's popular and crowded, however, especially during the weekends. Nearby is the mouth of the Wailua River and the Wailua Beach. To get there, follow the green sign just south of the Wailua Bridge on Kuhio Highway.

Anahola Beach Park

Anahola has the beige, fine sand of brackish water beaches near streams and river mouths. It's on a long and friendly bay with a state park on one end and a diverse network of pools bordering a stream on the other. You can have your pick here, from shallow, gently lapping waves to the less protected area of the bay. And if you're adventurous, you can head north toward the stream and go exploring. Anahola's sand is not like the dazzling, pearly white sand of the south shore, nor does it have the high drama of Polihale. It's quiet and unpretentious, with softer, more muted colors and all the conveniences of a county park. To get there, turn down Anahola Beach Road from Route 56 (Kuhio Highway) and follow it to the ocean.

Secret Beach

Word is getting out about Secret Beach, but the long and arduous walk downhill (and uphill coming back) puts natural controls on the traffic.

Secret Beach is the beach of your dreams, a wide, white-sand bay that, if you're lucky, you'll have all to yourself. You can find sunset seashells and walk the shoreline while the famous Kilauea cliffs hover behind you. Porpoises may frolic offshore, and if it's whale season, all the better.

Swimming is not recommended, but there's plenty to explore on either side. On the other hand, you may want to do nothing but look for shells, read a book, or gaze at the horizon contemplating not ever returning home.

Go prepared for a steep hike downhill, and take your provisions for the day. Once you get there, you won't want to casually leave for supplies. To get there, turn makai (toward the beach) on the dirt road just north of the service station on Route 56 in Kilauea. It's the first of two roads between the service station and Kalihiwai Bridge, but go slowly because it's easy to miss. Follow it through the pasture to the end. You can park and follow the trail to the left, past goats and cows. Be careful; it's a tricky walk to the beach below.

Kalihiwai Bay

Kalihiwai Bay borders the Kalihiwai stream and is popular for bodysurfing at the shorebreak and, at the point beyond, board surfing by the advanced. It's one of those stops that has everything: good seashell hunting; a wide beach for beachcombing; long, even breaks; and freshwater dipping in the adjoining stream. There are no facilities here, and you have to be extremely cautious. Don't even enter the water during winter months or periods of high surf.

You'll have to pass Kalihiwai on the way to the north shore. Continue on Route 56 past the service station that signals the road to the Kilauea Lighthouse. When Route 56 begins to dip and a canopy of trees shades the highway, a paved road to the right, Kalihiwai Road, appears. Take it to the end and you'll end up at Kalihiwai Bay.

Hanalei Bay

It has gotten busy and crowded of late, but Hanalei is a big, wide bay with lots of room. If the area around the old pier (across and below the bluff where the Sheraton Princeville is located) is too crowded, just drive along until you come to the pavilion or a part of the bay that's less full.

More than a beautiful beach, Hanalei Bay is the stuff of legend, a total package. Backlit by the purple chasms of the Waialeale mountain range, it evokes images of twangy crooners singing "Hanalei Moon" in vintage aloha shirts, or Mitzi Gaynor and France Nuyen as they dazzled the men in *South Pacific*. Like Lumahai Beach, Hanalei was immortalized in that 1950s movie.

The pier is rusty and dangerous and no longer viable for diving off into the water. The waves usually break gently here, and outside of the reef you can often see the island's better surfers tackling the waves. Many people enjoy the park area on the river side of the bay, called Hanalei Black Pot Park, with its boat ramp, canoeing, cookouts, and activities.

To get there, make a right turn after the Ching Young Village Museum and shops. Drive to the end of that short road, where you will hit the road that parallels the beach. Turn right. You can't miss the pavilion, and if you drive until the end you'll wind up at the Hanalei Black Pot Park by the boat ramp.

Lumahai Beach

Lumahai, too, is a legend. Although by now the *South Pacific*, Bali Hai image is overworked and a little tired, there is good reason for Lumahai's continuing renown. The white-sand beach just gleams as it reaches for the sea from the hala grove backshore. The thick growth of hala forms a shady area for descending onto the beach from the lookout above. It's a steep climb downhill and parking is always a problem, but if you can do it, do. The water is electric—some painters have dubbed it the "Lumahai blue"—and the black lava outcroppings cradling the bay add greater dimension and are fun to explore.

Because the bay is unprotected, extreme caution is advised, and swimming is discouraged during winter. Also, a certain hardiness is required for maneuvering the trail down from the lookout on Route 56.

To get there, drive north on Route 56, the main highway, past Hanalei. The road will ascend a bluff. There will be a red-and-yellow Hawaii Visitors Bureau marker designating Lumahai at a scenic overlook with parking. The steep trail down to the beach begins near the overlook.

Ke'e Beach

The "beach at the end of the road" is what Kauai folks call it. Indeed, the highway that almost encircles the island ends here in Haena on the north shore. Between Haena and Kokee at the other end of the Na Pali Coast (where the road ends in the other direction), are the magnificent Kalalau Valley and the sculpted sea cliffs that continue to awe the growing waves of visitors.

The disadvantage at Ke'e is that it is always crowded with the cars of hikers who have ventured into Hanakapiai Valley—the Na Pali Coast trails start here—or of sightseers who have reached the end of the road. The advantage of Ke'e is that it is a historic site and an unforgettable spot, bordered on one side by Hawaii's most significant hula temple, the Lohiau heiau. Remnants of the platform are close to the road; a coastal trail from the beach leads to a complex of house and hula sites where Pele is said to have fallen in love with the young prince Lohiau. Hula dancers throughout Hawaii still perform the ancient chants depicting the tumultuous events of this period and place. This is indeed an awesome site, and offerings can be found at the heiau today.

Ke'e is also a beautiful beach with good swimming most of the year. Sunsets viewed from Ke'e have been known to produce the unusual "green flash" seen only in Hawaiian sunsets.

To get there, simply take Route 56, Kuhio Highway, north—past the Waikapala'e and Waikanaloa wet caves—until the road ends at Ke'e Beach.

SHOPPING

....

WEST, SOUTH, AND EAST KAUAI

KILOHANA
3-2087 Kaumualii Highway
Puhi
Telephone: (808) 245-5608

Kilohana is a combination of museum, art gallery, and shopping complex. Every store in the beautifully restored manse is excellent, of good taste and adhering in some way to a Hawaiian motif. Island Memories is one of the shops, an especially worthy boutique filled with remarkable Hawaiian crafts, from feather hatbands to replicas of stone implements and beautiful hand-carved woods from throughout Hawaii. It's amazing what they've managed to get into such a little shop.

For clothing, Cane Field Clothing Company upstairs at Kilohana has the best selection of contemporary sportswear on the island. The boutique is small as well, and the merchandise is carefully selected. There are all price ranges, with some good buys in tropical prints by the local label, Kauaiana, and the more expensive Fresh Paint. Cool cotton knits, dressy linens, Carole Little silks, Eileen West dresses, flashy earrings, sarong skirts with matching jackets in tropical prints are some of the items that make good wearables for friend or self.

Highly recommended while you're at Kilohana is a foray into the Hawaiian Collection Room, where you'll see fantastic Niihau shells and Hawaiian jewelry. On the second floor, a display of dance headbands and masks from Papua, New Guinea, add a Pacific dimension to the plantation motif.

Stones at Kilohana gets our vote for the best gallery and gift shop. All items are handiworks of the Pacific, so there are selected works from outside of Hawaii as well. Primarily, however, it's Hawaii's finest local artists who exhibit here. The gallery is in a restored house outside of the main Kilohana complex and should definitely be checked out. There are posters of Pegge Hopper; photography by Franco Salmoiraghi; baskets, tapa, and mats from the South Pacific. Also wonderful are the fiber baskets, Pam Barton's hand-made paper, and the fine wearables hand-screened by the Big Island's Sig Zane. Gifts to go will abound here.

At Half Moon Trading Company, you can lose yourself in the Japanese esthetic. Cherry boxes, antique tansu chests, kimonos, Japanese handmade paper, a black persimmon merchant chest from 1868—these are some of the items carried here. The tatami square in the middle of the room houses an early-1800s sea chest and mirror stand, made of mulberry wood.

Kilohana's stores are open 9:30 A.M. to 6:30 P.M. daily. Major credit cards accepted.

STONES GALLERY
Kukui Grove Shopping Center
Lihue
Telephone: (808) 245-6653

Follow the aroma of fresh coffee to the natural wood doors and you'll find yourself in a bookstore. At the back of the bookstore is Kauai's nicest gallery, a treasure trove of Hawaii's contemporary fine art and made-in-Hawaii crafts in all media. There are original paintings, prints, and pastels, and there is the full range of weavings, fiber work, wood turning, jewelry making, and other crafts by Hawaii's finest artists. Everything from hand-painted silks to handwoven bullrush sandals made by a ninety-two-year-old Hanalei man are in the works here, mingling merrily with the nonfunctional pieces adorning the walls and counters. Stones is recommended as the most fun and tasteful gallery you could drop into, and it's full of possibilities for gifts to go. The staff is excellent, too; they'll make you feel right at home.

Open 9:30 A.M. to 6:00 P.M. Monday through Thursday, until 9:00 P.M. Friday, until 5:30 P.M. Saturday, and from 10:00 A.M. to 4:00 P.M. Sunday. Major credit cards accepted.

NORTH SHORE

HANALEI CAMPING AND BACKPACKING, INC.
Ching Young Village
Hanalei
Telephone: (808) 826-6664

Everything you could possibly need for the outdoors is here. The shop carries the most complete selection of camping and hiking gear in the state. And why not? They're at the gateway to the Na Pali Coast, the wilderness nonpareil, and they're here for those who want to explore without schlepping their 50 pounds of gear cross-country.

Snorkeling equipment, rainwear, knives, tents, maps (very important!), backpacks and day packs, stoves, accessories, freeze-dried food, sporting equipment—it's all here, everything you could possibly need for your trip, and you can rent it, too. Tents for rent include two- to four-person domes at anywhere from $10 to $16 a night, with a smaller charge after the first night. Campstoves, six-pack coolers, backpacks, and day packs are also for rent, along with Gerry child carriers and toddler totes. Not for rent but always there with information are the camping experts of the company, who can give you all the trail information you need. With this shop, no one need feel unprepared to explore Kauai's wilderness.

Open 8:00 A.M. to 7:00 P.M. Monday through Saturday and 9:00 A.M. to 6:00 P.M. Sunday. Major credit cards accepted.

KONG LUNG COMPANY
Kilauea Plantation Center
Kilauea
Telephone: (808) 828-1822

Kong Lung is at the gateway to the north shore, Kilauea, where the Kilauea Lighthouse is located. It's an old plantation store that was restored and converted into one of Hawaii's most interesting and popular shops. Most of its customers are regulars, many come from Oahu to shop, and they all agree that Kong Lung and its "Gump's of the Pacific" concept is entirely successful. The shop still has a plantation feeling—items range from quality muumuus and aloha shirts, including the classic palaka, to fine china, jewelry, purses, Crabtree and Evelyn soaps, made-on-Kauai crafts, and a fine selection of costume and antique jewelry.

Open 9:00 A.M. to 6:00 P.M. Monday through Saturday and until 5:00 P.M. on Sunday. Major credit cards accepted.

OLA'S
Hanalei
Telephone: (808) 826-6937

Ola's is named after the chief of the menehune, who made a work of art called the Menehune Ditch. Ola's is full of works of art, the work of island craftsmen and their counterparts from all over the country. More than seventy-five craftsmen are represented here, in everything from handcrafted jewelry to koa wood chopsticks. Glass, wood, metal, fiber, mixed media, and ceramic are among the selections represented here.

Open 10:00 A.M. to 9:30 P.M. daily. Major credit cards accepted.

EVERYDAY GOOD THINGS

Bookstores

STONES BOOKS
Kukui Grove Shopping Center
Lihue
Telephone: (808) 245-3703

One of Kauai's lasting favorites, Stones is singularly pleasant for browsing and the thoughtful perusal of Hawaiiana's newest and best. Under the same roof as Stones Gallery and Rainbow Coffees, the bookstore specializes in Hawaiian and Pacific island books covering natural and cultural histories. The selection is extensive. The shop is moving out of mass market titles into a strong focus on Hawaiian selections, quality children's books and materials, and self-help books. The bookstore/gallery/coffee shop complex is one of the island's most pleasant stops, with cheerful, knowledgeable help and a delightful ambience that encourages lingering.

Open 9:30 A.M. to 6:00 P.M. Monday through Thursday and on Saturday, until 9:00 P.M. on Friday, and 10:00 A.M. to 4:00 P.M. on Sunday. Major credit cards accepted.

WALDENBOOKS
Kukui Grove Shopping Center
Lihue
Telephone: (808) 245-7162

Everyone knows the national chain, so the sight of a Waldenbooks store is immediate reassurance that your mass-market, mainstream tastes will be satisfied here. This particular Waldenbooks does particularly well with hard-cover best-sellers and paperback fiction, as well as a booming video business with film classics. As with all the Waldenbooks, you can also participate in the chain's discount clubs in romance novels, science fiction, and mysteries, and for senior citizens and children.

Open 9:00 A.M. to 4:00 P.M. Monday through Thursday and on Saturday, until 9:00 P.M. on Friday, and 10:00 A.M. to 4:00 P.M. on Sunday. Major credit cards accepted.

Coffeehouse

RAINBOW COFFEES
Kukui Grove Shopping Center
Lihue
Telephone: (808) 245-6564

There are a lot of good reasons for coming here. One is the adjoining bookstore and gallery, the other is the quality of its coffees and pastries. Two to three dozen different coffees from around the world are offered, from Guatemalan Antigua to Sumatra and, of course, pure Kona coffee. You can choose your bulk coffees by the pound, or you can sit and sip espresso, cappuccino, and other favorites with fresh banana cake, mango pie during mango season, croissants, carrot cake, and other worthy accompaniments. There are a few tables for sipping, meeting, and lingering in a cordial atmosphere redolent with the fragrance of coffee and cinnamon.

Open 9:30 A.M. to 6:00 P.M. Monday through Thursday and on Saturday, until 9:00 P.M. on Friday, and 10:00 A.M. to 4:00 P.M. on Sunday. Major credit cards accepted, with a $10 minimum.

Drugstore

LONGS DRUG STORES
Kukui Grove Shopping Center
Lihue
Telephone: (808) 245-7771

On every island with a branch, Longs Drugs is the proverbial one-stop convenience store, with everything from a pharmacy to liquor department to extensive cosmetics and such oddball items as rubber zoris, the newest designer games such as Pictionary, and even, in some branches, fresh produce. Food items and automobile accessories are surprisingly good here, as well as camera needs and a one-to-three-day color print processing service. Longs has great sales and specials, too.

Open 8:30 A.M. to 9:00 P.M. Monday through Saturday and until 5:00 P.M. on Sunday. Major credit cards accepted.

Fruit Stands

BANANA JOE'S FRUIT STAND
Kilauea
Telephone: (808) 828-1092

Look for the sign by the roadside in Kilauea and turn into the parking lot. Banana Joe's is the most pleasant fruit stand you'll ever see. They make healthy frozen fruit frosties here that are pure ambrosia. Pure frozen fruit is put through the juicer, and a fluffy ice cream–like mound is the result. They also sell fresh mangoes, island oranges, locally grown bananas, and the obligatory pineapple. You'll want to try the dried banana and papaya strips too; they're sun dried and make great snacks. The banana–macadamia nut bread with whole wheat flour is a special treat as well.

Banana Joe's will also break and husk a coconut for you. It's no small thrill to drink the coconut milk and then partake of its white meat. If it's mango season or passion fruit is available, they'll be here too.

Open 9:00 A.M. to 6:00 P.M. daily. No credit cards.

FARM FRESH FRUIT STAND
4-1345 Kuhio Highway
Kapaa
Telephone: (808) 822-1154

If you're lucky enough to be in Hawaii during mango or lichee season, Farm Fresh will have the best selection around. They also carry a year-round supply of pineapples and Kauai sunrise papayas, preinspected for shipping or ready for a simple picnic. Coconuts, avocados, apple bananas, and the occasional pomelo or rare local fruit are also available here, all fresh and, except for the pineapple, grown on Kauai.

Open 7:00 A.M. to 7:00 P.M. daily. Major credit cards accepted.

Photo Processing

FOTO FREDDIE
Coconut Plantation
Kapaa
Telephone: (808) 822-9090

Ching Young Village Shopping
 Center
Hanelei
Telephone: (808) 826-7453

Kukuiula Shopping Center
Poipu
Telephone: (808) 742-9240

Foto Freddie was the first one-hour color print processing service on Kauai. Part of a chain, Foto Freddie has shops in Hilo and California as well as three strategic locations on Kauai. They offer one-day service from all the Kauai booths, with one-hour service from the Coconut Plantation location only. Those who use Foto Freddie tout its dependable service and good quality. Some of Kauai's prominent dive operators use Foto Freddie with good results, and they do guarantee their service. If you're not satisfied, they will redo your prints at no charge and will even mail them to you. Although there are some reports of a decline in quality, Foto Freddie tries hard to please its customers and there are many who swear by it.

Open 9:00 A.M. to 9:00 P.M. Monday through Saturday and until 5:00 P.M. Sunday in Kapaa, 8:30 A.M. to 5:00 P.M. Monday through Saturday and until 3:00 P.M. Sunday in Hanalei, and 8:30 A.M. to 5:00 P.M. Monday through Saturday and until 2:00 P.M. Sunday in Poipu. Major credit cards accepted.

POIPU FAST PHOTO
Kiahuna Shopping Village
Poipu
Telephone: (808) 742-7322

They do color prints only, they're big on quality, and they are nice to deal with as well. Poipu Fast Photo requires 1½ hours to process your color film in its own lab. Because they're owner operated, they take a special interest in details and service (such as checking the processing chemicals and electronics every day) and will pick up and deliver at three major Poipu hotels.

Open 9:00 A.M. to 9:30 P.M. Monday through Saturday and 10:00 A.M. to 8:00 P.M. Sunday. Major credit cards accepted.

FLOWERS AND LEIS

FUJIMOTO FLOWERS
2985-A Kalena Street
Lihue
Telephone: (808) 245-8088

They are the best in Lihue, providing good service and selection, especially if you order ahead. Although Fujimoto's carries a regular selection of orchid, ginger, royal ilima, and other favorite leis in stock, the really special leis should be ordered. Kauai is known for its maile, a green vine with small leaves that release an aniselike scent. Kauai maile is the cream of the crop and should be ordered ahead. So should the mokihana, a rare mountain fruit about ½ inch in diameter, found only on Kauai. Leis of mokihana release a sweet, spicy fragrance that is intoxicating and unforgettable. The cube-shaped capsules are so potent the lei must be worn on top of a garment or it burns the skin. At Fujimoto's, these rare leis are available on special order. They will also ship cut flowers and have a good supply of anthuriums and protea on hand.

Open 8:00 A.M. to 5:00 P.M. Monday through Saturday. Major credit cards accepted.

IRMALEE POMROY FLOWERS
60 Lihau Street
Kapaa, HI 96746
Telephone: (808) 822-3231

Irmalee Pomroy and her sister, Marie McDonald, were recently named the best lei makers in Polynesia. That's quite a distinction. Pomroy is the doyenne of lei making on the island, an artist who will haku (braid), wili (wind), string, and make the consummate custom lei for you with materials she farms or gathers in the wild. Pomroy is the in-house floral designer for the new Westin Kauai; it's her artistry that adorns its rooms and halls. Pomroy specializes in haku and wili leis for the head and neck—full, stately garlands with materials carefully selected according to preference, purpose, and time of year. Her fresh or dried leis can go back to the mainland, but all leis must be ordered ahead. Pomroy will ship special orders too, but she asks that orders be placed by calling her home in the evenings. No credit cards accepted.

MARINA FLOWERS
Wailua Marina
Telephone: (808) 822-5971

Leis are the specialty here—thick, regal carnations, colorful orchids, and rose and plumeria. Whatever is in season is available. If it's spring, fragrant pakalana will be available, and if you're really lucky, they'll have the rare white vanda orchid to string into leis for you. That is a rare treat worth asking about; we've never seen white vanda anywhere else.

Open 8:30 A.M. to 5:00 P.M. daily. No credit cards accepted.

GIFTS TO GO

Gift giving is a big deal in Hawaii, even if the gifts are small. Families traveling interisland invariably take armloads of goodies from their island as presents for their friends on the next. Usually the gifts are edible, and they are available on their island and nowhere else.

Kauai's Tip Top Macadamia Nut Cookies were an early favorite. Neatly bundled in pink cartons, they went all over the islands as gifts, and when visitors left this island, they took armloads with them as well. Although Tip Top cookies were the original, they're somewhat overshadowed now by the cookies that followed, which are now big sellers among residents and visitors. Of these, the most highly recommended is Popo's Cookies in Waipouli. Popo's makes cookies that melt in your mouth, with chocolate chips, macadamia nuts, coconut, and other tropical morsels in various combinations. The most popular are the ones with chocolate chips—they're indecently good. You can find Popo's at the bakery in Waipouli and a few selected stores on the island. Also popular are the Kauai Kookies brand of chocolate chip and macadamia nut cookies, more widely distributed and available in most stores.

Jacques Bread is another local phenomenon, the product of a baker from the north shore who was forced to work regular hours once word got out about his whole wheat bread. Jacques has his bakery in Kilauea, on the way to the Kilauea Lighthouse near Kong Lung Store, but his breads are available at various outlets throughout the state. Many chic restaurants serve his breads and rolls. When they were finally distributed in Honolulu, his outlets dropped his name as if it were Gucci.

And then, of course, there are the legendary Hamura's saimin noodles, made fresh daily at the tiny Lihue shop. They're versatile, they have a real insider's cachet, and like the pioneer Tip Top cookies, they come in crisp pink cartons that fit neatly under the airplane seat.

If you want to be different, Hanapepe Honey is the designer line, gathered from beehives all over the island and then bottled and sold as a benefit for the restoration of Hanapepe town. Hanapepe Honey delivers—it's tasty, made from the best nectars of the kiawe and Christmasberry flowers, and carefully packed so the nutrients are not destroyed. Hanapepe Honey is available in—where else?—Hanapepe town.

Those with heftier pocketbooks may want to consider the jewel of Kauai, the Niihau shell leis. These rare, intricately strung, and authentically Hawaiian garlands are museum pieces, made from the shells found on Niihau's shores and picked so arduously off the white sand. The shells are tiny and the work is demanding, hence the high prices commanded for these lovely strands. As Niihau's closest neighbor, Kauai has always had a better supply than most of Niihau shell leis, usually available in museums, galleries, and finer stores.

Feather leis are also a Hawaiian art, one requiring inordinate skill and patience as the minuscule feathers are sewn one by one onto the hatband in glimmering colors and patterns. In Hawaii, you can't get much better than a blue pheasant lei around your favorite hat. Watch for Chosaburo Terui's work. He's considered Kauai's best in the art, but his work is not widely displayed. Frank Enos Medeiros makes exquisite feather leis as well—watch for them in the galleries.

There are wearables galore, from Kauaiana tropical dresses and skirts to Fresh Paint hand-painted cotton knit dresses, most of them with island themes. Hand-painted T-shirts also abound on Kauai, and the best place to find the best of them is Stones Gallery in Kukui Grove Shopping Center.

By far the most unique, heartwarming, and highly recommended gift suggestion is a pair of bullrush sandals by Kenichi Tasaka, a man in his nineties who started his new career as a crafstman at age eighty-four. The oldest and favorite inhabitant of Hanalei, Tasaka gathers the bullrush himself from the mountain stream beds near the taro fields he's tended all his life. With patient concentration, he weaves the bullrush into beautiful sandals that look and smell of the woods. Tasaka sells his sandals from his Hanalei home and at galleries such as Stones in Kukui Grove.

There are many potters, photographers, and fiber artists making crafts from Kauai's natural materials. Galleries such as Stones and the Kauai Museum, as well as stores such as Island Memories at Kilohana, have an ample array of fine work by local artists and craftsmen.

HAWAII: THE BIG ISLAND

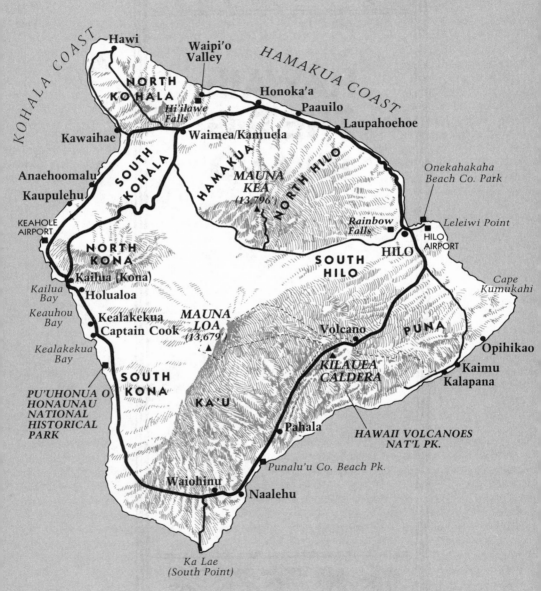

HAWAII: THE BIG ISLAND

KOHALA COAST

Hawi

Waipi'o Valley

HAMAKUA COAST

NORTH KOHALA

Hi'ilawe Falls

Honoka'a

Paauilo

Laupahoehoe

Kawaihae

Waimea/Kamuela

SOUTH KOHALA

Anaehoomalu

Kaupulehu

MAUNA KEA (13,796')

HAMAKUA

NORTH HILO

Onekahakaha Beach Co. Park

KEAHOLE AIRPORT

Rainbow Falls

Leleiwi Point

HILO AIRPORT

NORTH KONA

Kailua (Kona)

Holualoa

SOUTH HILO

HILO

Kailua Bay

Keauhou Bay

Kealakekua

Captain Cook

MAUNA LOA (13,679')

Cape Kumukahi

Volcano

PUNA

Opihikao

Kealakekua Bay

Kaimu

Kalapana

KILAUEA CALDERA

SOUTH KONA

PU'UHONUA O HONAUNAU NATIONAL HISTORICAL PARK

KA'U

HAWAII VOLCANOES NAT'L PK.

Pahala

Punalu'u Co. Beach Pk.

Waiohinu

Naalehu

Ka Lae (South Point)

0   5   10   15 Miles

A BRIEF HISTORY

The island of Hawaii, called the Big Island, is the largest, the youngest, and the most changeable of the Hawaiian islands. It was the last island in the chain to be formed and, to this day, is still creating and recreating itself. Lava flowing to the ocean in a sustained, years-long eruption of Kilauea, the world's most continuously active volcano, has added 30 new acres to the island's topography, a number that can grow by the day.

This is an island of inexorable creative fury, the home of the Hawaiian volcano goddess Pele, the southernmost point in the United States, the two tallest peaks in the world when measured from their ocean base, and Mauna Kea's Lake Waiau, at an elevation of 13,020 feet, one of the highest lakes in the world. It was on this island, at South Point, that Polynesian voyagers are believed to have first set foot in Hawaii around 700 or 750, and it was here that Kamehameha the Great was born and died and Captain James Cook was killed. This is also an island of great geological diversity, from vast ranchlands and moonlike terrains of lava to misty volcanic uplands and blinding white ski slopes. Some 300 miles of coastline frame the island in black lava or green-, white-, black-, and gray-colored sand. Although the Big Island's sobriquets include the "Orchid Island" and the "Volcano Island," neither begins to capture its parameters.

Spread across 4,037 square miles—nearly twice the size of all the other Hawaiian islands combined—the Big Island's 109,000 residents have a lot of ground to cover. They live on five large shield volcanoes that form an island 93 miles long and 76 miles wide, which occupies 63 percent of the state's total land area. The fabled Mauna Kea, the "white mountain," towers 13,796 feet high, dominating the island with its powerful and blinding presence. Although Mauna Kea has not erupted in many hundreds of years, its neighbor, the 13,677-foot-high Mauna Loa, last erupted in 1984 in a fiery and unprecedented duet with Kilauea, which has been in its current eruptive cycle since 1983. The other volcanoes are the Kohala mountain, 5,480 feet high and the Big Island's oldest volcano, as well as the 8,271-foot-high Hualalai. Although Hualalai last erupted around 1801, it rumbled in 1929 and emitted a strong tremor that rocked the state as recently as 1987. Scientists say Hualalai will certainly erupt within the next two centuries, perhaps even in the next few decades.

These massive geological features comprise a living laboratory, a microcosm of creation that has the world's top volcanologists and astronomers perched atop Mauna Kea and in the Hawaii Volcanoes National Park, the island's two dominant geological presences. While astronomers study the origins of the universe with the world's most powerful telescopes, volcanologists probe the mysteries on the other side of the island, deep within the earth's core where magma and primal forces roil without pause.

No wonder there is such diversity in weather, activities, and natural phenomena here. While Hilo, the island's county seat, averages 129 inches of rainfall a year, Kawaihae on the leeward side of the Big Island averages 9 inches a year. During winter months skiers dot the slopes of Mauna Kea while at the same moment within a 40-mile radius, other adventurers may be enjoying some of the world's best snorkeling and marlin fishing down at the South Kohala and Kona coasts. On the other side of the island, southeast of the Kilauea Crater, Big Island residents may be simultaneously evacuating their homes or watching helplessly as Kilauea's lava mows them down. At the time of this writing, more than fifty homes have been claimed by the eruption that began in 1983.

These awesome phenomena are a part of everyday life for Big Islanders, who are accustomed to sharing their land with extraordinary forces and Hawaiian deities of ancient legend. Most clearly felt is the temperamental Pele, the legendary goddess of the volcano, who is still worshipped by some Hawaiians and who is honored in many hula chants. In ancient Hawaiian lore, it was Pele's favorite sister, Hi'iaka, who made the first known mention of the hula in a chant about her friend Hopoe, the originator of the dance. It was on this island, in fact, in the eastern flank called Puna, that the first hula is said to have been performed. Today an active community of hula dancers and Hawaiian artists still makes offerings to Laka, the goddess of the dance, and to Pele, perpetuating ancient practices on an island rich in pre-Christian history.

Kamehameha the Great was born here in the 1750s, and it was to this island that he returned for his final days. His bones are believed to be buried near the westernmost point of the island, and his birthplace is near the Mo'okini Heiau at the northern tip of the island. The heiau, enormous and powerful, dates back to 480 and is said to have been built with stones passed hand to hand from the coastline 9 miles away.

The western coastline is rich with historical sites, from the Pu'ukohola Heiau, Kamehameha's monument to his family war god, to petroglyphs at Anaeho'omalu and the Mauna Lani Resort complex. Along this coastline ancient fishponds ring fields of lava from the Kaniku lava flow, predating 1500 and, further south, Hualalai's flows of 1800 and 1801.

The long stretches of black lava along the South Kohala coast lead to some of the most beautiful beaches in Hawaii, beaches that were populated and fished by ancient Hawaiians. Today the South Kohala coast is undergoing upscale tourist development as resorts such as Mauna Lani and Waikoloa—with its soon-to-be Hyatt Waikoloa—capitalize on the area's history and weather in seeking their share of the world's market.

In the stunning Kealakekua Bay, South Kona District, you come upon the place where Captain Cook was both greeted as a god and put to death. In 1779, one year after he anchored off Kauai to discover Hawaii, he sailed into Kealakekua Bay on the Big Island and was regaled with gifts, ceremonies, and entertainment. It is well known (but disputed too) that the Hawaiians mistook him for the reincarnation of the god Lono, whom they were honoring with their Makahiki festival. Cook accepted the honors, departed after two weeks, and returned for repairs after sustaining damage to his ship in a storm. This time the greeting was different. While investigating the theft of a cutter from his ship, Cook and several of his men were killed by some Hawaiians. Today a marker at the far end of Kealakekua Bay points to the site of Cook's demise.

It was years before foreigners returned, and when they did it was Kamehameha the Great who took an interest in them. From the westerners he acquired weapons and military acumen and systematically took over the islands, winning his home island in 1791 after a series of battles with other chieftains. In the several years before his death in 1819, he lived in Kailua (Kona) near the Ahu'ena Heiau, on the grounds of what is today the King Kamehameha Hotel.

In the same village not long after his death, Kamehameha's favorite wife, Ka'ahumanu, helped topple the ancient kapu system by dining with the young Liholiho (Kamehameha II), in open defiance of the taboo system that prohibited, among other things, men and women from dining together. Whiskey figured prominently in this historic occasion. After a hefty bout with the bottle, the story goes, Liholiho attended a feast in Kailua and was badgered by Ka'ahumanu into sitting down with the women. Mark Twain, in writings resulting from his trip to Hawaii in 1866, summarized the event as "probably the first time whiskey ever prominently figured as an aid to civilization."

Twain continued: "They saw him eat from the same vessel with them, and were appalled! Terrible moments drifted slowly by, and still the king ate, still he lived, still the lightnings of the insulted gods were witheld! . . . Thus did King Liholiho and his dreadful whiskey preach the first sermon and prepare the way for the new gospel that was speeding southward over the waves of the Atlantic."

Soon after, the missionaries did, indeed, arrive. In 1820, one year after Kamehameha's death, Hawaii's first missionaries arrived off Kawaihae on the North Kohala coast. They settled in at Kailua where Hawaii's first Christian church, Moku'aikaua, still stands.

In Kailua and along the drive south you will see many Christian churches, a testament to the missionary presence, juxtaposed among such sites as the Pu'uhonua O Honaunau, the Place of Refuge, where in ancient times criminals and outcasts were given sanctuary. All along the coastline there are sea caves, ancient trails and heiau, ruins, bays, lava tubes, and petroglyphs interspersed among the macadamia nut, coffee, and papaya farms. It is said that well-constructed slides for *holua*, Hawaiian sleds, once traversed Mauna Kea and there are vestiges still in evidence along the Kona coast. As you move through the town of Waiohinu, the Ka'u District, and the Hawaii Volcanoes National Park, the terrain changes dramatically and some of Hawaii's rare and endangered birds may come into view as you move to higher altitudes and some of the best hiking trails in the state.

A notable feature of the Big Island is its thriving community of artists, centered mainly around Holualoa in North Kona District and in Volcano and its environs. In greater numbers and seemingly with more vitality than on any other island, the artists celebrate old and contemporary Hawaii through the use of native woods, fibers, themes, and techniques that are of the highest quality and distinctively Hawaiian. Claiming to receive inordinate measures of creative energy from living on a volcano, the artists express a dimension of Hawaii that should not be overlooked. Along with the burgeoning numbers of accomplished hula dancers, they represent a relatively new dimension in the Big Island's social matrix.

Tourism, of course, is the bright hope of the Big Island, with activities and development centered in Kona (more affordable than Kohala, but a bit tired) and the South Kohala coast. With its fine restaurants and excellent weather, its beautiful beaches and good snorkeling, and its wide-open spaces and historical sites, the South Kohala coast is a destination of note. It is, however, expensive, catering specifically to the gold and platinum card set that can afford hundreds of dollars a night for a hotel room.

On the other side of the island is Hilo, the fourth largest city in the state and the main seaport and commercial center of the Big Island, the state's largest sugar producer. In and around the district are flower farms, waterfalls, seacoast towns with long Hawaiian names, sugarcane fields, and agriculture. While the Puna district is famous for its orchids and papayas, Hilo is known for its anthuriums, its many yards with lichee trees, its ancient architecture, and a predominantly Oriental community with roots in the plantation era. It is a provincial town but a charming one, in spite of a reputation for rain that has dampened things considerably for hotels and businesses in the area.

Watch this town, however. It's a sleeper that has much more going for it than meets the eye—a new crop of fine restaurants, including Roussels, one of Hawaii's finest; a restoration effort that is reviving downtown businesses and attracting new ones; and the abiding charm of one of Hawaii's last genuine old towns add up to something special. With Hilo, however, you take a chance on the weather.

Those who know Hilo are also staggered by its courage, by the way it has rehabilitated itself after several natural disasters. A tsunami in 1946 obliterated the town, which rebuilt itself only to be hit by another tsunami in 1960. A monument in the town center pays tribute to victims of the tsunami.

On clear days you can see Mauna Kea from Hilo and from along the Hamakua Coast to the north. A drive along this coastline takes you past old plantation towns, wood-framed churches, and tranquil villages with an unhurried pace. Waipio Valley to the north is one of the premier pleasures of this island, a serene, historic patch of paradise where a sizable community of taro farmers and fisherman once thrived. With its taro fields, black-sand beach, ancient legends, and narrow, steep walls leading to waterfalls, it offers a taste of old Hawaii much different from that of Waimea, where flower farmers and *paniolo* (Hawaiian cowboys) ride, rope, and brand in one of the country's largest privately owned ranches, the Parker Ranch. In Waimea (also called Kamuela) cowboy boots, fireplaces, and upcountry chill offer an interlude of a different sort before you reach the sun-drenched beaches of the South Kohala coast.

Hidden among the hills and valleys are truck farmers and conscientious pioneers who have found rich volcanic soil and some of the most affordable land in the state. Many of them manage to live self-sufficiently by growing their own food, storing water in their own catchments, and harnessing solar energy in "off-power" areas without electricity. Responding to the volcanic energy of this young and rugged island, they live close to the land and enjoy the seclusion it offers. Many of them could not afford to own land anywhere else in Hawaii.

The volcanic soil is also the reason that "Puna butter," "Kona gold," and other potent strains of *pakalolo* (marijuana) are grown in considerable quantities on the Big Island. In the international marijuana hierarchy, Big Island dope is considered by many to be the best in the world and a mainstay of the Big Island economy. This is an embarrassment to the county government, which goes to great lengths to conduct regular "Green Harvest" helicopter operations that scour the countryside for contraband. According to the Hawaii Criminal Justice Data Center, in 1986 authorities confiscated 742,238 marijuana plants on the Big Island alone. For every plant confiscated, officials estimate there are three more growing undetected. At an estimated market value of $1,000 per plant, that comes to $742 million in the Big Island's destroyed plants alone, making it the top grower in what is estimated to be a $4.2 billion industry throughout Hawaii.

For now, however, all eyes have turned to the Big Island's new frontier: astronomy. The eyes of the world's astronomers are on Mauna Kea, where revolutionary new telescopes are being built at the 13,796-foot summit. Recognized as the world's finest astronomical site, Mauna Kea will soon house the world's largest telescope, the $150 million, 600-inch National New Technology Telescope. Several other telescopes are operating or under construction, all representing the cutting edge of astronomy and reaching farther back in time than has ever been touched before.

As you will see when you visit this island, there is more than distance that separates. Centuries elapse between Big Island miles and eons of Hawaii's history are written in its lava. This is not an island to rush through. More than any of the other islands, planning and priorities are important here. Do you want beach, volcano, or both? Will it be Waipio Valley up north or a sunset cruise in Kailua? Without time, patience, and planning it can be totally exhausting, even unforgiving, especially if weather conditions sabbotage your plans. But remember, this is an island of consummate beauty and diversity, offering access to experiences normally available only across continents and hemispheres. And on this island, more than the others, you touch the primal energy of creation, rooted deep in its rumbling volcanoes.

GETTING AROUND

....

TRANSPORTATION

The two major airports of the Big Island are east Hawaii's Hilo Airport, officially named the General Lyman Field, and the Keahole Airport in west Hawaii. The three major interisland airlines—Aloha, Hawaiian, and Mid Pacific—fly into Hilo. These three airlines plus United Airlines also fly into Keahole Airport, which serves most of the South Kohala and Kona hotels and therefore the bulk of the visitor traffic to the island. Visitors flying in to see the volcano sometimes fly into Hilo and take the half-hour drive into Hawaii Volcanoes National Park. Princeville Airways offers three flights a day into the tiny Waimea-Kohala Airport up north and is the only commercial carrier serving that airport.

Gray Line Hawaii ([808] 834-1033 or 836-1883) offers transportation to and from Hilo and Kona airports, usually with advance arrangements and prepayment. There is also taxi service at both airports, but the long distances on this island make taxicabs prohibitive. Be sure to see if your hotel has airport pickup; most west Hawaii hotels do.

Major national car rental companies have booths at Hilo and Keahole airports. Avis, Dollar, National, Hertz, Budget, Tropical, Alamo, and others are at both airports and allow drop-offs on the other side of the island, but only with about a $25 to $30 additional fee. There's no mileage charge on the island.

The island's public transportation system consists of the Hele-On Bus, (808) 935-8241 (*hele* means to go or to move). The bus runs daily except Sundays and holidays, departing from Hilo in the afternoons and winding up in Kailua via a northern route. It also goes south from Hilo to Waiohinu in Ka'u, stopping at Volcano on the way. The Hele-On leaves Kailua on the same days, leaving early in the morning to cross the island toward Hilo. Fares are about $5.

Unless you have a lot of time to spend on the road or plan to spend your time close to the hotel, the vast distances between attractions on this island just about necessitate a rented car.

If you land at west Hawaii's Keahole Airport you will find yourself facing Hualalai and beyond it, on either side, Mauna Kea to the north and Mauna

Loa to the south. These three mountains form a triangle, with the Kohala Mountains to the north and Kilauea to the southeast. Directly east on the other side of the island is Hilo, connected to west Hawaii between Mauna Kea and Mauna Loa by the old, rugged, 54-mile Saddle Road, not favored for conventional vehicles.

Most visitors land at Keahole Airport, stay at Kohala coast or Kona hotels, and plan their sightseeing and recreation in manageable increments. You can take helicopters over Volcano (best, of course, if there's fountaining) and drive just about anywhere around the coastline. Highway 19 is a paved, well-maintained, and scenic route that traverses the island from Hilo north to Honokaa, west through Waimea to the coastline, and south along the South Kohala coast into Kona. The straight, long stretch of road from Kawaihae down to Kona is also called the Queen Ka'ahumanu Highway. The highway changes from Number 19 to Number 11 in Kailua and continues south through South Kona and Ka'u districts. It veers north into the 4,000-foot Hawaii Volcanoes National Park area and continues northeast to Hilo, making a complete circle of the island except for the coastal route through Puna to the Kaimu and Kalapana black-sand beaches. Some coastal sites, such as the Queen's Bath, have been destroyed or made inaccessible by recent lava flows.

The route around the island is about 225 miles and should only be attempted in increments. The distance between the Keahole Airport and Kailua is about 8 miles; from Keahole to the Kohala coast resorts, about 20 miles. It's more than 40 miles from Kailua to Waimea, whether you take the Ka'ahumanu Highway or the older Mamalahoa Highway slightly upland (a beautiful, underrated drive). From Waimea to Hilo it's 55 miles, and from Hilo to Volcano on Highway 11 the distance is 30 miles.

Helicopters

When Kilauea Volcano is fountaining, Hilo hotels are booked and helicopters swarm in from Kona and Hilo to watch the fiery spectacle. Most of the helicopter companies operate out of the Kona and Kohala areas because of the higher concentration of visitors in those areas, and most of them have hotel pickup service. There are also tours over Waipio Valley, the rugged Kohala Mountains, the Parker Ranch, and Mauna Loa. Rates hover around $250 to $270, with some deluxe longer tours going for about $335.

Among the Big Island's most popular:

Kenai Helicopters, probably the biggest, operating out of Waikoloa ([808] 885-7361) and Kailua ([808] 329-4861). They offer a two-hour volcano tour that also takes in Waipio Valley and Parker Ranch for about $268 per person.

Kona Helicopters, operating out of Keauhou ([808] 322-9166) and Keahole ([808] 329-0551), with a helipad also at the Mauna Lani. They have tours covering the Kohala Mountains to Volcano. Rates range from $135 for the most basic to $335.

Volcano Heli-Tours ([808] 967-7578), the only one with a helipad at the Volcano Golf Course, 1 mile away from the visitor center. It's noteworthy because it offers an alternative for those who want to drive the beautiful Ka'u coastline and the black-sand beaches on the way to Hawaii Volcanoes

National park. A 45-minute tour of the volcano is $105, often $15 less with a published coupon and less than half what it would cost to fly from Kona. Although the flight is shorter than those with the other companies, it's just fine for volcano viewing. You must book with them well in advance because they're very busy, and you must drive up to Volcano.

Hilo Bay Air ([808] 969-1545), operating out of Hilo Airport. An hour-long tour covers the Volcano and black-sand beach areas, going up to see some waterfalls along the Hamakua coast. Rates are about $115 to $160; hotel pickup in Hilo area.

TOURS

Tour operators on the Big Island include Gray Line, Roberts ([808] 329-1688 or 935-2858), Akamai Tours ([808] 329-7324), Jack's Tours ([808] 961-6666), and B.J. Limousine Services ([808] 325-1088). Each company will have its own assortment of vans, vehicles, and programs to take you to to the volcanoes, Kona, Kohala, Hilo, and around the island.

CAMPING

The Big Island's camping facilities include several beach parks and the most spectacular camping and hiking area, the Hawaii Volcanoes National Park. The National Park Service offers three campgrounds in the Volcano area: Namakani Paio, 3 miles from the visitor center; Kipuka Nene, 11.5 miles from the visitor center; and Kamoamoa, 35 miles away at the beach. Namakani, the most convenient, consists of ten cabins and a campground. You can reserve the cabins for $16 a night from the Volcano House, but no reservations are required for the campgrounds, which have walk-in, bare-bones camp shelters with tables and grassy areas. The campgrounds at Namakani, Kipuka Nene, and Kamoamoa are all on a first-come, first-served basis.

The Namakani cabins are unfurnished, with one double and two bunk beds and running water. A separate bathroom and shower are shared with the other nine cabins. There is a grill outdoors and an electrical outlet indoors, but that's all. For more information on the cabins: The Volcano House, Hawaii Volcanoes National Park, HI 96718; telephone (808) 967-7311.

The best beach parks for camping are on the South Kohala coast, where the weather is consistently sunny. Recommended camping sites are the Hapuna Beach Park (only five minutes away from the Mauna Kea Beach Hotel) and the Spencer Beach Park in Kawaihae. The Harry K. Brown Beach Park, a black-sand beach near Kalapana on the other side of the island, is gorgeous, historic, and a more isolated alternative. Hapuna and Spencer have beautiful white-sand beaches popular among local folks; Harry K. Brown has black sand and is popular among residents of Puna district.

Camping permits for Hapuna cost $7 a night, a flat rate for an A-frame shelter that sleeps up to four. Although well used and not very isolated, this is the best camping spot on the island, with comfortable, screen-enclosed shelters, a cabinlike recreational area for cooking, with refrigerator, stove, and hot water, and a stunning and popular beach. All you need here is your sleeping bag. Hapuna is a white-sand crescent with good swimming during summer but a treacherous riptide in winter months or periods of high surf. To reserve at Hapuna: Division of State Parks, P.O. Box 936, Hilo, HI 96721-0936; telephone (808) 961-7200.

Spencer Beach Park is a county facility that is extremely popular, well maintained, and comfortable. There are basketball courts nearby, lots of shade under kiawe trees (watch those kiawe thorns!), barbecue facilities, picnic tables, and a beautiful old stone pavilion looking out to sea. On one side is a small, rocky black lagoon; on the other side is a white-sand beach. Campgrounds for tents are off to the side, not far from all the conveniences, including a large, cafeteria-size sink and a new bathroom facility made of stone. Permits cost $1 a day per adult, with children free and teenagers at $.50. For permit: County of Hawaii, Parks and Recreation, 25 Aupuni Street, Hilo, HI 96720; telephone (808) 923-8311.

HOTELS AND
ALTERNATIVES

Budget Hotels

KONA HOTEL
765908 Mamalahoa Highway
Holualoa, HI 96725
Telephone: (808) 324-1155

It's more than sixty years old, a ramshackle hotel on the slopes of Holualoa, 4.5 miles above Kailua, with a gorgeous view of macadamia, papaya, and coffee trees sloping down to the ocean. This is an unbelievable bargain: $12 a night for a single. The rooms are clean and airy, with high ceilings, hardwood floors with small rugs, a dresser, towels, double or twin beds, abundant windows, and crisp mountain air. There aren't many places where you can sit on a porch with a book at sunset and look down 1,500 feet to the ocean, over rooftops, banana trees, sloping hills, and orchards. There are communal bathrooms, but the stellar attraction is the toilet at the end of a long walkway in its own pavilion, a throne overlooking an Eden clear down to the ocean. Inside the hotel, guests congregate around a small TV set downstairs and enjoy the quiet warmth of Goro and Yayoko Inaba. Their guests from Germany, France, Japan, and points beyond include world-famous cellists, students on strict budgets, fishermen, artists, and all kinds of travelers who keep returning—and there are only eleven rooms.

KONA TIKI
P.O. Box 1567
Kailua-Kona, HI 96740
Telephone: (808) 329-1425

Right on the ocean on Alii Drive, the Kona Tiki—one of the oldest hotels in the area—is a find for those who would forego a TV set, air conditioner, and telephone for a comfortable room with an ocean view. You must reserve far in advance because it's nearly always full, especially during peak season. There's a small parking lot, a pool, a hutlike office with marvelous managers, and a three-story walk-up so close to the ocean that the sound of the waves helps drown out traffic noises. Some rooms have kitchenettes, others don't; all have tiny refrigerators, dishes, lanais, ceiling fans, and great views of the ocean. The bathrooms have showers but no tub, and there is a short, narrow stretch of lawn for sunbathing. A three-night minimum is required, and there's a complimentary continental breakfast. The hotel is owned by an elderly gentleman who built it after World War II out of surplus army materials—so you know it's sturdy and the walls aren't thin. The major disadvantage is that there's only one pay phone in the lobby. Rates are $33 for a "mini-standard" room with a queen bed, $35 for a standard with a queen bed and a twin bed, and $40 for a standard with a kitchenette.

MANAGO HOTEL
P.O. Box 145
Captain Cook, HI 96704
Telephone: (808) 323-2642

The hotel's been here, overlooking Kealakekua Bay, since 1917. The Manago Hotel in the middle of Kona's coffee country is everyone's favorite, from its fresh fish lunches to its inexpensive rooms and its lobby with the stupendous old photos. The varnished post in the lobby is a coconut tree trunk from the hotel's inception in 1917. The Manago has charm. There are forty-two rooms in the new section, built in 1978, and twenty-two rooms with community bathrooms in the original building. The Japanese room is on the third floor, with tatami floor, futon, and sliding doors that open and look out to the sea. The rooms are all very clean, with tile showers, dressers, carpets, and no TV. Rooms in the old building begin at $15; in the new building, with private baths and lanais, they begin at $21 for a single.

SHIRAKAWA MOTEL
P.O. Box 467
Naalehu, HI 96772
Telephone: (808) 929-7462

Shirakawa's is where you'd stay if you're driving to South Point from Kona, or to Volcano and don't want to spend the night there. It's been here in Waiohinu since 1928, a town with gorgeous trees and churches on the way to Naalehu before the highway veers north toward Volcano. It's a way station, certainly not an end in itself, but for what it is it's fine: thirteen units, mostly studios, some with light cooking facilities and refrigerators, most with single beds. All rooms have two beds. They're humble but clean, and they're no more than 100 yards from the second generation of a monkeypod tree that Mark Twain planted more than a century ago. The Shirakawas have been here since 1928, and there's a family feeling to their place. Rooms start at $21 and go up to $25 for those with kitchenettes.

Moderate Hotel

HOTEL KING KAMEHAMEHA
75-5660 Palani Road
Kailua-Kona, HI 96740
Telephone: (800) 227-4700, (808) 329-2911

In all honesty, this is not a very exciting hotel. The lobby and shopping arcade are like Kailua's Disneyland and the rooms are perfunctory. However, this area is where King Kamehameha chose to live out his final days after conquering the other islands. On the grounds is the Ahu'ena Heiau, built in the sixteenth century and restored as one of Kailua's premier historical sites. This is also where Queen Ka'ahumanu, the queen regent and Kamehameha's favorite wife, broke the ages-old kapu by having Kamehameha II dine among women for the first time. There are two towers to the hotel, with 460 rooms on a small white-sand cove at the end of Kailua's main drag. The rooms face in all directions so only from the deluxe rooms and the higher floors can you actually see the ocean. The shopping arcade downstairs is tacky, but you can look beyond the stores to admire the feather cape and helmet, the Hawaiian quilts and weapons displays, and the fishing and canoe displays scattered across the complex. The best part of the King Kam Hotel is Ulalia Berman, kumu hula extraordinaire. She leads the free "Hula Experience" lecture tour at 10:00 A.M. Mondays and Wednesdays and chants to the kahiko (ancient hula) numbers performed by her students. (See The Best in Hawaiiana.) Room rates begin at $75 and go up to $130 for deluxe oceanfront rooms.

Superior Hotel

KONA SURF
78-128 Ehukai Street
Kailua-Kona, HI 96740
Telephone: (800) 367-8011, (808) 322-3411

This is the nicest hotel in the Keauhou area. On a point of black lava near Keauhou Bay outside of Kailua proper, the white four-tower structure faces the sea in a terraced design that widens at the base to face a crashing sea. The atrium-style building has wide terraces that leave room for strolling and lingering at sunset. It is decidedly a romantic hotel. If you're lucky, you'll see the full moon rising over Holualoa as the sun sets into the ocean. This is also the largest convention facility on the island, with 535 rooms on 14 acres, one freshwater and one saltwater pool, and conference rooms that open up to the lawn and then the ocean. The rooms have pink stucco walls, refrigerators, TV, and the usual amenities, with lanais that at their best overlook the ocean and at their worst overlook the parking lot and beyond it, Holualoa. Because it's on a private peninsula, you are not hemmed in by the towers of other hotels and you don't feel as closed in as you do in the middle of town. Also available are tennis, volleyball, and golf at the twenty-seven-hole Kona Country Club. Room rates during peak season range from $95 to $150 for an oceanfront room and $350 for a suite.

Deluxe Hotels

KONA VILLAGE RESORT
Box 1229
Kaupulehu-Kona, HI 96745
Telephone: (800) 367-5290; (808) 325-5555

Besides being the only full American Plan resort on the Big Island, the Kona Village is also the most private and one of the most romantic. First you drive more than 2 miles from the front gate to the hotel, and once you check in you're taken to your room in a jitney. These Polynesian-style thatched *hales* have high ceilings and porches overlooking the ocean or the lagoon and will make you feel that you are in a remote hideaway in the Pacific. Your room will be a comfortable—although not new—bungalow of your own, with ceiling fan, rattan *punees* (movable couches), and touches of lauhala. The tones are brown, rust, and yellow—none of the slick, modern marbles, tiles, and Art Deco posters ubiquitous in Hawaii hotels. There's no telephone, TV, or radio, and everything in the room is either hardwood or woven. The feeling is of utmost privacy and low-key luxury; you can loll on the gorgeous beach, dine morning, noon, and evening in the Polynesian-style restaurant, or lounge on your veranda listening to the winds rustling through the palm fronds. Or you can go snorkeling or sailing in one of the resort's two boats or take a walk to the petroglyphs on the property or take classes in Hawaiian crafts. The sandy cove is visited regularly by a large sea turtle; loud peacocks roam freely on the grounds. (At dawn, however, they sing a noisy duet with the sprinklers.) Casual dress is encouraged. The one hundred hales are scattered among the remains of an ancient Hawaiian village called Ka'upulehu. Rates for 1988 begin at $310 for two for a standard hale to $510 for a hale right on the beach, with several categories in between. Prices include all activities, meals, and the Monday and Friday night luau, unequivocally the best in Hawaii.

MAUNA LANI BAY HOTEL
P.O. Box 4000
Kawaihae, HI 96743
Telephone: (800) 367-2323, (808) 885-6622

The $72-million, 350-room hotel opened in 1983 and set about distinguishing itself as a luxury resort with an allegiance to the unique history of the area. There are 3 miles of shoreline; several inlets and bays; pre-Christian Hawaiian fish ponds, petroglyphs, and historic preserves; a nineteenth-century footpath called the King's Trail; a thirteenth-century cave complex; and all around, the green and black fields of lava from the Kaniku lava flow that predates 1500. The land is part of an area called Kalahuipua'a, which once belonged to King Kamehameha III and which eventually was acquired by "Mr. Golf," Francis I'i Brown, a direct descendant of one of Hawaii's ruling chiefs. The fish ponds were for the use of Hawaiian royalty and today are part of only a handful of such royal ponds left in Hawaii.

People who can afford to stay here often have to decide between the Mauna Lani and the Mauna Kea because they are the two world-class luxury resorts in the area, each with its own stunning golf course. The

Mauna Kea is immediately impressive, but the Mauna Lani grows on you. The greeting, service, and the room may seem derivative, but after you take a walk along the beach, with its four sandy coves and rough lava out-croppings, or along the fish ponds and ancient trails, you can feel the raw, tranquil beauty of the area. Not to be missed is the historical tour of the grounds by Kaniela Akaka, or a lazy afternoon in one of the hammocks by the sea. The Bay Terrace and the Third Floor are among the finer restaurants on the coast.

A mountain-view room costs $195; other choices include a partial–ocean-view room for $240, ocean-view for $270, and on up to $500 for a suite.

WESTIN MAUNA KEA
P.O. Box 218
South Kohala, HI 96743
Telephone: (800) 228-3000, (808) 882-7222

You are greeted by name and with a lei as you enter the spacious lobby. The atrium-style, open-air lobby (much imitated by newer developments) immediately relaxes you, unlike hotels that assault you with their opulence. What you see first is a large Thai Buddha at the entrance—then open air and plants, a large stairway, and the ocean. All of this is merely a prelude to a feast of art and antiques that pepper the complex, making the Mauna Kea a gallery without walls and making this hotel, created by Laurance Rocke-feller, the doyen of deluxe hotels and resorts in Hawaii. An extensive collection of Pacific and Asian antiques and artifacts is unpretentiously displayed in hallways, near elevators, at the edges of ponds and gardens; an intelligently narrated art tour is also offered.

You don't have to worry about a view here. If you don't get an ocean-view room, which is better than beachfront here because you're higher up and have a spectacular, unobstructed view, you can still get a room with a view of the water that isn't skimpy, or a mountain view that takes in the sweep of Mauna Kea. Space—wide hallways, large stairways, long walks between restaurants—and an unhurried pace, plus peerless service by many beautiful Big Islanders who have been there since the hotel's beginnings, are the hallmarks of this hotel. Many guests return year after year to the same room on the same floor with the same housekeeper.

There are 310 rooms in the Mauna Kea. The first four of eight floors are taken up with such things as restaurants and galleries, shops, pool, sauna, and other amenities. The rooms are tastefully appointed with rattan furni-ture, balcony, spacious bathrooms, and small refrigerators. In keeping with the hideaway nature of the hotel, there are no television sets. There is, however, some of the best swimming on the island a mere elevator ride away. From some of the oceanfront rooms, you can even see manta rays in the water, a sight that becomes surreal when they feed at night off the brightly lit Kaunaoa Point. There are parrots, garden paths, burbling pools, and many strategic areas for sitting and reading around the beautifully landscaped hotel. Here they have refined the art of pampering without intruding.

Activities range from horseback riding (they have their own stables in nearby Waimea) to snorkeling and sailing, windsurfing lessons, and a spate of golf, honeymoon, and tennis packages. The eighteen-hole Robert Trent Jones golf course is ranked as one of "America's One Hundred Greatest" golf courses by *Golf Digest* and is widely recognized as the one of the best and most challenging courses in Hawaii.

For years the Mauna Kea only offered the Modified American Plan (mandatory during peak season), but now the European Plan is available, too. The MAP is worthy because the Mauna Kea has more than its share of award-winning restaurants and the dining is always exceptional, especially in the Batik Room and Café Terrace. Rates for 1988 were unavailable at the time of this writing, but 1987 rates ranged from $198 a night, EP and mountain view, to $278 for ocean view, EP, single or double occupancy. MAP rates range from $248 for mountain view, single occupancy, to $318 for beachfront and $328 for ocean view, $50 more for double occupancy.

Alternatives

HALE KONA KAI
75-5870 Kahakai Road
Kailua-Kona, HI 96740
Telephone: (808) 329-2155

This three-story, thirty-nine-unit condo is on the ocean and next door to the Kona Hilton near Keauhou, which adds a measure of convenience. All the units have ocean views, and all are one-bedroom, with living room, lanai, kitchenette, bath and shower, and a washer/dryer on each floor. The building is fourteen years old; each unit is furnished differently. Ask about the corner units with the wraparound lanais. There are daily, weekly, and monthly rates, ranging from $65 a night ($390 a week) for an interior unit to $75 a night for the corner unit. Prices are based on double occupancy.

KANALOA AT KONA
78-261 Manukai Street
Keauhou-Kona, HI 96740
Telephone: (800) 367-6046, (808) 322-2272

The Kanaloa is listed as an alternative because technically it's a condominium; yet it has just about all the amenities of a hotel, including maid service, one of the best restaurants in west Hawaii, tennis courts, phone service, and three pools on its 17 acres. This luxury oceanfront property is one of the newer condos and certainly the best in the Kailua-Keauhou area; the thirty-seven low-rise buildings are excellently managed and maintained. All the living rooms are on the outer side of the building, the bedrooms on the inner area. Views are of the ocean, the golf course, neighboring buildings, or the mountains. The tallest building is four stories high, and some units have two levels and a loft. There's no air-conditioning, but ceiling fans and the sea breeze suffice. There are one-, two-, and three-bedroom units; all are very spacious, modern, and immaculate, set in well-landscaped surroundings offering privacy and elegance. The bathrooms are memorable: large showers with double heads are made for honeymooners, and even the regular small bathrooms have Jacuzzis. All units have full kitchens. No minimum number of nights required. Rates start at $115 for up to four persons to $205 for up to eight people and three bedrooms—a bargain for sure.

KONA BY THE SEA
75-6106 Alii Drive
Kailua-Kona, HI 96740
Telephone: (808) 329-0200

It's one of the newer condominiums in Kailua, a four-story, oceanside luxury property with 80 units not far from the center of activity in town. There's daily maid service for the one- and two-bedroom units, each with two baths. The units are large and tasteful, with full kitchens and ample lanais facing the ocean. The condo opened six years ago and is a favorite among kamaaina islanders and mainlanders in the know. The beach is small but sandy, and at night it's transformed into a candlelit gourmet haven, the Beach Club. Rates range from $135 to $165 a night.

KONA WHITE SANDS
P.O. Box 594
Kailua-Kona, HI 96740
Telephone: (808) 329-3210

One of the older buildings in the area, the Kona White Sands is a two-story, cement block walk-up with terrific prices but only ten units for rent. It's very modestly decorated. The studios are 450 square feet and the two-room units have a queen-size bed and, in the other room, two punees that pull out into beds. Each is equipped with a full kitchen and a large refrigerator. It's on Alii Drive, right across the street from the Magic Sands beach about 3.5 miles from the center of town. Rates range from $37 to $48.

Coming Attractions

HYATT WAIKOLOA
South Kohala

This $360-million development is expected to be developer Chris Hemmeter's fantasy hotel—and, he hopes, everyone else's. The hotel will have 1,244 rooms, a spa, a tournament-class stadium, professional sports training facilities, and a mile-long water transportation system sprawled across 60 oceanfront acres. There will be three separate buildings of six stories. Scheduled to open in the fall of 1988, the hotel will also feature lagoons, gondolas, and air-conditioned, three-module trains with cocktail bars, as well as nine restaurants and thirteen lounges. The Hyatt Waikoloa is expected to be an extravaganza of sybaritic indulgences for travelers with fat pocketbooks. More a metropolis than a simple hotel, it will no doubt be less personal and intimate than your everyday luxury hotel.

EAST HAWAII

As charming as it is, Hilo is not known for its hostelries. Most of its hotels are along Banyan Drive facing Hilo Bay, with great views but distressing decor and inflated prices. Hilo hotels bear another idiosyncrasy. Unlike sunny resort areas where guests lounge on the beach and never leave, a Hilo hotel is a place to sleep between trips to the volcano and up the Hamakua coast and points between. This is unfortunate and caused partly by the weather (Hilo's worst enemy) and partly by the mistaken notion that Hilo is the same sleepy town it's always been. If the truth be known, this town has excellent restaurants, a lovely park, and historical tours and attractions that bear exploring. The hotels, however, have never had it easy, and it shows.

Budget Hotel

WAIAKEA VILLAS
400 Hualani Street
Hilo, HI 96720
Telephone: (808) 961-2841

This is the best deal in Hilo, an astounding value. Located in the heart of town bordering a freshwater reserve, the 14-acre, low-rise, brown wooden complex features ponds and lagoons, carp and parrots, lush ferns and bamboo. It is also conveniently located not far from the airport and close to Hilo's major attractions. Formerly a Sheraton hotel with an ersatz zoo, the operation has resurrected itself as a hotel-condominium complex with the major amenities (except a restaurant and room service) of a standard hotel.

This is not for those who need to be pandered to and pampered, for service is less than adequate and the grounds, lush as they are, are not as well maintained as they should be. But for those seeking a clean, modern room in a hotel that's not a dive, this is it.

Because 1988 rates were unavailable at the time of this writing, only 1987 rates are provided here. There are 147 rooms, ranging from standards without kitchen—$27 a night—to superiors with kitchen for $32 and a large studio deluxe for $40. The big spenders here go for the $55 one-bedroom suite, with a king or two doubles, or the $90 honeymoon suite, very large. There is a $5 charge for an additional person.

The rooms are rather dark, in browns and deep rusts, but they are carpeted, clean, and large. There is wicker furniture, a lanai with table and chairs, color TV, and air-conditioning. The rooms with kitchenettes are very self-sufficient, with dishes, sink, stove, etc. There are no telephones, however, so the pay phones in the lobby will have to do.

Moderate Hotels

ASTON NANILOA
93 Banyan Drive
Hilo, HI 96720
Telephone: (800) 367-5360, (808) 935-0831

This is the largest hotel on Hilo Bay, and certainly the most pleasant. The rooms overlooking the bay have a gorgeous view of the ocean, Mauna Kea, and, from certain sections, a small islet, called Coconut Island, bordering the grounds where kids jump off stone walls and play among the ironwoods.

You can see boats motoring into the Suisan Fish Market, and on a sunny day you can actually sunbathe by the tide pools. This is a middle-of-the-road kind of place, far from elegant or dashing, but functional. The lounge here is one of Hilo's few spots for name acts from Oahu; when the Cazimeros or Melveen Leed arrive, the place starts jumping. There are close to 400 rooms in the eight-floor and eleven-floor towers, ranging from $135 suites to $50 standard rooms without lanais (1987 rates). Rooms have a telephone, color TV, table with chairs. Be cautious with your choice—many of the rooms seem overpriced. The new management of Aston and a $2.7-million renovation should upgrade things considerably, but prices are expected to rise.

VOLCANO HOUSE
P.O. Box 53
Hawaii Volcanoes National Park, HI 96718
Telephone: (808) 967-7321

Built in 1877, the Volcano House is Hawaii's oldest hotel and a part of Big Island history. Paintings of Pele adorn the walls of the lodge, and a comfortable living area with leather chairs invites lingering before the fire. Take out your parka, boots, and invoke your bird-watching skills and you're all set for the stay.

This is the only hotel in the Volcano area (Hilo is a half hour away) and is surrounded by hiking trails, craters, steam vents, fern forests, and a myriad possible activities for nature lovers. The Volcano Art Center is a stone's throw away.

The restaurant is always overrun with tour buses at lunchtime, a signifi-cant detraction for those who are around. The food is so-so, although some of their seafood dinner entrées are fine. For all its rarity and legendary merit, the ohelo berry pie—a Volcano House specialty—is overrated. But there are no complaints about the ambience, for the windows overlook a landscape of ohia, ferns, gingers, and other Hawaiian plants kissed by the elusive mists floating in and around the crater.

The rooms are nothing special, but you don't come here for luxury and many enjoy the modest, lodgelike atmosphere. In fact, it's more a budget hotel than a moderate one, except that its superior and deluxe rooms are recommended over the less expensive standards. There are thirty-seven units in the hotel, from $40 for a standard to $51 for a deluxe. Whatever you do, try to avoid a room by the parking lot or you'll never sleep.

Alternatives

THE HOUSE AT KAPOHO
Glenetta Bennett
2916-E Ainaola Drive
Hilo, HI 96720
Telephone: (808) 959-3488, 935-1121

The two-bedroom, one-bath home sits on a clear, large, blue-black warm spring that's like your own private lagoon. It's a scene out of Somerset Maugham: a clear pool surrounded by large hala and coconut trees with one side leading to the deck and to the neighbor's house. Concrete steps lead down to the pool from an immense porch and deck—it's stunning.

On the way to the rocky beach a short walk away you will pass other homes with their own warm springs heated by the nearby volcanoes. The area, Kapoho, is at the easternmost point of the island, a point that was extended by the 1960 lava flow. The ground here is largely cinder or rock, with greenery that still looks new and must be tended because of the scarcity of rain in the area.

It's gorgeous, secluded, and clearly restorative—but it's not for everyone. It's a long drive to the nearest store in Keaau, forty-five minutes from Hilo, and there's no telephone or television. You must also bring your own drinking water; the Kapoho well is not well maintained. For those who don't mind these inconveniences and want solitude and a healing environment, however, it's quite an exciting prospect.

The home is light and airy, with sliding glass doors leading to the deck, a bedroom with stacked mattresses for bigger groups, a living room, bathroom, and kitchen with large refrigerator and a four-burner stove. Around it are hibiscus bushes, ferns, sago palms, and, by the pond, a lava rock grill. The wall of the pond is where the 1960 lava flow stopped.

You will share the pond with the two neighboring houses, but they're hardly ever occupied and you're likely to have this entire dreamy scenario all to yourself.

Rates are $40 a night or $250 a week.

KALANI HONUA
P.O. Box 4500
Kalapana, HI 96778
Telephone: (808) 965-7828

Kalani Honua is for those seeking a healthy vacation in unrivaled surroundings. The 20-acre oceanfront center includes an ancient Hawaiian school site, a pasture with Arabian horses and an equestrian program, a store and restaurant, a new Olympic pool, a Japanese spa area with sauna, and four cedar lodges with private or shared baths. New at Kalani Honua is a three-bedroom, two-bath guesthouse that sleeps up to six.

In addition to its physical facilities, Kalani Honua is also known for its educational programs, including a dance retreat every summer and live-in programs in the arts, business, language, yoga, and the martial arts. Located near Opihikao and the Kalapana black-sand beach, Kalani Honua is an unbeatable choice for the health-conscious traveler seeking a salutary environment and the people to guide him. You will be directed to beautiful black-sand beaches, warm springs and underground steam vents, and good snorkeling and hiking. Massage is available, and bicycle tours can take you to lava tubes and swimming at secluded beaches. And when the volcano is erupting, Kalani Honua's helipad comes in handy for the throngs of sightseers wishing to fly over the eruptions for less than it would cost from Kona or South Kohala.

For those staying three nights or more, a room with a shared bath is $30 a night, single or double; for private bath, $40. Those staying for fewer than three nights will pay more. The guesthouse rents for $150 a day for up to six persons.

WAIPIO "HOTEL"
Tetsuo Araki
25 Malama Place
Hilo, HI 96720
Telephone: (808) 775-0368

If you're eccentric, adventurous, and not easily intimidated, Tom Araki's barrackslike "hotel" is certainly worth exploring. You won't find anything else like it in Hawaii. After descending the steep valley walls on the Waipio Valley Shuttle (see Special Outings: On Land), you'll come across this five-room retreat with its taro fields in front, plain rooms with hurricane lamps, and windows that look over to two robust waterfalls. This is a haven for reclusive writers, urbanites in hiding, and romantics who can rough it.

The kitchen (with a Coleman stove) is downstairs, and the bathroom is down the hall. There is no electricity, and you bring your own food, drinking water, towels, and flashlight. The shower—well, if you want hot water you'll have to use owner Tom Araki's shower next door, with its ninety-year-old bathtub from the old Waipio schoolhouse. The rooms, however, are more than adequate, with beds, a chair, wood floors, and windows that look out toward both ends of the valley. The building was constructed in the mid-1960s as headquarters for a Peace Corps camp.

You are in a valley of historical significance, a valley that once contained several small villages, stores, schools, restaurants, jails, churches, and homes—all destroyed in the 1946 tsunami. One mile wide at the ocean and stretching six to eight miles inland, Waipio was a Hawaiian cultural center before westerners arrived.

You can take long walks among the taro fields and wild horses, the streams and wild fruit trees that grow in abundance. It's quiet, peaceful, and isolated, except for the four-wheel drives carrying tourists. Your name in the guest book will be among those from Tibet, Bombay, Brooklyn, Tokyo, Queensland, Hollywood, Christchurch—people like you who have paid $5 a night to sleep in the lap of history.

DINING OUT

WEST HAWAII

Many of these restaurants do not have street addresses but are on the main highway or easy to find. As with all restaurants in this book, we strongly recommend that you call ahead.

ALOHA CAFÉ
Kainaliu
Telephone: (808) 322-3383

The Aloha Theatre complex is one of the more pleasant stops on the Big Island. You can dine on healthy, scrumptious, mostly vegetarian meals while sitting on the veranda that wraps around a vintage theater and overlooks coffee fields, horse pastures, and the ocean. Tropical fresh fruit syrups, the island's best corn bread and whole-grain pancakes, and excellent omelets and brownies make this a great breakfast stop. There are fresh-squeezed juices and fruit smoothies, too. Charbroiled hamburgers are very popular, and so are the lasagne and eggplant burgers. Fresh fish, tostadas, superb salads, sandwiches, quiches, and a plethora of generous desserts make this a local favorite.

Inexpensive—prices range from $5.25 to $10.95. Serves breakfast, lunch, and dinner. Open 8:00 A.M. to 8:00 P.M. daily except Sunday. Major credit cards accepted.

BAY TERRACE
Mauna Lani Bay Hotel
South Kohala
Telephone: (808) 885-6622

Besides serving, at breakfast, the best malasadas—Portuguese dumplings, from an employee's secret family recipe—the Bay Terrace also has a notable fettucine primavera and some fine fresh fish dishes in the evenings. A different menu is offered every night. Breakfast, lunch, and dinner are served at typically high hotel restaurant prices, but at least you're not getting typical hotel restaurant fare here. (A nice touch: all juices are freshly squeezed.) Jackets are required of men in the evenings, but the rest of the day it's pretty casual. The light, airy room is tiered, opening out to al fresco dining. The room is accented with designer floral arrangements and koa shutters—tasteful and pleasant.

Moderately expensive—breakfast from $6 to $10, lunch $8 to $10, and dinner $18 to $28. Open 6:00 A.M. to 9:30 P.M. daily.

BEACH CLUB
Kona by the Sea
75-6106 Alii Drive
Kailua-Kona
Telephone: (808) 329-0290

You drive into an underground garage and keep walking. Soon the white tablecloths with hurricane lamps under umbrellas in the sand will hit you like a mirage. The effect is startling, one of Casablanca unfolding before you. The Beach Club is the best restaurant in west Hawaii, a well-kept secret known only by word of mouth. You will dine amid coconut trees and torches at the ocean's edge; to the right is a saltwater pool, behind you is the indoor part of the restaurant. Owner Margo Elliopoulos and executive chef Mark Tuhy come with many credentials; the wall is plastered with awards from their days in San Francisco, where Tuhy worked at the Alexis restaurant. His forte is seafood and sauces with a Mediterranean touch: blackened spearfish fillet, Thai lobster curry, paella, Kona lobster, fresh fettucine with baby clams, moussaka, couscous. They go to great lengths for quality: the coconut milk for the curry is made from scratch, the angel hair pasta is made fresh, the "painted plate" comes with delicately flavored puréed vegetables in artistic patterns. This is gourmet fare in a fantasy setting; you'll return many times. If you can't, owner Elliopoulos's Bluewater Cuisine Catering will come to you.

Casual but elegant; dinner for two, about $60. Open 6:30 P.M. to 9:00 P.M. Tuesday through Saturday. Reservations a must. Major credit cards accepted.

LA BOURGOGNE
77-6400 Nalani Street
Kailua-Kona
Telephone: (808) 329-6711

Out of the mainstream of Kailua eateries, La Bourgogne is in the Kuakini Plaza South. The cozy, dark woods, floral wallpaper, and blue velvet booths make an appropriate backdrop for chef Guy Chatelard's French specialties: lamb with mustard sauce, shrimp Provençale, veal with cream sauce, fresh island fish.

Everything is à la carte; main courses range from $11.50 to $22. Open 6:00 P.M. to 10:00 P.M. nightly except Sunday. Major credit cards accepted.

BREAD DEPOT
Opelu Plaza
Waimea
Telephone: (808) 885-6354

Waimea's newest sensation is a small bakery with a few tables that are always full at breakfast when the cinnamon rolls come out of the oven, and at lunch when the clam chowder—the best on the island—always sells out. An array of delicious, freshly baked breads goes quickly too. Also popular are the deli items (i.e., salami au poivre) and sandwiches on your choice of just-baked bread. Chef Georges Amtablian's cinnamon rolls can be detected from blocks away, and in the afternoon the fragrance of fresh passion fruit (for cheesecake topping) fills the shop. Hot specials—shrimp curry, fettucine—are also offered, making this a depot worth finding.

Inexpensive—lunch costs about $9 for two. Open about 7:30 A.M. to 5:30 P.M. daily except Sunday. Major credit cards accepted.

CAFÉ TERRACE
Westin Mauna Kea
South Kohala
Telephone: (808) 882-7222

It's impossible not to gush over the Café Terrace's famous buffet. At lunchtime more than a hundred colorful dishes are offered in a gorgeous, sumptuous presentation that highlights the Big Island's best in fresh produce. Fern shoots from Waipio Valley, sashimi, Waimea strawberries, smoked marlin from Kailua, an array of salads and fish dishes, and hot and chilled entrées in infinite varieties make this a worthy stop. The terrace overlooks the bay and gardens and, if it doesn't rain, the lunchtime experience is flawless. In the evenings, Japanese cuisine with a nouvelle twist is offered: fillet of fresh fish with miso sauce, fresh catch with ginger shoyu, king crab meat with a tart plum sauce.

Buffet costs $17; expect to pay more at dinner. Open noon to 2:30 P.M. for lunch and 6:30 P.M. to 8:30 P.M. for dinner daily. Reservations requested. Major credit cards accepted.

DON'S FAMILY DELI
Kapa'au, North Kohala, across from the Kamehameha Statue
Telephone: (808) 889-5822

Vegetarian home-cooking is the fare here: lasagne, nachos, pasta, quiche, eggplant Parmesan, and other simple delectables to fortify you for the long drive back. Don Rich and his parents, Bill and Marion, emigrated from New York and opened this minuscule corner deli a few years ago. You can have cold cuts in giant heros, French rolls, or sourdough, and for some local color there's Portuguese bean soup. It's modest and inexpensive, hearty and wonderful, especially the macadamia nut pie fashioned after the traditional—and caloric—pecan pie.

Inexpensive—prices under $6. Open 10:00 A.M. to 6:00 P.M. Monday through Saturday, noon to 5:00 P.M. on Sunday. No credit cards accepted.

DORIAN'S
77-6452 Alii Drive, next to Magic Sands Beach
Kailua
Telephone: (808) 329-3195

The old Kailua favorite has just been remodeled, making its oceanfront dining even better. The restaurant is light and airy, with tables outdoors and the ocean on two sides. During lunch the seafood bar is popular, and in the evening the candlelit tables bear a bountiful parade of some of the town's best dishes. The Silver Platter is a popular choice, an elegant combination of meat or seafood dishes and combinations, sautéed, broiled, or in other methods of preparation. Fresh fish is blackened Cajun-style, and fresh oysters, clams, lobsters, veal, and other items are creatively presented. A Dorian's winner is the macadamia nut pie, prepared according to an old family recipe.

Cost is about $25 a person, with cocktails. Open 11:30 A.M. to 2:30 P.M. Monday through Friday, 6:00 P.M. to 10:00 P.M. nightly, and 10 A.M. to 2:00 P.M. Sunday. The Sunday champagne brunch is a Kailua favorite. Major credit cards accepted.

EDELWEISS
Kawaihae Road
Waimea
Telephone: (808) 885-6800

Chef and owner Hans-Peter Hager has people driving long distances for his veal, rack of lamb, and fish dishes, served in a cozy, chaletlike room with high ceilings and koa panels. He opened Edelweiss four years ago, after establishing a reputation at such places as Mauna Kea and Mauna Lani, which he helped open as executive chef. The menu is creative but is heavy on the meats, leaving not many choices for vegetarians or light eaters in the nouvelle cuisine tradition. Nevertheless, the soup changes daily, the fish is versatile, and the restaurant continues to pack them in.

Prices start at $7.75 for a light meal up to $36 for a rack of lamb dinner. Opens at 11:30 for lunch and at 5:00 P.M. for dinner daily except Monday. No reservations; first come, first served. Major credit cards accepted.

FISHERMAN'S LANDING WATERFRONT WONDERLAND RESTAURANT
75-5744 Alii Drive
Kailua
Telephone: (808) 326-2555

It sounds like Disneyland, and actually it's a little bit like it. It seats 400 people, has ponds, elaborate foliage, and four dining rooms inside and three dining rooms outside. But the view is the best in Kailua because it's on a point with a bay on each side and water all around. The chef, formerly of the Kona Village, is known for his presentation of local favorites: poke (raw fish with seasonings), shrimp tempura, chicken stir-fried with pineapple and lichees, stir-fried vegetables Japanese- and Chinese-style. Most popular are the steak and lobster, and the fresh fish that changes daily. The restaurant is impersonal and the service may plod, but the view is spectacular and the food is fine.

Fish entrées are about $16; steak and lobster, $20 and up. Open 11:30 A.M. to 2:30 P.M. daily, 5:30 P.M. to 10:00 P.M. Sunday through Thursday, and until 10:30 P.M. Friday and Saturday. Major credit cards accepted.

THE GALLERY
Mauna Lani Resort
South Kohala
Telephone: (808) 885-7777

This delightful little restaurant has an elevated dining area surrounded by glass and a creative, accommodating menu. Known for its fresh seafood, The Gallery will prepare dishes according to customers' requests but has its own repertoire of sautés, sauces, and preparations. At lunch the Philadephia cheese steak–sirloin sandwiches are very popular. Of note is the chef's Hawaiian Plate, an array of lomi salmon, poke (raw fish with seasonings), lau lau (pork steamed in taro leaves), and occasionally, the raw limpets called opihi, beloved by Hawaiians but decidely an acquired taste. The menu is daring and full of imagination, and the staff is cordial. Do not forego dessert—the fruit tarts and pastries are scrumptious. It's casual fine dining tucked away near the resort's racket club.

Lunch entrées are in the $5 to $10 range; dinner entrées, up to $25. Open 11:00 A.M. to 2:00 P.M. and 6:00 P.M. to 9:00 P.M. daily. Major credit cards accepted.

MANAGO RESTAURANT
Manago Hotel
Captain Cook
Telephone: (808) 323-2642

The Manago is a favorite of residents and loyal patrons who love the low prices and home-cooked fresh fish, the unpretentious decor, the nice view and family feeling. The Japanese and American food is simple, reasonable, and delicious, from the fresh opelu to the fresh ahi and the dishes of limu, or seaweed, they serve you. When you dine at Manago, you're eating at the area's favorite local hangout.

Inexpensive—lunch for two can be had for $12. Open 7:00 A.M. to 9:00 A.M. and 11:00 A.M. to 2:00 P.M. daily, 5:00 P.M. to 7:30 P.M. Monday through Thursday, and 5:00 P.M. to 7:00 P.M. Friday through Sunday. Major credit cards accepted.

OCEANVIEW INN
Alii Drive, across the seawall
Kailua
Telephone: (808) 329-9998

The Oceanview Inn borders on tacky, but it does have inexpensive local dishes and a healthy dose of local color. It's best for those who don't care about ambience but love watching the elderly local *tutus* (grandmothers) with haku leis and grandchildren in tow. The lovely island women who lunch here often look as if they came straight down from the mountain, wearing their dew-fresh *liko lehua* leis while eating saimin or beef stew and rice. The large, funky room has served Big Islanders for half a century with its Chinese, American, and Hawaiian dishes. The service is often brusque, but the Oceanview Inn has a perverse charm. It's such a shame they put jalousies instead of clear glass on the wall fronting Kailua Pier.

Inexpensive. Open for breakfast, lunch, and dinner daily. No credit cards accepted.

POKI'S PASTA
Kailua Bay Shopping Mall, across the seawall
Kailua
Telephone: (808) 329-7888

Poki Goold has eight kids and started out with a sandwich wagon. Then Dorian's hired her when it opened in the mid-1970s. Now Goold has her own eatery, a tiny hole-in-the-wall in the heart of Kailua. It's the hottest new restaurant in town—small (capacity of twenty-five, including the counter), with wholesome, fresh Italian dishes such as homemade pastas, minestrone made daily, fried mozzarella with marinara sauce (a big seller) and roasted whole elephant garlic, along with the veal and calamari steak that are so popular in the evenings. The lunchtime crowd fills the restaurant for its sandwiches, pasta salads, and hot specials. At dinner the crisp white napkins come out and diners tote their own bottles of wine to Poki's for a casual, wonderful Italian meal. Someone down the road makes their sorbets and gelati, a hot rival to the Oreo cookie cheesecake. Poki's is definitely a find and a great value.

The most expensive sandwich is $5.50; entrées go up to $13.95. Open 11:00 A.M. to 3:00 P.M. Monday through Saturday and 5:30 P.M. to 9:30 P.M. daily. Major credit cards accepted.

SIBU CAFÉ
Banyan Court, Alii Drive
Kailua
Telephone: (808) 329-1112

This is a real find in the middle of crowded, noisy Kailua. There are a few tables outside on the mall, where you can relax over Indonesian food under a plumeria tree with Kailua Bay in the distance. It's very informal and reasonable. Gado gado, a salad with spicy peanut dressing and lime, is a good choice for under $6. Balinese chicken, vegetable and beef sates (skewered and cooked on open flame), and many combinations of vegetarian and beef dishes make this a fine place for an inexpensive lunch. Beer, including Watney's and Anchor Steam, wine, and lilikoi juice also served.

Inexpensive—lunch for two can run about $15. Open 11:30 A.M. to 10:00 P.M. daily, with free lunch delivery in the area. No credit cards.

THE TERRACE
Kanaloa at Keauhou
Telephone: (808) 322-9625

You can dine watching whales at breakfast and porpoises at lunch. Like The Beach Club, The Terrace is a Kailua winner under wraps, a cozy restaurant of excellent fare, stupendous view, and quietly tucked away in a condominium, away from the crowds. This is al fresco dining at its best, a very small, intimate, and informal sprinkling of tables at a dramatic spot very close to the ocean and next to the Kanaloa's pool. There are palms and ferns around you, the 8,000-foot-high Hualalai behind you, and behind that, Mauna Loa. Over breakfast and lunch, the ocean dazzles; if there's a moon at night, the mountains beckon. But there's more than atmosphere. The Terrace's habitués come for the fresh fish and the creative presentation, from nouvelle vegetables to seafood Wellington and royal ulua. The fresh catch is always good, especially the rare fish called mu, which tastes like lobster and is exceedingly hard to get. The menu, on a chalkboard, changes daily.

Moderately expensive, with dinner entrées $10.75 to $20. Open 8:00 A.M. to 2:30 P.M. and 5:30 P.M. to 9:30 P.M. daily, and reservations are a must—it's such a small restaurant. Major credit cards accepted.

TESHIMA'S
Honalo
Telephone: (808) 322-9140

It's a local hangout; you can tell by the folks who gather for breakfast before work. The food is adequate but the prices are good, and the ambience is ersatz Japanese with original oils adorning the walls. Service at breakfast can be terrible but the lunchtime scene is much more promising. Japanese dishes such as shrimp tempura, sashimi, sukiyaki, teriyaki beef sticks, and teishoku combinations prevail then and at dinner.

Inexpensive—prices are $3 to $9.50. Open Monday through Friday 6:30 A.M. to 2:00 P.M.; 5:00 to 10:00 P.M. Saturday; and Sunday hours are 7:00 A.M. to 2:00 P.M., 5:00 P.M. to 10:00 P.M. No credit cards accepted.

....

EAST HAWAII

Restaurants

HOTEL HONOKAA CLUB
Route 240
Honokaa
Telephone: (808) 775-0678

Residents love to come here for fresh lobster and other local and American favorites at rock-bottom prices. Open for breakfast, lunch, and dinner, it offers everything from 80-cent papaya and two eggs for a dollar to mahimahi, filet mignon, seafood platters, and shrimp curry for less than hefty pocketbooks. You can get steak and lobster or a lobster tail for under $14. (The demand for the lobster is high, so they prefer you order ahead for those.) Even if you don't, you'll have a versatile selection of dishes. You must, however, keep your humor about the ambience. The large, strange room is partially redeemed by the light coming in from its windows, but you still must contend with the linoleum floor and vinyl tablecloths complementing the color TV in the corner. The restaurant serves the hotel upstairs (some good budget rooms), but it's the local folks who keep coming back.

Inexpensive. Open 6:00 A.M. to 2:00 P.M. and 5:30 P.M. to 8:00 P.M. daily. Major credit cards accepted.

REFLECTIONS RESTAURANT
Hilo Lagoon Center
101 Aupuni Street
Hilo
Telephone: (808) 935-8501

Hilo's newest fancy restaurant has all the elements: beautiful ambience, an imaginative menu, good food and service. You enter on a bridge over a carp pond into a chic dining room accented with ceiling fans, beveled glass, private wooden booths with etched glass panels, and touches of brass throughout. The dinner choices include lobster bisque, rack of lamb, steak au poivre, and a small but satisfying seafood selection, from island lobster to the fresh catch. Specials, such as fettucine Bolognese with lobster, appeal to the adventurous but the servings are excessive.

This is the newest oasis where people gather for lunch, happy hour, dinner, and late-night drinks to the sounds of a contemporary band from the mainland. Generous complimentary appetizers and Hilo's best appetizer menu draw many local residents for drinks after work. Dress is casual, but for a sophisticated restaurant in a not-so-fancy town, Reflections is a departure—and so far a successful one.

Moderately expensive, with entrées from $8.95 to $25.95. Open 11:00 A.M. to 2:00 P.M. and 5:00 P.M. to 9:30 P.M. daily. Major credit cards accepted.

RESTAURANT FUJI
Hilo Hotel
142 Kinoole Street
Hilo
Telephone: (808) 961-3733

Hilo's nicest Japanese restaurant has a full range of offerings, from poolside teppanyaki dining, their specialty, to sashimi, tempura, and the delicate teishoku assortment of vegetables, soup, rice, and appetizers. You can dine indoors or by the pool, and you can count on quality. Local favorites include yaki sakana (grilled fish), wafu steak (marinated and barbecued), and the tempura dishes.

Prices range from about $8 to $24 for teppanyaki. Open 11:00 A.M. to 2:00 P.M. and 5:00 P.M. to 9:00 P.M. daily except Monday. Major credit cards accepted.

ROSEY'S BOATHOUSE
760 Piilani Street
Hilo
Telephone: (808) 935-2112

Known for its sprawling salad bar, Rosey's is an old favorite with several things going for it. It's fairly consistent, it's comfortably casual, and it does have good food. There are about forty items in the salad bar, always fresh and most grown on the Big Island. The fresh catch, broiled over kiawe or sautéed, is always a safe choice. Others prefer the teriyaki steak. Desserts are marvelous, especially the famous macadamia nut cheesecake.

You can dine well here for under $20 a person. Open daily 4:30 to 9:00 P.M. Major credit cards accepted.

ROUSSELS
60 Keawe Street
Hilo
Telephone: (808) 935-5111

The Oliver brothers arrived from New Orleans two years ago, liked Hilo, and renovated the old welfare office into a restaurant people are excited about. The gray-and-red motif is accented with very high ceilings (it was a bank before it was a welfare office), polished hardwood floors, cane-backed chairs, and the pièce de résistance, tall columns and arches that lend a wonderful drama to the ambience. French Creole is the cuisine here, made with an enthusiasm, integrity, and excellence unsurpassed on the island and perhaps in the state. Chef Andrew Oliver, brother of owner Spencer Oliver, has combined more than twenty years of experience in New York restaurants with well-known and hidden family recipes from New Orleans. The freshest fish from the Suisan Fish Market and other uncompromising ingredients ensure that even Chef Andrew's grandmother would approve of his renditions of her secret recipes. The blackened fresh mahimahi, à la Paul Prudhomme, is the best in Hawaii, even surpassing attempts by Hawaii's more established, better-known restaurants. You can have the fresh catch (mahimahi, opakapaka, and onaga fresh from Suisan daily) prepared any way you want, and if that's not enough the shrimp creole or shrimp etouffé will do. The meal can be topped off with a hot, freshly baked beignet whose aroma lingers seductively. From start to finish it's a satisfying meal; you will surely want to return. Many people do, for the poor-boy sandwiches of oyster or soft-shelled crab inside a French bread loaf served at lunch. It's a sensation too.

Dinner, about $20 to $25 per person without drinks; lunch is less. Open 11:30 A.M. to 2:30 P.M. weekdays, 3:00 P.M. to 6:00 P.M. for appetizers daily except Sunday, and 5:30 P.M. to 10:00 P.M. daily except Sunday. Major credit cards accepted.

TEX DRIVE INN AND RESTAURANT
Highway 19
Honokaa
Telephone: (808) 775-0598

Tex Drive Inn is a roadside stand made famous statewide for its Portuguese donuts sans holes. Malasadas, they're called—doughy, yeasty dumplings made according to an old family recipe and then deep-fried and rolled in sugar. This morsel of indulgence attracts customers from all over the island, many of whom cart them off by the bundle for friends on the neighbor islands. The takeout counter has been on the Honokaa roadside for years, a comforting presence to its many fans.

Inexpensive. Open 5:00 A.M. to 10:00 P.M. weekdays and until 11:00 P.M. Saturday and Sunday. No credit cards accepted.

TING HAO
Puinako Town Center
Puinako
Telephone: (808) 959-6288

They're generous with the garlic, as in the skinned eggplant with large garlic chunks, a popular Mandarin dish. People drive long distances for it, or for the spicy tofu or mu shu pork with fungus and eggs. Ting Hao is a typical Chinese restaurant—linoleum floors, Formica-topped tables, fluorescent lights—with atypical food. You can dine heartily for $5 here, with good choices ranging from pot stickers—a favorite— to steamed fish and smoked chicken, all with that assertive Mandarin quality.

Inexpensive. Open 10:30 A.M. to 2:30 P.M. Monday through Saturday and 4:30 P.M. to 9:00 P.M. nightly. Major credit cards accepted.

TOMI ZUSHI
68 Mamo Street
Hilo
Telephone: (808) 961-6100

The fare here is delicious Japanese food at unbeatable prices. Those who discover Tomi Zushi are astounded at its generous offerings: affordable sushi, tempura, teriyaki, and bento, prepared by diligent, grandmotherly ladies working in a kitchen as large as the dining room. Watch those bountiful trays of steaming tempura and fish stream out of the kitchen to the handful of tables, and you'll know why the locals keep returning. It's very satisfying, and they serve beer and sake too.

Inexpensive—two can dine well for $12. Open 11:00 A.M. to 2:00 P.M. and 4:30 P.M. to 8:30 P.M. daily except Wednesday, when it's closed; Saturday, when lunch only is served; and Sunday, when dinner only is served. Cash only.

Coffee Shops

BEARS' COFFEE
106 Keawe Street
Hilo
Telephone: (808) 935-0708

Bears' is *the* haven for Hilo's coffee lovers, the classic sidewalk café located in the center of town with tables outdoors and a counter indoors. It's small and pleasant, with a bright tile floor and an *intime* crowd choosing from among bagels, deli sandwiches, croissants and rolls, quiches and soups, and, of course, the bean, from au lait to iced mochaccino. The menu is quite democratic, including a smattering of healthy foods (from Greek salad to bean burritos) to the caloric splendors of coffee cake, sour cream walnut cake, cinnamon rolls, and other enticements. For a small coffee-house, it has a versatile menu and a happy corps of habitués who gather from early in the morning to closing.

Inexpensive. Open 7:00 A.M. to 5:00 P.M. weekdays and 8:00 A.M. to 4:00 P.M. Saturday, closed Sunday. No credit cards accepted.

DICK'S COFFEE HOUSE
Hilo Shopping Center
Hilo
Telephone: (808) 935-2769

Dick's is the local hangout where morning patter consists of who won at last night's softball game or who didn't show up at the PTA meeting. On the walls are pennants for the Green Bay Packers and assorted teams who share the space with deer antlers. One corner wall is covered with oversized dollars and foreign currency. But Dick's is also known for its food.

You can get great mahimimahi with eggs, toast, and rice or hash browns, all for under $2. That's the morning special, and there are others like it, from steak and eggs for $2.50 to omelets for under $3. The efficient, old-timer waitresses bustle about with caps on their coifs, waiting on residents who know each other and start their day regularly here.

Very inexpensive. Open 7:00 A.M. to 10:30 P.M. daily, and 10:30 A.M. to 2:00 P.M. and 4:00 P.M. to 9:30 P.M. daily except Sunday. Major credit cards accepted.

....

THE BEST LUAU

THE KONA VILLAGE LUAU
Ka'upulehu-Kona
Phone: (808) 325-5555

The Kona Village Luau is the best in Hawaii. It's not flawless, mind you, but it does have a healthy balance of good cuisine, atmosphere, and entertainment. This is a Polynesian, not exclusively Hawaiian, luau, which means there's Tahitian dance among the kahiko numbers and other borrowings from our South Pacific relatives. The imu ceremony is held in a kiawe grove where every Monday and Friday night a pig stuffed with hot rocks and wrapped in leaves bakes underground for six hours. More than anything else, it's the buffet that succeeds: banana pudding, papaya pudding, lomi salmon, squid with miso, poisson cru, taro, poke, lau lau (pork steamed in taro and ti leaves), the kalua pig, and a medley of other Hawaiian, Tahitian, and ethnic foods that are delicious and authentic. Most impressive is the presence of opihi, perhaps the rarest, most expensive, and most daring of Hawaiian foods, a potent-tasting limpet much loved by locals but rarely loved by newcomers. You dine in an open-air thatched pavilion with the moon behind you and the Polynesian show a small galaxy away, on elaborate stages on the other side of the lagoon. You'll see some good ancient hula with real ti leaf skirts and some mesmerizing Tahitian, and you'll wonder why all luaus aren't like this. Cost is $42 per person. Monday and Friday evenings only.

NIGHTLIFE AND ENTERTAINMENT

WEST HAWAII

In Kailua, the Kona Surf (322-3411) has a Polynesian show on Tuesday and Friday nights on the Nalu Terrace overlooking the ocean. There's no charge but a two-drink minimum is required. The nearby Puka Bar, a dark, claustrophobic cave, features contemporary and Hawaiian entertainment from 8:00 to 11:00 P.M. Those wishing to dance can wait until Tropical Storm hits the stage Friday and Saturday nights.

On Alii Drive in the heart of Kailua, the Spindrifter (329-1344) is making efforts to reformat its entertainment. There is nightly entertainment, and at the time of this writing they're attempting to include Hawaiian music. Entertainment goes from 9:00 P.M. to closing at 1:30 A.M. If the entertainment is good, you can't get better than this—tables outdoors, very close to the ocean, the bright Kona moon ascending. A pleasant place for late-night drinks; with Hawaiian music, so much the better.

The disco crowd is filling Mitchell's (322-9966), the sleek, chic new night spot in the Keauhou Shopping Village where outdoor tables offer a cool alternative to the packed room inside. A combination of retro and high tech, Mitchell's is the better of Kailua's two discos. However, the younger crowd and those without cars often head for the Eclipse (329-4686), closer to the center of town, located on Kuakini above Alii Drive.

Many head for the swank lounges in the South Kohala hotels for light jazz or Hawaiian music. Watch for the Lim Family. This very talented family of Hawaiian entertainers is everywhere, from the Mauna Kea's luau (882-7222) and the open-air Café Terrace to the Mauna Lani's Atrium bar (885-6622) in the middle of the hotel lobby. The Lims usually include at least one hula dancer in the show. Also at the Mauna Lani, at The Bar, Bill Noble plays jazz saxophone with his trio nightly.

The Sheraton Royal Waikoloa (885-6789) has its own lounge show in its showroom, where Hana Ho Hawaii holds forth six nights a week with everything from Broadway imitations to Hawaiian paniolo music and a Hawaiian variety show.

If you ever get a chance to hear Clyde Sproat, a paniolo singer and storyteller extraordinaire, don't miss him.

EAST HAWAII

Hilo's nightlife, in East Hawaii, may receive a massive infusion of new life if the very chic Roussels (935-5111), a popular restaurant, follows through with its plans to feature renowned mainland jazz ensembles after dinner. Programs in the past have included Richie Cole and Wyndham Hill artists, appearing only on special prearranged occasions. Call them to check if something's happening, although you may want to go there for dinner anyway. Also popular is the new Reflections Restaurant (935-0861), the hot spot for contemporary music and dancing, with a regularly changing roster of mainland groups that fills the lounge with young late-nighters.

Always swinging is Rosey's Boathouse, which has good contemporary Hawaiian music that draws a big crowd. Other than that, and some jazz piano at Harrington's (961-4966), the choices are slim and sporadic.

The Aston Naniloa (935-0831) may have a hula halau performing or a name group from Oahu, such as the Brothers Cazimero, Brother Noland, or Melveen Leed. When entertainers like them arrive, Hilo comes alive and the Crown Room is full.

Local entertainers to watch for: Beloved Hawaiian songbird Diane Aki, who plays a custom-made six-string ukelele and who has an admirable repertoire of old Hawaiian favorites. Although she rarely performs these days (much to her fans' chagrin), when she does it's usually in the Volcano area. Also watch for Kuulei Ahuna, one of the Big Island's best in contemporary Hawaiian music, and Nelson Waialae, easy-listening Hawaiian and contemporary music.

And don't ever miss an opportunity to see Johnny Lum Ho's hula halau perform. Ho is a noted kumu hula (hula master) and regular winner of the Merrie Monarch hula competition, whose dancers perform publicly on occasion.

SPECIAL OUTINGS: ON LAND

Golf

WESTIN MAUNA KEA GOLF COURSE
South Kohala
Telephone: (808) 882-7222

The rolling terrain and uphill lies makes this a challenging course with few plain old straight putts. Meliculous care is given to the greens and fairways so it's a fast course and one of the most challenging, if not the most challenging, in the state. *Golf Digest* calls the Mauna Kea one of the top one hundred in the country. When you play at this status course, you play where all the golf greats have played—on terrain ranging from brown lava to green grass to ocean's edge, with a view of the ocean from every green and tee. Golfers applaud the diversity of the course, from the third and eleventh holes—the ocean spectaculars—to the dramatic fourteenth with its Cypress Point effect. The eighteen-hole, par 72 course was designed by Robert Trent Jones, and has four sets of tees for varying degrees of difficulty. You can't get much better than playing with Mauna Kea, the mountain, on one side, and the ocean on the other.

Green fees are $60 for someone who's not a guest at the hotel and $30 for a guest, with a $12 charge for his or her share of the cart.

FRANCIS I'I BROWN GOLF COURSE
Mauna Lani Resort
South Kohala
Telephone: (808) 885-6655

The Mauna Lani course is celebrated for its dramatic lava sculptures amid stretches of chartreuse—an ebony and onyx landscape that has golfers reeling with its beauty. Literally carved into an ancient lava flow, the 6,813-yard, par 72 course is considered one of the most beautiful in the world. Ocean views and views of Mauna Kea and Hualalai dominate, but the landscaping and immaculate greens make this a course to remember. It's a course of color drama, with some challenge to the average player.

Fees are $50 for a hotel guest, which include the cart, and $60 for a nonguest.

Hiking

If you wish more detailed information on hiking on the Big Island, *Hawaiian Hiking Trails* by Craig Chisolm and *Hiking Hawaii* by Robert Smith are highly recommended. Or you can write to the park headquarters and request information on camping and hiking.

HAWAII VOLCANOES NATIONAL PARK
Hawaii, HI 96718
Telephone: (808) 967-7311

The best hiking on the island is in the Hawaii Volcanoes National Park, where you can explore lava tubes, fern forests, moonlike terrains, and steaming vents while Kilauea busily continues her own private show. One of the island's two active volcanoes, Kilauea has been in a steady eruptive phase since 1983.

According to a new program imposed by Congress, anyone who enters the park has a choice of paying $5 a car, $2 a person, or $15 for an annual pass. You pay as you enter the park at the headquarters just off Highway 11. If you plan to stay overnight, you must register at park headquarters. You should check on weather and trail conditions and replenish your water supply before you begin your hike. There are several types of detailed maps for sale at park headquarters that will help you get your bearings and outline your course. Also, because volcanic activity is constantly changing the area's topography and road access, it's important you are fully briefed on conditions.

There are at least eight major trails in the park, ranging from short one-hour loop trails from easily accessible trailheads to the three-day, 18.3-mile (one way) Mauna Loa Trail, one of the most difficult in the state and recommended only for the inveterate. Most hikers will choose something less debilitating, such as the vigorous four-hour Kilauea Iki Trail to the Thurston Lava Tube and back. The Kilauea Iki Trail, is a 4.5-mile loop at about a 4,000-foot altitude, crossing fern forests and the Byron Ledge looking into the crater.

There are short, pleasant strolls as well, such as the fifteen-minute walk to the Thurston Lava Tube from its parking area. A pleasant one-hour loop is the Bird Park Trail (Kipuka Puaulu), which takes you through meadows and one of the richest examples of native Hawaiian forest. If you're lucky you'll see rare honeycreepers such as the apapane and the i'iwi, both red-and-black birds that love the koa, ohia, and mamani trees found in the area.

While petroglyphs and several fishing villages have been found near Kamoamoa and Pu'u Loa at the coastline, ruins of only two heiau, or precontact temples, have been found near Kilauea caldera. Some observers speculate that the ancient Hawaiians kept a respectful distance from the domain of Pele, whose wrath they greatly feared.

Today, offerings such as gin wrapped in ti leaves still are made to the goddess of the volcano. There are other elements of protocol that bear remembering as well, the most important of them the caveat against removing any pieces of lava from the park. It's considered bad luck to remove any of Pele's outpourings. Superstition or not, those who defy the rule often send back their booty after sustained bouts of misfortune. At the Kilauea

Visitor Center, mounds of lava are received daily, accompanied with humorous, contrite, or fearful notes. Some of them are on display.

KONA HIKING CLUB
Telephone: (808) 332-3302

Although most of the Big Island's hiking trails are in the Hawaii Volcanoes National Park, there is some good hiking on back roads and through private gates in the Kailua area. The Kona Hiking Club leads hikes to accessible and not-so-accessible areas the first Saturday and third Thursday of each month. The hikes are free and are listed beforehand in *West Hawaii Today* and the *Hawaii Tribune Herald*. The outings range from historic sites in Kohala to gorgeous beaches with private access. A terrific service, and it's free.

Horseback Riding

IRONWOOD OUTFITTERS
Waimea
Telephone: (808) 885-4941

The ride takes you deep into the Kohala Mountains, at a 4,000-foot elevation that looks down over the western coastline and the rolling terrain of two ranches that sprawl over 30,000 continuous acres. The guides keep the rides personalized, with no more than ten to a group, and the views, over hills and misty ironwoods down to the ocean, are unequaled. The morning ride departs at 9:00 for three hours; the afternoon ride, by special arrangement only, leaves at 2:00. There are horses for both seasoned riders and neophytes. Rates, which may change, are about $48 for the morning ride or $22.50 per hour.

WAIONO MEADOWS
Holualoa
Telephone: (808) 329-0888

There's nothing like it in Hawaii: mountain rides and trout fishing in vast ranchlands, with a spectacular view of Kailua and the myriad greens cascading down to the coastline. The rides go through a 1,800-acre cattle ranch to a 3,000-foot elevation, with fishing on the way. Rides range from one hour ($17) to a lunch or breakfast ride for $38, which includes a two-hour mountain ride. The four-hour mountain and fishing ride ($65) allows half of the time for rainbow trout fishing at a reservoir, with lunch at water's edge. Riders return with unabashed enthusiasm while the anglers wax poetic about the trout fishing experience.

Museums and Historic Sights

LYMAN MUSEUM
276 Haili Street
Hilo
Telephone: (808) 935-5021

This is that rare entity, a comfortable, manageable, and enjoyable museum that will not exhaust you with its magnitude. Named after one of the original missionary families in Hilo, the museum was established in 1932 and houses an extensive collection of Hawaiian artifacts, from canoe paddles and stone implements to fiber work and *haku hulu*, the intricate art of featherwork. Impressive examples of kapa cloth and pili grass structures are here, as well as the Taoist shrines and antique Japanese stoneware that came later with the waves of immigrants beginning in 1885. Not to be missed is the Earth Heritage Gallery with the Pacific's largest mineral collection—26,000 specimens—and the world's only museum collection of Hawaiian land shells. It is also enlightening to peer into the Maui moonstones or the white bloedite crust from Mauna Loa or the epsomite stalactite from Kilauea's Mauna Ulu Crater. Next door is the Lyman Mission House, listed in the State and National Registers of Historic Places. The museum gift shop has an admirable selection of island books, jewelry, crafts, and gifts. Closed Tuesday and Sunday. Admission is $3.

While you're at Lyman Museum, pick up a copy of their walking tour of Hilo, a brochure that will guide you through sixteen of the city's ethnic and cultural delights, from historic buildings to old churches and wharves from the nineteenth century. You'll learn that this quaint, provincial town was populated by Hawaiians in 1100, and that they traded their goods along the rushing Wailuku River in the northern part of town.

PUAKO

The Puako petroglyph field is the largest on the island, one of many remnants of the ancient culture that thrived on the western shoreline. The petroglyphs are a substantial walk from the road in a residential area not far from Hapuna beach just south of the Mauna Kea. These are some of Hawaii's finest and largest rock carvings, some of them reaching several feet in size. To get there, take Puako Beach Road and follow the shoreline. Watch for the petroglyph sign on the mountain side of the road.

PU'UKOHOLA HEIAU NATIONAL HISTORIC SITE
Kawaihae

Built by Kamehameha I in 1790–91, Pu'ukohola, or "hill of the whale," is the last major religious structure of the ancient Hawaiians to be built in Hawaii. Today visitors must view the massive structure from below because the temple site is crumbling. Platforms, terraces, thatched houses, a prayer tower, and other religious features were built and in use at the turn of the century, but today only the stone structure remains. Kamehameha built the heiau in honor of his family war god, Kuka'ilimoku. It is said the heiau helped him fulfill the prophecy that he would conquer the islands. Indeed, his rival from the other part of the island was slain near the heiau and offered as a sacrifice to the family war god. The heiau is near Spencer Beach Park off of the north Kohala coastal route.

Skiing

SKI GUIDES HAWAII
P.O. Box 2020
Waimea, HI 96743
Telephone: (808) 885-4188

Chris Langan was a ski guide for nine years on Mauna Kea, learning the ins and outs of the "pineapple powder" that blankets the 13,796-foot-high summit. Now he and his partner run Ski Guides Hawaii, the unofficial information center on skiing on Mauna Kea and also a rental, guide, and tour service with a full menu of choices. You don't need anything to ski with them; they provide transportation, clothing, equipment, lunches, and instruction, if needed. They have thirty different brands of skis to choose from, will pick you up at designated points and then, conditions permitting, take you on a day tour (12,000 to 13,796 feet), single runs, five-mile runs, designer tours (completely personalized), and the "ski to the sea" special of skiing in the morning and swimming in the afternoon. Because access is by four-wheel drive vehicles and ski areas may harbor hidden rocks, their service and expertise are valuable. The new water-ski service offers water-skiing on the South Kohala coast year-round, picnics on secluded beaches, ski instruction, and access to otherwise unreachable bays and coves. Rates vary; the snow-skiing day tour is about $120, the super-deluxe "ali'i ski tour," twice as much.

Special Excursions

AKAKA FALLS
Honomu

The path to the lookout over the waterfall meanders through vegetation so thick the sun can barely shine through. All around is the sound of water—first from the stream, and then, as you near the falls, from the powerful cascade of the 420-foot Akaka Falls. It's a hike to the lookout from the parking lot and there aren't many places to sit down, but it's an easy uphill hike on a well-paved path. Azaleas, hapu'u ferns, lush bamboo, impatiens, gingers, and mosses line the path beside the stream. No swimming is allowed, however, and when you finally get there you must view the waterfalls from a distance. Kahuna Falls is the smaller of the two; Akaka, at the end of the walk, is a thundering, deafening cascade that drops like a fern-covered tube. The moist, sweet air is refreshing on this invigorating nature walk. To get there, drive to Honomu on Route 19, then take Route 22 to the end.

HAWAII TROPICAL BOTANICAL GARDEN
Onomea Bay
Telephone: (808) 964-5233

If it's not raining and if you've come prepared to wage battle against mosquitoes and pay $6 to see beautiful plants, this could be for you. Nature lovers will delight in this 17-acre Eden of lily ponds, waterfalls, streams, wildlife, and irrepressible fecundity. More than 1,000 species of plants, some extremely rare, flourish here along with forest and shore birds. The real coup is the garden's location, combining the best of valley and shoreline. The drive to the garden is itself an adventure: a 4-mile detour from Highway 19 that leads you along a pristine shoreline of black-pebbled coves and tree-covered promontories, across ancient bridges and overlooks. This is a drive you must not miss, if not for the sheer beauty of the landscape, then surely for the tantalizing fruit that may dangle from the trees like so many enticements. Shuttle service offered from parking lot to the garden. Open 9:00 A.M. to 5:00 P.M. daily.

NORTH KOHALA

There are two routes to the top of the island: one on the coastline and the other inland, through pasture and ranchland where velvet of a million greens has blanketed the Big Island's oldest mountains. The inland route to Hawi or Kapa'au, where the King Kamehameha statue stands, is what residents commonly call "the best drive on the island." On an island where driving never ends, that's quite a distinction. See for yourself: At the top of Waimea, past the Opelu Plaza, a sign points to Hawi via Highway 250, the Kohala Mountain Road. The road leads through mist-covered pastureland, heading straight through the Kohala Mountains at a nearly 4,000-foot elevation. Sky-high ironwoods and eucalyptus trees border the cinder cones that have long been covered with green, and the salutary air is a relief. When you get to Hawi, continue on to the Pulolu Valley lookout for a consummate view of the north coast.

VOLCANO ARTISTS STUDIO VISITS
Volcano Artists

The rarefied atmosphere of the Volcano area attracts artists like a magnet. They work quietly in the creative atmosphere of a 4,000-foot-high live volcano, producing works that are displayed nationally as well as locally. Five of these artists, working in different media, have opened their studios to the public, free, on an appointment basis. These visits are highly recommended, as an adventure off the beaten track. You won't find tour buses, crowded elevators, air pollution, or condescending tour guides. What you will find are some fine people in pristine surroundings, offering you a more personal view of Hawaii and of how islanders live and work.

Pam Barton: Barton's fiber art is well known in Hawaii, where the environment and its plants are an integral part of her work. She gathers vines, leaves, bark, and the sheddings of trees and nature and then fashions them into hangings, baskets, and sculptures of many dimensions. She greets you with a warm smile and when you sit amid the vines and roots of her exquisite nature sculptures, it's like taking a cool walk in the forest. Telephone: (808) 967-7247.

Marian Berger: You don't have to be a naturalist to appreciate her watercolors of native birds and flora. Most of the birds are endangered and some of them, such as the o'o, extinct. Hawaii's premier wildlife watercolorist, Berger paints with meticulous detail, studying skins from the Smithsonian and other museums and from her own findings from many years in Volcano. Her precision and skill are astounding: the palila on the mamane tree (it's only found on Mauna Kea) and the apapane with the akala blossoms are too good to be true. Telephone: (808) 967-8195.

Chiu Leong: A Chiu Leong pot has cachet. He is best known for his moonlike raku but also does pit firing and high-fire ceramics with mysterious, lustrous glazes. Although his pots are generally nonfunctional, some of them have limited uses, such as the classic bowls for the tea ceremony and his wonderful collection of stoneware and porcelain and, most recently, the handmade, hand-painted, ultra-deluxe tiles. Leong works in an airy, geometric studio accented by otherworldly pots and surrounded by giant ferns and sugi pines. Telephone: (808) 967-7637.

Boone Morrison: Morrison has been photographing the hula, the landscape, and volcanic eruptions for years, and he does it with a ceaseless passion. He has done books, posters, and exhibits and is represented in galleries throughout the state, primarily in black and white. Morrison also knows the Big Island as few people do, having captured in print the character of some of its more remote, isolated communities, which he defends and protects with zeal. Telephone: (808) 967-7512.

Ira Ono: Ono's work—ceramic masks, wall hangings, body ornaments— and his view of life make him an artist you won't forget. His masks evolved into the Trashface Collection, the current rage in stylish New York boutiques. Found objects, from minuscule stamps to Japanese rice paper, are arranged with miniature masks into one-of-a-kind compositions for the ear, throat, and wrist. Working in his glassed-in aerie, Ono continues to compose his bold accessories, such as the hand-held opera mask encrusted with objects. Besides being esthetic, bold, and imaginative, his pieces have a sense of humor. Telephone: (808) 967-7261.

Tours

MAUNA KEA SUMMIT TOURS
P.O. Box 5128
Kukuihaele, HI 96727
Telephone: (808) 775-7121

Customized van tours will take you to the heights of Mauna Kea and to everything in between, with a tour guide who is pleasant, informed, and trained to handle emergencies that might arise from the thin air of such high altitudes. The five- to six-hour tour includes lunch at slightly below the 9,000-foot level, hotel pickup at an extra charge, a visit to the observatory at the summit, and a comfortable, informative foray into one of the world's great wonders, Mauna Kea. The van holds four to twelve people, which means you won't be part of a herd. The moonlike terrain toward the summit is surreal; you can have a snowball fight during some months, and when the skies are clear the view is incomparable. There are a number of advantages to the tour over attempting Mauna Kea on your own: Car rentals forbid use of their cars on the Saddle Road, which provides access to Mauna Kea; after the visitor center at the 9,000-foot level, the road becomes passable by four-wheel-drive vehicles only; and standard automobiles often fail at such high altitudes. The summit tour departs from Waimea and is run by the owners of the highly reputable Waipio Valley Shuttle, who know all about educational, lively excursions to remote and exotic places. Cost is about $65. Tours run daily.

WAIPIO VALLEY SHUTTLE
P.O. Box 5128
Kukuihaele, HI 96727
Telephone: (808) 775-7121

Waipio Valley opens the door to the lush northern tip of the island, where the deep valleys of the Kohala Mountains—the island's oldest—line the shoreline one by one in a series of splendid sweeps. Only the intrepid, the inordinately strong, and the most determined of hikers will ever glimpse the island's hidden northern shore. Pololu Valley is the sentinel to the north, Waipio Valley the door to the south. Waipio is the crown of the island, the last accessible valley before the remote north-shore valleys begin.

Waipio is also the Big Island's largest valley, 6 miles long and 1 mile wide at the shoreline. Most visitors approach the valley on the Waipio Valley Shuttle and its four-wheel-drive vehicles that can negotiate the steep, rugged road to the valley floor. But first, the lookout: It offers a glimpse of waterfalls plunging to the sea, of white waves on black sand where more than a few tsunami have crossed. A switchback trail, very steep, climbs up the other side of the valley.

The guide, who is likely to have grown up in Waipio, will tell you that it's five hours to the next valley by foot or horseback, and that the valley was populated by nearly 2,000 Hawaiians who fished, grew taro, and worshipped their gods before westerners arrived. Only a handful of people live in the valley today amid the taro, coconuts, mountain apples, kamani, lichees, avocados, bananas, and waterfalls, including the 1,200-foot Hi'ilawe twin falls. A few of the residents pick Waipio Valley fern shoots, or fiddleheads, for restaurants and the South Kohala hotels that feature them as a gourmet item. The guide will stop at the beach, pick medicinal plants on the way, and perhaps break a coconut for the tasting. It is a wonderful escape to the past.

To get there, take Route 240 to Kukuihaele. The tour is an hour and a half long; the starting point is an hour and a half from Kona and the same distance from Hilo. Cost is $15 for adults, $5 for children. Tours are offered daily.

SPECIAL OUTINGS:
IN AND ON THE WATER

Fishing Charters

Kailua is brimming with able captains and commercial fishing charters. After all, the waters here are considered the premier blue marlin fishing grounds in the world. A few of the old-timers and respected skippers considered the tops in town are Fred Rice, the *Ihunui;* Rick Rose, the *Aerial IV;* Bobby Brown, the *No Problem;* Jeff Fay, the *Humdinger;* Peter Hoogs, the *Pamela;* Del Cannon, the *Annetta;* Tom Rogers, the *Kona Safari;* Steve Rooney, the *Holiday;* John Llanes, the *Island Girl;* John Tanaka, Adobie Sport Fishing.

The Kona Charter Skippers Association, Inc., (808) 329-3600, is the place to call for charter fishing information and bookings. Located across the Kailua Pier, they book all the activities in the area and will book share charters and full charters on more than fifty boats in all price ranges. Rates range from $250 to $500 for a full day to $175 to $350 for a half day. On shares, the rates are $85 on a half day and $125 on a full day.

The Kona Coast Activities Center, (808) 329-2971, has desks at various hotels in town and will also book charters, cruises, and the full gamut of activities. Like the Skippers Association, they'll tell you what you can expect in the way of boat size, meals, whether there are restrooms on board, etc.

One thing to remember is that usually the catch stays with the boat. If that is a problem for you, make that clear before you book.

An invaluable resource on any ocean activity is Kamuela Leisure's Sheri Shaw, telephone (808) 322-2023 or 322-6501. Shaw knows everything: who's doing what, who's good, and how to match you with what you need in all aspects of ocean activities, from snorkeling to fishing and scuba. Most important, she puts your needs and budget first.

Snorkeling, Scuba, and Dinner Cruises

CAPTAIN BEAN'S
Kailua
Telephone: (808) 329-2955

Everybody has fun on Captain Bean's cruises. The Tahitian drums begin before you board, easing away your inhibitions so you can join in the fun.

The Polynesian-style *Tamure* is 150 by 50 feet and run by a cordial, professional staff.

The morning cruise begins at 8:30 and goes to Kealakekua Bay for forty-five minutes of snorkeling, with lunch, Polynesian dancers, coconut hat weaving, and the like. Ideal for children, seniors, and less demanding snorkelers. It costs $20 for the four-and-a-half-hour cruise. There's also a glass-bottom boat cruise that leaves Kailua at 1:30 P.M., one hour long and $10 per person.

The dinner cruise is one of Kailua's most popular activities, departing daily at 5:15 P.M. for two hours. There's an open bar, entertainment, and laughs galore as even blue-haired ladies from Hoboken learn to sway their hips in the famous Kona sunset. Adults only for the dinner cruise, $35 per person.

FAIR WIND
Keauhou Bay
Telephone: (808) 322-2788

Fair Wind serves lunch on board and offers the most snorkeling time, which makes it the boat for serious snorkelers. There are two trips a day: at 8:30 A.M. and 1:00 P.M. to Kealakekua Bay, where you spend two and a half hours hours snorkeling in a state marine preserve. It is protected, calm, and the visibility is always good. *Fair Wind* is the only boat with a mooring in the cove area because they've been going there for fifteen years. It costs $45; the vessel is a 50-foot trimaran with an upper sundeck, glass bottom, a shaded cabin, two restrooms, and a bar. They'll troll for fish on the way back.

The afternoon trip offers an hour and a half of snorkeling, with lunch. There is every kind of gear imaginable, from inner tubes to view boxes and prescription masks—even underwater cameras for an extra charge. Scuba diving also offered.

HAWAIIAN PRINCESS
Kailua
Telephone: (808) 329-6411

This is the cruise for those seeking a quieter, more romantic, and more intimate ambience than the party-hearty Captain Bean's. The 95-foot monohull, *Hawaiian Princess,* has a bowsprit for unequaled sunset viewing; there's an open bar and dinner seating over white linens indoors. At the stern, a kiawe charcoal grill puts out barbecued steaks and fish. In summer months when ono (wahoo) is running and during other fish seasons, you get grilled fresh catch. Over a Kona sunset, that's hard to beat. The entertainment is low-key, mostly Hawaiian with a few hula numbers and rudimentary hula lessons on demand. For dinner, the maximum number carried is usually seventy-five. Cost is $29.50 for the dinner cruise, departing at 6:00 P.M. nightly from Kailua Pier.

KONA SEA ADVENTURES
Keauhou Bay
Telephone: (808) 322-6501

The 40-foot sailing catamaran, called the *Kaliana*, is a good choice for families who want to snorkel and scuba dive on the same trip, and without spending a fortune. Snorkeling, scuba, and sunset cruises are offered, and the prices are right: $20 for snorkelers on a three-hour trip with one and a half hours of snorkeling; $55 for a one-tank dive on the same three-hour trip. Usually they go to Kealakekua Bay, but they will go north to other sites when conditions are right. The food is light—appetizers and drinks only—but this is a good choice for serious snorkelers. Also available are a 15-foot glass-bottom boat and bookings on charter boats with lower rates than most.

Whale Watching

The first whales of the year are usually sighted in November, when they begin arriving for their annual winter sojourn. Most whale-watching operations, however, begin their cruises in December or January when there are more of them to be seen and they are more comfortable in Hawaiian waters. The season continues until mid-April. The best whale-watching operations are those that employ naturalists or research biologists who can provide good insights on whales while looking out for their well-being.

Vessels are required to remain 100 yards away from the whales, but many don't. It's important to choose an operation that doesn't exploit or harass the whales, for they are sensitive creatures who come to Hawaiian waters to give birth.

HAWAIIAN CRUISES
Kailua
Telephone: (808) 329-6411

They have two boats, the *Hawaiian Princess*, a sleek 95-footer, and the *Captain Cook VII*, a 96-foot glass-bottom boat. Both offer various snorkel and dinner cruises all year and, during whale season, comfortable cruises among the friendly leviathans.

What makes their whale-watching cruises the best is their research biologist Dan McSweeney, who has been researching whales in Kona for fourteen years. Employed by the West Coast Whale Research Foundation headquartered in Canada and the mainland, McSweeney specializes in humpback and pilot whales in Hawaii and killer whales and humpbacks in Alaska. Experts like him enhance the trip with their educational insights and up-to-the-minute contacts with sighting networks. McSweeney conducts whale-watching cruises on both *Captain Cook VII* and the *Hawaiian Princess*. The 3¼-hour swim and snorkel cruise and the whale-watching cruise on both vessels cost $17.30. If you want more information on whales, write the West Coast Whale Research Foundation, P.O. Box 139, Holualoa, HI 96725.

BEACHES

....

WEST HAWAII

The beaches are listed going north to south along the west Hawaii coastline. For more information on Big Island beaches, their legends, and history, *The Beaches of Hawaii County* by John Clark is an excellent resource. (East Hawaii beaches follow this section.)

Samuel M. Spencer Beach Park

Spencer is very popular and therefore never empty. On one side of the large pavilion is a white-sand crescent; on the other, a small, rocky black lagoon. Concrete steps from the stone pavilion lead right into the water, which is clear and inviting, rocky but fine for snorkeling. Besides great swimming and snorkeling, there are facilities for camping, picnicking, and tennis, plus large restrooms and extensive grassy areas. On a hill overlooking the beach is the Pu'ukohola Heiau of Kamehameha the Great.

Hapuna Beach

With its modern facilities and clean, wide sweep of white sand, Hapuna is the Big Islanders' favorite beach. On good days the bodysurfing is peerless and the waves ideal for children and adults. The beach stretches for more than a half mile and during summer months, the sand builds up to a width of hundreds of feet. You can bodysurf but not board surf at Hapuna, making this a haven for the island's bodysurfers, many of whom drive here from the other side of the island. During winter months, be extremely cautious; the riptide may be treacherous.

Waialea (Beach 69)

Only minutes south of Hapuna, Waialea Beach, called Beach 69, is the favorite of local residents who brave the rocky road to it with their four-wheel drives for lazy summer days on a wide, sloping, sheltered beach. The small bay also attracts windsurfers and sailors, so there can be considerable beach activity on a sunny day. You're on your own here; there are no showers or running water. It's located just minutes south of Hapuna, down a dirt road by a pole numbered 69.

Honokohau Beach

Hundreds of archaeological sites have been found in the area, including three major fish ponds and several smaller ones that infuse the bay with brackish water. Pockets of white sand alternate with lava outcroppings, and a protective reef provides good snorkeling. This is a popular spot for Big Island nudists, who like the seclusion and excellent snorkeling along the rocky part of the shoreline. Although fishermen love this beach too, and so do swimmers and bodysurfers, it is largely the domain of the nudists. To get there, park near Honokahau Harbor, off Queen Ka'ahumanu Highway, and walk along the shoreline.

Anaeho'omalu

Anaeho'omalu Bay is at the very edge of the Kaniku Lava Flow and marks the point where the South Kohala District meets the North Kona District. The Sheraton Royal Waikoloa is situated on this gorgeous beach, a beach close to petroglyphs and fish ponds and frequented by sunbathers, swimmers, fishermen, and windsurfers. There are park and restroom facilities for the public at the edge of the beach and in the middle of it, beach equipment rentals. Because the hotel is on it, however, the beach is never deserted; a short walk south to Kapalaoa may be more rewarding. Access to Anaeho'omalu is through the entrance to the Sheraton Royal Waikoloa.

White Sands Beach

Aside from the small beach fronting the King Kamehameha Hotel, White Sands is the only beach for swimming in the main part of Kailua. When there's enough sand, the beach can be crowded. And when the waves are good, the waters are dotted with happy bodysurfers and boogie boarders. White Sands Beach is also called Magic Sands and Disappearing Sands Beach (the sand "leaves" in the winter) and is an unforgettable sight along Alii Drive. In summer months when the sand returns, the wide, white-sand beach is in its glory, and so are the million sunbathing bodies lying end-to-end on the small shore.

Napo'opo'o Beach Park

It's crowded and rocky, but the snorkeling, if you find safe entry, is fantastic. Kealakekua Bay offshore is a marine preserve, making this a bay of spectacular underwater sights in spite of its hordes of visitors and boaters. Many are drawn by the historic significance of this area: This is where British explorer Captain James Cook met his demise in 1779. On the far side of the bay, a white marker points to the site. Residents who swim here before the crowds arrive rave about the crystal clarity of the deep teal waters. To get there, take the road to Kealakekua Bay from Highway 11.

Pu'uhonua O Honaunau Park

There is a picnic and beach area worth exploring in the southern section of the grounds of Pu'uhonua O Honaunau, the Place of Refuge and National Historic Park. There are cliffs and tidal pools for beautiful shoreline exploration and, to the south, a small bay. The park discourages use of the beach in certain areas of the park, but snorkeling is good from the boat ramp adjoining it. Caution is always advised in the waters, expecially in the winter months.

Ho'okena Beach Park

Ho'okena was once a thriving fishing village. Hala (pandanus) trees planted by families of old still line the shoreline in some areas. Fish ponds, housing sites, and salt ponds are still visible in the area as well, even though the community has long since moved to higher ground. At the shoreline is Kauhako Bay, bordered by low cliffs and patches of sandy shoreline. There is a small white-sand beach near the park, but the currents are tricky. You can drive down to the park from Highway 11 in a rented car, and if you're lucky the gate on the north side of the park, near a residential section, will be open, giving you access to some great snorkeling areas.

EAST HAWAII

Apart from a few exceptions, east Hawaii beaches are anything but white. Black and gray beaches (and a few green) are the norm here, the result of years of erosion over the a'a—slow-moving, crumbly lava—that flowed to the sea in past eruptions. This lends an exotic, primal air to the business of beach going on the Big Island. In its most general terms, east Hawaii covers the beaches from Naalehu and up the east coast. We have made an exception here and included the Green Sand Beach near South Point. The beaches are listed north to south. For more information on Big Island beaches, facilities, and water safety, see John Clark's handy reference, *The Beaches of the Big Island.*

ONEKAHAKAHA BEACH PARK
Hilo

When the sun is out, all of Hilo can be found at its only white-sand beach, Onekahakaha. It will be crowded, and it won't compare with Hapuna and south Kohala's more glamorous beaches. However, the shallow, protected pool of Onekahakaha is popular among Hilo residents and children, who line the shoreline with their picnics on sunny Hilo days. If Onekahakaha is too tame or too crowded, nearby shoreline areas harbor tidal pools and pretty inlets ideal for picnics and exploring.

LELEIWI BEACH PARK
Hilo

Located right next to the Richardson Ocean Center in Hilo, this beautiful black-sand beach is at the easternmost point of Hilo, directly east of Hilo

Bay. There are ponds and coves in this area of shallow, clear waters where Hilo residents love to snorkel and swim. There is a retaining wall in the area next to the Richardson Ocean Center. This is a dramatically scenic part of the shoreline, particularly when Hilo fishermen can be seen throwing their nets in the inlets and surfers are riding the waves offshore. There are pavilions in the park, and the seawall is a great spot for quiet contemplation of the ocean's beauty. The infusion of fresh water from the pools nearby adds a crystalline clarity to the water, particularly in the lee areas of the point.

KALAPANA BEACH
Harry K. Brown Beach Park
Kalapana

Many people refer to the nearby and better-known Kaimu Black Sand Beach as Kalapana, but this is the real Kalapana. Kalapana Beach, fronting the Harry K. Brown Beach Park, is recommended over its more celebrated neighbor because it's equally beautiful and safer for swimming. Bordered by coconut and hala trees, the broad, black curve is a favorite of swimmers, sunbathers, and surfers. The surrounding area includes a heiau, remnants of an ancient village, and a large freshwater pond where there used to be a canoe landing. Kids like to swim in the lovely, sandy pond because the ocean is often too rough for the inexperienced. Offshore is Drainpipes, a favored Big Island surfing spot and site of an annual surf meet. Caution is advised for those unfamiliar with the waters. Pavilions and restrooms nearby.

PUNALU'U BEACH
Punalu'u

This black-sand beach is the only accessible swimming site in Ka'u. The long curve is fringed by one of the district's few coconut groves, and to the southeast are concrete remnants from its days as a thriving commercial pier. Not far away are a heiau, churches, and other signs of a once-thriving village, as well as the last spring-fed pond to have survived the tsunamis that have hit the area. During some periods of the year Punalu'u residents can be seen picking seaweed and fishing near this gentle slope of black sand while their children swim in the safer northern area of the bay. Punalu'u is the site of the so-called "birth pebbles," pebbles that emerge out of others when the lava that bonds them is washed away. There are showers, tables, campsites, and restrooms in the park.

GREEN SAND BEACH
(Papakolea Beach)
South Point

If you have a four-wheel-drive vehicle you can explore Green Sand Beach near South Point and many other spots that don't accommodate standard vehicles. Also called Papakolea or Mahana, the green-sand beach is illuminated and colored by crushed olivine, one of the minerals occurring in lava. The green-sand beach is about 3 miles north of South Point and is reached via a rugged dirt road less than 3 miles from the Kaulana Boat Ramp. There are no lifeguards or conveniences on this isolated beach, so extreme caution is advised, even when negotiating the hike down the cliff to the cove below. The beach should only be approached in extremely calm conditions, for the small cove can be covered with water when the seas are rough. An outing to Green Sand Beach is recommended only for the hardy, or for those seeking seclusion and novelty.

SHOPPING

··

WEST HAWAII

In addition to the chic and pricey boutiques in the Mauna Lani and Mauna Kea resorts, the following west Hawaii shops offer good browsing in a variety of areas and for all pocketbooks.

ALOHA VILLAGE STORE
Route 11
Kainaliu
Telephone: (808) 322-9941

You can find everything from Caswell-Massey soaps to Big Island pottery and woven bags from Indonesia, South America, or Africa. You can also stock up on health foods and produce, such as the famous Sam's Big Island pumpkins that always sell out. This is a health food store with Big Island macadamia nut butters, cards, jewelry by Big Island artists, and those proverbial souvenirs, hand-screened T-shirts.

Open 8:00 A.M. to 8:00 P.M. weekdays, until 6:00 P.M. on Saturday, and 9:00 A.M. to 4:00 P.M. Sunday. Major credit cards accepted.

GALLERY OF GREAT THINGS
Waimea Design Center
Waimea
Telephone: (808) 885-6171

You can shop the Pacific here, from New Guinea artifacts to Hawaiian white lehua honey and Sumatra woven bags. If the nineteenth-century Thai silver box doesn't do, there are always the shell necklaces from Rarotonga or baskets from the Cook Islands. The parade of Big Island gifts is long and varied, from locally made chopsticks of exotic and elegant woods to cards and beautiful bowls made of native woods. Gifts to go abound here.

Open 9:00 A.M. to 5:00 P.M. Monday through Saturday. Major credit cards accepted.

HOBIE SPORTS
Kona Inn Shopping Village
Kailua
Telephone: (808) 329-1001

The store is a must for any beach goer—not only to stock up on the best surfboards and flip-flops, but also to scope out the swimwear, visors, and towels as well. State-of-the-art body boards and everything from aloha shirts and T-shirts to sun gels, blocks, lotions, and glasses (all the best lines, including Vuarnet and Revo)—everything you need for sunning or swimming—fill this colorful, tiny shop with its helpful, tanned sales clerks. Start here if you're going to spend time in the sun.

Open 9:00 A.M. to 9:00 P.M. daily. Major credit cards accepted.

KEALAKEKUA'S GRASS SHACK
Route 11
Kealakekua
Telephone: (808) 323-2877

The sign beckons from the main road like a postcard from the past. At first it looks like so many trinkets, but look closer. Niihau shells and Kamaka ukeleles, sugi pine bowls, feathered gourds for hula dancing, coffee wood walking sticks, and such novelties as coffee wood *lomi lomi* (Hawaiian massage) sticks and $4 koa chopsticks make this an eventful stop. Magnificent milo bowls and rare island hardwoods fill the store, which contains 98 percent locally made items.

Open 9:00 A.M. to 5:30 P.M. Monday through Saturday and noon to 4:00 P.M. Sunday. No credit cards accepted.

KIMURA LAUHALA SHOP
Mamalahoa Highway
Holualoa
Telephone: (808) 324-0053

Tsuruyo Kimura is in her eighties; the shop is one of a kind and is a legend among weavers. It began in the old days of bartering and represents a slice of Hawaiian history, when hala (pandanus) trees were abundant in Kona and there were many to weave its leaves in the old Hawaiian way. But today the weavers are elderly, the work remains arduous, and many people have long since chopped down their hala trees to plant coffee instead. Kimura has maintained the tradition and kept some of her weavers, doing the finishing herself on many of the items. And although lauhala weaving is a dwindling art, Kona lauhala (woven hala leaves) is still distinctive because of its suppleness, sheen, color, and resilience. The shop is filled with mats, purses, hats, coasters, hangings—all manner of lauhala and other fiber handicrafts. Kimura's is one of a handful of places left in Hawaii where you can find high-quality, made-in-Hawaii lauhala hats in stock.

Open 9:00 A.M. to 5:00 P.M. Monday through Saturday. If it's urgent, you can call on Sunday and she'll open for you if she's home. No credit cards.

NOA NOA
Kona Inn Shopping Village
Kailua
Telephone: (808) 329-8187

This is a fascinating shop of Balinese handicrafts, from baskets and carved wooden implements to rattan lombok baskets of a tight, solid weave. Hand-painted Balinese cottons and pareus—those exotic long wraps of hand-painted or screened prints—wave in the breeze while the scent of wood and reeds fills the shop. There are Balinese masks, Timor ikat bags, and even Balinese versions of the aloha shirt, in batik or silk-screened cottons. Delightful.

Open 9:00 A.M. to 9:00 P.M. daily. Major credit cards accepted.

SUZUMI
Ironwood Center
Waimea
Telephone: (808) 885-6422

This is the stop for the new swimsuit you've been coveting or the cotton muumuu that's a cut above. Suzumi has a large selection of made-in-Hawaii sportswear: swimwear by Raisins, silk-screened T-shirts, Kauaiana tropical dresses, Laura Lewis hand-painted silks. From the casual and inexpensive to the more discriminating, Suzumi has a great representation of island sportswear that has nothing to do with the matching-aloha-shirt-and-muumuu polyester pairings that are so tacky. Ask about the J. C. Designs muumuus by a Waimea designer—dainty cotton with a surprise in front, a silk-screened quilt design. Not your ordinary muumuu by any means.

Open 9:30 A.M. to 5:30 P.M. Monday through Thursday, until 6:00 P.M. on Friday, and until 5:00 P.M. on Saturday, and from 11:00 A.M. to 4:00 P.M. on Sunday. Major credit cards accepted.

UNISON
75-5695 H Alii Drive
Kailua
Telephone: (808) 329-2343

Go to the ocean corner of the shop and check out their Sensi rubber zoris made in Italy and definitely the haute couture of beach sandals. Their perforated tops and polyurethane material will send sand through the sandal and out—without squeaking or rubbing! You can spend about $15 for a fashionable pair in pastel and gray and change your beachcombing life forever. Jimmy Z sportswear (the rage among teens), Italian Boys T-shirts, and a spate of sweatshirts (Ton Sur Tons, made in Portugal) and casual wear round out the very hip sportswear selection.

Open 9:00 A.M. to 9:00 P.M. Monday through Saturday and 10:00 A.M. to 6:00 P.M. Sunday. Major credit cards accepted.

WAIMEA GENERAL STORE
Waimea Design Center
Waimea
Telephone: (808) 885-4479

What else could it be but an old-fashioned country store? Heady with the fragrance of Crabtree and Evelyn soaps and peppered with exotic teas and preserve jars, the general store is a worthy stop. Native wood crafts, a goodly selection of Hawaii books, Japanese yukatas and hapi coats, and gorgeous, handwoven cotton shawls also beckon from the crowded shelves.

Open 9:00 A.M. to 5:00 P.M. Monday through Saturday and 10:00 A.M. to 4:00 P.M. Sunday. Major credit cards accepted.

YUGEN
Spencer House
Mamalahoa Highway
Waimea
Telephone: (808) 885-7007

Waimea batik artist Carolyn Ainsworth has a large selection of her fluttering silk dresses here, as well as linen jackets and suits for mature women with elegant taste. Natural fiber clothing is in abundance, most of it fashioned by the best designers on the Big Island. This is the kind of clothing you'd wear to brunch at the Mauna Kea or to a dance concert at Volcano—chic, imaginative, art-to-wear. No wonder this tiny, tony boutique has a big following. Ask about the Ira Ono Trashface earrings—the best—and Sig Zane's quilted jackets, Laura Lewis's Silks by Hand, or C. Marie's upscale jackets and suits. They're world class—and made right on the island.

Open 11:30 A.M. to 5:00 P.M. Monday and Tuesday, 10:00 A.M. to 5:00 P.M. Wednesday through Friday, and noon to 4:00 P.M. Saturday. Major credit cards accepted.

....

EAST HAWAII

BASICALLY BOOKS
169 Keawe Street
Hilo
Telephone: (808) 961-0144

Consider this the most necessary first stop on the Big Island. The bountiful selection of maps and miscellany makes this the best place to get your bearings. You can browse interminably among its travel books, nautical charts, U.S. Geological Survey maps (the Cadillacs of cartography), street maps, plastic raised relief maps, out-of-print books, and wonderful assortment of globes, compasses, atlases, and such. The store specializes in material about Hawaii and the Pacific and is suited to anyone with an interest in Hawaii. The company will ship anywhere and will even order USGS maps that are not kept in stock.

Open 9:00 A.M. to 5:00 P.M. weekdays and 10:00 A.M. to 4:00 P.M. Saturday. Major credit cards accepted.

HAWAIIAN HANDCRAFT
760 Kilauea Avenue
Hilo
Telephone: (808) 935-5587

Dan Deluz is a prolific and gifted artist who shapes native woods into fine, luminous pieces. His shop, Hawaiian Handcraft, has the largest selection in Hilo of bowls made of rare woods: curly koa, olopua, Portuguese cypress, ohia, Hawaiian sandalwood, milo, kamani, mango, macadamia, and many others from Hawaii's forests. Glistening koa boxes and calabashes fill this shop, along with smaller gift items such as rice paddles and lauhala headbands. Interspersed among the Deluz bowls are pieces by noted Big Island wood sculptor Jay Warner, who makes museum quality koa boxes. A softspoken man with a big heart, Deluz has been turning wood for nearly twenty years; many have been collecting his bowls for as long.

Open 9:00 A.M. to 5:00 P.M. weekdays, 10:00 A.M. to 3:00 P.M. Saturday. Major credit cards accepted.

SIG ZANE DESIGNS
140 Kilauea Avenue
Hilo
Telephone: (808) 935-7077

Head for the bright yellow awning and leave ample time for browsing. This shop deserves it. From its lauhala mat on the floor to the bright pareus on the wall, it expresses the joie de vivre of Hawaii and the creativity of its contemporary artists. Big Island designer Sig Zane's distinctive Hawaiian prints appeared first in T-shirts (a big seller at the Bishop Museum), then in aloha shirts, and now in the spectrum of sweatshirts, pareus, muumuus, and the queenly quilted jackets sold in only the best of boutiques. Although distributed statewide, the biggest selection is right here. Known for his original presentations of classic Hawaiian motifs such as the ti leaf and kukui leaf, Zane has elevated Hawaiian wear to new heights.

The muumuus and dresses are designed by Zane's wife, Nalani Kanaka'ole, the Big Island's best known kumu hula. They use 100 percent cotton in everything from the screen-printed visors and handmade cotton slippers to the more upscale designer quilted jackets. The patterns and styles are identifiably theirs, offered with the perfect ensembles: bullrush sandals by Lorna Omori; Iona Kanetake's hand-painted batik slippers; lauhala purses; gourds; and carved bone fishhook pendants, a traditional Hawaiian ornament, by other local artists. If you're looking for the best local gifts by those who know and love Hawaii, this is the store to try. "I liked this store from the beginning because it used to be a poi shop," Kanaka'ole recalls, surveying the Hawaiian prints and fibers that took up where the dry-land taro left off.

Open 9:30 A.M. to 4:30 P.M. weekdays, 9:00 A.M. to 1:00 P.M. Saturday. Major credit cards accepted.

WAIPIO WOODWORKS
Kukuihaele
Telephone: (808) 775-0958

Some of the finest woods on the island end up here in gleaming bowls, screens, and sculptures. *Ipus* (gourds used in hula) by Malu Aina find their way here from the gourd slopes of Kilauea. Hand-carved bowls of pheasant wood, red sandalwood, false wiliwili, and other rare woods share space with works of mountain apple wood, the rare kamani, and textured treasures made of bamboo root. The world's most tactile letter opener, a sculpture of gnarled bamboo root shaped and polished to a magnificent sheen, sits among the pit-fired pots of Chiu Leong. Some seventy local artists, most of them from the Big Island, have their work displayed here. Seeing and touching their work tells you much about the islands, but the salespeople help, too. They love the pieces and will happily tell you stories of the trees, the woods, and the artists represented in this gallery near Waipio Valley.

Open 9:00 A.M. to 5:00 P.M. daily. Major credit cards accepted.

ZEUS
64 Keawe Street
Hilo
Telephone: (808) 935-7022

Located right next to the restaurant Roussels, Zeus is conspicuously Yuppie in a non-Yuppie town. However, its small selection of men's American and European sportswear offers tasteful alternatives to island wear. Crisp cottons in Italian stylings and expensive trousers for power lunches next door are only the beginning. There are linens, ramies, and the latest fabrics for comfortable living in the tropics, but nothing you'd wear to Waipio Valley. Visiting jet-setters love the selection; they didn't think you could come to Hilo and find such stylish city duds.

Open 10:00 A.M. to 6:00 P.M. weekdays and 10:00 A.M. to 4:00 P.M. Saturday. Major credit cards accepted.

ZEUS FOR WOMEN (FORMERLY LE MIRAGE)
Prince Kuhio Plaza
Hilo
Telephone: (808) 959-7111

The boutique is small, but good taste abounds. Contemporary women's sportswear and surf wear with a European twist can be found among the T-shirts, dresses, and separates on the racks. Jimmy Z, the popular surf line, offers trendy beachwear while Laise Adzer dresses and Lanvin purses beckon for dressy evenings. The shop will not overpower; it's very low-key and unassuming. Big Island artist Ira Ono has his marvelous Trashface earrings here; they'll make you smile.

Open 9:30 A.M. to 5:30 P.M. Monday through Wednesday and on Saturday, until 9:00 P.M. Thursday and Friday, and 10:00 A.M. to 4:00 P.M. Sundays. Major credit cards accepted.

EVERYDAY GOOD
THINGS

WEST HAWAII

Photo Processing

BIG ISLAND PHOTO
75-5669 Alii Drive
Across from Kailua Pier and King Kamehameha Hotel
Telephone: (808) 329-4221

They are fast and they are excellent, serving everyone from professional photographers to fisherman and visitors. Because it's a small shop, the service is personalized and friendly, and your color slides are always done in an hour. Enlargements are done in an hour, too, but black-and-whites are an overnight job.

Open 6:30 A.M. to 7:00 P.M. Monday through Saturday, and until 5:00 P.M. Sunday. Major credit cards accepted.

Edibles

KTA SUPER STORES
Kona Coast Shopping Center
Corner Palani and Kuakini
Kailua
Telephone: (808) 959-9111

Hilo-grown rainbow trout, Kona smoked marlin, colorful trays of red *aweoweo*, an island fish, and such things as Big Island pomelo (like a large, sweet grapefruit), taro chips, and other offbeat local delicacies make this a supermarket worth looking for. Macadamia nuts on sale are a great bargain here, and when the Pu'ueo Poi *kulolo*—a dense, tasty taro-coconut steamed pudding—is on the shelves, the pleasure is bountiful.

Open 6:00 A.M. to 11:00 P.M. Monday through Saturday and until 10:00 P.M. on Sunday. No credit cards accepted.

KAMUELA ROADSIDE VEGETABLE STAND
Kawaihae Highway
Waimea
Telephone: (808) 885-7056

From its plump tomatoes to luxurious fresh shiitakes, Waimea (also known as Kamuela) is like one small truck farm. In fact, Kohala chefs rely on locally grown produce for those opulent buffets and culinary coups that grace the pages of gourmet magazines. The Kamuela roadside stand is really a small market, limited and simple, but always full of plump Kona oranges, local tangerines and grapefruit, shiitakes in season, and the full range of local produce. If you're lucky, they'll have some fresh, inexpensive Waimea roses too.

Open 8:30 A.M. to 5:00 P.M. Tuesday through Saturday. No credit cards accepted.

SUMMER RAIN FISH MARKET
Honalo
Telephone: (808) 322-3354

So what do you do if your fishing trip yields zilch? Head for the Summer Rain Fish Market, where fresh clams and oysters, fresh poke (sashimi with seasoning) in many versions, smoked marlin, smoked ahi, dried opelu, fresh mahimahi, and myriad types of seafood beckon from the counters. The next best thing to catching your own for the Friday night barbecue is getting it here.

Open 9:30 A.M. to 8:00 P.M. daily except Sunday. No credit cards accepted.

EAST HAWAII

Edibles

SUISAN FISH AUCTION
1965 Kam Avenue
Hilo
Telephone: (808) 935-9349 (store), 935-8051 (auction)

The company was formed in 1907, the fish auction began in 1914, and to this day the Suisan Fish Market still draws fishermen and viewers to its colorful daily spectacle. Fishermen bring their catch in by boat or by truck from all corners of the island (except Kona), where chefs, grocers, and all manner of wholesalers, retailers, and fish sellers bid their way through another day's catch. The Hilo boats coming into the bay at sunrise and unloading their shiny fish are something to see.

The auction starts at 8:00 A.M. and normally goes for about half an hour; if it's a big haul, it may go up to an hour. Spectators are welcome; it's best to be there about 7:00 A.M.

Next door is the retail fish store, open 8:00 A.M. to 5:00 P.M. weekdays and until 4:00 P.M. Saturdays. No credit cards accepted.

THE BEST IN
HAWAIIANA

The Big Island is the hot spot for the Hawaiian arts and crafts, as well as for contemporary fine arts. In fact, galleries and an exceptionally active community of Hawaiian artists and craftspeople abound on the Big Island, in communities from Holualoa to Volcano and all the way up to North Kohala. In quiet little corners of this large and vital island, artists collect materials from their gardens, and from mountains, valleys, forests, and shorelines and transform them into living works of art. Many of them receive from the environment nothing more than inspiration. Many of the finest artists in lauhala weaving, lei making, and featherwork are elderly, working with consummate skill and little recognition as they compose great works out of Hawaiian materials. Here are some of the Big Island's best in the traditional Hawaiian crafts, along with the island's best galleries. Most of the artists work out of their homes and require advance notice on orders.

DAVID GOMES GUITARS
P.O. Box 5
Kapaau, HI 96755
Telephone: (808) 889-5100

David Gomes grew up in North Kohala and knows the forests well. He also plays classical guitar and knows tuning, the instrument, and music. It was only natural that he would learn to make guitars, and to make them out of native woods.

He is a world-class builder of guitars and ukeleles and uses such materials as kolohala, or pheasant wood, Australian cedar, the rare kou, curly koa, and other precious woods from the mountains of Hawaii. He orders other woods from the four corners of the world: ebony, Brazilian rosewood, Honduran mahogany, spruce, and many others. He shapes the instrument and finishes it with abalone shell inlays on the fretboard, or an ivory gardenia (fashioned from the keys of an antique piano) on the sandalwood, or perhaps an orchid or maile vine made of abalone for the final flourish on the fretboard. The materials are the best, the workmanship astounding.

Gomes learned to build these instruments when he met one of the world's premier guitar makers on a trip to Madrid. He returned home to the land of Martin and Kamaka ukeleles and paniolo music, and set out to develop his own craft. Today his work has been displayed at the Honolulu Academy of Arts and his instruments have been purchased by such performers as George Benson, who years ago ordered a David Gomes ukelele. It takes about forty hours to make a ukelele and eighty to make a guitar. It is made to order—by shape, type of wood and trimmings, and with the neck shaped to the player's hand. Cost is about $375 to $450 for a ukelele and $950 for a steel string guitar and $1,200 for a classical guitar. They are booked months in advance, but they're worth the wait.

Gomes works in Kapa'au, North Kohala, in a dusty workshop filled with fragrant shavings and designer sawdust. Each work is numbered; when it's finished, he cleans it and tunes it. "People just glow when they pick up their instruments," he says.

TOSHI IWAMASA
P.O. Box 385
Kamuela, HI 96743
Telephone: (808) 885-4534

Toshi's specialty is haku leis, in which flowers, ferns, and greens are intricately braided, or plaited, into lush garlands for the neck, head, or hat. Although she works often with pansies and baby roses, she also uses palapalai ferns, liko lehua (the new red leaves of the ohia tree), and the velvety pink flower called akulikuli that is strung by the hundreds into thick, luxurious strands.

The time-consuming haku leis may be her signature, but she does combine flowers and greens in other styles, such as the ilima stung with cigar flowers, or the pikake that is strung end to end. The work is labor intensive: Materials must be gathered from her gardens and the mountains, and the leis take time to make. Leis range from $12.50 to $20 and more. Advance notice is necessary, at least two to three days except holidays and special occasions, when more time is needed. If you do meet Toshi Iwamasa, ask her about the time she won first place in Frank Sinatra's lei contest.

TSUGI KAIAMA
P.O. Box 763
Kamuela, HI 96743
Telephone: (808) 885-4869

Kaiama's feather leis are legendary on the Big Island, where cowboy hats and feather hatbands are firmly entrenched in the ranching community. A lei maker for half a century, she uses feathers from the skins of pheasant, partridge, francolin, and other game birds that are hunted seasonally on the island, sewing them one by one into intricate patterns that match their colors and qualities. You can imagine the time and commitment required. The prestigous blue lei, made from tiny feathers around the pheasant's ear, requires about three months. Leis of larger feathers may be a few days in the making. The feather leis may cost anywhere from $65 to more than $1,000 and must be ordered ahead. Kaiama's strawflower hatbands in the *humu papa* style are equally a sensation.

SOPHIA KAIAWE
P.O. Box 361
Captain Cook, HI 96704
Telephone: (808) 323-2574

She is in her eighties and has a good many lauhala hats under her belt. She has made them for decades, beginning with gathering the leaves from the old hala grove at the beach nearby. After collecting the long dried leaves of the hala tree, she removes their thorns, flattens and softens them, and strips them to prepare them for weaving. It's time-consuming and arduous, which accounts in large measure for the fact that there are few lauhala weavers left in Hawaii.

Kaiawe's hats are distinctive, made of extremely fine—⅛-inch wide—strips of lauhala woven into three basic styles. The sheen of the fiber, the mastery of the weave, and the ultra-fine handiwork make each hat a work to be treasured. In each is the ocean, the land, and many generations of tradition. Kaiawe makes lauhala hats for her son's store, Joe's Village in Kainaliu (322-9577), but she will make hats to order with enough lead time. The hats sell at about $25, which doesn't even approach their worth.

NALANI KANAKA'OLE
Halau O Kekuhi

You won't see Nalani Kanaka'ole dance unless you happen to be around during a cultural festival or hula competition. She does not perform commercially, preferring to work solely with her students in the rigors and traditions of a five-generation hula school. She is a serious, powerful presence in the firmament of Hawaiian dance, the daughter of the late Edith Kanaka'ole, a leading proponent of the art. The dances of their school—many of them 300 years old—are a vital link to a rich past. If you see Kanaka'ole's name on any concert program, don't miss her.

MARIE MCDONALD
Honopua Flower Growers
P.O. Box 1258
Kamuela, HI 96743
Telephone: (808) 885-4148

Known as the grande dame of lei making, Marie McDonald has been teaching, designing, researching, and making leis for several decades. The author of *Ka Lei*, the definitive book on leis, McDonald is a leader in an art form that is evolving even today. Using leaves, flowers, vines, berries, and other materials from the land, she makes intricate wili (wound) leis that evoke the fresh mountain mists of Waimea. Her leis dry well, many of them made of liko lehua or dried materials, and all of them local. McDonald and her sister, Kauai's Irmalee Pomroy, were selected the best lei makers at a cultural festival of Pacific nations in 1985. Because lei making is an art of the Pacific, that distinction could be extended to mean they're the best lei makers in the world. Her prices range from about $10 to $20, and she'd like at least two days' notice.

BARBARA MEHEULA
Westin Mauna Kea
South Kohala
Telephone: (808) 882-7222

There is nothing casual about a Barbara Meheula lei. If you order one from her it will be custom designed according to occasion, attire, and the wearer's sensitivities. (A blind customer once received the most fragrant lei possible in a freshly cut, tactile bamboo boat with her name carved in it.) Her techniques are haku (braided or plaited), wili (wound), kui (strung), and others, depending on the materials available and the wearer's needs. Unless they're out of season or available only on other islands—such as the fragrant mokihana fruit, grown only on Kauai—Meheula uses Big Island materials of all textures, colors, and origins. She's renowned for her packaging: the leis may come in handmade baskets of coconut frond, banana leaf, ti leaf, bamboo, bark, and other living fibers. She'll make a simple single strand as well, but the more elaborate custom versions run about $30. Ask about her baskets, too—they're large, strong vessels of local bark, roots, and vines in unimaginable colors and textures. Orders must be placed through the Mauna Kea.

KAMAILE MONIZ
P.O. Box 451
Kamuela, HI 96743
Telephone: (808) 885-4125

Moniz loves to make leis of pansies, roses, ferns, and liko, blending colors and textures into her famed haku leis. But she also makes strung leis that are exquisite, from the intricate cigar lei to the akulikuli, or ice plant, which rests so nobly on the shoulders. Moniz gathers her own flowers and plants: the palapalai (a native fern), a'ali'i (a small, leaflike flower in greens and pinks), pansies, tuberoses, and many others. And then, using any of several techniques she has mastered, she'll compose the right garland in the right style for you. Her leis are $12 to $15.

ULALIA SCHOOL OF HAWAIIAN DANCE
P.O. Box 5166
Kailua-Kona, HI 96745
Telephone: (808) 325-7539

Ulalia Berman is the highlight of the King Kamehameha Hotel, where she dances, leads tours, and presents her students in the art of kahiko, ancient hula. She dances as much with her eyes as with the rest of the body, engaging the viewer with her distinctive style and an infectious love of the dance. Hula has been her love since the age of three. Now she shares it with others, through her classes, demonstrations, and performances. Her teacher, the late Ma'iki Aiu, was one of Hawaii's treasures. Visitors are welcome to watch her halau practice at the Keauhou Shopping Village on Saturday mornings, and to her free tour at the King Kamehameha Hotel at 10:00 A.M. Monday and Wednesday.

GALLERIES

ACKERMAN GALLERY
961 Kapa'au, across from the Kamehameha Statue
North Kohala
Telephone: (808) 889-5971

Painter Gary Ackerman and wife, Yesan, who buys the handicrafts, combine fine art with crafts in their remote North Kohala gallery. Fabulous gifts abound here, from earthy, textured ceramic bowls to hand-blown glass by Wilfred Yamazawa and other noted Holualua artists. There is a smattering of Oriental antiques and primitive artifacts, plus bowls beautifully carved out of milo and other rare native woods. Ackerman's oil and watercolor landscapes adorn the walls; finely crafted jewelry, hand-painted fabrics, and collected works from the Big Island and beyond round out a distinctive selection. Ask to see their selection of Dan Lily's bowls, ornaments, and vases made of Big Island bamboo—very textured, imaginative, and affordable.

Open 9:30 A.M. to 5:30 P.M. daily. Major credit cards accepted.

BLUE GINGER GALLERY
Highway 11
Kainaliu
Telephone: (808) 322-3898

Impeccable in taste, this new gallery is already a winner. Owners David Bever and Jill Ami Meyers, who paints silks, have transformed an old wooden house into a sparkling gallery showcasing the best in island crafts. There are things to wear—hand-painted silk scarves and jewelry—and there is furniture—koa chairs or a regal table in curly koa by cabinetmaker Marcus Castaing. Etched glass of the highest quality and bracelets of native woods, plus a small selection of imported Asian jewelry, round out a small but rich collection. The work of forty different artists is represented here, from furniture to stained glass, including that of several of the Big Island's finest potters.

Open 9:00 A.M. to 5:00 P.M. daily except Sunday. Major credit cards accepted.

NIKKO GALLERY
Spencer House
Mamalahoa Highway
Waimea
Telephone: (808) 885-7661

The gallery, a newcomer to Waimea but not to the Big Island, makes a strong statement with its selection of artists. The artists may not be widely known, but they are the best on the island and among the best in the state. Marilyn Wold's handmade wauke (paper mulberry) paper is hanging art. Jay Warner's sugi, milo, and koa boxes with ohia or bamboo hinges are of museum quality. There are Japanese boxes of cherry bark, a samurai money chest, a woven obi of handmade paper yarn, and a selection of antiques, collectibles, paintings, prints, and sculptures that would make a sultan envious. With its understated good taste and pristine Japanese esthetic, the gallery sings paeans to the treasures of the Big Island, from its exotic natural materials to the people who shape them. Yet, with its silks, fibers, metals, and elements from many different cultures, it is far from a regional gallery.

Open 9:00 A.M. to 6:00 P.M. Monday through Saturday and 10:00 A.M. to 4:00 P.M. Sunday. Major credit cards accepted.

THE POTTER'S GALLERY
Corner Waianuenue and Keawe
Hilo
Telephone: (808) 935-4069

A bright, airy gallery in the middle of town, the Potter's Gallery showcases the work of Big Island artists in all media, from jewelry to batik to pit-fired pottery and an occasional piece of handmade koa furniture. The name artists and craftsmen are represented here with works for all pocketbooks and tastes. Chiu Leong pots, Wilfred Yamazawa glass, and a host of other works from fiber arts to porcelain, stoneware, functional pottery, and wood make this a pleasant introduction to the island.

Open 9:00 A.M. to 5:00 P.M. Monday through Saturday. Major credit cards accepted.

STUDIO 7 GALLERY
Mamalahoa Highway
Holualoa
Telephone: (808) 324-1335

Many artists consider this the best gallery on the Big Island. It's small, unpretentious, and eminently tasteful. Folk and fine art blend in a collection that includes original paintings by Hiroki Morinoue, Jennifer Pontz's glassware, Chiu Leong's raku tea bowls, hand-blown glass by Wilfred Yamazawa, and fiber baskets, woodblock prints, and other treasures. Gallery owner Morinoue is one of Hawaii's best, whose talents include painting, raku, and metal sculpture. The selection of contemporary fine arts and crafts, set in an environment of stream pebbles, dark woods, and other Japanese elements, takes on a Zen purity that refreshes and delights.

Open 10:00 A.M. to 4:00 P.M. Tuesday through Saturday. Major credit cards accepted.

VOLCANO ART CENTER
Hawaii Volcanoes National Park
Telephone: (808) 967-7511

The art center opened in 1974 when an artists' community was just taking shape on the Big Island. It's a nonprofit, tax-exempt educational center that also exhibits fine work by about 175 artists. You'll find works in all media here, from handmade cards to jewelry, large koa sculptures, paintings, photographs, ceramics, baskets, glass, T-shirts, and prints. The building in which these treasures are displayed is the original Volcano House, built in 1877, so you know those hardwood floors have been around.

Open 9:00 A.M. to 6:00 P.M. daily. Major credit cards accepted.

WESTIN MAUNA KEA
South Kohala
Telephone: (808) 882-7222

It would take you days to see the Mauna Kea's art collection. In fact, the hotel itself is a gallery without walls, an astounding collection of Asian and Pacific art discreetly arranged amid the gardens, stairways, hallways, and foyers of this remarkable labyrinth. More than 1,000 objects of folk, tribal, and fine art, from a seventh century Indian Buddha to Thai dragons and Sepik River fighting shields, greet you at every turn. Even the hotel's brilliantly narrated art tours barely scratch the surface of all there is to absorb. Included in the collection are temple and ritual art from New Guinea, Ceylon, India, Thailand, Japan, and points beyond—the best of the world's cultures melding with the quilts and tapas of Hawaii. Not to be missed are the fifth and sixth floor galleries of Hawaiian quilts.

FLOWERS AND LEIS

I n Hilo, excellent flowers and leis, including the Big Island's signature, anthuriums, may be found at stores that carry groceries as well, such as Ebesu's (301 Keawe Street, Hilo, telephone [808] 935-3361). Other good sources of flowers and leis include: The Floral Mart, 738 Kinoole Street, (808) 935-6344; the Greeters of Hawaii Lei Shop, Hilo Airport, (808) 959-6355; and the Hilo Pau Nani Florist, 284 Kam Avenue, (808) 935-8409. Most of them will ship flowers as well, or prepare them for travel. Among the larger, reliable orchid farms that specialize in Hilo's famous blooms are Akatsuka Orchid Gardens in Glenwood, (808) 967-7660, and Orchids of Hawaii, 2801 Kilauea Avenue, (808) 959-3581.

GIFTS TO GO

I t's impossible to leave the Big Island without a cache of Kona coffee or macadamia nuts. Like lox from Zabar's and onions from Kula, they are the luxury gifts of the area, the regional specialties and authoritative offerings from the place that does them best.

Among the best Kona coffees are the Bong Brothers Kona coffee and Kona mauka (mountain) coffee by Rooster Farms. Rooster Farms is situated 1,600 feet high on the slopes of Mauna Loa, where the arabica beans are grown organically. A lot of personal attention is given to these beans in the growing and natural processing, and their chemical-free state is a plus. A caveat: Watch the shelf life on these and any other coffees that aren't vacuum packed.

Bong Brothers coffee comes in a 1.3-ounce fractional size, which makes eight to ten cups, and a 10-ounce size, both vacuum packed with a one-way valve. Besides being visually stunning, the packaging ensures freshness and is a major consideration among connoisseurs. Bong Brothers uses classified coffee and is able to pack the beans warm because of the efficient packaging. They also put out a chocolate-covered Kona coffee bean, the only product of its kind. Expect to pay for Kona coffee; any way you cut it, it's expensive.

It you'd like to be different, there are alternatives galore. Smoked marlin from Kona, available at KTA Super Stores and many others, is a tasty alternative for the adventurous, as are Atebara's jumbo taro chips—the best. The chips are as big as Frisbees, made from dry-land taro, hand-sliced and hand-packed and then distributed to selected points on the island. They're crisp and nutty, a little denser than potato chips but so much more exotic. (Hilo Airport almost always has them.) Atebara's also has a host of other comestibles, including Hawaiian Crunchies, an imaginative melding of their famous Atebata's potato chips, crushed, with chocolate and macadamia nuts. Other worthy food items include Kona's Best macadamia nut brittle, made with butter and honey, and Kailua Candy Company's preservative-free, butter-rich macadamia nut chocolates.

The ultimate gift idea is a line of products called Tropical Dreams. You won't want to leave without these ambrosial concoctions: macadamia nut butter, macadamia creme, macadamia mocha java, macadamia butter chocolate, macadamia butter ambrosia, and more. They're as good as they sound. These couture spreads and condiments feature the Big Island's specialties and are widely distributed throughout the island. They come in small bottles wielding big calories, but you should tackle them with abandon.

For those croissants and Sunday brunches, you might also consider some of the island's gourmet preserves, among them Pu'ukapu Farms' poha-papaya jam. They're the best. Don't forget flowers, too. Hilo anthuriums are quite the sentimental favorite, available at grocery and flower shops around town. They travel well and are a symbol of the island. If you're taking flowers out of a state, be sure they are agriculturally approved.

Artists—and the Big Island has many of them—are also putting out numerous works that make ideal gifts for those with discriminating taste. Ask about the posters and paintings of noted Hawaiian artist Herb Kane, linoleum block prints by Volcano artist Deitrich Varez, photographer Franco Salmoiraghi's black and white prints of the Big Island, and Boone Morrison's photographs and posters of the hula. Along with originals by these artists, they can be found in stores and galleries around the island. Jack Straka's works in wood and Kathy Long's photographically detailed drawings of Hawaiian scenes also occupy prominent positions in the vast amalgamation of contemporary Hawaiian art. Don't forget, too, to ask about Henry Bianchini's bronze sculptures depicting Hawaiian legends, chanters, goddesses, and dancers—for the high roller and definitely worth exploring. All these works are by fine artists, all have a Hawaiian theme, and all capture the essence of Hawaii with resounding sincerity.

Big Island wearables include the handmade bracelets of Cloud Forest Woodworks, which uses koa, ohia, naio (also known as false sandalwood, because of its fragrance), macadamia nut, mango, lichee, silk oak, and other woods grown on the Big Island. The bracelets, laminated and labeled on the inside, make inexpensive gifts from Hawaii. They're available at many galleries and gift shops across the island.

The most avant-garde of the Big Island wearables is Ira Ono's Trashface jewelry, each earring a sculpture of found objects and snippets from Ono's travels. Also eminently wearable are Laura Lewis's Silks by Hand, poetic expressions for women. Also wearable, and distinctive, is Volcano Glass jewelry in its medley of different forms. Made with a special process using volcanic ash, Volcano Glass jewelry will catch your eye from gallery counters with its iridescent glow. From pale yellow to the deepest indigo, glass is treated to create various shades and degrees of opalescence and then shaped into necklaces and earrings. The simpler styles are more appealing.

Woodworks, hand-painted silk scarves, hand-screened T-shirts and dresses, and a plethora of other items are all over the Big Island, making sure you know there's more to life than Kona coffee and macadamia nuts. For other ideas, see Shopping and the Best in Hawaiiana.

ACKNOWLEDGMENTS

Laulima. Cooperation; group of people working together; . . . to work together. *Lit.*, many hands. (from Mary K. Pukui and Samuel Elbert's *Hawaiian Dictionary*.)

Many hands and many minds helped me through this. It was impossible even to approach this book alone.

For their time, encouragement, support, and assistance, I am grateful to Rose Fuerte, Annette Fujii, Milton Goto and Aloha Airlines, Grady Timmons, Stephen Long, Paul Mitchell, Michael Kwock, Val Kim, Franco Salmoiraghi, Nalani Kanaka'ole, Sig Zane, Dennis Keawe, Marie McDonald, Philip Spalding III, Connie Wright, Carl Lindquist, Sheila Donnelly, Lindy Boyes, Marcie Carroll, Maile Semitekol, Duane Black, Brooks Takenaka, Carol Hogan, John Clark, Sam Lee, and countless other generous souls. Thanks also to Frances Dote, who flew to my rescue at the eleventh hour.

I especially thank Bob Toyofuku, who, by publishing my first book on the best of Honolulu, indirectly made possible this new book. It is to Bob that I attribute the good things spawned by our modest venture five years ago. Besides being a rare and generous friend, Bob has knowledge, insights, and tastes that contributed prominently to the reviews in this book.

I wish also to thank Marcia Sult, whose friendship and extraordinary assistance on the Maui chapter were integral to this project. She unstintingly shared her insights on Maui, her home, and gave me direction and guidance on a difficult section.

I am also greatly indebted to Jane von Mehren, who gave me this opportunity in the first place, and who fulfilled the monumental task of editing this book with patience and equanimity. It was her skillful editing that gave the book its coherence and identity; it was my good fortune to have worked with her.

For their support from the beginning, from that first phone call to the publisher from their New York home, a special thank you goes to Anne and Lloyd Moss.

And for his constant patience and assistance, I owe a special debt to Bradley Shields. This is the third book he has seen me through; it has not been easy. He spent countless hours helping in research, and when his work was done, had the presence and generosity to encourage me as only the best of friends can.

For his compassion and guidance throughout, I am grateful to Tanouye Roshi.

And finally, a heartfelt mahalo to all those in this book, particularly the Hawaiians, who are the soul and the majesty of our island home.

INDEX